Holding Out

This is a ground-breaking study of German operational command during a critical phase of the First World War from November 1916 to the eve of the third battle of Ypres. The situation faced by the German army on the Western Front in 1917 was very different from the one anticipated in pre-war doctrine, and *Holding Out* examines how German commanders and staff officers adapted. Tony Cowan analyses key command tasks to get under the skin of the army's command culture, internal politics and battle management systems from co-ordinating the troops, matériel and different levels of command needed to fight a modern battle to continuously learning and applying lessons from the ever-changing Western Front. His detailed analysis of the German defeat of the 1917 Entente spring offensive sheds new light on how the army and Germany were able to hold out so long during the war against increasing odds.

Dr Tony Cowan is a retired diplomat and member of the British Commission for Military History, Society of Military History and Western Front Association. He co-edited a translation of the German official monograph on the battle of Amiens (2019).

Cambridge Military Histories

Edited by

GREGORY A. DADDIS, USS Midway Chair in Modern US Military History and Director of the Center for War and Society, San Diego State University

HEW STRACHAN, Professor of International Relations, University of St Andrews and Emeritus Fellow of All Souls College, Oxford

GEOFFREY WAWRO, Professor of Military History and Director of the Military History Center, University of North Texas

The aim of this series is to publish outstanding works of research on warfare throughout the ages and throughout the world. Books in the series take a broad approach to military history, examining war in all its military, strategic, political and economic aspects. The series complements *Studies in the Social and Cultural History of Modern Warfare* by focusing on the 'hard' military history of armies, tactics, strategy and warfare. Books in the series consist mainly of single author works – academically rigorous and groundbreaking – which are accessible to both academics and the interested general reader.

A full list of titles in the series can be found at: www.cambridge.org/militaryhistories

Holding Out

The German Army and Operational Command in 1917

Tony Cowan

Independent Scholar

CAMBRIDGE
UNIVERSITY PRESS

Shaftesbury Road, Cambridge CB2 8EA, United Kingdom

One Liberty Plaza, 20th Floor, New York, NY 10006, USA

477 Williamstown Road, Port Melbourne, VIC 3207, Australia

314–321, 3rd Floor, Plot 3, Splendor Forum, Jasola District Centre,
New Delhi – 110025, India

103 Penang Road, #05–06/07, Visioncrest Commercial, Singapore 238467

Cambridge University Press is part of Cambridge University Press & Assessment,
a department of the University of Cambridge.

We share the University's mission to contribute to society through the pursuit of
education, learning and research at the highest international levels of excellence.

www.cambridge.org
Information on this title: www.cambridge.org/9781108830232

DOI: 10.1017/9781108900553

First published 2023

Printed in the United Kingdom by CPI Group Ltd, Croydon CR0 4YY

A catalogue record for this publication is available from the British Library.

Library of Congress Cataloging-in-Publication Data
Names: Cowan, Tony, 1953– author.
Title: Holding out : the German Army and Operational Command in 1917 /
Tony Cowan.
Other titles: German Army and Operational Command in 1917
Description: Cambridge, United Kingdom ; New York, NY : Cambridge
University Press, 2023. | Series: Cambridge military histories | Includes
bibliographical references and index.
Identifiers: LCCN 2022056942 | ISBN 9781108830232 (hardback) | ISBN
9781108820516 (paperback) | ISBN 9781108900553 (ebook)
Subjects: LCSH: Germany. Heer – History – 20th century – Case studies. |
World War, 1914–1918 – Campaigns – Western Front. | World War, 1914–1918
– Germany. | Operational art (Military science) – Case studies. | Command of
troops. | Military doctrine – Germany – History – 20th century – Case studies.
Classification: LCC D531 .C69 2023 | DDC 940.3/43–dc23/eng/20221220
LC record available at https://lccn.loc.gov/2022056942

ISBN 978-1-108-83023-2 Hardback

In memory of my grandfather, Captain Alexander Comrie Cowan, MC and Bar, 16th Battalion The Royal Scots

Contents

Figures

Maps

Tables

Acknowledgements

This book grew out of my doctoral thesis at the University of Liverpool and King's College London, so my first thanks go to my supervisors, Dr Robert T. Foley, who did the heavy lifting, and Professor Charles Esdaile, who asked the left-field questions. Warm thanks too to my examiners, Dr Annika Mombauer and Professor David Stevenson, for their rigorous inquisition of my thesis, which suggested further avenues of research, and for their helpful advice on publishing.

I owe particular gratitude to Professor Sir Hew Strachan for his generous support of my book proposal to Cambridge University Press, starting from our time on the same syndicate of a British Army staff ride in 2018 as part of the First World War centenary. Dr Jim Beach and Professor David French gave me much good advice on drafting the proposal. I should also thank Cambridge University Press's two anonymous readers for their enthusiastic reception of it and my draft chapters: their suggestions have undoubtedly made this a better book. And I have received much help from Michael Watson and his editorial team at Cambridge University Press, who have helped steer this inexperienced author through what can seem the impenetrable thickets of publishing.

Among friends and colleagues, I cannot thank enough those who read and commented so valuably on my manuscript in whole or part – Jim Beach again, Jonathan Boff, John Bourne, Aimée Fox, Tim Gale, Brian Hall, Markus Pöhlmann and Andy Simpson; some of them had read my thesis in draft as well, and this double service really was above and beyond the call of duty. I have been fortunate too to receive much help and support from others including Florian Altenhöner, Phylomena Badsey, Stephen Badsey, David Blanchard, Simon Chapman, Marcus Faulkner, Will Fletcher, Kay Fraser, Bruce Gudmundsson, Paul Hederer, Sylvia Hoenig, Alan Judd, Mungo Melvin, Christopher Newton, Michael Orr, David Pearson, Mike Ramscar, Élise Rezsőhazy, Krisztina Robert, Klaus Schmider, Christian Stachelbeck and Daniel Whittingham.

More broadly, I have greatly benefitted from various organisations I belong to, and two in particular. The first is the British Commission for Military History, which I joined in the heyday of revisionism about the First World War in the early 1990s. Its battlefield tours are both fun and educational. One I helped organise on the centenary of the two battles at the core of this book, the battle of Arras and the Nivelle offensive, was particularly useful in crystallising my thinking on what went wrong for the British and French armies, and whether their efforts were doomed to failure. The second organisation is the Coal Hole Club – formally, the King's College London First World War operational study group, chaired by Professor William Philpott – which provided a friendly environment for exchanging ideas with fellow PhD students. Presenting papers to its members was a stimulating challenge, which also played a formative role in developing my thinking.

I am hugely grateful to Barbara Taylor for her skill, speed and attention to detail in producing the excellent maps and Figure 1.1; she retains the copyright, and the maps and figure are not to be reproduced in any format without her express permission. I also owe warm thanks to my cousin Justin Lyon, who found the cover photograph, and to Tom Thorpe for his advice on setting up the website which will provide supporting material for this book.

I have made extensive use of German documentary material, and I could not have written the book without the help I have received over many years from the seven German archives in which I have researched. So I am very grateful to the archivists and staff in the Archiv des Hauses Württemberg, Altshausen; the Bayerisches Hauptstaatsarchiv, Abteilungen III, Geheimes Hausarchiv and IV, Kriegsarchiv, Munich; the Bundesarchiv, Abteilung Militärarchiv, Freiburg im Breisgau; the Generallandesarchiv, Karlsruhe; the Hauptstaatsarchiv, Dresden; and the Hauptstaatsarchiv, Stuttgart.

Of these, I am perhaps most indebted to the Kriegsarchiv in Munich. Thirty years ago, I wrote to them about my grandfather, Captain Alexander Comrie Cowan, whose military service first sparked my interest in the First World War and to whom this book is dedicated. He was briefly captured by a Bavarian regiment at the beginning of the battle of Arras, and I wanted to know if there were any German records about this. The Kriegsarchiv took the trouble to locate and transcribe the report of the platoon that captured him, and from this kindness I first realised the richness of information still available in German archives despite the destruction of so many records since 1918.

I would also like to express my gratitude to the staff of four libraries which I have made frequent use of – the Bayerische Staatsbibliothek, Munich, the British Library, the German Historical Institute London and the London Library.

Last and by far the most important, my heartfelt thanks go to my family for all their love, support, interest and indeed patience over the many years since I set out on my PhD. Sadly neither my father nor mother are still alive to see this book, but I hope they would have been proud of it. My mother used to ask, more or less from when I started the PhD, what I was going to do next. I have always been able to dodge this question, but now the book is finished, the family – and I – will finally discover the answer.

Comparative Ranks

German	British
German	**British**
Generalfeldmarschall	Field Marshal
Generaloberst	General
General der Infanterie (Kavallerie, Artillerie)	Lieutenant-General
Generalleutnant	Major-General
Generalmajor	Brigadier-General
Oberst	Colonel
Oberstleutnant	Lieutenant-Colonel
Major	Major
Hauptmann (Hauptleute)	Captain (Captains)
Rittmeister	Cavalry Captain
Oberleutnant	Lieutenant
Leutnant	Second Lieutenant

Chronology

Date	Western Front	Other fronts	Political, political-military and diplomatic
13–18 Nov. 1916	Battle of the Ancre (Somme)		
15–16 Nov. 1916			Inter-allied conferences in Chantilly (military) and Paris (political)
21 Nov. 1916			Archduke Karl succeeds Franz Josef as Austro-Hungarian Kaiser
1 Dec. 1916	First edition of new German defensive doctrine issued		
6 Dec. 1916		Germans capture Bucharest	
7 Dec. 1916			Lloyd George becomes Prime Minister
12 Dec. 1916			Central Powers peace proposals
12 Dec. 1916			Nivelle appointed commander-in-chief of the Armies of the North and North-East, replacing Joffre
15–16 Dec. 1916	Second French counter-offensive at Verdun		

(*cont.*)

Date	Western Front	Other fronts	Political, political-military and diplomatic
18 Dec. 1916			President Wilson calls on belligerents to state their peace terms
26 Dec. 1916			Joffre resigns as general-in-chief of the French Armies
26–7 Dec. 1916			London conference on extension of British front in France and on Salonika
4–7 Jan. 1917			Anglo-French-Italian conference in Rome
15–16 Jan. 1917			Anglo-French conference in London on extension of British front in France
31 Jan.–3 Feb. 1917			Nivelle visit to Italy
1 Feb. 1917			Germany begins unrestricted submarine warfare
1–20 Feb. 1917			Inter-allied conference in Petrograd
3 Feb. 1917			United States breaks off relations with Germany
15 Feb. 1917	Germans capture new French attack doctrine		

(*cont.*)

Date	Western Front	Other fronts	Political, political-military and diplomatic
22–3 Feb. 1917	German withdrawal from Bapaume salient		
26–7 Feb. 1917			Anglo-French conference in Calais on unified command
11 Mar. 1917		British capture Baghdad	
12 Mar. 1917			Russian Revolution begins
12–13 Mar. 1917			Anglo-French conference in London on unified command
14 Mar. 1917			Resignation of Lyautey, French Minister of War
16–18 Mar. 1917	German withdrawal to the Hindenburg Line		
17 Mar. 1917			Fall of Briand government
20 Mar. 1917			Formation of Ribot government
23 Mar. 1917			Anglo-French-Italian meeting at Udine
24 Mar. 1917			Kaiser Karl makes secret overture for a separate peace

(*cont.*)

Date	Western Front	Other fronts	Political, political-military and diplomatic
4 Apr. 1917	British bombardment for battle of Arras begins		
4 Apr. 1917	Germans capture part of French attack plan		
6 Apr. 1917			United States declares war on Germany
6 Apr. 1917			Compiègne conference on Nivelle offensive
7 Apr. 1917			The Kaiser's 'Easter Message' offering Prussian voting reform
8 Apr. 1917	French bombardment for Nivelle offensive begins		
9–14 Apr. 1917	Battle of Arras first phase		
9–16 Apr. 1917			Lenin travels from Switzerland to Russia
11 Apr. 1917	First battle of Bullecourt		
13 Apr. 1917	Nivelle offensive (Oise)		
15 Apr. 1917	German attack at Lagnicourt (Arras)		
16–20 Apr. 1917	Nivelle offensive (Aisne) first phase		

Date	Western Front	Other fronts	Political, political-military and diplomatic
17–20 Apr. 1917	Nivelle offensive (Champagne) first phase		
17 Apr. 1917	First mutiny in the French army		
19 Apr. 1917			Anglo-French-Italian conference on Salonika
20 Apr. 1917			Anglo-French conference in Paris on continuing the offensive
23–4 Apr. 1917	Battle of Arras second phase		
24 Apr. 1917			Haig meeting with Nivelle
26 Apr. 1917			Haig meeting with Painlevé
28–29 Apr. 1917	Battle of Arras third phase		
29 Apr. 1917			Pétain appointed French chief of the general staff
30 Apr.–7 May 1917	Nivelle offensive (Champagne) second phase		
3 May 1917			Haig's first meeting with Pétain as chief of the general staff

(*cont.*)

Date	Western Front	Other fronts	Political, political-military and diplomatic
3–4 May 1917	Battle of Arras fourth phase		
3–17 May 1917	Second battle of Bullecourt		
4–5 May 1917			Anglo-French political and military conferences in Paris
4–9 May 1917	Nivelle offensive (Aisne) second phase		
12 May–8 Jun. 1917		Tenth battle of the Isonzo	
15 May 1917			Nivelle removed, Pétain appointed commander-in-chief of the Armies of the North and North-East
15 May–30 Jun. 1917	Peak of French army mutinies		
18 May 1917			Haig's first meeting with Pétain as commander-in-chief
20–5 May 1917	Nivelle offensive (Champagne) third phase		
22–5 May 1917	Nivelle offensive (Aisne) third phase		
28–9 May 1917			Anglo-French conference in London on Greece and Salonika

(*cont.*)

Date	Western Front	Other fronts	Political, political-military and diplomatic
7–14 Jun. 1917	Battle of Messines		
9–29 Jun. 1917		Battle of Asiago (South Tirol)	
1–28 Jul. 1917		Kerensky offensive	
10–11 Jul. 1917	German attack at Nieuport		
13 Jul. 1917			Fall of Chancellor Bethmann Hollweg
19 Jul. 1917			Reichstag passes Peace Resolution
19 Jul.–3 Sept. 1917		German and Austro-Hungarian counter-offensive	
31 Jul. 1917	Third battle of Ypres begins		

Abbreviations

a.D.	*außer Dienst* (retired)
AFGG	*Les Armées françaises dans la grande guerre* (French official history)
AHW	Archiv des Hauses Württemberg
AK	Armee-Korps
AOK	Armee-Oberkommando (headquarters of an Army)
BArch	Bundesarchiv, Abteilung Militärarchiv (formerly BA/MA), Freiburg im Breisgau
BID	Bayerische Infanterie-Division
BK	Bayerisches Korps
BOH	*Military Operations France and Belgium* (British official history)
BRD	Bayerische Reserve-Division
BRK	Bayerisches Reserve-Korps
CGS	Chef des Generalstabes
f.	folio
GID	Garde-Infanterie-Division
GHQ	Großes Hauptquartier (General Headquarters)
GLAK	Generallandesarchiv Karlsruhe, file series 456
GQG	Grand Quartier Général (French General Headquarters)
GRD	Garde-Reserve-Division
HAM	Bayerisches Hauptstaatsarchiv, Munich, Abteilung III, Geheimes Hausarchiv
HDK	Heeresgruppe Deutscher Kronprinz (Army Group Crown Prince)
HHA	Heeresgruppe Herzog Albrecht (Army Group Albrecht)
HKR	Heeresgruppe Kronprinz Rupprecht (Army Group Rupprecht)
HSAD	Hauptstaatsarchiv Dresden
HSAS	Hauptstaatsarchiv Stuttgart
ID	Infanterie-Division

KAM	Bayerisches Hauptstaatsarchiv, Munich, Abteilung IV, Kriegsarchiv
KTK	Kampftruppenkommandeur (combat troop commander)
LIB	Landwehr-Infanterie-Brigade
MGFA	Militärgeschichtliches Forschungsamt der Bundeswehr
NARA	US National Archives and Records Administration
OHL	Oberste Heeresleitung (German Supreme Army Command)
RD	Reserve-Division
RIR	Reserve-Infanterie-Regiment
RK	Reserve-Korps
SHD	Service historique de la Défense
USPD	Unabhängige Sozialdemokratische Partei Deutschlands (Independent Social Democratic Party)
z.D.	*zur Disposition* (retired on half pay)

General key to maps

BR British

FR French

BE Belgian

☐ German formations

XXXXX
☐ Army group

XXXX
☐ Army

XXX
☐ Gruppe/Corps

•••••• Canals

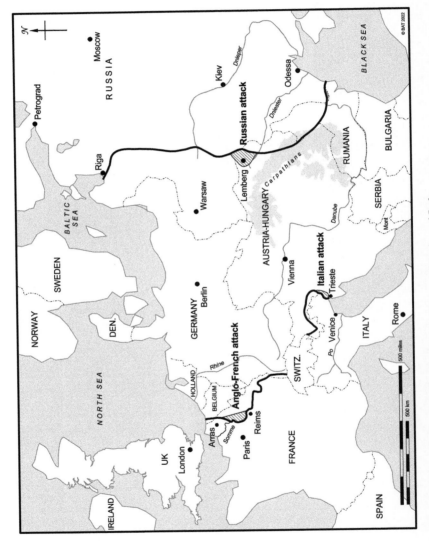

Map 1 Plan for co-ordinated offensives in France, Russia and Italy

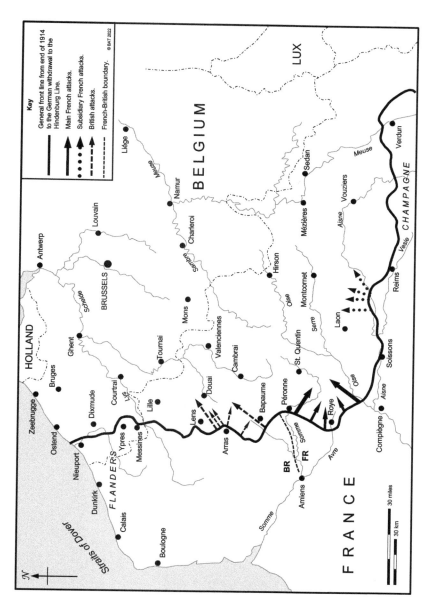

Map 2 Joffre's plan for the 1917 Western Front offensive

Key

General front line from end of 1914
to the German withdrawal to the
Hindenburg Line.

Main French attacks.

Subsidiary French attacks.

British attacks.

French-British boundary.

© BAT 2022

HOLLAND

BELGIUM

LUX

FRANCE

Straits of Dover

N

30 km
30 miles

Boulogne

Calais

Dunkirk

Zeebrugge

Ostend

Nieuport

Bruges

Dixmude

Ypres

Messines

Courtrai

Lille

Lens

Arras

Amiens

BR

FR

Péronne

Bapaume

Roye

Compiègne

Soissons

Douai

Cambrai

Valenciennes

Mons

Tournai

Ghent

BRUSSELS

Louvain

Antwerp

Charleroi

Namur

Liège

St. Quentin

Hirson

Laon

Montcornet

Mézières

Sedan

Reims

CHAMPAGNE

Vouziers

Verdun

Soissons

FLANDERS

Schelde

Sambre

Meuse

Lys

Somme

Avre

Somme

Oise

Serre

Oise

Aisne

Aisne

Vesle

Meuse

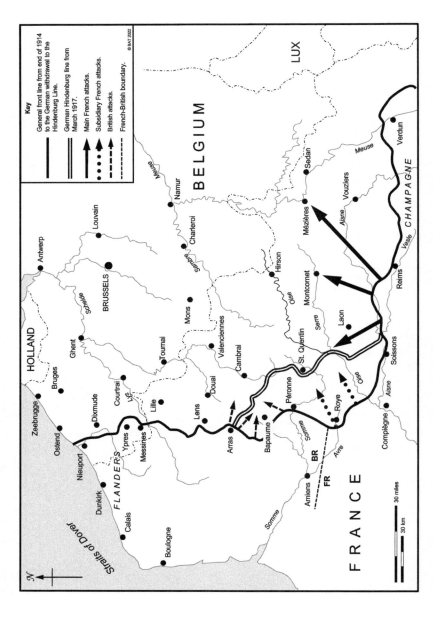

Map 3 Nivelle's initial plan, the German withdrawal to the Hindenburg Line and its effect on the plan

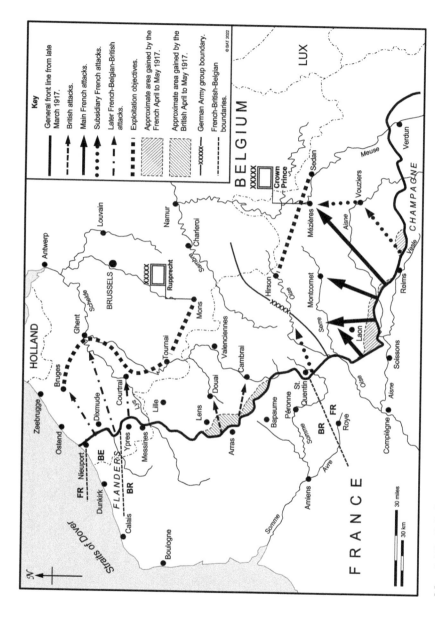

Map 4 Nivelle's final plan including exploitation objectives, and ground actually gained

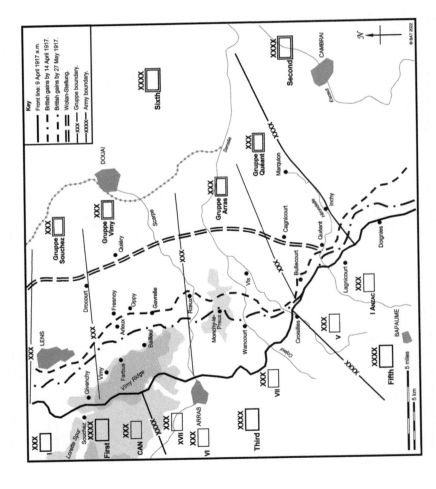

Map 5 Arras

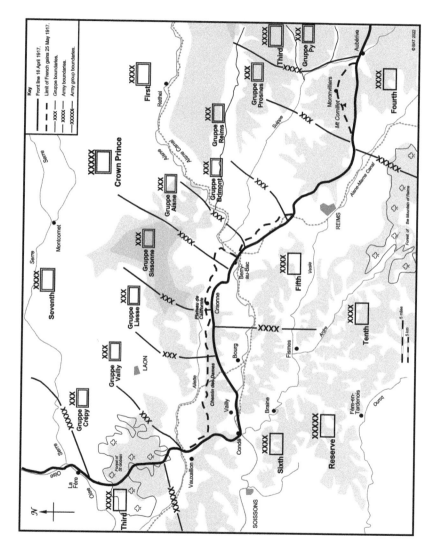

Map 6 Nivelle offensive

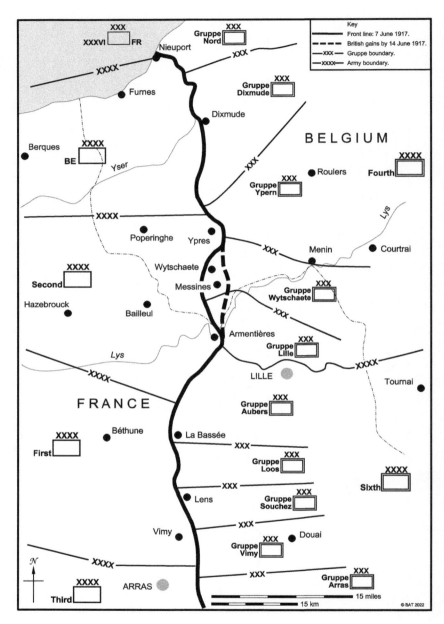

Map 7 Messines

Introduction

> Things that might seem obvious now were far from obvious then. What to us is the past, unalterable and fated, was to them still the future, full of possibility, confusion and doubt.[1]

At 5.30 a.m. on 9 April 1917, a wintry Easter Monday, British and Canadian troops advanced to assault the German positions at Arras. Within two days they had seized the important Vimy Ridge, and further south had broken through all the prepared German defensive positions in the area. They had made the longest advance by Entente forces in a single day since trench warfare had begun on the Western Front, capturing thousands of prisoners and hundreds of guns. This was victory, and the British commanders gave orders that risks must be freely taken in the pursuit of the defeated enemy.[2]

On the German side, something like panic set in. The commander of the forces facing the British, Crown Prince Rupprecht of Bavaria, asked himself anxiously in his diary whether his troops would be able to hold further attacks, and even whether it made sense to continue the war.[3] First Quartermaster-General Erich Ludendorff described the situation as extremely critical; he had looked forward to the offensive with confidence, based on the recent introduction of new defensive tactics, and was now deeply depressed.[4] His chief, *Generalfeldmarschall* Paul von Hindenburg, hinted at Ludendorff's shaken nerves: 'I pressed the hand of my First Quartermaster-General with the words: "We have lived through more critical times than to-day together." To-day! It was his birthday!'[5]

---

[1] Alan Allport, *Britain at Bay 1938–1941: The Epic Story of the Second World War* (London: Profile Books, 2020), 100.

[2] Captain Cyril Falls, *Military Operations: France and Belgium 1917*, vol. 1, *The German Retreat to the Hindenburg Line and the Battles of Arras* (London: Macmillan, 1940), 259 (hereafter, BOH 1917, 1).

[3] Kronprinz Rupprecht von Bayern, *Mein Kriegstagebuch*, ed. Eugen von Frauenholz (Munich: Deutscher National Verlag, 1929), 2:136 (9 April 1917).

[4] General Erich Ludendorff, *My War Memories 1914–1918* (London: Hutchinson, 1919), 421.

[5] Marshal Paul von Hindenburg, *Out of my Life*, trans. F. A. Holt (London: Cassell, 1920), 265. In formal terms, the Kaiser was Supreme Commander [*Oberster Kriegsherr*] of all

However, this British success was the high point of the Entente joint spring offensive that it opened.[6] The British made little progress in the rest of the battle of Arras. When the French launched the main effort of the joint offensive on 16 April – the Nivelle offensive – they made only tactical gains that bore no relation to their casualties, the strategic vision of the commander-in-chief, General Robert Nivelle, or the hopes of the troops. As the German official history commented, it was clear on the evening of the first day that the breakthrough had failed.[7] The collapse of the French assault and attempts to renew it led to mutiny in the French army, affecting its offensive capabilities for much of the rest of the year.[8] Both battles continued for weeks, but strategically the Germans had won.

This book explains the dramatic reversal of fortunes from the German side. In formal terms, it is a case study analysing the five key tasks of German operational command in the battles. The tasks – defined later in this Introduction – were co-ordinating the masses of troops, matériel and different levels of command needed to fight a modern battle, including striking the correct balance between decentralisation and control; selecting the right men for command and staff positions; using intelligence and communication to reduce the uncertainty caused by the chaotic nature of war so that it could be exploited; continuously learning and applying lessons from the ever-changing Western Front; and crucially, winning, both by preventing an Entente breakthrough and inflicting more casualties than suffered.

These tasks are derived from contemporary German and modern thinking on command, as well as from the current state of research on the Entente spring offensive and on the German army as an institution. But an even more important source is how German commanders and staff officers viewed the problems they faced and what to do about them. The book systematically compares pre-war thinking on these issues and developments in the early war period with what was going on in 1917, and it distinguishes the German army's doctrine and reputation from what actually happened.

German armed forces, Hindenburg was his top military adviser with the title Chief of the General Staff of the Field Army [*Chef des Generalstabes des Feldheeres*] in Supreme Army Command [*Oberste Heeresleitung* or OHL] and Ludendorff was Hindenburg's deputy as First Quartermaster-General [*Erster Generalquartiermeister*]. In fact, Ludendorff exercised the real power in the army.

[6] Formally speaking, the Triple Entente powers (Britain, France and Russia) became the Allies with the signing of the Pact of London in September 1914. However, the Germans often continued to refer to the Entente, and this book adopts the same usage. 'Entente spring offensive' means the principal Anglo-French operations of April–May 1917.

[7] Reichsarchiv, *Der Weltkrieg 1914 bis 1918: Die militärischen Operationen zu Lande*, vol. 12, *Die Kriegführung im Frühjahr 1917* (Berlin: E. S. Mittler, 1939), 403.

[8] BOH 1917, 1:505.

The concluding chapter shows that the findings from this case study apply well beyond early 1917 and in fact illustrate the story of the German army throughout the First World War. In this way, the book contributes to the debate on what has been described as the real question of the war: how was Germany able to hold out for over four years despite growing Entente dominance in both matériel and manpower?[9] This is the first strand to the meaning of 'holding out'. Holger Afflerbach's aptly named book *Auf Messers Schneide* [*On a Knife Edge*] is an important reminder that the conclusion of the war was not inevitable and that for much of its duration German defeat was by no means certain. Afflerbach argues that throughout the war the Central Powers, particularly Germany, were more militarily effective than their enemies and that this counterbalanced the latter's numerical and material superiority.[10] A pre-eminent component of this effectiveness was German fighting power, which only began to decline in summer 1918. Afflerbach further suggests that an unshakeable pride and confidence in German military superiority permeated German society from before the war till late in 1918, leading to the belief that the way out of the war must and could be found through military means.[11]

The second strand of 'holding out' in the book's title is how the German army held out against the Entente assault in early 1917. It is easy to dismiss this offensive as doomed to failure, the victim of the iron laws of early twentieth century warfare on the Western Front – the force/space ratio, with too many men and too much matériel in a small area, preventing manoeuvre; the added constraint on manoeuvre imposed by firepower's contemporary dominance over mobility; and the fragility of battlefield communications, which particularly disadvantaged the attacker. But this is hindsight. As we shall see, before the event the German army viewed the offensive as the decisive moment of the war, and afterwards thought its success in holding out was an 'absolutely extraordinary' achievement.[12] Furthermore, different operational choices by the Entente high command would almost certainly have produced much better results for the attackers. Even as it was, the

---

[9] Holger Afflerbach, *Auf Messers Schneide: Wie das Deutsche Reich den Ersten Weltkrieg verlor* (Munich: C. H. Beck, 2018), 8, quoting Professor Jay Winter on the real question of the war.

[10] The Central Powers were Germany and its allies Austria-Hungary, Bulgaria and the Ottoman Empire (Turkey).

[11] Afflerbach, *Auf Messers Schneide*, 21, 512–13 and 519.

[12] General der Infanterie a.D. Georg Wetzell to the Kriegsgeschichtliche Forschungsanstalt des Heeres [Army Research Institute for Military History], 19 January 1939, BArch, RH61/1901. In spring 1917, Wetzell was head of the First Section (Operations) in OHL's Operations Department [*Abteilung Ia/Operationsabteilung*].

German army only achieved its defensive victory at great and lasting cost to itself.[13]

The book examines the role of German operational command in this victory. 'Operational' here means relating to military operations rather than the operational level of war discussed in the next section. What the German army referred to as *Führung* [command] or *Truppenführung* [unit and formation command] would probably now be called command and control. One typical modern explanation describes command as what a commander does, and control as how he does it; the two are closely related and the boundaries between them are so blurred that they may become indistinguishable.[14] This suggests that there was logic behind the German army's treating the two concepts as one. The Germans themselves wrote much about command without defining it. German pre-war thought focused on mobile, offensive operations aimed at bringing about decisive battle. Conceptually, this was the core role of what was seen as 'high command' [*höhere Truppenführung*]. In organisational terms it was the realm of divisions, corps and, once they were formed in wartime, Armies and later army groups: these were the formations that comprised units of all arms and were therefore capable of conducting major battle.[15]

The third strand of the title is the paramount duty of German soldiers at all levels to hold out.[16] Most obviously, this means ordinary soldiers at the front facing the terrors of an attritional war. But it also refers to more senior officers in headquarters, who were subject to ferocious mental strain. The book is not about the experience of individual soldiers, but in reading its academic analysis of operational command, we must always remember the human consequences in all the combatant armies. For me, this means my paternal grandfather Comrie Cowan, a 20-year-old British company commander in 34th Division who was seriously wounded at the battle of Arras. A few days later, he wrote to his father:

I had wonderful good luck the day that I was hit on 7th [April] as I took a bombing raid of three officers and 100 men over. I was struck by a piece of shell just behind his second line and had my leg broken above the knee. I couldn't get away and about 2 hours afterwards I was taken prisoner and luckily remained in their fourth

---

[13] More on all this in Chapter 8.
[14] Gary Sheffield and Dan Todman, eds., *Command and Control on the Western Front: The British Army's Experience 1914–1918* (Staplehurst: Spellmount, 2004), 1.
[15] The book uses 'Army' with a capital letter to refer to specific field formations such as First Army, and 'army' in lower case for generic organisations such as the German army.
[16] On the centrality of holding out [*Durchhalten*] to German soldiers' duty during the war, especially in 1916–18, and to their subsequent interpretation of their experiences, see Anne Lipp, *Meinungslenkung im Krieg: Kriegserfahrungen deutscher Soldaten und ihre Deutung 1914–1918* (Göttingen: Vandenhoeck & Ruprecht, 2003), particularly 129–72 and 320.

line until after the attack when I was released by our own fellows. Pretty lucky!!
I am afraid that I have lost my leg, but I'll soon get used to that.

Holding out indeed.

Significance of the Entente Spring Offensive

> ... this gigantic struggle, which can really only be compared with our
> 1918 attack.[17]

The Entente spring offensive of 1917 is well-suited as a case study of
German command because it was a significant event at each of the four
different levels of war where military activity takes place. At the risk of
oversimplifying, a short explanation may be helpful here. The top level is
national or grand strategy, which concerns 'the co-ordinated use of the
three principal instruments of national power: economic, diplomatic and
military'. Next comes military strategy, the military component of grand
strategy. Third is the operational level at which campaigns are planned
and executed. Finally, the tactical level is where 'warfighting actually
takes place'.[18] These levels should not be seen as totally distinct, and
indeed one of the themes of this book is the linkages between them.

The year 1916 had been very difficult for all the main participants in the
war. As David Stevenson has put it, 'The European nations had dug
themselves into a war trap, and on one level the story of 1917 is of their
efforts to escape it.'[19] At the beginning of the year, both the Central
Powers and the Entente looked for a quick-fix conclusion to the war,
but not at the cost of abandoning their war aims. Throughout 1917,
military operations interacted with various peace initiatives. These initiatives all failed, partly because respective war aims were far apart and partly
because of the political–military interaction. Stevenson again: 'The diplomatic impasse set the context for decisions to launch offensives, and the
military balance shaped responses to the peace bids.' Both sides still had
reason to believe that military operations would win them more than
diplomacy.[20]

---

[17] Wetzell to the Kriegsgeschichtliche Forschungsanstalt des Heeres, 19 January 1939,
BArch, RH61/1901.
[18] Ministry of Defence, *British Defence Doctrine (Joint Warfare Publication 0–01)*, 2nd ed.
(London: Ministry of Defence, 2001), 1–2 and 1–3. This edition, rather than more recent
ones, is used here because for analytical purposes its terms are clearer, especially on grand
strategy. British and allied doctrine now refers to three levels of war, confusingly putting
national and military strategy on the same level.
[19] David Stevenson, *1917: War, Peace, and Revolution* (Oxford: Oxford University Press,
2017), 9.
[20] Ibid., 234 and 395.

In grand strategic terms, the Entente objective in spring 1917 was to launch a knock-out blow by concentric offensives on the Western, Italian and Eastern Fronts. Failure to co-ordinate these efforts, partly caused by the Russian Revolution beginning in March, was one of the chief factors in the defeat of the Anglo-French offensive.[21] German grand strategy for the year was to beat off the Entente attacks on land while a greatly intensified U-boat campaign at sea – unrestricted submarine warfare – brought Britain to its knees. The German assessment, or gamble, was that the campaign would succeed in five months. It would almost certainly cause the United States to enter the war on the Entente side, but Britain would collapse before American military forces could have any significant effect in the crucial theatre.[22]

So the two sides' grand strategies, including the Entente spring offensive, affected and were affected by the Russian Revolution and the United States' entry, events that shaped the rest of the war and indeed the twentieth century. As an illustration of the chronological links, the United States declared war on the day of an important and controversial French conference that finally gave the go-ahead for the Nivelle offensive. Lenin left Zurich in the famous sealed train on 9 April, the day the battle of Arras started, and arrived in Petrograd on 16 April, the day the Nivelle offensive started.[23] The dates are of course coincidence, but nevertheless underline the linkages between political and military developments.

Taking Russia first, the revolution highlights how what is obvious now was not at all obvious then. By the end of 1917, Russia was about to leave the war, a major victory for the Central Powers. But this only became clear after the Bolsheviks' coup in November, with their policy of peace at any price. Earlier in the year, everything was uncertain. Even a senior officer like *General der Infanterie* Moriz Freiherr von Lyncker, one of the Kaiser's closest confidantes, changed his mind almost daily about the future of Russia in the first half of the year – sometimes believing the country was about to collapse, sometimes that it was recovering; sometimes that events there would help the Entente, sometimes the Central Powers.[24]

---

[21] See Chapter 8. Dates in this book relating to Russia follow the Gregorian calendar rather than the Julian used in Russia at the time, which was thirteen days behind.

[22] Stevenson, *1917*, chapter 1 gives a full account of the evolution of the unrestricted submarine warfare campaign.

[23] Catherine Merridale, *Lenin on the Train* ([London]: Allen Lane, 2016), 179 and 226.

[24] Holger Afflerbach, ed., *Kaiser Wilhelm II. als Oberster Kriegsherr im Ersten Weltkrieg: Quellen aus der militärischen Umgebung des Kaisers 1914–1918* (Munich: Oldenbourg, 2005), 99 for a summary, and in more detail Lyncker's letters to his wife, 475–81 (March–April 1917), 483, 487, 491, 494, 496–9 (May), 503–4, 506–8, 511 (June) and 514–15 (July).

Such uncertainties affected decision-making on both sides. OHL's chief operations officer, *Major* Georg Wetzell, assessed in late May that it was premature to place too much hope in a Russian collapse. In his view, OHL should act on the worst-case scenario, that the present stalemate on the Eastern Front would continue and the Central Powers would have to keep strong forces there.[25] From the western allies' point of view, Russia's failure or inability to co-ordinate an offensive with them greatly reduced the pressure on the German army in spring 1917. But by remaining a belligerent and indeed taking the offensive later on – the so-called Kerensky offensive – Russia provided relief right up till November. This affected operations throughout the year: the British government saw Russia continuing to pull its weight and pin significant forces on the Eastern Front as a factor in the success or failure of the offensive at Ypres that summer and autumn.[26]

Conversely, the need to support Russia in its difficulties was one reason why Britain and France decided in early May to continue their offensive. Similarly, the Italian high command feared that a Russian collapse would enable the Germans and Austro-Hungarians to transfer strong forces to their front. So relieving pressure on the Russians was a factor in the decision to keep attacking on the Isonzo. Indeed, the defeat of the Kerensky offensive in Russia did allow the Central Powers to divert forces to Italy for what became their very successful attack at Caporetto.[27] And Russia's disintegration at the end of 1917 enabled a German build-up on the Western Front for the huge spring offensives in 1918.

Not long after the United States declared war on 6 April, British War Cabinet member Lord Milner wrote to his colleagues, 'The entrance of America into the war has introduced a new factor, of great ultimate promise but small immediate value.'[28] The Germans certainly agreed with the latter point, and indeed had earlier assessed the United States as militarily less important than Bulgaria.[29] Given its small size, the US army would be unable to make a significant contribution on the Western Front till 1918. This would be too late, since Germany expected that the U-boat campaign would already have forced Britain out of the war by then. The US part of this assessment was well founded, as there were in fact only 130,000 American troops in France by December.[30]

---

[25] Reichsarchiv, *Weltkrieg*, 12:549.   [26] Stevenson, *1917*, 145, 168 and 190–1.

[27] Ibid., 179, 210–11 and 222.

[28] David R. Woodward, *Trial by Friendship: Anglo-American Relations, 1917–1918* (Lexington, KY: University of Kentucky Press, 2003), 68.

[29] Afflerbach, *Auf Messers Schneide*, 189.

[30] Brigadier-General Sir James E. Edmonds, *Military Operations: France and Belgium, 1918*, vol. 1, *The German March Offensive and Its Preliminaries* (London: Macmillan, 1935), 35 (hereafter BOH 1918, 1).

In the longer term of course, the huge accession of strength represented by the United States' entry into the war was a decisive factor in the eventual Allied victory. But the expectation alone of the US army arriving on the Western Front influenced Entente thinking from much earlier. Even before the United States actually declared war, the French government considered whether to defer the spring offensive until American help could make itself felt.[31] As soon as General Philippe Pétain replaced Nivelle after the offensive had failed in May, he stressed the need to wait for the Americans.[32] In June, British prime minister David Lloyd George worried that if Russia dropped out on the Entente side but Austria-Hungary remained with the Central Powers, the Germans could transfer 1.5 million men to the Western Front, greatly outnumbering the half a million Americans expected at that time. The Allies would then have no chance of victory.[33]

In Germany, when Hindenburg and Ludendorff had formed the 'Third OHL' in late August 1916, they faced a crisis on the Western Front:

We had heavy losses in men and material ... The strain on physical and moral strength was tremendous and divisions could only be kept in the line for a few days at a time ... The number of available divisions was shrinking ... The supply of ammunition was steadily getting shorter ... The situation on the Western Front gave cause for greater anxiety than I had anticipated ...[34]

Germany's rapid success against Rumania in late 1916 gave it an end-of-year fillip. But this was balanced by a sharp local defeat at Verdun in December and anyway the reality was that in the west at least the Entente had the initiative: OHL was well aware that they would aim to launch multiple attacks in different theatres early in 1917. Austria-Hungary was a particular worry, and Lyncker for one feared that it was finally falling apart and might even become an open enemy.[35]

By now, Germany's economic and political situation was also turning to crisis. A hard winter and growing problems of food supply led to strikes and the foundation of the radical Independent Social Democratic Party [USPD] promoting a compromise peace with no annexations or reparations. As one sign of the increasing strain, OHL's department IIIb

[31] Ministère de la Guerre, *Les Armées françaises dans la grande guerre*, tome V, vol. 1, *L'offensive d'avril 1917 (1er novembre 1916 – 15 mai 1917)* (Paris: Imprimerie Nationale, 1931), 561 (hereafter, AFGG, V/1, etc.).

[32] AFGG, V/2, *Les opérations à objectifs limités (15 mai – 1er novembre 1917)* (Paris: Imprimerie Nationale, 1937), viii.

[33] Stevenson, *1917*, 190.

[34] Ludendorff, *My War Memories*, 244–6. The First OHL was headed by *Generaloberst* Helmuth von Moltke, the Second by *General der Infanterie* Erich von Falkenhayn.

[35] Lyncker to his wife, 14–15 April and 12–19 June 1917, in Afflerbach, *Kaiser Wilhelm II. als Oberster Kriegsherr*, 480–1 and 507–10.

(the military secret intelligence service) set up a section to study the growing number of attacks on the monarchy, OHL and morale in the civilian population and the army.[36] In a political concession, the Kaiser's 'Easter Message' promised a more democratic voting system in Prussia – the largest federal German state – once a successful peace was concluded.

The increasing political and economic tensions had a direct effect at the front, as the strikes included armaments workers and contributed to difficulty replacing aircraft losses in May. So concerned was OHL that it called for reports on the effect political developments in Germany were having on the troops, and issued orders to 'educate' them on the army's right to demand the highest possible production of munitions from the homeland.[37] *Generalleutnant* Otto von Moser, commanding a corps at Arras, raged that the strikes were taking place 'when our brave troops are fighting with all their strength against such a superiority in men and matériel and when every rifle, gun, shell and aircraft which does not arrive or arrives late must be replaced with German blood!'[38] More generally, the tensions in Germany mirrored the growing and continuous strain to which the army was subjected throughout the year.

In France, the disappointing results and heavy casualties of over two years of war triggered increasingly vociferous parliamentary attacks on the commander-in-chief, General Joseph Joffre. At the same time, morale in the army dropped to crisis point.[39] To save his government, Premier Aristide Briand restructured his cabinet in December 1916, brought in General Hubert Lyautey as Minister of War, side-lined Joffre (who soon resigned) and appointed Nivelle commander of the armies in France. Briand's reformed government did not last long. A row with parliament in March 1917 led to Lyautey's resignation and the fall of the government.

Two main factors lay behind these changes. First was concern that France was running out of time, given the exhaustion of the army and declining manpower. Both Joffre and Nivelle supported a decisive offensive in 1917. But whereas Joffre wanted a step-by-step Somme-style advance, Nivelle planned to adopt the rapid and violent tactics that had

[36] Michael Epkenhans, Gerhard P. Groß, Markus Pöhlmann and Christian Stachelbeck, eds., *Geheimdienst und Propaganda im Ersten Weltkrieg: Die Aufzeichnungen von Oberst Walter Nicolai 1914 bis 1918* (Berlin: de Gruyter, 2019), 366.

[37] General der Infanterie Otto von Below, 'Ausarbeitungen zu Kämpfen und Feldzügen des Ersten Weltkrieges. Bd. 22: Sommerkrieg in Artois 27. Apr.–8. Sept. 1917', unpublished manuscript in BArch, Otto von Below Nachlass, N87/61, 6 and 18 May 1917 (hereafter, Otto von Below diary); Lipp, *Meinungslenkung*, 258 and 290–2.

[38] Otto von Moser, *Feldzugsaufzeichnungen 1914–1918 als Brigade-, Divisionskommandeur und als kommandierender General*, 3rd ed. (Stuttgart: Belser, 1928), 297. More on Moser in Chapter 4.

[39] Robert A. Doughty, *Pyrrhic Victory: French Strategy and Operations in the Great War* (Cambridge, MA: Harvard University Press, 2005), 317.

brought him two smart victories in Verdun in October and December 1916. Everyone knew that Nivelle meant risk, but this was balanced by the risk that if the Entente could not bring about victory before autumn 1917, France would be forced to negotiate for peace on unfavourable terms. Nivelle promised a way of winning the war; more cautious methods advocated by commanders such as Pétain did not. As Lyautey's successor Paul Painlevé said, 'In war one must take the gravest decisions in uncertainty about the exact state of the enemy, and none is without risk.'[40]

The second factor was the desire to reassert parliamentary and governmental control of military affairs. But there were sharp differences of view about war aims and how to achieve them militarily.[41] President Raymond Poincaré supported wide-ranging French demands, including some kind of control over the Rhineland and possibly dissolving Germany as a unified state. He therefore backed first Joffre's and then Nivelle's plans for a decisive campaign in 1917, which might equally well have been named the Poincaré offensive. Painlevé on the other hand believed in a more moderate peace involving the return of Alsace-Lorraine to France and guarantees of security. Militarily, he sought a third way between the all-out offensive represented by Nivelle and defeatism espoused by some politicians to his left. To achieve this, he backed Pétain's plans for a defensive posture while waiting for the Americans. From entering office on 20 March 1917, he was therefore hostile to Nivelle and his offensive.

In Britain, disappointment over the results of the battle of the Somme and an escalating commitment to the war had contributed to Lloyd George becoming prime minister in December 1916. He was as determined as anyone to secure victory, but equally he was appalled by the casualties on the Somme. When his attempts to promote offensives away from the Western Front failed, he eagerly accepted Nivelle's proposal that France should make the main effort in early 1917. His subsequent plot to subordinate the British commander-in-chief, Field Marshal Sir Douglas Haig, to Nivelle for the period of the joint offensive was one of the lowest ever points in British civil–military relations.[42]

One of Lloyd George's most immediate problems was Britain's increasingly poor financial situation, dependent as it was on American loans to pay for strategic imports. US government restrictions on loan

---

[40] Stevenson, *1917*, 119–21, 143–4 and 398.

[41] What follows draws heavily on Georges-Henri Soutou, 'Poincaré, Painlevé et l'offensive Nivelle', in Jean-Claude Allain, ed., *Des Étoiles et des Croix* (Paris: Economica, 1995), 91–109.

[42] Elizabeth Greenhalgh, *Victory through Coalition: Britain and France during the First World War* (Cambridge: Cambridge University Press, 2005), 133–48.

conditions in November 1916 immediately damaged British credit, leading the Chancellor of the Exchequer to warn that by June 1917 the American President would be able to dictate his terms to Britain. It has been suggested that during this crisis the Entente came closer to defeat than at any time since the battle of the Marne in 1914. This may be exaggerated, but ultimately only the prospect and then reality of the United States' entry into the war eased the Entente's financial danger.[43]

It will be sufficient here simply to outline the significance of the Entente spring offensive at the other three levels of war, as they are covered in detail later. At the strategic and operational levels, Nivelle planned to fight a series of linked British and French battles to destroy the German army in the field.[44] The German defeat of this ambitious plan was a strategic victory, boosted by the subsequent mutinies in the French army. Finally, on the tactical level, the spring fighting saw the introduction of new methods by all three armies based on experience from 1916. The Entente would use much greater artillery fire and improved all-arms co-operation, including better infantry tactics, to launch a more powerful and faster assault. However, the Germans too had learned from their harrowing experiences on the Somme. As well as introducing new, more mobile defensive tactics, Hindenburg and Ludendorff had reorganised the higher-level handling of battle; and they had begun training on these new techniques from divisional commander to private.

The Entente spring offensive saw the first test of these new methods. Although not as prominent in First World War historiography or popular memory as Verdun, the Somme and Third Ypres, it was a major military event, as Georg Wetzell reflected in the quote heading this section. The British had fourteen divisions in the front line on 9 April, the same number as on 1 July 1916. The French had sixty active infantry divisions waiting to go into battle, compared with forty-nine in August 1914. Facing the French, the Germans deployed forty-five divisions compared to ten attacking or otherwise taking part on the first day of Verdun. Over 200 divisions from all three armies were involved in the two battles and related fighting, totalling at least 2 million men. Huge quantities of matériel were committed too, including thousands of guns and aircraft.

---

[43] Stevenson, *1917*, 48–9 and 60. Niall Ferguson, *The Pity of War* (London: Allen Lane, 1998), 326–9 downplays the seriousness of the Entente's financial problems at this time.
[44] Doughty, *Pyrrhic Victory*, 324–6.

Current State of Research

> There are few notions in modern history more secure than that of German military excellence.[45]

Despite the importance of the Entente spring offensive, there is no satisfactory modern account. In German historiography it plays a much smaller role than the dramatic events of 1914 and 1918.[46] This is part of a broader trend in Germany, where operational military history was traditionally the monopoly of the military; before 1945 civilian historians were kept out of it and since then have generally shunned it.[47] Jack Sheldon has provided the only modern English-language work on the German army in the offensive. His book relies mainly on published regimental histories and portrays the battles largely from the perspective of participants below battalion level; about two-thirds of the book covers the opening few days of the offensive, with a lot more on the British than the bigger French effort. It contains much useful material, particularly on the damage done to the German army, but the structure and limited sources preclude a full over-view or analysis of the offensive.[48]

Historians of the French army have paid more attention to the mutinies triggered by the offensive than the fighting itself, the classic work being Guy Pedroncini's *Les Mutineries de 1917*.[49] Leonard V. Smith's important research on the French 5th Division follows suit: though not in action during the offensive, the division was one of those worst affected by mutiny.[50] David Murphy's *Breaking Point of the French Army* gives a general account of the offensive but is too thinly sourced to be authoritative.[51] Denis Rolland has partly covered the gap in his biography of Nivelle, centring on Nivelle's period as commander-in-chief. Rolland is particularly illuminating on the troubled relations between government

---

[45] Robert M. Citino, *The German Way of War: From the Thirty Years' War to the Third Reich* (Lawrence, KS: University Press of Kansas, 2005), xii.

[46] Benjamin Ziemann, 'Le Chemin des Dames dans l'historiographie militaire allemande', in Nicholas Offenstadt, ed., *Le Chemin des Dames: De l'événement à la mémoire* (Paris: Éditions Stock, 2004), 341.

[47] Stig Förster, 'The Battlefield: Towards a Modern History of War', 2007 annual lecture to the German Historical Institute London (London: German Historical Institute, 2008), 7–8 and 11.

[48] Jack Sheldon, *The German Army in the Spring Offensives 1917: Arras, Aisne and Champagne* (Barnsley: Pen & Sword, 2015).

[49] Guy Pedroncini, *Les Mutineries de 1917*, 4th ed. (Paris: Presses Universitaires de France, 1999). For more recent research, see André Loez and Nicolas Mariot, eds., *Obéir/ désobéir: Les mutineries de 1917 en perspective* (Paris: Éditions La Découverte, 2008).

[50] Leonard V. Smith, *Between Mutiny and Obedience: The Case of the French Fifth Infantry Division during World War I* (Princeton, NJ: Princeton University Press, 1994), chapter 8.

[51] David Murphy, *Breaking Point of the French Army: The Nivelle Offensive of 1917* (Barnsley: Pen & Sword, 2015).

and military and between senior French officers. However, he covers the operational aspects of the offensive in less depth, has little to say about the British contribution and ultimately veers too far towards an attempted rehabilitation of Nivelle.[52] Nicolas Offenstadt's edited book *Le Chemin des Dames* contains some material on operations, but the focus is on social history issues. Elizabeth Greenhalgh's *The French Army and the First World War* gives a good summary of the Nivelle period, particularly the poor civil–military relations, but as a general work covering the whole war inevitably cannot go into much detail about the operations. Michel Goya's thematic *La chair et l'acier* on the development of the French army during the war is important but again cannot devote much space to the Nivelle offensive.[53]

For many years, British historians of 1916–17 concentrated on the battles of the Somme and Third Ypres, which were larger-scale than the battle of Arras as well as being emotionally more charged. Recent work has improved our understanding of Arras. The main account is now Don Farr's *A Battle Too Far*, which is largely non-analytical but covers the French as well as British sectors and replaces Jonathan Nicholls' older *Cheerful Sacrifice*. Other books deal with specific aspects rather than the whole battle, such as those by Jim Smithson (first six days of Arras), Jonathan Walker (Bullecourt), Geoffrey Hayes and others (Canadians) and Peter Hart (air).[54] Finally, Spencer Jones' edited work *The Darkest Year* publishes the latest scholarship on the British army in 1917; particularly relevant to this book are chapters by Meleah Hampton on Bullecourt, Harry Sanderson on the 'Black Day of the British Army' (the 3 May attack at Arras) and Tim Gale usefully comparing the British and French tank forces.[55]

What can the voluminous thematic coverage of the German army as an institution contribute to our understanding of its ability to hold out in

---

[52] Denis Rolland, *Nivelle: L'inconnu du Chemin des Dames* (Paris: Éditions Imago, 2012); see also André Loez's review in *Vingtième Siècle*, no. 116 (2012), 176.

[53] Elizabeth Greenhalgh, *The French Army and the First World War* (Cambridge: Cambridge University Press, 2014), chapter 5; Michel Goya, *La chair et l'acier: L'armée française et l'invention de la guerre moderne (1914–1918)* (Paris: Tallandier, 2004).

[54] Don Farr, *A Battle Too Far: Arras 1917* (Warwick: Helion, 2018); Jonathan Nicholls, *Cheerful Sacrifice: The Battle of Arras 1917* (London: Leo Cooper, 1990); Jim Smithson, *A Taste of Success: The First Battle of the Scarpe. The Opening Phase of the Battle of Arras, 9–14 April 1917* (Solihull: Helion, 2017); Jonathan Walker, *The Blood Tub: General Gough and the Battle of Bullecourt, 1917* (Staplehurst: Spellmount, 1998); Geoffrey Hayes, Andrew Iarocci and Mike Bechthold, eds., *Vimy Ridge: A Canadian Reassessment* (Waterloo, ON: Laurier Centre for Military Strategic and Disarmament Studies, 2007); Peter Hart, *Bloody April: Slaughter in the Skies over Arras, 1917* (London: Weidenfeld & Nicolson, 2005).

[55] Spencer Jones, ed., *The Darkest Year: The British Army on the Western Front 1917* (Warwick: Helion, 2022).

early 1917? Here we confront a running argument about the quality of the army and its command methods. As illustrated by the quote leading this section, Holger Afflerbach is by no means alone in suggesting that Germany was more militarily effective than its enemies and that a major reason for this was the German army's fighting power. On the other hand, while writing this book and the doctoral thesis on which it is based, various scholars have suggested to me that viewing the German army as a benchmark of military excellence is now something of a straw man. Daniel J. Hughes and Richard L. DiNardo comment judiciously that careful study over many years has chipped away at the reputation of the German army, but its image as 'capable of operational and tactical brilliance in both world wars remains strong, especially in the popular imagination and even in professional military circles'.[56]

The idea of German military superiority is particularly prevalent in older scholarship, an obvious example being Trevor N. Dupuy's *A Genius for War*.[57] Dupuy was not blind to problems in the German military system, but thought it was an example of institutionalised military excellence, resulting in a combat performance in different ages and situations almost invariably superior to any enemy. The key elements were the army's characteristic command methods and principles, especially the standardisation of general staff work at a high level of efficiency. Even before Dupuy, Graeme C. Wynne's *If Germany Attacks* had proposed that in terms of doctrine, the outstanding feature of the First World War was the development of German defensive tactics. In Wynne's view, German tactical expertise and learning consistently outclassed the less adroit British. Later works that have drawn heavily on Wynne include the now rather dated but still much quoted studies by Timothy T. Lupfer, Bruce I. Gudmundsson and Martin Samuels.[58]

The most substantial of these works is Samuels' *Command or Control?*, which looks at both the British and German armies. Samuels rightly

---

[56] Daniel J. Hughes and Richard L. DiNardo, *Imperial Germany and War, 1871–1918* (Lawrence, KS: University Press of Kansas, 2018), xi.

[57] Trevor N. Dupuy, *A Genius for War: The German Army and General Staff, 1807–1945* (London: Macdonald and Jane's, 1977).

[58] Graeme C. Wynne, *If Germany Attacks: The Battle in Depth in the West*, ed. Robert T. Foley (Brighton: Tom Donovan, 2008); Timothy T. Lupfer, *The Dynamics of Doctrine: The Changes in German Tactical Doctrine during the First World War* (Fort Leavenworth, KS: Combat Studies Institute, U.S. Army Command and General Staff College, 1981); Bruce I. Gudmundsson, *Stormtroop Tactics: Innovation in the German Army, 1914–1918* (New York: Praeger, 1989); Martin Samuels, *Command or Control? Command, Training and Tactics in the British and German Armies, 1888–1918* (London: Frank Cass, 1995). See also Christian E. O. Millotat, *Das preußisch-deutsche Generalstabssystem: Wurzeln-Entwicklung-Fortwirken* (Zurich: Hochschulverlag, 2000), passim.

stresses what he calls the comparatives of effectiveness; in other words, the least ineffective army wins.[59] His core argument revolves round the German use of mission command. A well-known military writer gave a contemporary definition of this concept: 'Orders give information on the situation and the intentions of the commander, and assign tasks, but leave the recipient free to choose the method of carrying them out.'[60] Samuels believes that the resulting decentralisation increased flexibility and was generally more effective in the chaotic environment of First World War battle than the British preference for restrictive control mitigated by what he calls the 'umpiring' system; by this term he means delegating control to the point of abdicating responsibility. Various objections can be made to this argument, including that Samuels' concept of umpiring is flawed.[61] Also, he concentrates on infantry tactics: if he had included the artillery, he would have had to allow for the view of many German experts that artillery worked better under restrictive control than mission command.[62]

There was in fact a contradiction at the heart of mission command as a principle in modern war. By 1914, German military thinkers understood the crucial role of all-arms co-operation in tactical success. However, this gave rise to conflicting needs for centralisation of command in order to synchronise combined arms battle, and for decentralisation to handle the extent and pace of modern combat with its associated uncertainties and heavy casualties.[63] A recent study of mission command argues that German practitioners were well aware of its weaknesses and viewed control to achieve unity of action as being at least as important. Finding the right balance between these two principles was one of the continuities of Prussian-German command beginning with Helmuth von Moltke the Elder. For Moltke, means of control included adherence to the order of battle and chain of command, as well as efficiently passing orders and information through the general staff.[64]

---

[59] Samuels, *Command or Control?*, 3.

[60] Colonel William Balck, *Tactics*, vol. 1, *Introduction and Formal Tactics of Infantry*, 4th ed., trans. Walter Krueger (Fort Leavenworth, KS: US Cavalry Association, 1915), 41.

[61] Andy Simpson, *Directing Operations: British Corps Command on the Western Front 1914–18* (Stroud: Spellmount, 2006), xx.

[62] Hew Strachan, Review of *Command or Control? Command, Training and Tactics in the British and German Armies, 1888–1918* by Martin Samuels, *Journal of Military History*, vol. 60, no. 4 (October 1996), 778–9.

[63] Antulio J. Echevarria II, *After Clausewitz: German Military Thinkers before the Great War* (Lawrence, KS: University Press of Kansas, 2000), 5–6.

[64] Marco Sigg, *Der Unterführer als Feldherr im Taschenformat: Theorie und Praxis der Auftragstaktik im deutschen Heer 1869 bis 1945* (Paderborn: Schöningh, 2014), 130–43 and 462.

Later on, Alfred Graf von Schlieffen was faced with the problem of directing armies even larger than Moltke's in a two-front war involving bigger and longer battles. His solution was to move the balance further in the direction of control, including by strengthening the general staff system. In contrast his successor, Helmuth von Moltke the Younger, was a proponent of greater independence for commanders on the spot.[65] The 1910 manual 'Essentials of High Command', reprinted without change in 1913, codified the doctrine with which the German army entered the war. As an amalgamation of the older Moltke's views – indeed as far as possible retaining his wording verbatim – with those of Schlieffen and of the younger Moltke, it attempted to balance a subordinate commander's right to independence and his duty to follow his superior's intentions.[66]

The situation faced by the German army on the Western Front after the onset of trench warfare and especially from 1916 was very different from the one assumed in the 1910 instructions. Most obviously, it was static not mobile. In addition, the German army had been forced onto the defensive, it had lost both numerical and material superiority and heavy casualties were eroding its quality. These problems were not entirely unforeseen. Although planning (and hoping) for a short war, many senior German commanders – including both Moltkes – feared that it might last much longer. Nor had the German army completely ignored preparations for a war of matériel.[67] Nevertheless, Ludendorff's description of the crisis on the Western Front in late 1916 shows the unprecedented strain on the German command system. OHL's response included ordering regular reports on the state of divisions as a management tool to handle the effects of attrition. Better known is its promulgation of new defensive doctrine in the series 'Regulations for Trench Warfare for All Arms'

---

[65] Good accounts of the two Moltkes' and Schlieffen's military thought in Daniel J. Hughes, trans. and ed., *Moltke on the Art of War: Selected Writings* (Novato, CA: Presidio Press, 1993); Robert T. Foley, trans. and ed., *Alfred von Schlieffen's Military Writings* (London: Frank Cass, 2003); and Annika Mombauer, *Helmuth von Moltke and the Origins of the First World War* (Cambridge: Cambridge University Press, 2001). See Sigg, *Unterführer als Feldherr*, 210 for Moltke the Younger's strong belief in granting independence to subordinates.

[66] Kriegsministerium [Ministry of War], *D. V.E. 53. Grundzüge der höheren Truppenführung: Vom 1. Januar 1910* (Berlin: Reichsdruckerei, 1913), 9 and 12; as with all references in German manuals here, these are section numbers [*Ziffer*] not pages. For an overview of German pre-1914 thinking, see Tony Cowan, 'German Army Command and Control in the Late Nineteenth and Early Twentieth Centuries', unpublished research paper, 2010, https://independent.academia.edu/CowanTony; and in more detail, Hughes and DiNardo, *Imperial Germany and War*, chapters 2 and 4.

[67] Hew Strachan, *The First World War*, vol. 1, *To Arms* (Oxford: Oxford University Press, 2003), 1005–11 and 1014–35.

[*Vorschriften für den Stellungskrieg für alle Waffen*]; as the title suggests, the doctrine covered the key issue of all-arms co-operation.

Led by Wynne, literature on the war has concentrated on the tactical developments described in the main manual of this series, 'Principles for the Conduct of the Defensive Battle in Trench Warfare' (hereafter, 'Defensive Battle'), particularly the introduction of mobile defence in depth. In fact this manual gave instructions for controlling the whole battle as it had developed by late 1916, including intelligence, top-down defensive organisation, handling of reserves and the management of attrition. The army also continued its traditional stress on the importance of personality.[68] These aspects of wartime command have generally not received systematic attention. Good work has been done on German intelligence before and at the beginning of the war. Markus Pöhlmann has provided an overview of its activities during the war, but highlights the need for further studies on the effect of intelligence on operations.[69] There has also been productive analysis of soldiers undergoing the horrors of a war of attrition: Alexander Watson's *Enduring the Great War* is especially valuable as a comparative study on the resilience of the British and German armies.[70] But such works do not address the management of attrition, in particular how the German army evaluated its formations' fitness for major battle as a basis for their most economical and effective deployment. Nor is there any detailed analysis of how personality fitted into German thought on command in a war of matériel.

Core to assessing the excellence or otherwise of the German army is the question whether it was a thinking army: this is in fact one of the liveliest areas of debate in the literature. The ability to learn – analysed fully in

---

[68] Chef des Generalstabes des Feldheeres, *Vorschriften für den Stellungskrieg für alle Waffen*, Teil 8, *Grundsätze für die Führung in der Abwehrschlacht im Stellungskriege: Vom 1. Dezember 1916. Neudruck vom 1. März 1917* (Berlin: Reichsdruckerei, 1916), 1, 3, 5 and 7–10 (hereafter, '*Abwehrschlacht*', March 1917); AOK 1, 'Erfahrungen der 1. Armee in der Sommeschlacht 1916, I: Taktischer Teil', Generallandesarchiv Karlsruhe, 456 F1/525, 7 and 24 (hereafter, AOK 1, 'Erfahrungen'). All Generallandesarchiv Karlsruhe references in this book are in the 456 series (hereafter, GLAK).

[69] Markus Pöhlmann, 'German Intelligence at War, 1914–1918', *Journal of Intelligence History*, vol. 5, no. 2 (winter 2005), 39. Lukas Grawe, *Deutsche Feindaufklärung vor dem Ersten Weltkrieg: Informationen und Einschätzungen des deutschen Generalstabs zu den Armeen Frankreichs und Russlands 1904 bis 1914* (Paderborn: Schöningh, 2017) is particularly important for the pre-war period. See also Robert T. Foley, 'Easy Target or Invincible Enemy? German Intelligence Assessments of France Before the Great War', *Journal of Intelligence History*, vol. 5, no. 2 (winter 2005), 1–24; Ulrich Trumpener, 'War Premeditated? German Intelligence Operations in July 1914', *Central European History*, vol. 9, no. 1 (March 1976), 58–85; and Holger H. Herwig, 'Imperial Germany', in Ernest R. May, ed., *Knowing One's Enemies: Intelligence Assessment before the Two World Wars* (Princeton, NJ: Princeton University Press, 1984), 62–97.

[70] Alexander Watson, *Enduring the Great War: Combat, Morale and Collapse in the German and British Armies, 1914–1918* (Cambridge: Cambridge University Press, 2008).

Chapter 7 – was of course crucial to coping with the unexpected emergence of trench warfare and the constantly evolving challenges of the modern battlefield. For many years, there have been two diametrically opposed schools of thought, one emphasising the German army's intellectual openness and progressive nature, the other its resistance to change. The former focuses on the army's military professionalism, the latter on its conservatism and its social and political role, especially suppressing unrest in Germany.

Broadly speaking, Wynne, Dupuy, Lupfer, Gudmundsson, Samuels, Sheldon and Terence Zuber belong to the first school.[71] So too does Arden Bucholz, who describes how the Prussians developed what he calls 'deep-future-oriented war planning', looking ahead one to five years, to help organise a mass army for war.[72] He portrays the thoroughness and process by which the German army evolved war plans and trained its staff officers to carry them out. Antulio J. Echevarria and Robert T. Foley are also generally in this school. Echevarria concludes that by 1914 German military thinkers had understood many of the problems mass armies would face in war, including how to use combined arms tactics to cope with modern firepower, and that at least some of their proposed solutions were valid.[73] Foley has argued that the German army was an example of 'institutionalised innovation' with a tradition of intellectual openness and continuous education. This mindset placed it in a good position intellectually to find answers to the problems of trench warfare when it began in late 1914.[74] Continuing his theme into the war years, he has analysed German horizontal innovation through circulation of *Erfahrungsberichte* [after-action reports] as the basic mechanism by which the army was able to assimilate and circulate experience rapidly and so continually improve tactics.[75]

However, scholars disputing the view of German military excellence also have much ammunition to hand. Bernd-Felix Schulte claims that the pre-war army was conservative, slow to innovate and focused more on the need to suppress internal unrest than on warfighting.[76] Eric Dorn Brose

---

[71] On Zuber, see Robert A. Doughty, Review of *The Battle of the Frontiers: Ardennes 1914* by Terence Zuber, *Journal of Military History*, vol. 72, no. 3 (2008), 965–6.

[72] Arden Bucholz, *Moltke, Schlieffen and Prussian War Planning* (New York: Berg, 1991), 12–17.

[73] Echevarria, *After Clausewitz*, 5–6 and 213–28.

[74] Robert T. Foley, 'Institutionalized Innovation: The German Army and the Changing Nature of War 1871–1914', *RUSI Journal*, vol. 147, no. 2 (April 2002), 89.

[75] Robert T. Foley, 'Learning War's Lessons: The German Army and the Battle of the Somme 1916', *Journal of Military History*, vol. 75, no. 2 (April 2011), 471–504; and 'A Case Study in Horizontal Military Innovation: The German Army, 1916–1918', *Journal of Strategic Studies*, vol. 35, no. 6 (December 2012), 799–827.

[76] Bernd-Felix Schulte, *Die deutsche Armee 1900–1914: Zwischen Beharren und Verändern* (Düsseldorf: Droste Verlag, 1977).

believes that 'stubborn adherence to the old ways' led to the failure of the initial German 1914 offensive in the west and the four-year stalemate of trench warfare.[77] Technical and organisational weaknesses of command and control certainly contributed to the offensive's failure. The German army had developed its communications, transport and logistics capabilities, but insufficiently to control and support the grandiose operational plan. These were serious deficiencies in the professional expertise of the general staff; indeed, Gerhard P. Groß labels the resulting gap between operational requirements and actual capability 'the suppression of reality'.[78]

Some writers have commented negatively on the general staff's increasingly narrow, operationally focused mindset: particular weaknesses were lack of understanding of political affairs, which mattered in terms of grand strategy, and technical subjects.[79] Annika Mombauer has graphically described the lack of co-ordination at the highest level of command caused by the Kaiser's 'often whimsical and usually ill-informed opinions' and his active encouragement of divisions between the army's command and administrative structures.[80] Indeed, senior foreign politicians were concerned to find that 'in this highly organised nation, when you have ascended to the very top storey you find not only confusion but chaos'; ultimately, was anyone actually in charge of policy?[81] Jonathan Boff argues that the First World War German army was 'far from the well-oiled machine of myth', and was instead 'a deeply flawed institution which reached poor battlefield decisions and by doing so contributed significantly to Germany's defeat'. Its problems, especially as pressure on it mounted in 1917–18, included overconfidence in its own abilities, increasing micro-management and decreasing delegation, distorted reporting from below leading to faulty analysis, decision-making and learning, and an officer corps part selected by merit and part riddled with cliques and personal intrigue.[82]

It seems from the literature that there were in effect two armies. Foley and Bucholz among others make a strong case for the 'thinking' part of

---

[77] Eric Dorn Brose, *The Kaiser's Army: The Politics of Military Technology in Germany during the Machine Age, 1870–1918* (Oxford: Oxford University Press, 2001), 5.

[78] Strachan, *First World War*, 1:233–4 and 239–41; Gerhard P. Groß, *Mythos und Wirklichkeit: Geschichte des operativen Denkens im deutschen Heer von Moltke d.Ä. bis Heusinger* (Paderborn: Schöningh, 2012), 142.

[79] Bradley J. Meyer, 'Operational art and the German command system in World War I', unpublished PhD thesis, Ohio State University, 1988, 62–4.

[80] Mombauer, *Moltke*, 18–20.

[81] Viscount Haldane, *Before the War* (London: Cassell, 1920), 71.

[82] Jonathan Boff, *Haig's Enemy: Crown Prince Rupprecht and Germany's War on the Western Front* (Oxford: Oxford University Press, 2018), 4, 159–61, 167, 261, 268 and a summary at 277–9.

the army, both before and during the war. Schulte and Brose are no doubt right that there was also conservatism and technophobia, but they exaggerate. For example, after a slow start the army moved competently to establish machine gun and aviation units. Also, following general staff analysis of the Russo-Japanese War, it developed weapons that turned out to be particularly useful in trench warfare. Such innovation continued throughout the First World War in many different weapons categories. In the case of aviation, Germany repeatedly regained technological superiority, a major factor in the survival of the air force as an effective combatant right up till November 1918.[83]

Nevertheless, there clearly was a 'you're not paid to think' attitude in parts of the army, illustrated by the story in which a divisional commander justified an action on grounds of strategy; his corps commander replied, 'His Majesty has only one strategist, and that is neither you nor I.'[84] There is also ample evidence in memoirs about the pre-war army of an anti-intellectual atmosphere in many regiments, with officers focusing on mess life and heavy drinking.[85] Of course, this could affect tactical training: when Walter Nicolai (later head of IIIb) made proposals to improve training of officers and NCOs in his regiment, the commanding officer – 'an old war horse from the Guards' – told him that the only things which counted were marching in review and shooting; everything else was rubbish.[86]

Even the *Kriegsakademie* [staff college] was affected. *Generalleutnant* Kurt Litzmann, its director from 1902 to 1905, recorded that instructor jobs there were not popular because of the army's prevailing emphasis on practical rather than intellectual performance. That attitude and the expanding size of classes affected the quality of tuition. But Schlieffen brusquely turned down Litzmann's proposals for reform because the Kaiser was simply not interested in the *Kriegsakademie*, and there was no way of changing his views. Students too found that instructors varied greatly from the excellent to the mediocre. Because of the large classes,

---

[83] Sönke Neitzel, 'Zum strategischen Mißerfolg verdammt? Die deutschen Luftstreitkräfte in beiden Weltkriegen', in Bruno Thoß and Hans-Erich Volkmann, eds., *Erster Weltkrieg – Zweiter Weltkrieg: Ein Vergleich. Krieg, Kriegserlebnis, Kriegserfahrung in Deutschland* (Paderborn: Schöningh, 2002), 169.

[84] Bernhard Schwertfeger, *Die Großen Erzieher des deutschen Heeres: Aus der Geschichte der Kriegsakademie* (Potsdam: Akademische Verlagsgesellschaft Athenaion, 1936), 122.

[85] Examples include 11th Grenadier Regiment: General der Infanterie a.D. Freiherr von Freytag-Loringhoven, *Menschen und Dinge wie ich sie in meinem Leben sah* (Berlin: E. S. Mittler, 1923), 80 and 87–8; 82nd Infantry Regiment: Theodor Steltzer, *Sechzig Jahre Zeitgenosse* (Munich: Paul List, 1966), 18–19; and 88th Infantry Regiment: Curt Liebmann, 'Lebenserinnerungen', unpublished manuscript in BArch, Liebmann Nachlass, N882/12, 14–19.

[86] Epkenhans, *Nicolai*, 81.

they could not know all students individually and this meant their final evaluations – which were decisive for the students' career prospects – were something of a lottery, particularly for the majority of officers who were in the mid-performance bracket, neither obvious stars nor duffers.[87]

Despite such problems, commentators on the German army, whether positive or negative, largely agree that general staff training acted as an important guarantor of the unity of command. General staff officers were to be interchangeable, and each knew how another would react in the current situation because that was what he himself would do.[88] This homogeneity had important practical advantages, but carried with it the less remarked risk of groupthink, defined in a modern British government inquiry as the development of a 'prevailing wisdom' and a resulting vulnerability to preconceptions.[89] General staff selection may have succeeded in choosing the most suitable and rejecting the least suitable officers, but it did so at the cost of excluding idiosyncratic characters who might have different points of view. The general staff and the army as a whole did not like uncomfortable subordinates, so groupthink was a potential problem everywhere. 'Fitting in' was often more highly valued than sharpness of judgement. Some senior officers welcomed dissenting views, but others saw a challenge to their authority. There was pressure to 'keep your trap shut whatever happens', as to do otherwise might not be career-enhancing.[90]

An insight from Hans-Ulrich Wehler helps us understand all these contradictions. He argued that the German army was a pre-eminent example of 'the deep ambivalence and unresolved dichotomy between modernity and defence of tradition' which permeated German society from at least the 1840s and which, unresolved, eventually led to the 1918 collapse.[91] This dichotomy expressed itself in different ways, an example being the army's efforts both to promote and to control officers' and ex-officers' published writing on military affairs.[92] The practical

---

[87] Karl Litzmann, *Lebenserinnerungen* (Berlin: R. Eisenschmidt, 1927–8), 1:125–9; Liebmann, 'Lebenserinnerungen', 28 and 31.

[88] Groß, *Mythos und Wirklichkeit*, 47; Bucholz, *Moltke, Schlieffen*, 320.

[89] Committee of Privy Counsellors report to the House of Commons, *Review of Intelligence on Weapons of Mass Destruction* (London: The Stationery Office, 2004), 16 (the 'Butler Report').

[90] Liebmann, 'Lebenserinnerungen', 32; Paul Freiherr von Schoenaich, *Mein Damaskus: Erlebnisse und Bekenntnisse*, 2nd ed. (Hamburg: Fackelreiter, 1929), 63 and 106; Generalmajor Gerold von Gleich, *Die alte Armee und ihre Verirrungen: Eine kritische Studie* (Leipzig: K. F. Koehler, 1919), 86.

[91] Hans-Ulrich Wehler, 'Der Aufbruch in die Moderne 1860–90. Armee, Marine und Politik in Europa, den USA und Japan', in Michael Epkenhans and Gerhard P. Groß, eds., *Das Militär und der Aufbruch in die Moderne 1860 bis 1890* (Munich: R. Oldenbourg, 2003), xxvi.

[92] Martin Kitchen, *The German Officer Corps 1890–1914* (Oxford: Clarendon Press, 1968), 58–63; Ralf Raths, *Vom Massensturm zur Stoßtrupptaktik: Die deutsche Landkriegtaktik im*

consequence was that in both peace and war the army clung to old methods but would accept new ones if they seemed necessary and effective. Learning therefore happened not as a smooth process but on a step-by-step basis with compromises between traditional and new approaches.[93] We shall see the effect on the 1917 battlefield.

Methodology and Sources

Er will blos zeigen, wie es eigentlich gewesen.[94]

In his well-received book *Command: The Twenty-First-Century General*, Anthony King argues that command is an executive decision-making function involving primarily the 'decisive and unique responsibility' of defining a mission, but also managing the mission and leadership, meaning motivating subordinates to carry it out.[95] King focuses on command at the divisional level, and in many ways his analysis fits well with German divisions in 1917, which had become the main battle-fighting formations. German thinking on command stressed the primacy of the commander's intention [*Absicht*], and devoted much thought to training the general staff as the main mechanism for implementing it. The ideal relationship between a commander and his chief of staff was collaborative rather than simply one of subordination, foreshadowing what King sees as a feature of command in the twenty-first century. Finally, the German army traditionally stressed the moral element of war, in which leadership and the character of the leaders were crucial to success. In the chaos and uncertainty of battle, one thing must be certain: the commander's decision.[96]

In other ways, though, we need to go further than King's definition. The principal reason for this is the nature of the Western Front by 1917, above all the issues of mass forces and mass casualties. Controlling the mass forces required many different levels of command, and this study looks at three – army group, Army and corps – in addition to division.

Spiegel von Dienstvorschriften und Publizistik 1906 bis 1918 (Freiburg: Rombach, 2009), 15–19.

[93] Christian Stachelbeck, *Militärische Effektivität im Ersten Weltkrieg: Die 11. Bayerische Infanteriedivision 1915 bis 1918* (Paderborn: Schöningh, 2010), 246–8; and Christian Stachelbeck, '"Lessons learned" in WWI: The German Army, Vimy Ridge and the Elastic Defence in Depth in 1917', *Journal of Military and Strategic Studies*, vol. 18, no. 2 (2017), 128.

[94] 'It [this book] simply aims to show how things actually were': Leopold von Ranke, *Geschichten der romanischen und germanischen Völker von 1494 bis 1514*, 3rd ed. (Leipzig: Duncker & Humblot, 1885), vii.

[95] Anthony King, *Command: The Twenty-First-Century General* (Cambridge: Cambridge University Press, 2019), 69.

[96] Kriegsministerium, *Grundzüge der höheren Truppenführung*, 3.

We can begin to understand the effect of mass casualties on command through the experience of British 34th Division referred to earlier. In its first major action on 1–3 July 1916, the war-raised division suffered over 6,500 casualties, some half of its infantry strength. It also lost one of its three brigade commanders and more than half of its battalion commanders; three weeks later, the divisional commander was killed. The division next went into action on 9 April 1917 at Arras, taking most of its objectives, and the remainder the following day. Opposition was relatively weak but the infantry suffered over 30 per cent casualties. Two weeks after being relieved, with two new brigade commanders and filled out by recently enlisted, poorly trained soldiers, the under-strength division attacked one of the toughest objectives on the Arras front, defended by a thoroughly alerted garrison. It failed completely and lost 40 per cent of its infantry. In early June, it made a successful limited attack in the same area, losing a 'mere' 1,291 men and taking its total casualties in two months to 6,700.[97]

King has set the historical context of his study carefully and acknowledges the problem of mass forces and mass casualties in an existential war of peer opponents, together with commanders' onerous responsibilities in these conditions. However, as one (very positive) review of his book suggested, he may perhaps underestimate the complexity and scale of the challenge faced by divisional commanders in the two world wars.[98] The 34th Division experience was paralleled by German and French formations and well illustrates this challenge. The division's operations took place in the organisational framework of command and support from corps and Armies, which was crucial to its effective functioning, and in the conceptual context of learning and coping with the effects of attrition. Compounding the challenge, all these factors mutually interacted, and the enemy had a vote too of course.

This study takes account of King's analysis of command but adopts a different approach based on contemporary German thinking as well as the current state of research on the Entente spring offensive and the German army as an institution. It pays particular attention to the reaction of German commanders and staff officers at the time to the challenge just described. It proposes that in early 1917 the German army faced five main command tasks. The size, duration, extent and depth of battle were even greater than envisaged before the First World War, increasing the

[97] Lieutenant-Colonel John Shakespear, *The Thirty-Fourth Division 1915–1919: The Story of Its Career from Ripon to the Rhine* (London: H. F. & G. Witherby, 1921), 52, 109–11, 123 and 132.

[98] Jonathan Boff, Review of *Command: The Twenty-First-Century General*, by Anthony King, *Journal of Military History*, vol. 84, no. 1 (January 2020), 343–5.

problem of co-ordinating the masses of troops, matériel and different levels of command. This co-ordination can be defined as the first task of command, and one of the issues it involved was the balance to strike between granting independence to and controlling subordinate commanders in the new type of warfare. As the army was well aware from before the war, personality was a basic factor in this and all other aspects of command. Selecting the right men for the job was therefore the second task.

The German army traditionally viewed battle as uncertain and chaotic. By late 1916, Germany had lost the initiative in the west and was generally inferior in men and matériel. Intelligence on enemy intentions and command mechanisms able to transmit reports and orders effectively were essential to preparing and implementing a strong defence. Reducing the uncertainty of battle by such means was the third task. Trench warfare was only static in a geographical sense, and despite the stagnation of the Western Front, the German, French and British armies continuously innovated in terms of technology, tactics and organisation. So learning was the fourth task. For the German army in 1917, the central point of this learning was combined arms battle, the key to tactical success and an area in which it had fallen behind its enemies.

Ultimately, these first four tasks were means to an end. The final and crucial task was therefore performance on the battlefield, in other words winning. The traditional aim of command was to bring about and win the decisive battle in manoeuvre warfare. By 1917, however, Germany was fighting a defensive war of attrition on the Western Front in which new tactical methods and skilful command could only partly offset its inferiority in men and matériel.[99] What counted as winning in such circumstances? The German army in effect divided this task into two, preventing an Entente breakthrough and managing attrition by inflicting maximum casualties on the enemy while preserving its own forces.

In keeping with Leopold von Ranke's famous words quoted earlier, this book adopts an empirical approach to analyse these five command tasks. Given its focus on the two battles at the centre of the 1917 spring offensive, an obvious starting point is mid-November the previous year when the Entente partners co-ordinated their plans. Finding a logical place to stop is less easy. The two battles had effectively ended by late May 1917 but German commanders were not sure of this: even in late June, many expected British and French attacks to continue, and this affected deployment of forces. The June–July period also includes the battle of Messines – which the German official history covers in the same volume

---

[99] Groß, *Mythos und Wirklichkeit*, 129–30.

as the Entente spring offensive – and continuous operations in the French sector as both sides struggled to improve the positions reached at the end of the main fighting. These had the effect of diverting German resources and attention from the forthcoming British attack in Flanders. Summing all these factors up, the book ends in mid-July 1917, when OHL decided to concentrate on Flanders (15 July) and the French official history considered the actions from the spring offensive as finally over (16 July).[100]

The book explores the existing literature but bases itself largely on primary sources, both documentary and printed, and on statistical analysis derived from them. Despite extensive destruction between 1939 and 1945, especially of the Prussian army archive, great quantities of relevant military records survive. Much valuable Prussian documentary material was captured by the Soviets in 1945, eventually passed to the East German authorities and is now in the Federal Military Archive in Freiburg.[101] Equally significant are holdings in regional archives of papers from the three other major contingents that constitutionally comprised the German army – Bavarian, Saxon and Württemberg. There is also an important collection of military documents in Karlsruhe, capital of the then Grand Duchy of Baden. Baden's forces were incorporated into the Prussian army from 1870, but First World War papers relating to them were nevertheless held in the local archive.[102]

Military organisation affected the survival of records. To ensure coordination, formations had to keep each other informed with side copies of orders and reports. By 1917, the top three levels of command covered in this book – army group, Army and corps – were all holding organisations rather than fixed formations. This meant that a Prussian division might serve in a Bavarian corps, or a Bavarian corps under a Prussian Army headquarters. Records relating to 15th and 16th Infantry Divisions show how this organisation could affect documentary survival. In autumn

---

[100] General der Infanterie a.D. Hermann von Kuhl, 'Persönliches Kriegstagebuch', unpublished manuscript in BArch, RH61/970, 15 July 1917; AFGG, X/1, *Ordres de bataille des grandes unités* (Paris: Imprimerie Nationale, 1923), 235.

[101] Uwe Löbel, 'Neue Forschungsmöglichkeiten zur preußisch-deutschen Heeresgeschichte: Zur Rückgabe von Akten des Potsdamer Heeresarchivs durch die Sowjetunion', *Militärgeschichtliche Mitteilungen*, vol. 51, no. 1 (1992), 143–9. See also Robert T. Foley, *German Strategy and the Path to Verdun: Erich von Falkenhayn and the Development of Attrition, 1870–1916* (Cambridge: Cambridge University Press, 2005), 10–12.

[102] For the federal nature of the German army, see Tony Cowan, 'A Picture of German Unity? Federal Contingents in the German Army, 1916–1917', in Jonathan Krause, ed., *The Greater War: Other Combatants and Other Fronts, 1914–1918* (London: Palgrave Macmillan, 2014), 141–60; Gavin Wiens, 'In the Service of Kaiser and King: State Sovereignty, Nation-Building and the German Army, 1866–1918', unpublished PhD thesis, University of Toronto, 2019.

1916, these two Prussian divisions were regarded as having failed in action on the Somme. They were sent to Seventh Army to recuperate, and the Army was ordered to hold an inquiry into their performance. Because it originally comprised mainly Baden formations, its papers are in Karlsruhe and the inquiry documents have therefore survived the large-scale destruction of the Prussian army's archive.[103]

Within the Entente spring offensive, the battle of Arras was fought by German Sixth Army under Army Group Rupprecht. Both formations were heavily Bavarian-influenced and their records are in Munich. Under Army Group Crown Prince, two Armies and part of a third faced the larger-scale Nivelle offensive. One of them was Seventh Army, and its files in the Karlsruhe archive contain much useful material on the offensive, including a fair number of documents from Army Group Crown Prince and the other two Armies involved. The Stuttgart central archive holds the papers of the six Württemberg divisions engaged in the spring fighting. Taken together, the various archives provide good coverage for the purposes of this book. In addition their spread is broad enough to avoid the problem of over-emphasis on one particular contingent, with the linked question whether Bavarian units, for instance, behaved differently from Prussian.

The book also draws extensively on officers' personal papers. Some officers were squirrels, assiduously collecting official documents. For example, *General der Kavallerie* Duke Wilhelm of Urach kept a complete set of handouts from a divisional command training course in March 1917: these show exactly what senior officers were being trained on just before the spring offensive.[104] A lot of officers left more personal records such as diaries and memoirs. Some were published, but many were not. These sources frequently give insights into the German army missing from or even concealed by official accounts. Naturally, as with all such documents they reflect the point of view of the writer and we must allow for this when reading them.

Generalleutnant Hermann von Kuhl, in 1917 chief of staff to Army Group Rupprecht, is one example.[105] As a senior general staff officer throughout the war, he was involved in many of its major events. In particular, he played a central role in the decision to retreat at the battle of the Marne in September 1914, which came to be seen as the decisive

---

[103] See GLAK files F1/430, 431, 432 and 547.

[104] In Hauptstaatsarchiv Stuttgart (hereafter, HSAS), Urach Nachlass, GU117 Nr. 362. These courses trained divisional commanders and their chief staff officers in particular on the new combined arms battle doctrine: see Chapter 7.

[105] This book uses the term 'chief of staff' to translate the German *Chef des Generalstabes*, the most senior general staff officer at corps, Army and army group level.

moment of the war. After the war, he became a prolific writer of military history, acted as an expert witness to the parliamentary inquiry into the causes of the defeat, served on the *Reichsarchiv*'s advisory board and edited a journal for officers.[106] This made him one of the *Reichsarchiv*'s most important collaborators, and not surprisingly secured favourable depiction in official history publications of his wartime actions, including crucially at the Marne. In addition, he was one of only two German generals to be awarded the civilian class of the *Pour le Mérite* as well as the military class and its oak leaves – the other was Moltke the Elder no less – and he outlived most of his contemporaries.[107] As we shall see in Chapter 4, many of them disagreed with the positive assessment of him usually presented by modern scholarship.

Having written a two-volume account of the war, in the early 1930s Kuhl sent extracts from his war diaries and phone log book to the *Reichsarchiv*. His motive was clearly to influence drafting of the official history, which by that stage had reached 1915. He explained that he had removed certain passages, while maintaining that he had not changed the actual text. In summer 1917, he commented cynically on the motives of Georg Wetzell in OHL who he believed was acting against Army Group Rupprecht's interests. We do not need to accept his view, but his inclusion of these opinions in a record sent to the *Reichsarchiv* means that they must have been both plausible and respectable.[108]

Published sources usefully supplement archival material, not least because many pre-Second World War works drew on documents subsequently destroyed. The starting point must be the various publications comprising German official history writing. Markus Pöhlmann argues that we should view this as a conceptual whole. Apart from the main work, *Der Weltkrieg 1914 bis 1918* [The World War 1914 to 1918], the corpus includes various side volumes, follow-ups and related publications

---

[106] The *Reichsarchiv* [Imperial Archive] was the central German military history organisation. In 1935, its Historical Department – which was in charge of writing the main official history – became the *Forschungsanstalt für Kriegs- und Heeresgeschichte* (later renamed the *Kriegsgeschichtliche Forschungsanstalt des Heeres*), and the next year all military archives were moved to the new office of the *Chef der Heeresarchive* [Head of the Army Archives]: see Markus Pöhlmann, *Kriegsgeschichte und Geschichtspolitik: Der Erste Weltkrieg: Die amtliche deutsche Militärgeschichtsschreibung 1914–1956* (Paderborn: Schöningh, 2002), 152 and 154. For convenience, '*Reichsarchiv*' is used throughout this book.

[107] Pöhlmann, *Kriegsgeschichte*, 192. For more on Kuhl's career, albeit hagiographical, see Hanns Möller-Witten, *Festschrift zum 100. Geburtstag des Generals der Infanterie a.D. Dr. phil. Hermann von Kuhl* (Berlin: E. S. Mittler, 1956). The military *Pour le Mérite* was the highest Prussian award for wartime services, and its oak leaves were a repeat award (a bar in British parlance).

[108] See Chapter 4.

such as the thirty-six-book *Schlachten des Weltkrieges* [Battles of the World War] series and well over 1,000 regimental histories. Looking across this breadth, Pöhlmann takes a more positive view of the qualities of German official history writing on the First World War than previous commentators, without ignoring its failings.[109]

The '*Weltkrieg*' volume covering the first half of 1917 contains material which is essential to this book, including both factual descriptions of the Entente spring offensive and details such as casualties, deployment and movement of units. It does not paint an entirely rosy view of events, recording stiff resistance by senior officers to the new defensive doctrine and describing the opening of the battle of Arras as a serious defeat. Against that, although it assesses the causes of the defeat it does not attribute blame; nor does it mention the sacking of the Sixth Army chief of staff and operations officer, and it glosses over the side-lining of the Army commander soon after.[110] It naturally writes positively about the successful German repulse of the offensive, but in doing so avoids discussing various problems of the defence. It also illustrates what some historians have seen as a general bias against the first two wartime Chiefs of the General Staff, Moltke the Younger and Erich von Falkenhayn, in favour of Hindenburg and Ludendorff.[111]

Many of the German regiments involved in the spring fighting published histories. As products of the official history process, they were susceptible to the same problems as '*Weltkrieg*'.[112] In addition, although the guidelines to which they were subject specified that they should honestly recount failures, regimental loyalty might dictate otherwise. This is of course not a problem confined to the German army or the First World War: a British officer warned a historian of the Troubles in Northern Ireland that when writing official reports or regimental histories, 'You put into it what you are going to admit to'.[113] There are German exceptions to this, such as a regiment recording that two of its companies broke and ran before a British tank at Arras.[114] The quality of German regimental histories naturally varies, but carefully used they can fill gaps

---

[109] Pöhlmann, *Kriegsgeschichte*, 162 and 199. For details of the *Schlachten des Weltkrieges* series, see the Editors' Introduction in Thilo von Bose, *The Catastrophe of 8 August 1918*, trans. and ed. David Pearson, Paul Thost and Tony Cowan (Newport, NSW: Big Sky Publishing, 2019). Franz Behrmann, *Die Osterschlacht bei Arras 1917*, 2 vols., Schlachten des Weltkrieges 28–9 (Oldenburg: Gerhard Stalling, 1929) covers Arras; there is no equivalent for the Nivelle offensive.
[110] Reichsarchiv, *Weltkrieg*, 12:32, 234–9 and 255.
[111] Pöhlmann, *Kriegsgeschichte*, 183–4; Foley, *German Strategy*, 7–10.
[112] Pöhlmann, *Kriegsgeschichte*, 198–200.
[113] Edward Burke, *An Army of Tribes: British Army Cohesion, Deviancy and Murder in Northern Ireland* (Liverpool: Liverpool University Press, 2018), 21.
[114] Smithson, *Taste of Success*, 230.

in the documentary record. This is especially true for Prussian formations, given the destruction of much of the Prussian army's archive. Regimental histories are very useful for detail such as the arrival of new equipment, training and casualties; there is no reason to doubt them on such factual information.

During the inter-war period many officers and ex-officers published other forms of historical writing, such as articles in professional journals, full-scale histories, monographs, commentaries, diaries and memoirs. The last two are especially important for this book. As with their unpublished equivalents, they were of course written from the authors' point of view and for their purposes: we need to allow for this in using them as sources. Many of these works were part of the 'Battle of the Memoirs'. Given the heated arguments over why Germany lost the war – *Generalleutnant* Wilhelm Marx light-heartedly claimed to have identified forty-eight separate factors or people held to have 'definitely' caused the defeat – such works might be pronouncedly defensive or self-serving.[115] Wilhelm Solger of the *Reichsarchiv* wrote of the well-known unreliability of printed memoirs, citing the examples of Falkenhayn and Fritz von Loßberg (Germany's chief defensive expert).[116]

These points are illustrated by Crown Prince Rupprecht's diaries, a valuable source. They were published as part of a sustained effort to defend Rupprecht's and the Bavarian army's wartime reputation, particularly relating to the opening 1914 campaign, and they were edited accordingly.[117] The original handwritten diary includes much material that is useful for this book but was cut from the published version. For instance, in February 1917 Rupprecht recorded the departure of his adjutant following a spat with Kuhl, his chief of staff; he then mused about the personalities involved and the problems of having a Prussian rather than Bavarian chief of staff; and from there to the need for Bavarian troops in future to form an integrated Army rather than act as a contingent of the imperial German [*Reich*] forces.[118] None of this was published.

---

[115] Generalleutnant a.D. Wilhelm Marx, 'Zur Psychologie der deutschen Kriegskritik', *Militär-Wochenblatt*, vol. 119, no. 5 (1934), 174–6.

[116] Pöhlmann, *Kriegsgeschichte*, 169. For an analysis of senior officers' memoir writing, including motivation, see Pöhlmann's '"Daß sich ein Sargdeckel über mir schlösse": Typen und Funktionen von Weltkriegserinnerungen militärischer Entscheidungsträger', in Jost Dülffer and Gerd Krumeich, eds., *Der verlorene Frieden: Politik und Kriegskultur nach 1918* (Essen: Klartext Verlag, 2002), 149–70.

[117] Pöhlmann, *Kriegsgeschichte*, 284–321, especially 303–6.

[118] Kronprinz Rupprecht von Bayern, unpublished diary, Bayerisches Hauptstaatsarchiv, Abteilung III Geheimes Hausarchiv, Munich (hereafter, HAM), Rupprecht Nachlass Nr. 705, 21 February 1917. Boff, *Haig's Enemy*, 6–7 discusses the different diary versions.

Although we need to be constantly aware of the personal aims and prejudices of the writers of memoirs and diaries, their value lies precisely in their expression of attitudes that do not toe the party line. An example here is a diary entry by the author Rudolf Binding, a divisional staff officer during the battle of Arras. In April 1917 he recorded:

What a mess we are in! The enemy attacks where he likes and stops where he likes. We have to stand fast and meet every thrust, even at points where it hurts us. Ludendorff must needs christen this "The Defensive Battle". His *Instructions for the Defensive Battle* [the new tactical doctrine] are in many cases not being followed, or else being misunderstood, or turning out to be impracticable.[119]

His personal opinion of course, and very different from the official view – reflected especially in Wynne – of the efficacy of the new tactics.

In addition to these primary and secondary sources, the book grounds parts of its analysis on statistics covering the prosopography of officers and military formations such as divisions. Using statistics to supplement the qualitative approach derived from documentary material produces a fuller picture than either could alone. As an example of the benefits, analysing the movement of divisions between theatres and their employment in battle provides evidence on how German commanders viewed the quality of different parts of the army and how this changed over time. It is important to note that the statistical evidence collated for the book covers the whole German army throughout the war.[120]

Approach and Structure of the Book

[F]rom the German Wars of Unification, the tension between doctrine and what commanders actually did characterised German operational and tactical command far more than historiography has yet recognised.[121]

Table 0.1 sets out schematically the German army's five main command tasks described in this Introduction. These tasks do not all translate directly into chapters, as many are interlinked. So, for instance, Chapter 4 is the main analysis of the second task, selecting the right men. But personality and personal relationships affected the willingness of superiors to delegate to subordinates, how commanders and their

---

[119] Rudolf Binding, *A Fatalist at War*, trans. Ian Morrow ([London]: Allen & Unwin, 1929), 159 (18 April 1917).

[120] It is not currently possible to publish the databases from which the statistical information is drawn, but I intend to post background workings on the Internet. Unless otherwise stated, statistics exclude cavalry formations.

[121] Sigg, *Unterführer als Feldherr*, 18.

Table 0.1 *German command tasks in 1917*

1. Co-ordinating a mass army: decentralisation versus control
2. Selecting the right men: the role of personality
3. Reducing uncertainty: intelligence and communication
4. Learning: lessons learned, doctrine and training for combined arms battle
5. Winning: preventing breakthrough and managing attrition

chiefs of staff worked together, the actual as opposed to formal authority of command organisations, the structure of intelligence, the handling of information, lessons learned and performance. Such linkages between the five tasks are an important aspect of command and therefore a theme that recurs throughout the book.

After this Introduction, Chapter 1 assesses the state of the German army in late 1916–early 1917 and efforts to improve it; Entente plans for their offensive and German countermeasures; and what actually happened. This provides the context for the analysis in the rest of the book. The next two chapters cover the first command task, how to co-ordinate a mass army by striking the right balance between decentralisation and control. Chapter 2 looks at the two principles that are perhaps seen as most characteristically German, mission command and the special relationship between commanders and general staff officers through which it was implemented. There was less scope for mission command in 1917 circumstances than commonly assumed, and despite much effort the army was only partly successful in creating effective commander–chief of staff teams to control its formations. The balance was shifting from decentralisation to control, exemplified both by the greater power accruing to general staff officers and by the continuing emphasis placed on two other principles, creating a *Schwerpunkt* [point of main effort] and maintaining the chain of command. Chapter 3 explains the function of each level of command through which these principles were put into effect, from army group to division; it argues that the relative importance of corps and division in particular has been misunderstood.

Many accounts of the German army stress its professional approach to mastering its business. But as Chapter 4 shows, officers were also professional in the sense of pursuing their careers in the army, giving full play to personal motivations and feelings. Even in a war of masses and matériel, personal factors and relationships therefore played a significant role in the performance of the army. This in turn complicated the second command task, selecting the right men, despite constant and systematic efforts to fulfil it.

The third command task was to reduce the inherent uncertainty of war to manageable levels so that it could be exploited by superior German command techniques. This task was fulfilled through intelligence on the enemy and communication of reports and orders to control German forces. German military intelligence during the war is not well understood. Chapter 5 helps fill this gap by describing the growing dependence on good intelligence in a situation where the German army no longer had the initiative or superiority; it takes German knowledge of and resulting countermeasures against the Entente spring offensive as a case study to assess the effectiveness of the intelligence organisation. German intelligence performance before the offensive was mixed – good on the French, poorer on the British. Chapter 6 assesses that the German communication system coped at least adequately with the requirements of battle, despite the growing volume of traffic and the constant risk of links to the forward troops being broken by enemy fire; French and British inability to achieve a high operational tempo helped here. However, the increasing problems of bureaucracy and falsified reporting were danger signals for the future.

Chapter 7 describes the German army's ability to learn, the fourth command task. Its analysis of how and what the army learned focuses on the crucial tactical issue of co-operation between the infantry, artillery and aviation, where the Germans had fallen behind the Entente. The army made effective use of both formal and informal learning mechanisms to catch up. The growing maturity of the learning system undoubtedly helped improve battlefield performance, and many accounts of this period emphasise German tactical sophistication. However, important aspects of German combined arms tactics remained problematic throughout the year.

In April–May 1917, the German army fulfilled its fifth command task, winning the battle, with a clear victory: it both prevented an Entente breakthrough and inflicted more casualties than it suffered. Chapter 8 shows that this was no foregone conclusion, and that in achieving its victory the army sustained lasting damage. Given that a large proportion of available formations were of too low a quality to participate in full-scale battle, this attrition was serious. The chapter explains how the German system for evaluating divisions helped manage the effects of attrition. It concludes though that the failure of the Entente offensive was as much due to the attackers' shortcomings as to good performance by the German defenders. A counterfactual argues that better Entente decision-making could have inflicted even greater damage on the German army and possibly even tipped it into crisis.

Summarising the findings of the book, the Conclusion shows that the German army's fulfilment of all five command tasks was patchy – certainly not disastrous, but by no means perfect either. The chapter also considers whether the book's findings on German command are more broadly applicable. It produces evidence that the command tasks did remain the same in different situations in the First World War, as did many or most of the factors that affected their implementation.

The book focuses on early 1917 but ranges much wider to analyse the five command tasks fully. In particular, it systematically compares pre-war thinking and developments in 1914–16 with events in 1917; and it distinguishes the German army's doctrine and reputation from what actually happened. In this way, it gets under the skin of the army's culture, internal politics and battle management systems to offer a comprehensive view of German operational command throughout the war. It therefore provides a fuller description of German command than accounts that either stress its excellence and so fall into 'a certain overenthusiasm for things German', or conversely portray the army as a kind of 'gang that couldn't shoot straight'.[122]

The new insights which emerge from this analysis of the German army's command tasks include the complex relationship between traditional command principles, military organisation and personal factors; the increasing role of intelligence in operations; the difficulty of converting lessons learned into practice and the resulting persistence of certain tactical problems; and the system for assessing the very differing qualities of formations to mitigate the effect of attrition. The book also throws new light on the Entente spring offensive itself, which as noted earlier is not well covered in the literature, despite its importance.

Through its empirical approach, broad use of archival material and detailed description of the German army as an institution, the book aspires to achieve four further aims. The first is to help future researchers mine the archival riches that still exist despite the destruction of records. Second, the book presents to an anglophone readership much new material on the German army which is not available in English. This includes important research published by the Centre for Military History and Social Sciences of the *Bundeswehr* (the modern German armed forces), little of which has been or will be translated. Third, the book is intended as a comparison with other armies in the First World War and therefore an aid to scholars working on those armies. It is not itself comparative but it does incorporate some comparative elements. Finally, the book presents a case study of what happens when you go to war against a peer enemy, and many of the concepts discussed are still relevant today – mission command is an obvious example. So hopefully it will contribute to the professional military education of modern-day officers as they prepare for the future.

---

[122] Citino, *German Way of War*, 142; Dennis E. Showalter, 'Even Generals Wet Their Pants: The First Three Weeks in East Prussia, August 1914', *War & Society*, vol. 2, no. 2 (1984), 63.

1   Context

The battle of the Somme is rightly seen as a victory. Less attention seems to be paid to the reverse side – that the tactics practised there indeed enabled us [the German army] to hold terrain, but led to very heavy losses, especially in junior commanders and trainers, thereby hastening the watering down of the army and weakening our powers of resistance in 1917. It has only now become really clear to many that we have hardly any manpower replacements available for 1917. Theoretically everyone knows that our supplies of ammunition, construction material and equipment of every type are limited. But it seems questionable how far they have drawn the practical conclusions. Almost no one realises the actual situation in this area – few reserves, especially of ammunition, and a serious threat to the hoped-for increase of production, perhaps even at the moment a partial decrease.[1]

This OHL commentary on Ludendorff's inspection of the Western Front in January 1917, downbeat though it is, nevertheless understates the poor condition of the German army following the attritional battles the year before. By the end of 1916, 60 per cent of all German divisions had fought at Verdun or the Somme or both. German casualties in the two battles reached some 750,000, giving a total for 1916 of 1.2 million (and 4 million since the beginning of the war).[2]

Despite these terrible figures, manpower in the German field army was in fact still increasing at this period, particularly through calling up younger year groups and combing out fit soldiers from non-combat units. The real damage to the German army was more to its quality and morale than its size. The German official history commented that what

---

[1] OHL memorandum, 'Gesamteindrücke der Westreise', 21 January 1917, BArch, Geyer Nachlass, RH61/924, f. 32.

[2] Alexander Watson, *Ring of Steel: Germany and Austria-Hungary at War, 1914–1918* (London: Allen Lane, 2014), 300 and 324; James H. McRandle and James Quirk, 'The Blood Test Revisited: A New Look at German Casualty Counts in World War I', *Journal of Military History*, vol. 70, no. 3 (July 2006), tables 8 and 11.

still remained of the old, peace-trained German infantry bled to death on the Somme. For the first time there was doubt whether Germany would win the war.[3] In an important memorandum, written in October 1916 after two tours as a corps commander on the Somme, *General der Infanterie* Max von Boehn discussed why most German attacks and counter-attacks during the battle had failed. Six different divisions had passed through his corps on the Somme; according to him none were fit to carry out a successful attack, and this was common to all corps on the Western Front. He saw the root cause as the lower quality of units, which he ascribed ultimately to inadequate training both in Germany and in the field. He believed that the army could have coped with inferior manpower if it had had good junior officers, but by the end of 1916 they too were lacking.[4]

Though Boehn may have been exaggerating to make a point, there is no doubt that the quality of many formations had suffered at this period. Hermann von Kuhl recorded in October 1916 that 15th Infantry Division, in Boehn's corps, had completely failed, serious indiscipline had occurred and the men had not moved forward into their positions. Boehn said he had never come across such an appalling unit.[5] Boehn himself told Crown Prince Rupprecht, the army group commander, that men had shot at their own officers. Following these events the divisional commander was sacked and there was a series of court martials.[6] Disciplinary problems and failures of performance continued well into 1917. The next divisional commander was also removed, as were other senior officers, including the chief staff officer. When the third commander, *Generalmajor* Gerhard Tappen, arrived in September 1917, he was horrified by the division's condition and the number of pending court martials.[7]

---

[3] Reichsarchiv, *Weltkrieg*, vol. 11, *Die Kriegführung im Herbst 1916 und im Winter 1916/17: Vom Wechsel in der Obersten Heeresleitung bis zum Entschluß zum Rückzug in die Siegfried-Stellung* (Berlin: E. S. Mittler, 1938), 105; Watson, *Ring of Steel*, 326. See also Tony Cowan, 'Muddy Grave? The German Army at the End of 1916', in Spencer Jones, ed., *At All Costs: The British Army on the Western Front 1916* (Warwick: Helion, 2018), 451–73.

[4] Boehn memorandum to Chef des Militär-Kabinetts [Head of the Military Cabinet], 24 October 1916, BArch, PH1/9, ff. 284–9 (hereafter, Boehn memorandum, October 1916); Kuhl, 'Kriegstagebuch', 7 November 1916. Jack Sheldon, *Fighting the Somme: German Challenges, Dilemmas and Solutions* (Barnsley: Pen & Sword Military, 2017), 173–6 translates extensive extracts from the memorandum.

[5] Kuhl, 'Kriegstagebuch', 13 October 1916.

[6] Rupprecht unpublished diary, 12 October 1916; Rupprecht, *Kriegstagebuch*, 2:116 (15 March 1917).

[7] Gerhard Tappen, 'Meine Kriegserinnerungen', unpublished manuscript in BArch, RH61/986, f. 191.

Rupprecht piously thanked God in his diary that a case such as 15th Infantry Division was rare.[8] It may indeed have been unusually bad, but the division was not the only one of concern. Rupprecht himself referred to problems in ten other divisions in autumn 1916. Of these, 12th and 16th Infantry and 5th Ersatz Divisions had failed in action; 183rd, 212th and 221st Infantry and 22nd, 44th and 53rd Reserve Divisions were shaky or under-performing; 9th Infantry Division had been badly battered at Verdun.[9] Including the divisions Boehn mentioned, there are indications of similar problems or concerns about performance in 27 of the 118 divisions that fought at Verdun or the Somme or both, over one-fifth of them. These divisions are of course the ones for which we have evidence: there may well have been others.

In OHL's judgement, by the end of 1916, the army was exhausted but morale was still good. A post-war *Reichsarchiv* analysis concluded that in general this was correct, as shown by the army's stubborn resistance on the Somme, but that there were warning signals, such as the large number of officers and men surrendering at Verdun in December. OHL was aware of these signals but because of its faith in the German soldier failed to appreciate the gravity of the morale problem.[10] Whether or not OHL's judgement on morale was right, it was clearly worried by the quality of its divisions and decided, for the first time, to assess formally the capabilities of German troops. In early November 1916, it therefore ordered formations to report weekly on the combat value, readiness for deployment or need for relief of every division.[11]

As '*Weltkrieg*' commented, despite efforts to make all divisions as homogeneous as possible, nowhere near all were suitable for major battle and the combat value of even those that were suitable constantly changed during action; the highest demands were made of the best divisions. This increased the risk that reliable divisions would suffer long-term damage from excessive deployment in major battle. We can identify twenty-four that fought and suffered appreciable casualties at both Verdun and the Somme: OHL apparently saw them as the workhorses of the army during 1916.[12] Strikingly, six of the divisions just described as of concern were

[8] Rupprecht, *Kriegstagebuch*, 2:116 (15 March 1917).
[9] Rupprecht, unpublished diary, 17, 18 and 29 October, 3, 8 and 13 November and 9 December 1916, 12 April 1917.
[10] 'Die Entwicklung der Stimmung im Heere im Winter 1916/17', unpublished Reichsarchiv research paper, BArch, RH61/1655, sections 1, 7 and conclusion.
[11] Reichsarchiv, *Weltkrieg*, 11:481. See Chapter 8 for a definition of the German term 'combat value', roughly equivalent to modern 'fighting power'.
[12] Calculated from Reichsarchiv, *Weltkrieg*, vol. 10, *Die Operationen des Jahres 1916 bis zum Wechsel in der Obersten Heeresleitung* (Berlin: E. S. Mittler, 1936), Anlagen 2 and 3, and vol. 11, Anlage 4. Appreciable casualties are defined as over 1,000 men.

from the workhorse group, implying that overuse had indeed caused them serious damage.[13]

When Ludendorff attempted to convince Chancellor Theobald von Bethmann Hollweg in January 1917 that Germany should launch unrestricted submarine warfare, his strongest argument was the need to relieve pressure on the army: 'We must spare the troops a second Somme battle.' The poor state of the army in late 1916 therefore directly contributed to what has been called 'the worst decision of the war', which, by instigating US entry, ultimately cost Germany victory.[14]

Efforts to Strengthen the German Army

> After we have held out in the current heavy fighting, next spring [1917] will again demand a supreme effort from us.[15]

From autumn 1916, OHL had been warning that the enemy offensive which was expected next spring would decide the very existence of the German people. This may have been partly propaganda aimed at the 'remobilisation' of the German war effort, but OHL undoubtedly did assess that the Entente would launch even heavier assaults than in 1916. The overall balance of forces – both Entente strength as well as German weakness – precluded German offensive action on land. As described in the Introduction, the army's role in grand strategy at this period was therefore to hold out for the five months believed necessary for unrestricted submarine warfare to knock Britain out of the war. On 6 January, OHL issued an order stating that the task on the Western Front was now to organise the defence in every detail, as well as to create and train reserves.[16] It took various steps to improve the German army's capabilities from the low point of late 1916. These included promulgating new defensive tactics, improving training at all levels, increasing the number of divisions available (including by withdrawing to the Hindenburg Line), reorganising the army on the Western Front and bringing new equipment into service.

The new tactics were known variously as mobile defence, elastic defence or defence in depth. Formally, they were introduced on 1 December 1916 with the issuing of the 'Defensive Battle' manual, but in fact they had grown up in stages since 1915, in particular during the

---

[13] 5th, 38th, 103rd and 113th Infantry and 22nd and 44th Reserve Divisions.
[14] Watson, *Ring of Steel*, 416–24 and 448–9.
[15] OHL letter to the Kriegsministerium, 14 September 1916, in Reichsarchiv, *Weltkrieg*, 11:42.
[16] OHL to HKR, Ia/II Nr. 1760 geh. op., 6 January 1917, KAM, HKR neue Nr. 31.

battle of the Somme. Tactical control of the combined arms battle would be delegated to the divisional commander. The defence should be mobile, in depth and offensive; it was mainly to be conducted by machines not men. 'Mobile' meant that the defence would be conducted around and not in the forward position; ground could be given up temporarily but must be recaptured by counter-attack. 'In depth' meant that there should be several successive positions which the enemy could not engage in one operation; that the ground must be properly prepared with fixed defences such as trenches, machine gun positions, shelters and wire obstacles; and that units should be deployed throughout the defensive zone. 'Offensive' involved both the counter-attacks and offensive use of the artillery. 'Machines not men' required thinner deployment of manpower, especially in the forward positions, and greater use of firepower from machine guns, mortars and artillery. The division would be the main battle unit and would be allocated important extra resources to conduct the new form of defence.[17]

It will be helpful to explain the nature of a defensive zone at this time in more detail. A position [*Stellung*] comprised several lines of trenches with barbed wire obstacles, as well as shelters – some made of reinforced concrete [*Mannschafts-Eisenbetonunterstände*] – and emplacements for machine guns and other infantry weapons constructed throughout a deep 'intermediate area' [*Zwischengelände*] to the rear.[18] A complete defensive zone now comprised a number of such positions one behind the other, to a depth of several kilometres (Figure 1.1).[19]

There were risks in introducing these new tactics in the middle of a war, and Hindenburg stressed two. Conservatism and misunderstandings complicated change even in peacetime. More seriously, in abandoning a rigid defence and stressing the need for independent action, the new system made greater demands on the troops. Given the concerns about the quality of the officers and men, could the army of 1917 actually carry out the new tactics?[20] In view of such doubts, it is not surprising that there was considerable opposition to certain aspects of the new tactics,

---

[17] Moser, *Feldzugsaufzeichnungen*, 267–8. Chapter 2 covers divisional organisation and firepower; Chapter 7 considers the new tactics in more detail.

[18] *Mannschafts-Eisenbetonunterstände* were known to the British as 'Mebus', though at least one unit mistook this as the singular form and used the plural Mebuses: useful discussion of the term with sketches in Great War Forum, 'Meaning of "Mebus" in WW1 Recollection', www.greatwarforum.org/topic/265830-meaning-of-mebus-in-ww1-recollection (accessed 21 March 2022). See also sketch of a position in Generalkommando 64 circular, 'Neues franz. Angriffsverfahren', Ic Nr. 61 geh., 21 March 1917, HSAS, Urach Nachlass, GU117 Bü 364.

[19] Sketch of Sixth Army positions before the withdrawal to the Hindenburg Line, compiled by Barbara Taylor from BOH 1917, 1: Map 1 and Reichsarchiv, *Weltkrieg*, 12: Beilage 9.

[20] Hindenburg, *Out of My Life*, 262–3.

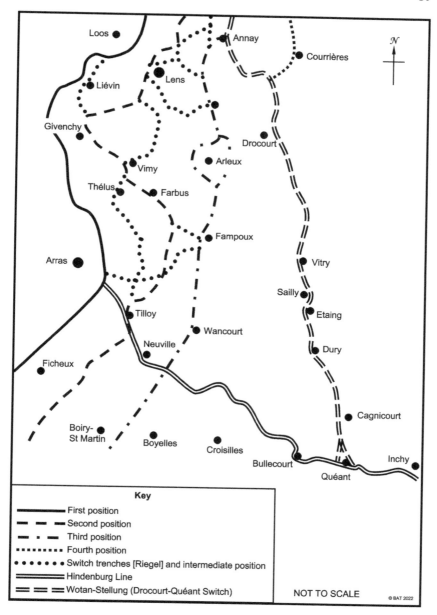

Figure 1.1 German defences at Arras in early 1917 (not to scale)

especially the authorisation to give ground if necessary when attacked and the level at which artillery should be controlled. These concerns were addressed in a second edition of 'Defensive Battle', published in March 1917 and therefore the version in effect at the time of the spring offensive.

OHL knew that doctrine had to be converted into reality by training, and it tackled this task at two levels. In February 1917, it introduced courses on the new tactics for division and brigade commanders and staffs. The courses were clearly important to OHL, considerable resources were devoted to them and throughput of students was impressive. OHL was pleased with the result, but as Chapter 7 explains, there are questions about just how effective the courses were. The second level was training for the field formations of the army. In early 1917, OHL tried to arrange at least three weeks' training for all divisions, but again Chapter 7 shows that how much divisions actually received varied widely.

OHL also took action to increase the number of divisions available on the Western Front. First, the withdrawal to the Hindenburg Line [*Siegfried-Stellung*] in February–March 1917 shortened the front, thus saving thirteen to fifteen divisions as well as considerable amounts of field and heavy artillery.[21] A further benefit was that the withdrawal disrupted a substantial part of the plan for the Nivelle offensive. All in all, the Germans considered it a great operational success and boost to morale. But as a major operation – thirty-six divisions from four of Army Group Rupprecht's Armies took part – it occupied much of the army group's attention in a crucial period before the Entente offensive. The French saved almost as many divisions from the shorter line, which they committed to another part of the offensive. The withdrawal also handed the Entente a propaganda victory by creating the impression that the Germans were retreating after being defeated in the battle of the Somme.[22]

Second, in November 1916, orders were given for the establishment of thirteen divisions, to be ready for action by the next March. They were a mixture of experienced soldiers and new recruits. The training of these units suffered badly from turnover of officers, late delivery of equipment, geographical separation of infantry and artillery – which affected practice

---

[21] Reichsarchiv, *Weltkrieg*, 12:128.

[22] On the withdrawal, see William Philpott, *Bloody Victory: The Sacrifice on the Somme and the Making of the Twentieth Century* (London: Little, Brown, 2009), 454–63, and Michael Geyer, 'Rückzug und Zerstörung 1917', in Gerhard Hirschfeld, Gerd Krumeich and Irina Renz, eds., *Die Deutschen an der Somme 1914–1918: Krieg, Besatzung, Verbrannte Erde* (Essen: Klartext, 2006), 163–201.

of all-arms co-operation – and the harsh winter.[23] The generals who inspected the new divisions in March noted other problems such as the insufficient skill of the mainly very young officers and NCOs. The physical and disciplinary state of the young recruits also left something to be desired. The inspecting officers' reports were nevertheless, surprisingly perhaps, generally satisfactory; but they did recommend more training in quiet sectors.[24] In keeping with the priority now given to the Western Front, ten of these divisions were deployed there. They were not fit to take part in the opening phases of the spring fighting, though they did start to appear later on. Meanwhile they could free up experienced divisions.

Another thirteen divisions were raised between November 1916 and the opening of the spring offensive. Formed largely from existing units, they were in principle immediately deployable. However, only four of them were fit for major battle on the Western Front: the others were a mixture of *Landwehr* and lower-quality formations that could only be used in quiet sectors in the west or on the Eastern Front.[25] This ratio suggests that even though the German army's manpower continued to increase at this period, it was scraping the barrel in terms of fully combat-capable divisions. Indeed, a draft for '*Weltkrieg*' commented that the increase in the number of divisions only partly resulted in an increase in fighting power.[26] But in terms of number alone, with the last of these creations, the total of infantry divisions in the field when the Entente offensive opened on 9 April 1917 was 228.[27]

The third step was to move divisions from the Eastern to the Western Front. Between mid-November 1916 and the opening of the spring offensive, twelve infantry divisions arrived in the west. Of these, eleven were in principle fit for major battle on the Western Front but their actual combat capability there could not be taken for granted.[28] Experience in 1916 had shown that divisions which performed well on the Eastern Front could fail in the west. Eight of the arriving divisions which had

---

[23] Theobald von Schäfer, 'Die Entwicklung der Gesamtlage an der deutschen Front vom Herbst 1916 – Frühjahr 1917', unpublished drafts for Reichsarchiv, *Weltkrieg*, vol. 11, BArch, RH61/1645, 7.

[24] Reichsarchiv, *Weltkrieg*, 12:4.

[25] The four were 5th Guard, 220th, 227th and 16th Bavarian Infantry Divisions. The term *Landwehr* is usually not translated; *Landwehr* units comprised older men and by 1917 were mainly employed in defensive roles on quiet fronts.

[26] Schäfer, 'Die Entwicklung der Gesamtlage', 9.

[27] Reichsarchiv, *Weltkrieg*, 12:4–5, using slightly different criteria and timings, says 232 by the end of April. Both sets of figures exclude the 10 cavalry divisions, 3 of which were now dismounted, and 3 coast defence divisions in Germany.

[28] 3rd Guard, 2nd, 20th, 37th, 41st, 187th and 11th Bavarian Infantry Divisions and 43rd, 49th, 79th and 80th Reserve Divisions; the twelfth division was 301st Infantry Division; three cavalry divisions also arrived during this period.

been in the east for a long time had to familiarise themselves with new Western Front techniques, but not all of them received the necessary training.[29] As we saw in the Introduction, OHL was reluctant to move more divisions from the east in early 1917. The Russian Revolution in March occurred too late to affect the initial deployment of divisions facing the Entente attack in France. Even in the second half of May, OHL's Operations Department was recommending caution in stripping further divisions from an already thinly garrisoned Eastern Front, though it was possible to exchange fought-out divisions from the west with fresh ones from the east.[30]

Hindenburg and Ludendorff also intended to increase further the ratio of firepower to manpower, in an effort to counterbalance Entente superiority in matériel. There were three aspects to this – production, introduction of new weapons and organisation of the army to use them. Immediately after taking over OHL they launched the so-called Hindenburg Programme. The objective was to secure a dramatic increase in the production of weapons and equipment by May 1917 when the Entente offensive could be expected. Modern research, however, stresses that production had already greatly increased before they took over, casts doubts on their ambitious targets and demonstrates the chaos which ensued. In the long term, the strain on German society inflicted by the programme's fantasy targets paved the way for revolution. In the short term, steel production actually fell in the six months to February 1917. In addition, at a time when military requirements for manpower continued to grow, the programme needed increasing numbers of workers who were in principle liable and fit for active military service. By early 1917, there were about 1 million men in this category. They could not, however, be called up because of the adverse effect on production for the programme. In fact, the army agreed to give up 125,000 skilled workers to help it.[31]

---

[29] Tappen, 'Kriegserinnerungen', f. 93; Heinrich Harms, *Die Geschichte des Oldenburgischen Infanterie-Regiments Nr. 91* (Oldenburg: Gerhard Stalling, 1930), 260; Reichsarchiv, *Weltkrieg*, 12:55–6.

[30] Reichsarchiv, *Weltkrieg*, 12:502. Twelve fresh divisions arrived from the east by early June 1917 (the Alpine Corps, 119th, 121st, 195th and 10th Bavarian Infantry and 3rd, 5th, 6th, 36th, 47th, 48th and 78th Reserve Divisions). In addition, three of the 1916 'problem' divisions that had been sent east to recuperate returned (12th, 15th and 16th Infantry Divisions). Only 15th Infantry and 78th Reserve Divisions were engaged against the spring offensive, right at the end.

[31] Watson, *Ring of Steel*, 377–80; Afflerbach, *Auf Messers Schneide*, 248, 250 and 255; Reichsarchiv, *Weltkrieg*, 12:10. Robert T. Foley, 'The Other Side of the Wire: The German Army in 1917', in Peter Dennis and Jeffrey Grey, eds., *1917: Tactics, Training and Technology* (Canberra: Australian History Military Publications, 2007), 159–62 considers that despite these problems, the Hindenburg Programme did increase the production of weapons at this period.

Under the Third OHL, new weaponry was introduced into each of the three main components of combined arms battle – infantry, artillery and aviation – though given the lead time Hindenburg and Ludendorff could not take the credit. This new equipment had the greatest effect in the air: Albatros fighters brought into service from September 1916 outclassed anything the Entente had and made a major contribution to regaining air superiority.[32] New equipment for ground troops had a less dramatic effect. The most important new infantry weapon was the MG 08/15 light machine gun that would equip infantry companies. It was an unloved wartime compromise and in any case production and distribution were so delayed that few divisions had it by the beginning of the spring fighting. The artillery were to receive model 1916 field guns and howitzers; both had increased range but at the cost of added weight, which impeded changing position, a key tactic to defeat enemy counter-battery fire. In addition, as with the light machine gun, wartime compromises caused problems of reliability. It also took time to equip all batteries, some only receiving the new equipment in early 1918.[33]

The Third OHL could take credit for the reorganisation of some of the units and formations employing this equipment. Once again, the most significant change was in aviation, which was established as a separate arm of service. A new post of 'commanding general of air forces' [*Kommandierender General der Luftstreitkräfte* or *Kogenluft*] took control of all air-related assets – including aircraft, airships, balloons, anti-aircraft guns and searchlights – in the field and in Germany. The number of squadrons continued to grow, and in particular the formation of specialist fighter units [*Jagdstaffel*] contributed to German predominance in the air at this period.[34] Field artillery batteries increased from 1,929 in autumn 1916 to 2,709 in summer 1917; the 7,130 heavy guns at the front in February 1917 represented the highest number reached during the war.[35] The bulk of this weaponry was controlled by divisional artillery commanders, a new post created in February 1917 to integrate handling of field and heavy artillery. Finally, from summer 1916 the original

[32] Hart, *Bloody April*, 30–3.
[33] Chapter 3 looks further at infantry equipment. On artillery, see P. E. Bielenburg, 'Erfahrungen mit der l.F.H. 16' and Major a.D. Drees, 'Die Geschütz-Ausrüstung unserer Feld- und schweren Artillerie im Weltkriege', *Artilleristische Monatshefte*, vol. 15, nos. 169/170 (January–February 1921), 19–26 and 62–71; Fritz Heidrich, *Geschichte des 3. Ostpreußischen Feldartillerie-Regiments Nr. 79* (Oldenburg: Gerhard Stalling, 1921), 106. Reichsarchiv, *Weltkrieg*, 12:13–18 gives a good summary of equipment introduced at this period.
[34] Reichsarchiv, *Weltkrieg*, 12:8–10 for an overview; Hart, *Bloody April*, 30 on fighter units.
[35] Generalmajor a.D. Ernst von Wrisberg, *Heer und Heimat 1914–1918* (Leipzig: K. F. Koehler, 1921), 39 and 58.

establishment of one medium machine gun company per infantry regiment had tripled to one company per battalion; and guns per company had doubled from six to twelve. A range of specialist units was also available for allocation to divisions as required, including extra machine gun units, flamethrowers, gas troops and especially storm troops. OHL ordered the creation of more storm troop units, stressing that their main role was to improve the assault capabilities of the ordinary infantry through training.[36]

In the longer term, the various steps taken to strengthen the German army would produce benefits, but not all the changes had actually been implemented by the time the Entente attacked in April 1917. As Boehn said in his memorandum the previous October, 'It therefore seems at least questionable whether the army will be up to the task of countering the great deployment of strength by our enemies in the West which OHL expects next spring.'[37]

Entente Plans, German Preparations

The impending battle was seen by everyone at the time as the deciding event of the war.[38]

The Entente were well aware of the low state of the German army in late 1916. In November, Joffre organised an inter-allied conference at his headquarters in Chantilly, with the aim of repeating the agreement on joint action reached the previous November which had put the Central Powers under such pressure in 1916. The conference decided that in order to exploit the damage done to the enemy, offensive action would be maintained as far as possible over the winter. All the allied armies would be ready to launch general offensives from early February 1917. These would begin as soon as they could be synchronised on the different fronts, meaning that they should start within three weeks of each other.[39]

Events soon nullified these intentions. In Russia's case, it was agreed that the Chantilly obligations would not come into force until ratified at a follow-up conference in Petrograd. When this finally began in February, it became clear that weather conditions and the deficiencies of the

---

[36] Hermann Cron, *Geschichte des Deutschen Heeres im Weltkriege 1914–1918* (Berlin: Siegismund, 1937), 118; Hellmuth Gruss, *Die deutschen Sturmbataillone im Weltkrieg: Aufbau und Verwendung* (Berlin: Junker und Dünnhaupt, 1939), 56–64 and Anlage 7.

[37] Boehn memorandum, October 1916, f. 283.

[38] Max von Boehn, 'Kriegserlebnisse des Generaloberst Max v. Boehn 1914–1918', BArch, Boehn Nachlass, N306/1, 5.

[39] Doughty, *Pyrrhic Victory*, 311–14 gives background on the Chantilly Conference; the agreement reached there is in BOH 1917, 1: appendix 1.

Russian and Rumanian armies precluded a major offensive before 1 May. By the end of March, the Russians were stating that the revolution and continuing transport problems would force a further delay to at least mid-May and possibly June or July. Nivelle, who had now replaced Joffre, tried but failed throughout this period to make the Russians adhere to the Chantilly programme.[40] Ideally, the Italian offensive would take place at the same time as the Russian in order to put maximum pressure on Austria-Hungary. However, the Italians feared, with some justification, that they themselves would be attacked. This delayed preparation of their offensive until an agreement was reached in March on what help their allies would offer if needed.[41]

As a result of these problems, only the French and British were in a position to launch an early offensive. Joffre's original agreement with Haig called for British and French offensives in the Arras-Bapaume and Somme-Oise areas, followed by subsidiary French attacks on the Aisne and in Alsace. All would take place on a broad front and consist of a sequence of assaults to the maximum depth that could be supported by artillery, following each other as quickly as possible and aimed at destroying the enemy's capacity for resistance.[42] Nivelle retained the idea of a number of attacks on a broad front to be carried out as quickly as possible. But he changed the overall aim as well as the respective importance of the attacks and greatly increased their tempo.

In his new scheme, the Anglo-French forces would break through and destroy the main enemy forces in open battle. To achieve this, the Arras-Bapaume and Somme-Oise attacks, though large-scale, would be preliminary operations to draw in German reserves. The French would then launch the main offensive on the Aisne. In choosing these sectors, Nivelle reasoned that the region between the coast and Flanders was too wet to allow an attack before summer. Arras-Bapaume was suitable for an early offensive, the British had already begun preparations and the German salient in the area was vulnerable to a converging attack. The Somme area to the south as far as the river Avre was unsuitable for operations because of the devastation wrought by the 1916 fighting. Next to it, the narrowness of the Oise sector made only a limited offensive possible. Eastwards, the Aisne-Champagne sector was the nearest area suitable for a major offensive. Its advantages included that an attack from here could converge with the British advance from Arras-Bapaume and that

---

[40] AFGG, V/1:226–41, 547–57 and V/2: Annexe 145.

[41] John Gooch, *The Italian Army and the First World War* (Cambridge: Cambridge University Press, 2014), 203–8.

[42] BOH 1917, 1:18–19 and 50–1; AFGG V/1:57 and Annexe 183; Doughty, *Pyrrhic Victory*, 315–16.

there was a favourable starting point for capturing the vital Chemin des Dames position. Nivelle apparently only formulated this reasoning after the offensive, but the British official historian at least found it 'certainly cogent'.[43]

For the main offensive on the Aisne front, Nivelle believed that the technique he had successfully used at Verdun, overwhelming artillery bombardment followed by a rapid and massed infantry assault, would enable him to break through the entire German defensive system in one day. He stressed to his subordinates that all operations were to be properly prepared but must be conducted with decisiveness, audacity and speed; the watchword was 'when lightning can be used it should be preferred even to cannon'.[44] This triggered an informal competition between generals as to whose infantry would advance furthest and fastest, easily won by General Charles Mangin, commanding French Sixth Army. No doubt the earlier sacking of two corps commanders for expressing doubt in a breakthrough encouraged the others.[45]

Nivelle's plan quickly ran into difficulties. Although Haig recorded a positive impression when they first met, he soon began to make various objections. He wanted the French to take over a greater length of the front; he was concerned that the offensive might be prolonged, thereby endangering the possibility of a later British attack in Flanders; and finally he wanted to delay the attack till May. Slightly later, Lloyd George's plot to subordinate the British army in France to Nivelle led to an outraged reaction from Haig and Sir William Robertson, the Chief of the Imperial General Staff. Lloyd George backed down, Nivelle's authority over the British was limited to the duration of the offensive, and even then there were exceptions to it.[46]

Still more seriously, senior French commanders expressed increasing doubts about the prospects for the offensive the closer it came. As early as December 1916, Pétain, commanding Army Group Centre [*Groupe d'armées du centre*] commented that the terrain chosen for the main attack was extremely difficult and suggested an alternative. Nivelle therefore established a new Reserve Army Group [*Groupe d'armées de réserve*] to command the attack. However, by late March 1917 even its commander, General Alfred Micheler, was expressing severe doubts. Such concerns culminated in an extraordinary politico-military council of war at

---

[43] BOH 1917, 1:47–51.
[44] AFGG, V/1:461 and Annexe 1169; Brigadier-General Edward L. Spears, *Prelude to Victory* (London: Jonathan Cape, 1939), 327.
[45] Spears, *Prelude to Victory*, 93 and 457.
[46] Greenhalgh, *Victory through Coalition*, 138–48.

Compiègne on 6 April, chaired by President Poincaré. Nivelle effectively only secured continued governmental backing for the offensive at this late hour by threatening to resign.[47]

Nivelle's final orders, issued on 4 April after the German withdrawal to the Hindenburg Line, set the overall aim of the offensive as the destruction of most of the German army on the Western Front. He would achieve this in two stages: a series of separate attacks to break through followed by exploitation. In order of implementation, the breakthrough operations were a powerful but subsidiary British attack at Arras; a comparatively minor French operation on the Oise; the main element of the offensive, the French attack on the Aisne northwest of Reims including on the Chemin des Dames position; and closely linked with that, a smaller but still important attack in Champagne just to the east of Reims. A decoy attack in Alsace would distract German attention from the real assault front. During the exploitation stage, French, Belgian and British forces from the coast to Ypres would join the attack on the weakened enemy. In this stage, Nivelle hoped to reach Bruges, Ghent and Mons in Belgium and Mézières in France.[48] An advance of this extent would have liberated most of France and much of Belgium (and was similar to the line actually reached in November 1918).

The planned operational role of the Arras attack was to draw in German reserves before the French offensive. The British would make a strong thrust to break through and advance towards Cambrai (some thirty-five kilometres from Arras). As Figure 1.1 shows, German defences in this area consisted of three and in some places four positions, with another being constructed further back (the *Wotan-Stellung*). This gave a depth of up to seven kilometres for the main positions, and fourteen kilometres including the incomplete *Wotan-Stellung*.[49] Following an unprecedentedly heavy bombardment, the British intended to penetrate the main German positions on the first day. The northern and southern flanks would be covered by capture of the commanding Vimy Ridge and the village of Bullecourt respectively. Cavalry would exploit any breakthrough by advancing to the *Wotan-Stellung*, then preparing to move towards Cambrai and if possible Douai.[50] Twenty-six infantry and three cavalry divisions would participate in these operations.[51]

[47] AFGG, V/1:179–80; Rolland, *Nivelle*, 152–61.
[48] AFGG, V/1:457–60 and 521–30. The operations between the coast and Ypres never got beyond the planning stage and are not further considered here.
[49] Details measured from Reichsarchiv, *Weltkrieg*, 12: Beilage 9; the British called the *Wotan-Stellung* the Drocourt-Quéant Switch.
[50] BOH 1917, 1:vi, chapter 7 and appendixes 29 and 31.
[51] As with the number of French divisions below, this includes divisions in reserve but intended to participate in the attack.

The subsidiary French offensive on the Oise had been intended to employ twenty infantry and two cavalry divisions.[52] The German withdrawal to the Hindenburg Line in March completely disrupted this plan, and most of the French formations in the sector were moved to take part in the Champagne attack. Under the revised plan, French Army Group North [*Groupe d'armées du Nord*] would attack two days after the British, on an eleven kilometre front between St Quentin and the Oise. How the attack developed would depend on how strongly the Germans resisted. Two divisions would launch an initial assault to determine this. If there was little resistance, three more would join in. If the Germans resisted strongly, artillery preparation would continue and an attack by all five divisions would be mounted three days later. Should this lead to a breakthrough, Army Group North would initially advance to Hirson (some fifty-five kilometres east of St Quentin).[53]

In the main offensive, French Fifth, Sixth and Tenth Armies, comprising forty-seven infantry and seven cavalry divisions in Reserve Army Group, would attack on a front of forty kilometres.[54] The breakthrough would take place on the first day. As an example of what the plan called for, II Colonial Corps in Mangin's Sixth Army was to advance up to ten kilometres (a depth never achieved on the Western Front since the start of trench warfare). This entailed penetrating four German positions in the Chemin des Dames sector, as well as crossing the difficult Ailette valley and three successive ridge lines. The exploitation stage would begin the same evening and the corps would advance to just east of Laon, fifteen kilometres from the start line. By the evening of the second day, the advance guard was to be thirty-three kilometres from the start line; cavalry would push twenty kilometres further.[55] Fifth and Tenth Armies would make similar progress. At about the same date, French Fourth Army east of Reims would attack with eight divisions on a front of ten kilometres. Its immediate objectives were to reach and cross a line of commanding hills to the north, advancing four kilometres and penetrating three strong German positions. Next day Fourth Army would link up with the Fifth Army attack and also begin exploitation towards the Aisne, forty kilometres from its start line.[56]

---

[52] AFGG, V/1: chapter 8.   [53] Ibid., 460 and 462–70.
[54] Ibid., chapter 17. Fifth and Sixth Armies also each had one territorial division, composed of older men and used for labour and guard duties. Not included in these figures, First Army, with eight divisions, was in GQG reserve south of the main attack front.
[55] Ibid., 488–9.   [56] Ibid., chapter 18.

What did the Germans know of these plans? At the turn of the year, OHL assessed that the German army faced multiple possible attacks, including in Italy, several areas on the Western Front, Rumania and the Eastern Front.[57] It could not permanently provide all threatened areas with forces and fixed defences sufficient for a long battle. Timely intelligence was therefore crucial to deploy reinforcements and complete defensive preparations; it would also prevent the French achieving surprise, an essential precondition if they were to reach their ambitious tactical objectives.

As Chapter 5 shows, OHL was uncertain about British intentions until shortly before the offensive at Arras opened. In particular, Army Group Rupprecht and Sixth Army did not submit their finalised request for extra forces till the end of March. By the time of the British assault on 9 April, reinforcements were on their way but too late to avoid a heavy defeat. German intelligence work was more effective against the French, allowing OHL to identify enemy intentions with increasing confidence from the end of February and to convert intelligence assessments into practical countermeasures. The defending forces were substantially increased, and much labour put into both forward and rearward defences. Preparations against the French were therefore well advanced by the time of the infantry assault on 16 April.

These preparations also involved a complex reorganisation to achieve the most effective chain of command, described in Chapter 3. From early March, three German army groups covered the Western Front. Army Group Rupprecht faced the British in the north and Army Group Crown Prince the French. The newly formed Army Group Albrecht controlled the sector from east of Verdun to the Swiss border, a quiet front where formations came to recover from battle and consequently a pool from which reserves could be drawn. Table 1.1 sets out these command arrangements in more detail, focusing on the formations facing the offensive in mid-April 1917. To explain two possibly unfamiliar terms, an Army Detachment [*Armee-Abteilung*] was a small Army with its own headquarters; and a *Gruppe* [group] was a corps-level formation comprising two or more divisions.[58] Table 1.2 shows the opposing forces, in the front and in reserve, once the two sides had concentrated before the opening of the Entente attack.

---

[57] Reichsarchiv, *Weltkrieg*, 12:64–6.
[58] See Cron, *Geschichte des Deutschen Heeres*, 81 for Army Detachments; and Chapter 3 for *Gruppen*.

Table 1.1 *German command organisation on the Western Front, spring 1917*

Formation	Commander	Chief of staff	Total formations under command
Army Group Rupprecht	*Generalfeldmarschall* Crown Prince Rupprecht	*Generalleutnant* Hermann von Kuhl	3 Armies
Fourth Army (7 June)	*General der Infanterie* Friedrich Sixt von Armin	*Major* Max Stapff	6 *Gruppen*
Sixth Army (9 April)	*Generaloberst z.D.* Ludwig Freiherr von Falkenhausen	*Generalmajor* Karl Freiherr von Nagel zu Aichberg	6 *Gruppen*
Sixth Army (28 April)	*General der Infanterie* Otto von Below	*Oberst* Fritz von Loßberg	7 *Gruppen*
Gruppe Souchez	*General der Infanterie* Georg Wichura	*Oberstleutnant* Kurt Auer von Herrenkirchen	3 divisions
Gruppe Vimy	*General der Infanterie* Karl Ritter von Fasbender	*Oberstleutnant* Hermann Lenz	3 divisions
Gruppe Arras	*Generalleutnant* Karl Dieffenbach	*Oberstleutnant* Albrecht von Thaer	4 divisions
Gruppe Quéant	*Generalleutnant* Otto von Moser	*Major* Friedrich von Miaskowski	3 divisions
Second Army (12 April)	*General der Kavallerie* Georg von der Marwitz	*Oberst* Wilhelm Wild	5 *Gruppen*
Gruppe St Quentin	*Generalleutnant* Viktor Albrecht	*Major* Leo von Caprivi	2 divisions
Army Group Crown Prince	*General der Infanterie* Crown Prince Wilhelm	*Oberst* Friedrich Graf von der Schulenburg	4 Armies
Seventh Army	*General der Infanterie z.D.* Max von Boehn	*Oberstleutnant* Walther Reinhardt	4 *Gruppen*
Gruppe Crépy	*General der Infanterie* Hugo von Kathen	*Oberstleutnant* Erich von Tschischwitz	2 divisions
Gruppe Vailly	*Generalleutnant* Viktor Kühne	*Oberstleutnant* Willi von Klewitz	4 divisions
Gruppe Liesse	*General der Infanterie z.D.* Eduard von Liebert	*Oberstleutnant* Günther Hassenstein	3 divisions
Gruppe Sissonne	*General der Artillerie* Maximilian Ritter von Höhn	*Major* Julius Ritter von Reichert	3 divisions
First Army	*General der Infanterie* Fritz von Below	*Major* Robert von Klüber	4 *Gruppen*
Gruppe Aisne	*General der Infanterie* Ferdinand von Quast	*Oberst* Wilhelm von Dommes	[created 17 April]
Gruppe Brimont	*General der Infanterie* Magnus von Eberhardt	*Oberstleutnant* Otto Hasse	3 divisions
Gruppe Reims	*General der Infanterie z.D.* Franz Freiherr von Soden	*Major* Max Stapff	3 divisions
Gruppe Prosnes	*Generalleutnant* Martin Chales de Beaulieu	*Oberstleutnant* Eberhard von dem Hagen	4 divisions
Third Army	*Generaloberst* Karl von Einem	*Oberst* Martin Freiherr von Oldershausen	3 *Gruppen*
Gruppe Py	*General der Infanterie* Horst Edler von der Planitz	*Major* Horst von Metzsch	3 divisions
Army Group Albrecht	*Generalfeldmarschall* Duke Albrecht	*Generalleutnant* Konrad Krafft von Dellmensingen	3 Army Detachments

Table 1.2 *The opposing forces at the opening of the Entente spring offensive*

Army	Divisions[59]	Guns[60]	Aircraft[61]	Tanks[62]
German	64	3,447	840	0
French	60	4,544	1,000	176
British	26	2,817	365	60

The Battles: Arras

Easter Monday [9 April] of the year 1917 must be accounted from the British point of view one of the great days of the War. It witnessed the most formidable and at the same time most successful British offensive hitherto launched.[63]

The English did not seem to have known how to exploit the success they had gained to the full.[64]

The battle of Arras divided into four main phases. In the opening phase, 4 to 14 April, a preparatory bombardment of unprecedented weight enabled a successful infantry assault by twenty-three divisions. The first day of the attack in particular, 9 April, saw appreciable British gains, including the capture of Vimy Ridge; units further south made the longest single advance on the Western Front to date, six kilometres, and broke through all German prepared defences in the area. In addition the Germans suffered heavy casualties and loss of matériel. The British made some further gains over the next few days but were seriously hampered by bad weather – in 34th Division some men died of exposure[65] – and the difficulty of getting forward over the shelled area. An even more significant factor was British inability to improvise and co-ordinate in the semi-open warfare which now began, especially when faced with increasingly effective German resistance.[66] The attack was

---

[59] Includes divisions in reserve and arriving, excludes two German *Landwehr* divisions working on the rearward defences, three British and seven French cavalry and two French territorial divisions.

[60] Reichsarchiv, *Weltkrieg*, 12: Beilage 28 gives establishments, rather than guns actually serviceable, for the British army on 9 April, French on 16 April and German on both; it excludes anti-aircraft guns and mortars as well as French and German artillery deployed for the Oise attack.

[61] Reichsarchiv, *Weltkrieg*, 12:180, 212 and 299 give the approximate total available for service in the sectors of the offensive on 9 and 16 April respectively (i.e. again excluding the Oise sector); Walter Raleigh and H. A. Jones, *The War in the Air: Being the Story of the Part Played in the Great War by the Royal Air Force* (Oxford: Clarendon Press, 1931), 3:334.

[62] AFGG, V/1:617 and 628; BOH 1917, 1:310, 360 and appendix 40.

[63] BOH 1917, 1:201.   [64] Hindenburg, *Out of My Life*, 265.   [65] BOH 1917, 1:284.

[66] Ibid., 297.

halted on 14 April. During this period one Australian and one British division made a failed assault at Bullecourt.[67]

The Introduction described the panic that the successful attack of 9 April caused in the German command. The reaction included sacking Sixth Army's chief of staff and operations officer; the new chief was *Oberst* Fritz von Loßberg, the defensive expert. Later in the month the opportunity arose to move the Army commander, *Generaloberst* Ludwig Freiherr von Falkenhausen, who was replaced by *General der Infanterie* Otto von Below. The Germans made a planned withdrawal to their original third position, and brought up sizeable reinforcements.[68]

Despite the decreasing progress by the end of this first phase, Haig had agreed to support the French – whose own offensive had not yet opened – so there was no question of stopping the battle. However, its subsequent three phases were much less successful for the British. Haig insisted on a pause in the attack in order to ensure proper co-ordination. His original plan was for parts of three Armies to attack on 20 April. In the event the second phase did not open till 23 April, was confined almost entirely to one Army and ended the next day. Conditions were now much more difficult for the British, especially because their artillery no longer had the advantage of engaging long-identified targets. By contrast, the German artillery had greatly increased and were more effectively employed. In addition, the pause in operations enabled the Germans to deepen their defensive positions and deploy reserves properly for counter-attacks. The British therefore made only limited progress at the cost of quite heavy casualties.[69]

By now Haig was aware that the French offensive – which was launched on 16 April and which was the motive for the battle of Arras in the first place – had generally failed. He also knew that the French government was considering stopping it and replacing Nivelle. A conference in Paris on 20 April attended by Lloyd George had agreed that operations should continue, but that progress should be reviewed two weeks later. However, a discussion with the French Minister of War, Painlevé, on 26 April revived Haig's concerns.[70] His thinking now was to pursue Arras operations while the French offensive continued; but if or when it stopped, to mount an attack in Flanders to clear the U-boat bases there. Because of

---

[67] On the two battles of Bullecourt, see now Meleah Hampton, 'Especially Valuable? The I Anzac Corps and the Battles of Bullecourt, April–May 1917', in Jones, *Darkest Year*, 337–59.

[68] BOH 1917, 1:352–6.   [69] Ibid., 378–408 and 557.

[70] Gary Sheffield and John Bourne, eds., *Douglas Haig: War Diaries and Letters 1914–1918* (London: Weidenfeld & Nicolson, 2005), 284–7 (diary entries for 17, 18 and 24 April 1917); BOH 1917, 1:410–12.

this possibility he was not willing to use troops in Flanders to relieve those at Arras. So the next phases of the offensive were fought mainly by British divisions that had already been engaged and were 'tired and depleted'.[71] The description earlier of 34th Division's experiences shows what this carefully chosen phrasing meant in human terms.

Phase 3 of the battle, a secondary British attack on 28–29 April to improve positions by gaining ground, was an almost complete failure.[72] Soon after, it became obvious that Nivelle was likely to be removed and the French offensive stopped. The original British objectives were therefore no longer relevant. Haig now intended to move the focus of operations to Flanders, where he would attack as soon as possible after the expected Italian and Russian offensives. At Arras, he merely aimed to improve British positions locally and pin down German forces.[73] Accordingly, the fourth phase of the battle there opened on 3 May; it lasted little over twenty-four hours. The equivalent of ten British divisions attacked seven German. The Canadian Corps captured the tactically important village of Fresnoy, but otherwise the attack was poorly co-ordinated and failed almost completely in the face of German artillery fire, unsuppressed by British counter-battery work, and small-scale but vigorous local counter-attacks. Notably, the Germans did not have to commit the divisions held back for counter-attack. For the British, Phase 4 'was nothing less than a disaster', and the Germans even retook Fresnoy a few days later.[74]

Although this was the last major engagement in the battle of Arras proper, related fighting continued into June. The largest-scale clash was the second battle of Bullecourt, lasting from 3 to 17 May, with three British and three Australian divisions engaged against the equivalent of four German. The British and Australians made very limited gains in a battle that had 'the reputation of a killing match, typifying trench warfare at its most murderous'.[75] Fighting continued in May over various localities, with both sides having some success. As late as 28 June, five British and Canadian divisions made a limited attack to gain tactically useful ground. At a strategic level, these operations were intended to distract German attention in the gap between the battle of Messines in early June and the opening of the Ypres offensive at the end of July; and

---

[71] BOH 1917, 1:411–12.   [72] Ibid., 413–26 and 557.   [73] Ibid., 427–8.
[74] Ibid., 430–54 and 557; Harry Sanderson, 'Black Day of the British Army: The Third Battle of the Scarpe 3 May 1917', in Jones, *Darkest Year*, 360–86.
[75] BOH 1917, 1:455–81.

to contribute to the wearing down of the German army agreed at Anglo-French conferences at the beginning of May.[76]

The Battles: The Nivelle Offensive

The aim remains the destruction of the main body of the enemy forces on the Western Front.[77]

But it's over because the *poilus* are all going to go on strike.[78]

The story of the first French action, the subsidiary attack on the Oise, can be quickly told. An initial attack by three divisions on 13 April met fierce German resistance and made very limited progress. It was clear that the Germans were not planning to withdraw from the Hindenburg Line. The second phase was therefore cancelled, and French artillery resumed the preparatory bombardment for an assault provisionally set for 19 or 20 April. However, this depended on the arrival of artillery reinforcements and was never mounted.[79]

As Pétain had commented when he first saw it, the ground chosen for the main offensive was extremely difficult. The western sector of the attack faced the steep and rugged Chemin des Dames ridge terminating in the locally dominating Plateau de Californie (Winterberg to the Germans); the valley of the little river Ailette, which had become a nearly impassable bog; and one or more further ridges. A particular feature of this area was the many caverns formed by underground quarries, which could be used to shelter defending troops. To the east of the Chemin des Dames position was flat, low country that offered better going, including for tanks, but could be commanded by artillery fire from both flanks. The eastern sector of the main assault and the subsidiary attack by French Fourth Army in Champagne both faced naturally strong lines of hills.

The assault phase of the French offensive began on 16 April and made some progress at various points of the line. The best results came from the flat terrain at Berry au Bac on the Aisne, where French infantry, for the first time supported by tanks, advanced four-and-a-half kilometres. In the central sector of the Chemin des Dames ridge, the advance was

---

[76] Brigadier-General Sir James E. Edmonds, *Military Operations: France and Belgium, 1917*, vol. 2, *7th June–10th November. Messines and Third Ypres (Passchendaele)* (London: HMSO, 1948), 24–5 and 112–16 (hereafter, BOH 1917, 2).

[77] GQG, 'Directive pour les armées britanniques, l'armée belge et les groupes d'armées français', 4 April 1917, AFGG, V/1: Annexe 1167.

[78] Anon., *La Chanson de Craonne*, http://crid1418.org/espace_pedagogique/documents/ch_craonne.htm/ (accessed 16 May 2022).

[79] AFGG, V/1:604–11.

about two kilometres. Over 10,500 German prisoners were captured during the day. These were respectable achievements compared with some earlier offensives but they fell far short of Nivelle's objectives. II Colonial Corps, which was to have advanced fifteen kilometres on the first day, at furthest penetrated one-and-a-half kilometres; most of its units fared worse. The gains that were made came at the cost of heavy casualties. The tanks gave some useful support to the infantry but in general did not fulfil the hopes placed in them and nearly half were knocked out. By the evening of 16 April, the Germans realised that the long-awaited and feared French breakthrough attempt had failed.[80]

But Nivelle had no thought of abandoning the offensive and gave orders for the main effort to be shifted to the apparently promising Berry area. However, the assault there made only minor progress over the next few days. In contrast, a concentric attack on the hinge of the German line on the western flank of the battle persuaded the Germans to withdraw on 18 April. This led to the biggest French territorial gains of the offensive, to a depth of seven kilometres on a twelve kilometre front. But it proved impossible to exploit this success and the first phase of the offensive ended on 20 April.[81]

Over this same period, French Fourth Army carried out its supporting attack in Champagne, east of Reims. On the first day, 17 April, it advanced up to two-and-a-half kilometres, penetrating two German positions at some points and taking over 2,000 prisoners. However, it did not capture the line of hills and their northern slopes which were the objective. In the next few days it made limited progress, including occupying some of the hills. But the attack had run out of impetus and, like the main offensive, it was halted on 20 April.[82]

Nivelle was now subject to conflicting pressures. His initial decision was to pursue the original aims of the offensive. On 21 April he asked the British to continue and even expand their operations.[83] However, the same day Micheler, the commander in charge of the main French effort, told Nivelle that a breakthrough was no longer possible. He cited the serious casualties, fatigue of the troops, bad weather and lack of ammunition; and there was no question of surprise. Micheler proposed instead two powerful but local attacks aimed at wearing down the enemy and improving French positions. In broadly accepting these ideas, Nivelle changed the nature of the offensive from breakthrough and rapid

---

[80] Ibid., 631–52; Reichsarchiv, *Weltkrieg*, 12:403. On the performance of British and French tanks in the spring fighting, see Tim Gale, '1917: The "Dark Days" of the Tank', in Jones, *Darkest Year*, 483–504.
[81] AFGG, V/1:654–63 and 673–89.   [82] Ibid., 663–72 and 689–701.   [83] Ibid., 704.

exploitation to much more limited objectives. By this stage too, the French government was increasingly concerned with the progress of operations and intervened to limit their scale. The 29 April appointment of Pétain as chief of the general staff with expanded powers signalled its loss of confidence in Nivelle.[84]

The new series of operations began on 30 April with a six-division attack by Fourth Army aimed at firmly capturing the line of hills to its front. The attack made little progress, at the cost of heavy casualties, and renewed efforts over the next few days suffered the same fate or worse.[85] Nor was the four-division assault by Fifth Army south of Berry on 4 May any more successful. In view of the German resistance, the Army commander recommended against continuing and this was agreed the same day.[86] On 4–5 May, a three-division attack by Tenth Army had better luck. In particular, it captured the Plateau de Californie, took almost 1,200 prisoners and beat off a series of counter-attacks. To its left, ten divisions of Sixth Army attacked with tank support on 5 and 6 May. They made a limited advance and captured 3,800 prisoners but failed to achieve their objective of taking the whole of the Chemin des Dames ridge; the attack was called off. On 15 May, Nivelle was sacked and Pétain became French commander-in-chief.[87]

In what may be seen as a third phase of the offensive from 20 to 25 May, the French captured the locally commanding Mont Cornillet in Champagne in a four-division attack; however, owing to poor co-ordination, an attack by elements of three divisions on the Aisne made limited progress.[88] By this stage mutiny had broken out in the French army following the high casualties and disappointing results of the battles since mid-April. The French therefore now ended full-scale offensive action. But this did not mean the end of fighting in the area: the German army recorded fifteen local actions from the beginning of June to mid-July, mainly German initiatives to recapture tactically important ground lost in April–May. Despite the mutinies, German attackers generally met fierce French resistance and this fighting drew in German formations that could better have been used against the British in Flanders. Operations gradually declined after mid-July, but nevertheless there were a further eight local actions up till the battle of Malmaison in late October, when a successful French attack finally captured the whole Chemin des Dames ridge.[89]

---

[84] Ibid., 706–13 and 725–7; Rolland, *Nivelle*, 182–9.
[85] AFGG, V/1:750–5 and 777–82.   [86] Ibid., 756–60.
[87] Ibid., 760–73; Rolland, *Nivelle*, 198–203.   [88] AFGG, V/2:369–72 and 387–8.
[89] AFGG defines the Aisne battle as finishing on 8 May and the Champagne on 16 July. This chronology was apparently adopted to protect Pétain's image after he replaced

The Battles: Messines

One of the [German army's] worst tragedies of the war ...[90]

While the fighting continued, Anglo-French conferences in Paris on 4–5 May agreed that a decisive breakthrough was no longer feasible in 1917. However, it was essential to prevent a German attack and to wear down German strength until American forces had arrived in sufficient numbers to enable a final offensive in 1918. These aims would be achieved by launching a series of powerful attacks with limited objectives; the British would take on the main operations.[91] Haig envisaged that these operations would be in three stages. First, the Arras battle would continue in order to wear down and mislead the Germans. Next, the Messines Ridge would be captured as a preliminary operation to the third stage. This final stage, the Flanders operation, would be launched some weeks later and would aim to secure the Belgian coast.[92]

By mid-May the British were beginning to doubt that the French would carry out their side of the Paris agreement, and the War Cabinet told Haig it would not authorise his offensive plans if the French did not co-operate. To clarify their intentions, Haig met Pétain as French commander-in-chief for the first time on 18 May. Pétain told him about the unrest in the French army, but said he nevertheless planned to make four attacks including at Malmaison on 10 June and Verdun in late July; in addition French First Army would take part in the Flanders offensive.[93] These French plans were badly disrupted by the mutinies, which were at their most serious between 15 May and 30 June. Pétain informed Haig on 2 June, five days before the opening of the battle of Messines, that he would be unable to launch the Malmaison attack; the earliest French attack would now be the Verdun operation in late July. Haig decided not to tell the War Cabinet that the French could no longer co-operate fully as originally agreed, and to go ahead with the battle of Messines anyway.[94]

The Messines plan called for an attack by twelve divisions on a front of sixteen kilometres, penetrating the defences to a depth of up to four kilometres; the assaulting infantry would be supported by the explosion

Nivelle in mid-May, since it separated him from the defeat on the Aisne and linked him to what could be claimed as victory in Champagne: Philippe Olivera, 'La bataille introuvable?', in Offenstadt, *Chemin des Dames*, 36–46.
[90] Hermann von Kuhl, *Der Weltkrieg 1914–1918* (Berlin: Wilhelm Kolk, 1929), 2:114.
[91] BOH 1917, 2:22–4.   [92] Ibid., 24–5.   [93] Ibid., 25–8.
[94] Ibid., 29–30. In the event, the Verdun attack began on 20 August and Malmaison on 23 October.

of nineteen long-prepared mines and by seventy-two tanks. The battle lasted from 7 to 14 June, with the main fighting taking place on the first day. The British took all their objectives, and the fifteen German divisions involved in the defence lost 7,400 men captured.[95] Hermann von Kuhl described Messines as one of the worst tragedies suffered by the German army during the war because the defeat could have been avoided by a local withdrawal, which had been considered but was rejected. A major reason for this decision was that intelligence on the scale of British mining activity was conflicting and that the German planning process therefore did not take full account of the severity of the threat.[96]

The Results of the Entente Offensives in Early 1917

As usual, performance had lagged behind promise.[97]

In defeating the Entente breakthrough attempt and inflicting many more casualties than it suffered, the German army won a strategically important victory. True, the French made some useful tactical gains as well as capturing almost 29,000 prisoners and 187 guns.[98] At an earlier period of the war, this would have been seen as success, but it bore no relation to Nivelle's objectives, to the hopes of the French soldiers or to the casualties. Of particular significance was the collapse of the French army into mutiny. Although the mutinies were comparatively short-lived, they and the steps needed to restore military effectiveness left the army in a weakened state for the rest of the year.[99] The British too made considerable tactical gains and captures at both Arras and Messines. The latter was a prelude to a much bigger operation, but the former had been intended as a breakthrough and in this light it failed completely. Nor did it achieve its operational role of attracting reserves from the French front.[100]

However, as Chapter 8 on performance shows, the German army itself was badly damaged by these battles and for the first time its field strength began to fall. Ludendorff believed that what saved the German army in early 1917 was the Entente's failure to co-ordinate assaults in different theatres. He may well have been right given the scale of the Italian and Russian offensives that finally took place in May–June and July, respectively. The Italians deployed twenty-eight divisions for the

[95] Ibid., 32–3, 38 and 87.
[96] Kuhl, *Weltkrieg*, 2:114; Reichsarchiv, *Weltkrieg*, 12:468–9.
[97] BOH 1917, 1:535.   [98] AFGG, V/1:782.
[99] For the rest of the war according to some British observers: BOH 1917, 2:30 fn. 1.
[100] Stachelbeck, '"Lessons learned" in World War I', 129 assesses the Arras offensive's success in pinning German reserves more favourably.

tenth battle of the Isonzo in May, the largest yet, and a further ten for the battle of Asiago in June. In both cases, they suffered severe losses for almost no gains. They did draw in six-and-a-half Austro-Hungarian divisions from the Eastern Front, but the delay in launching the Kerensky offensive cancelled out the effect. The Russians and Rumanians attacked with 134 infantry and 27 cavalry divisions. They made good initial progress against the Austro-Hungarians, but were then pushed back by a powerful counter-offensive.[101]

All this came too late to support the Anglo-French offensives. Nevertheless, as the Introduction described, the Italian and especially Russian attacks did have a significant effect on the Western Front: knowledge of the coming threats was one of the reasons why OHL refused to release forces to attack the French army at the moment of its maximum weakness during the mutinies. The British minor attacks at Arras, continuing into June, had the same effect.[102] Joffre's and Nivelle's grand strategy may not have worked for the offensive, but it contributed to saving France later.

---

[101] Reichsarchiv, *Weltkrieg*, 12:514, 518 and Beilage 26; Reichsarchiv, *Weltkrieg*, vol. 13, *Die Kriegführung im Sommer und Herbst 1917: Die Ereignisse außerhalb der Westfront bis November 1918* (Berlin: E. S. Mittler, 1942), 150 and 181. Stevenson, *1917*, chapter 6 argues that the Kerensky offensive had a calamitous political effect in paving the way for anarchy and Bolshevik dictatorship in Russia.

[102] Max Schwarte, 'Die Grundlagen für die Entschlüsse der Obersten Heeresleitung vom Herbst 1916 bis zum Kriegsende', in Max Schwarte, ed., *Der Weltkampf um Ehre und Recht* (Leipzig: Ernst Finking, n.d.), 3:27; Reichsarchiv, *Weltkrieg*, 12:547 and 559.

2 Principles

Where have our old Prussian principles gone? We are really losing our pleasure in our own work and our willingness to take responsibility.[1]

In this plaintive diary entry from April 1917, *General der Artillerie* Max von Gallwitz, commanding Fifth Army, expressed his annoyance at what he saw as the latest encroachments on his authority by Army Group Crown Prince and OHL. His and other memoirs frequently refer to the modern commander's decreasing autonomy and even powerlessness at certain moments.[2] This is a far cry from the common view of such autonomy – in other words, mission command – as the cornerstone of a distinctively German way of command that underlay the army's many operational successes through different historical periods.[3] Apart from mission command, lists of traditional principles include commanders and general staff officers as partners, function overriding rank and setting a *Schwerpunkt* for every operation.[4] These principles undoubtedly did exist, but were not necessarily defined or even identified by a specific term or set out in official doctrine.

However, the principles were developed to meet the requirements of the first command task, co-ordinating a mass army, in a mobile, offensive war aimed at bringing about and winning a decisive battle. In particular, they were intended to help strike the correct balance between granting independence to enable subordinate commanders to cope with the uncertainties and exploit the fleeting opportunities of battle, while exerting enough control to fulfil the mission and avoid chaos. Modern scholarship tends to cover application of the principles in mobile war and has little to say about what happened in the very different static warfare that emerged

[1] Max von Gallwitz, *Erleben im Westen 1916–1918* (Berlin: E. S. Mittler, 1932), 180.
[2] Ibid., 29, 83, 130 and 147.   [3] Sigg, *Unterführer als Feldherr*, Vorwort.
[4] David T. Zabecki, ed., *Chief of Staff: The Principal Officers behind History's Great Commanders* (Annapolis, MD: Naval Institute Press, 2008), 1:9–13; Samuels, *Command or Control?*, 8–10.

on the Western Front. This chapter and the next fill the gap by analysing the role of the principles in carrying out the first command task under 1917 trench warfare conditions, when the German army was on the defensive and facing an increasingly superior enemy.[5]

Mission Command

> [I]n the trench warfare of today we can no longer survive only on the mission procedure [*Auftragsverfahren*] to which we gave priority in peacetime by stressing the independence of the subordinate commander. It is rather the duty of all levels of command *to intervene in the arrangement of detail* much more frequently than before.[6]

The Introduction quoted a contemporary definition of mission command: 'Orders give information on the situation and the intentions of the commander, and assign tasks, but leave the recipient free to choose the method of carrying them out.' By the outbreak of war, mission command was a well-established concept in the German army at both operational and tactical levels. It was generally seen as part of a spectrum of control ranging from loose to strict. As early as the 1890s, the British military commentator Spenser Wilkinson had pointed to the dilemma – which he thought the German army had solved – that free criticism might undermine discipline, and that unconditional obedience destroyed independent judgement.[7] The 1906 infantry regulations addressed the balance to strike between the two by emphasising the inculcation in the individual soldier of both initiative and discipline, which defined the limits of his autonomy.[8]

---

[5] Function overriding rank is covered in Chapter 4.

[6] AOK 6 to corps and divisional commanders, 'Erfahrungen aus den Ereignissen bei Verdun Ende 1916', Ia No. 450 geh., 15 January 1917, KAM, AOK 6 Bd. 369 (emphasis in the original). Many terms were used for mission command, *Auftragsverfahren* – rather than *Auftragstaktik* – being one of the most common: the terminology is discussed in Stephan Leistenschneider, 'Die Entwicklung der Auftragstaktik im deutschen Heer und ihre Bedeutung für das deutsche Führungsdenken', in Gerhard P. Groß, ed., *Führungsdenken in europäischen und nordamerikanischen Streitkräften im 19. und 20. Jahrhundert* (Hamburg: E. S. Mittler, 2001), 177. It is worth noting that important prewar documents such as the infantry regulations of 1906, the field service regulations of 1908 and 'Essentials of High Command' use *none* of the terminology employed by modern commentators to describe German mission command at this period, such as *direktive Befehlsführung, Weisungführung, Weisungsführung* with a second 's', *Führen durch Direktiven* and *Führung nach Direktive*; all mean commanding through broad directives rather than detailed orders.

[7] Meyer, 'Operational Art', 134–5; Spenser Wilkinson, *The Brain of an Army: A Popular Account of the German General Staff*, 2nd ed. (Westminster: Constable, 1895), 191.

[8] Raths, *Vom Massensturm zur Stoßtrupptaktik*, 28–30.

Early twentieth century thought on mission command stressed that a precondition for its successful application was a highly trained officer corps. Proper training was essential to achieve the uniform approach needed for the integrated handling of combat. Mission command required 'independently thinking obedience' and hence mutual trust between superior and subordinate. Officers given latitude to adopt their own solutions to missions might choose a good one but equally might not. Mistakes and misunderstandings happened quite often in manoeuvres even with a professional and well-trained officer corps. So what might be expected in wartime given personnel churn and the presence of many inexperienced reserve and *Landwehr* officers?[9] The level of training reached by individual officers defined how much autonomy they could be granted; full account had to be taken of personalities and circumstances.[10]

Descriptions of German army methods in the First World War tend to assume that mission command played an important role throughout the war. The application of mission command at all levels has even been claimed as one reason why the German army made fewer mistakes than its enemies and generally remedied those it did make more quickly.[11] The introduction of the new defensive tactics at the end of 1916 in theory at least specifically emphasised mission command at divisional level:

The essence is above all that responsibility for the tactical control of action by all arms in the defensive battle is expressly passed to the division, i.e. the divisional commander. He is given only the main points for this by corps, Army and army group.[12]

Below divisional level there was undoubtedly still scope for mission command in early 1917, but its application was uneven. 3rd Bavarian Infantry Division adapted its methods at Arras on the basis of advice from its regiments, and its successful defensive action was regarded as a model application of the new tactics. The British ruefully admired the skill with which German infantry from another division infiltrated forward even in

---

[9] Dirk W. Oetting, *Auftragstaktik: Geschichte und Gegenwart einer Führungskonzeption* (Frankfurt: Report Verlag, 1993), 18–19; Balck, *Tactics*, 1:402.

[10] Otto von Moser, *Ausbildung und Führung des Bataillons, des Regiments und der Brigade: Gedanken und Vorschläge*, 4th ed. (Berlin: E. S. Mittler, 1914), 189; Leistenschneider, 'Entwicklung der Auftragstaktik', 186–7.

[11] Samuels, *Command or Control?*, 282–5; Millotat, *Generalstabssystem*, 115. Cf. *Generalfeldmarschall* Erich von Manstein's comment that mission command was the secret of German operational success in the Second World War: Manstein, *Verlorene Siege* (Bonn: Athenäum-Verlag, 1955), 57.

[12] Moser, *Feldzugsaufzeichnungen*, 267.

unfavourable ground and under heavy artillery fire.[13] But 5th Bavarian Reserve Division on the Aisne believed that its junior commanders were only capable of the simplest tasks; if the situation required new orders, they must come from the regimental or battalion commander since the tactical understanding needed was completely lacking below that level.[14] This is a striking comment on the restricted application of mission command given that the division had recently been the demonstration unit at a divisional command course, and was therefore well versed in the new defensive tactics. The comment also reflects the pre-war concerns about mission command in wartime, following the influx of non-professional officers.

Further up the military hierarchy, it is a commonplace in senior officers' post-war writings that application of mission command on the Western Front during the trench warfare phase was restricted. Hermann von Kuhl commented that army group and Army headquarters had to limit subordinates' freedom of action compared with peacetime because they needed closer supervision: 'We were unable to get by with the mission procedure of peacetime training.'[15] Among many others, Gallwitz and *General der Infanterie* Hans von Zwehl agreed. Otto von Moser even referred to the 'blind obedience' [*Kadavergehorsam*] demanded from above.[16]

Many wartime documents illustrate the limitations on mission command. In December 1916 Seventh Army's chief of staff wrote that the headquarters responsible for an operation must prepare and check the co-operation of all arms down to the smallest detail; general staff officers must know how to draft the much increased contents of orders briefly and clearly.[17] A pamphlet circulated throughout the army on how divisions should make limited attacks stressed that their parent corps should check every detail beforehand. At about the same time, OHL began taking a much more restrictive approach to doctrine than was traditional, insisting that all manuals in the 'Regulations for Trench Warfare for All Arms' series were absolutely binding.[18]

---

[13] 3.BID, 'Erfahrungen aus den Kaempfen bei Arras', 6 May 1917, KAM, AOK 6 Bd. 419, ff. 30–51 (hereafter, 3.BID, 'Erfahrungen'; first and subsequent references for such reports from other divisions treated similarly); BOH 1917, 1:555.

[14] 5.BRD, 'Gegenstoß aus der Tiefe', No. 2973 Ia, 18 March 1917, KAM, XV.BRK 174.

[15] Hermann von Kuhl, *Der deutsche Generalstab in Vorbereitung und Durchführung des Weltkrieges*, 2nd ed. (Berlin: E. S. Mittler, 1920), 187.

[16] Hans von Zwehl, *Generalstabsdienst im Frieden und im Kriege* (Berlin: E. S. Mittler, 1923), 32; Moser, *Feldzugsaufzeichnungen*, 346.

[17] AOK 7 to its corps, CGS Ia Nr. 78/Dez. 16, 15 December 1916, GLAK, F1/374.

[18] Chef des Generalstabes des Feldheeres, *Anlage kleiner Angriffs-Unternehmungen bei Gruppe Vailly (XI. Korps) im Mai/Juni 1917* (GHQ: Druckerei des Chefs des

Three main factors limited the application of mission command on the Western Front at this period: the nature of the front and the complexity of battle there; shortages of skill and matériel; and the current state of technology. On the first point, Zwehl – a corps commander from the outbreak of war till late 1916 – regretted the near disappearance of mission command but understood the reasons. Attacks on prepared positions were so difficult that unless all details were carefully worked out in advance, misunderstandings and mistakes would lead to failure. In addition, the enemy were watchful, tough and superior in numbers and matériel: they would not often let mistakes go unpunished.[19] This perception of risk, especially at a period when German commanders worried about the declining quality of their troops, precluded the sort of operational stroke at which the army traditionally excelled. Offensively minded senior officers disliked the new defensive doctrine because it stressed a purely tactical defence, enabled OHL to exert control right down to divisional level (and below) and avoided risk. Such officers saw rejection of proposals for a larger-scale and more aggressive defence in spring 1917 against the obviously impending French assault as an example of this cautious attitude.[20]

By 1917 tactical success in battle required effective all-arms co-operation; the operational level of war added the problems of co-ordinating neighbouring formations, deep battle and the battle of matériel. Co-ordination could only be effected by higher echelons of command. There is a noteworthy clash here between the views of pre-war commentators, who stressed German formations' willingness during the Franco-Prussian War to help each other, and those of First World War practitioners such as *Oberst* (later *Generalmajor*) Friedrich Graf von der Schulenburg. Having served as a corps, Army and army group chief of staff, he commented acidly that neighbouring formations could never be relied on to reach agreement for mutual support and that higher levels of command therefore had to issue clear and exhaustive orders. The sheer number of formations on the Western Front aggravated this issue.[21]

Generalstabes des Feldheeres, 1917), 4; Chapter 7 discusses OHL's new approach to doctrine.

[19] Hans von Zwehl, *Maubeuge, Aisne – Verdun. Das VII. Reserve-Korps im Weltkriege von seinem Beginn bis Ende 1916* (Berlin: Karl Curtius, 1921), 149. For a modern take on armies' use of increasing management to eliminate uncertainty by reducing errors, see David R. Segal and Joseph J. Lengermann, 'Professional and Institutional Considerations', in Sam C. Sarkesian, ed., *Combat Effectiveness: Cohesion, Stress and the Volunteer Military* (Beverly Hills, CA: Sage Publications, 1980), 161.

[20] Generalleutnant August Fortmüller, 'Die Heeresgruppe Deutscher Kronprinz 1917 bis März 1918', in Schwarte, *Weltkampf um Ehre und Recht*, 3:175.

[21] Oetting, *Auftragstaktik*, 114 on mutual support in the Franco-Prussian War; Friedrich Graf von der Schulenburg-Tressow, 'Erlebnisse', unpublished manuscript in BArch,

The complexity of battle in 1917 also demanded greatly increased managerial co-ordination and therefore control from above. New formations such as army groups wanted oversight of activity by subordinate organisations.[22] The maintenance of operational reserves at different command levels, the need to manage attrition and the increasing number of independent specialist units, particularly artillery, all added to the burden. When OHL ordered regular assessment of divisions' combat value, it had to reassure army groups and Armies that checking on the condition of the units at the front was not infringing on subordinates' authority, an interesting comment on the sensitivities involved in mission command.[23] In a battle of matériel, proper organisation of logistics was crucial.[24] Intelligence had to be acquired and fitted into the overall command system. Against this background it is not surprising that efforts throughout 1917 to rein in bureaucracy failed.[25]

In Western Front circumstances it was difficult to strike the right balance between issuing orders and granting independence. Mistakes in this regard were an important cause of at least four heavy local defeats in 1917 – Arras on 9 April, Messines, Verdun and Malmaison. At Arras, Army Group Rupprecht failed to ensure that Sixth Army had brought up its reserves close enough to the front. At the other three battles, Army Groups Rupprecht and Crown Prince suggested local withdrawals to pre-empt clearly impending attacks, but in each case allowed themselves to be persuaded by the Army concerned that withdrawal was unnecessary or impossible.[26] Kuhl later commented that the defeat at Messines could have been avoided if the army group had simply ordered the evacuation of the position; but the united advice of local commanders had opposed this, and to reject their advice would have gone against the customs of the German army.[27]

Writing about the failure to withdraw before the attacks at Verdun and Malmaison, Schulenburg realised with hindsight that one could not expect the two Armies involved voluntarily to evacuate ground they had

---

Schulenburg Nachlass, N58/1, 144 (hereafter, Schulenburg, 'Erlebnisse'); Gallwitz, *Erleben im Westen*, 98.

[22] HDK telegram to its AOKs, Id 2251, 12 April 1917, GLAK, F1/374.

[23] OHL to CGS AOK 7, Ia No. 2812 geh. op., 12 April 1917, GLAK, F1/374.

[24] HDK circular, 'Zusammenstellung von Erfahrungen aus den Schlachten an der Aisne und in der Champagne betreffend Munitionsnachschub', Mun./1391/17, 14 June 1917, GLAK, F1/536.

[25] See Chapter 6.

[26] For the German investigation of the Arras defeat, see Jack Sheldon, *The German Army on Vimy Ridge 1914–1917* (Barnsley: Pen & Sword, 2008), chapter 8; and Boff, *Haig's Enemy*, 159–62. Messines: Kuhl, 'Kriegstagebuch', 1 May 1917. Verdun and Malmaison: Schulenburg, 'Erlebnisse', 157–8.

[27] Kuhl, *Weltkrieg*, 2:114.

won at great cost. It was the job of the higher command, in this case the army group, to think more broadly and to give a clear and binding order to withdraw.[28] Withdrawal, especially the permanent evacuation of positions, was always a sensitive issue during trench warfare. On the Somme, Army commanders were said to hesitate over withdrawal out of fear they would be accused of being soft; at least one divisional commander was sacked for withdrawing without orders.[29] The first edition of the 'Defensive Battle' manual, issued shortly after this in December 1916, placed responsibility for ordering withdrawal on division, or in urgent cases brigade or regiment. In March 1917 the second edition moved the responsibility firmly upwards, to Army or corps; divisions could decide only in the most urgent cases, and lower levels were excluded.[30] This shift again demonstrates how trench warfare eroded mission command.

The second factor limiting higher-level mission command was shortages, especially of skilled general staff officers, manpower and munitions.[31] As already described, good and uniform training was a precondition of successfully implementing mission command. One reason Kuhl gave for increased supervision from above was inexperience in divisional headquarters, which frequently had to be allocated young general staff officers. This was a widespread concern of commanders and is discussed further below. Lack of manpower and matériel, especially ammunition, resulted in the need to check rigorously that even minor actions were proportionate to the resources they would use. This requirement was formally included in the new doctrine.[32] Many divisions were not of high enough quality to be used in major battle, with the consequence that those which were had to be carefully husbanded. For much of the first half of 1917, ammunition supply was thoroughly unsatisfactory and heavy expenditure during the spring fighting greatly outstripped production. As a result, OHL constantly worried about sinking reserves and regularly issued orders for ammunition economy. This disparity between the needs of the front and the means available to satisfy

---

[28] Schulenburg, 'Erlebnisse', 160.

[29] Oberstleutnant (later Generalmajor) Hermann Ritter Mertz von Quirnheim's tenth report to the Bavarian Kriegsminister [Minister of War], 20 November 1916, NARA, Mertz von Quirnheim papers, Publication Number M958, Roll 1; Mertz was a section head in OHL's Operations Department. The divisional commander was *Generalleutnant* Heino von Basedow of 5th Ersatz Division: see AOK 1 letter, Ia 174 pers., 31 October 1916, KAM, HKR neue Nr. 378.

[30] 'Einleitender Vortrag des Kursleiters', lecture to the fifth divisional command course in Valenciennes, 10–16 April 1917, HSAS, Urach Nachlass, GU117 Bü 362, 20–1; '*Abwehrschlacht*', March 1917, 6b.

[31] Kuhl, *Generalstab*, 187.   [32] '*Abwehrschlacht*', March 1917, 17.

them was a further cause of the more detailed orders now found necessary.[33]

The contemporary state of technology limited mission command on the Western Front in two ways. First, it was a key part of the all-arms battle and hence itself contributed to complexity. This was particularly true of artillery and related services such as aviation, flash-spotting and sound-ranging. Every aspect of artillery work had to be co-ordinated with the infantry and other arms. A complicating factor here was that not all senior commanders were up to the task of controlling the masses of artillery involved, and not all artillery officers had mastered the increasing technical sophistication of their art – another illustration of the link between mission command and skill sets.[34] As the importance of specialist arms grew, there was an increasing need for staff officers in headquarters at different levels to service them and of course a corresponding growth of the headquarters. The new staff functions were themselves responsible for a part – possibly a large part – of the increased bureaucracy of the war, in terms of the questionnaires, reports and lessons learned which they generated. Gallwitz commented that what was simply an idea when expressed by senior officers became an avalanche of paper in the hands of the young specialists.[35]

The second way in which technology limited mission command was through the means of communication and mobility available during the war. Battlefield communications in an age before radio telephony were all too likely to fail at the vital moment, with a disastrous effect on all-arms co-operation. This problem was aggravated by the need for staffs to remain out of the worst of the danger zone if they were to function at all. Similarly, genuine all-terrain vehicles did not yet exist, limiting movement across the battlefield; in particular, it was difficult to bring artillery and ammunition forward once attacking infantry had passed out of range. These two factors together greatly reduced the flexibility on which mission command at anything above local level depended, as the Germans found in their 1918 offensives: the necessary co-ordination could only be achieved by non-flexible methods such as controlling artillery support by the clock.[36]

The availability of technology linked to communications and mobility, especially the car, the railway and the telephone, also influenced mission

[33] Reichsarchiv, *Weltkrieg*, 12:82.
[34] Generalleutnant a.D. Ziethen, 'Die Artillerie-Führung', in Franz Nikolaus Kaiser, ed., *Das Ehrenbuch der Deutschen Schweren Artillerie* (Berlin: Wilhelm Kolk, 1931), 62.
[35] Gallwitz, *Erleben im Westen*, 161.
[36] Reichsarchiv, *Weltkrieg*, vol. 14, *Die Kriegführung an der Westfront im Jahre 1918* (Berlin: E. S. Mittler, 1944), 49.

command. The short distances on the Western Front made it easy for superiors to meet their subordinates, with the associated possibility of face-to-face intervention in decision-making. Having just arrived in the west from Macedonia, Sixth Army commander Otto von Below was struck that he was able to visit three corps headquarters between breakfast and lunch.[37] The phone was a crucial tool in enabling command at all during trench warfare, but it negatively affected mission command in three ways. First, it made intervention by superiors much easier: commanders' memoirs are full of complaints about interference from above by phone.[38] Second, the phone centralised the flow of information and empowered those who were able to make most regular use of it. This was usually the staff, and the phone's essential role in communications strengthened the predominance of the staff officer over the commander.[39] Third, the phone enabled superiors to bypass levels of command and to control events from a distance; and it enabled subordinates to consult superiors when faced with problems. In this way, it diminished commanders' sense of the need to take independent action on the basis of their own judgement.[40]

It is clear then that Western Front conditions limited mission command in the trench warfare period. A good example of the effect on operations is a plan evolved by 16th Bavarian Infantry Division in the Vimy Ridge area in March 1917. Codenamed *München*, the aim of the operation was to improve observation, increase the depth of the German position and interrupt any enemy mining preparations. It was basically a regimental 'attack with limited objectives'. We could expect it to require authorisation by brigade, division and perhaps corps; but in the event it also needed approval by Sixth Army, the army group and OHL. Rupprecht, the army group commander, mentioned it four times in his diary. Preparations and changes of mind entailed correspondence between all the levels of command involved, and the brigade orders included details such as that each man was to carry two water bottles.[41]

Theoretically, a large-scale counter-attack from the rear [*Gegenstoß aus der Tiefe*] – as we will see, a controversial aspect of the new tactics – offered the opportunity for mission command at corps and divisional level. But it had been established since late 1915 that the sort of counter-attack

---

[37] Otto von Below diary, 30 April 1917.

[38] Moser, *Feldzugsaufzeichnungen*, 319 for one.   [39] Ibid., 335.

[40] Max von Gallwitz, *Meine Führertätigkeit im Weltkriege 1914/1916. Belgien – Osten – Balkan* (Berlin: E. S. Mittler, 1929), 298.

[41] For *München*, see Sheldon, *Vimy Ridge*, 248–66; Rupprecht, *Kriegstagebuch*, 2:119, 121, 128–9 and 132–3 (diary entries for 20 and 22 March, 3 and 7 April 1917). In the end, the operation was pre-empted by the opening of the battle of Arras.

a corps or division might be able to launch on its own initiative, in other words of medium force and beginning after a few hours, fell between two stools and almost inevitably failed. Experience of attempting this sort of counter-attack in the spring fighting was mixed: some succeeded, many did not. A more carefully prepared counter-attack could be delivered with greater force; but as the equivalent of an attack with limited objectives, it was subject to the same control and micro-management from above as operations like *München*.

Commanders and General Staff Officers as Partners

In this unification of two personalities lies the security of command.[42]

A traditional way of describing the ideal relationship between a commander and his chief of staff was as a happy marriage. It should combine 'the genius of Gneisenau and the aggression of Blücher'.[43] The commander took decisions and was responsible for them; the chief of staff was not only fully responsible for the advice he gave his commander, he was also jointly responsible for the commander's decisions. If he and the commander disagreed, he had the unwritten right to have his view formally recorded. However, he was then faithfully to carry out his commander's orders.[44] This form of partnership marked a sharp difference between the German system of command and the British or French, where the commander–chief of staff relationship was more that of a senior and his subordinate. Good partnerships were also crucial to successful mission command, which depended on a common understanding of how to act based on a high level of training of commanders and general staff officers, and of trust between them.

To use modern parlance, the commander and his chief staff officer were a command team. Various definitions have been proposed for such teams. Jonathan Boff's analysis of British Third Army in 1918 includes directly subordinate infantry and artillery commanders.[45] The German army did not use the term 'command team', but in effect saw the staff as a series of concentric circles for purposes such as briefing and

---

[42] General Hans von Seeckt, *Thoughts of a Soldier*, trans. Gilbert Waterhouse (London: Ernest Benn, 1930), 115.

[43] Citino, *German Way of War*, 141.

[44] Cron, *Geschichte des Deutschen Heeres*, 72; Wiegand Schmidt-Richberg, *Die Generalstäbe in Deutschland 1871–1945: Aufgaben in der Armee und Stellung im Staate* (Stuttgart: Deutsche Verlags-Anstalt, 1962), 53.

[45] Jonathan Boff, *Winning and Losing on the Western Front: The British Third Army and the Defeat of Germany in 1918* (Cambridge: Cambridge University Press, 2012), 215–16.

quartering.[46] The commander and his chief staff officer were clearly at the centre, and because of their special relationship it is appropriate to focus on them as the core command team.

At army group, Army and corps level, the chief of staff had formal rights and responsibilities. Theoretically the chief general staff officer in a division, titled the *Ia*, did not have these rights.[47] But at this level too, the trend was towards centralisation on the *Ia* so that from February 1916 he increasingly if informally became a chief of staff. A year later, the new divisional command courses stated that the *Ia* was the commander's right hand and that his work would be eased the more his position resembled that of a corps chief of staff. The importance of the commander–*Ia* relationship was further emphasised by new reporting on divisions introduced during the 1917 spring fighting. This covered three points: a general assessment of the division's performance and then judgements on the commander and the *Ia*.[48]

Commanders

In German thinking about command, the commander traditionally played the starring role. Clausewitz believed that in the danger, exertion, uncertainty and chance of war, a commander needed two qualities above all – intellect to understand what was happening and courage then to take the right decision and implement it, leading his troops through all friction and failure to victory. Military genius meant possessing these qualities to a high degree and at the highest level of command.[49] Moltke the Elder too stressed the uncertainty of war, and consequently the need to make and execute decisions quickly rather than waste time looking for ideal solutions; improvisation over doctrine; and the greater importance of the moral factor in war compared with peace.[50] Building on such thoughts, later manuals emphasised that in all the uncertainty, one thing at least must be certain: the commander's decision. His intention was the core

---

[46] More on this in Chapter 6.

[47] The term '*Ia*' (pronounced *Eins-A* in German) designated the senior general staff officer of the operations section (*Abteilung I*) of any headquarters from division up. In a division, the *Ia* was directly responsible to the commander; above division, to the formation's chief of staff. More junior general staff officers in the operations section were designated *Ib*, *Ic* and so on.

[48] Stachelbeck, *Militärische Effektivität*, 43–4; 'Organisation des Divisionsstabes in der Abwehrschlacht', lecture to the second divisional command course in Sedan, 21–7 March 1917, HSAS, Urach Nachlass, GU117 Bü 362; HDK circular, IIa Nr. 1249, 14 May 1917, HSAD, 11355–0268.

[49] Carl von Clausewitz, *On War*, trans. and ed. Michael Howard and Peter Paret (Princeton, NJ: Princeton University Press, 1976), book 1, chapters 3 and 7.

[50] Hughes, *Moltke*, 5.

element of mission command.[51] And of course the whole purpose of mission command was to cope with and exploit the uncertainty and fleeting opportunities of war, wherever possible by offensive action. Indeed, it has been said that the German way of war centred less on staff officers and their careful professional training, and more on aggressive operational manoeuvre by commanders in almost all circumstances.[52]

We can easily understand how men such as Blücher – 'Marshal Forwards' – and even Moltke the Elder fit the heroic image of a commander and his leadership described by Clausewitz. But did this role survive in First World War conditions, especially trench warfare? The analysis of mission command showed how commanders' freedom to operate was circumscribed at this period. One post-war commentator thought modern technology had killed off 'the romantic idea of the independently acting commander' and there seems little doubt that the balance of power did indeed swing towards the staff. Many commanders particularly disliked their staff not keeping them properly informed, or pre-empting their decisions by exploiting general staff channels.[53] Wilhelm Deist and Michael Geyer among others have therefore argued that commanders became marginalised as the increasing complexity of the war demanded managerial and technical skills rather than the traditional leadership functions of the commander; the general staff officer and general staff channels became predominant.[54]

However, we should not exaggerate commanders' loss of influence. We saw Hindenburg steadying Ludendorff's shaken nerve on 9 April 1917, one of several occasions when he had to do this. Senior general staff officers agreed that commanders remained important. Schulenburg commented that the troops wanted to see and know their commanders: it was only the commanders they thought were important, not the staff. The commander was crucial to the performance of the troops. If he was good, the troops performed excellently; but if they lacked confidence in him, their performance slumped.[55] According to *Oberstleutnant* Albrecht von Thaer, chief of staff to IX Reserve Corps, the corps' good state at the end

---

[51] Kriegsministerium, *Felddienst-Ordnung (F.O.)* (Berlin: E. S. Mittler, 1908), 50; Kriegsministerium, *Grundzüge der höheren Truppenführung*, 3.

[52] Citino, *German Way of War*, 307 and 309.

[53] Generalleutnant a.D. Wilhelm Marx, 'Die entschwindende Führerromantik', *Militär-Wochenblatt*, vol. 119, no. 27 (1935), 1052–5; Rupprecht, *Kriegstagebuch*, 2:130–1 (5 April 1917).

[54] Wilhelm Deist, 'Zur Geschichte des preußischen Offizierkorps, 1888–1918', in Hanns Hubert Hofmann, ed., *Das deutsche Offizierkorps, 1860–1960* (Boppard am Rhein: Harald Boldt, 1980), 55–7; Michael Geyer, 'The Past as Future: The German Officer Corps as Profession', in G. Cocks and K. H. Jarausch, eds., *German Professions 1800–1950* (Oxford: Oxford University Press, 1990), 193 and 196.

[55] Schulenburg, 'Erlebnisse', 98–9 and 250.

of 1916, despite heavy losses on the Somme, was entirely due to its commander, Max von Boehn.[56]

Typically in the trench warfare period, commanders played an important role in maintaining the quality of units and the officer cadre, including by deciding what lessons to draw from experience, oversight of training, inspections and writing personnel reports.[57] They still bore formal responsibility for all decisions, even if the main influence had been their chief of staff. *General der Kavallerie* Georg von der Marwitz, Second Army commander, noted cynically that chiefs of staff tended to involve their commanders only superficially when things were going well; but if there were problems, the chiefs were always very keen for the general to be responsible for the decision.[58]

On the outbreak of war, senior commanders were figures of real authority and well able to hold their own against their staff.[59] By spring 1917, most of these men had left their jobs. But the commanders of 1917 – certainly at army group and Army, to some extent at corps too – were still senior officers. Their position and views could not just be ignored. A general like Gallwitz, while expressing his frustration that he had many responsibilities but little freedom of action, not only spoke and wrote as if he was in charge but was criticised for excessively controlling his staff.[60] As always, much depended on personalities and personal relationships. Rupprecht had three chiefs of staff during the war, and his relationships with them varied. The longest lasting was Hermann von Kuhl, but even with him, sometimes Kuhl was the dominant partner, sometimes Rupprecht, and sometimes 'it is hard to see the join between the two men'.[61]

Writing shortly after the war, Schulenburg identified various weaknesses in the cadre of commanders. In peacetime, there had been too much emphasis on unconditional obedience, and men who were not comfortable subordinates were little promoted. In addition, slow promotion and hard service wore many officers out by the time they reached the level of corps command. Very few officers got the chance to command an all-arms formation. Finally, many lacked the time and inclination for the study needed to equip themselves for high command. In short, many

---

[56] Albrecht von Thaer, *Generalstabsdienst an der Front und in der O.H.L. Aus Briefen und Tagebuchaufzeichnungen 1915–1919*, ed. Siegfried A. Kaehler (Göttingen: Vandenhoeck & Ruprecht, 1958), 99.

[57] Ibid., 23; Stachelbeck, *Militärische Effektivität*, 353.

[58] General der Infanterie a.D. Erich von Tschischwitz, ed., *General von der Marwitz: Weltkriegsbriefe* (Berlin: Steiniger, 1940), 278–9.

[59] Dennis E. Showalter, *Tannenberg: Clash of Empires* (Hamden, CT: Archon Books, 1991), 142.

[60] Gallwitz, *Erleben im Westen*, 83 and 235–6.   [61] Boff, *Haig's Enemy*, 113–15 and 257.

senior officers were not fully up to their job as high commanders, and this was precisely the reason why general staff officers gained such predominance. Schulenburg also criticised the appointment of royal personages to senior command positions.[62] How justified were his comments?

By 1914 the division of German officers into Blücher-types and Gneisenau-types was in fact disappearing. The increasingly technical demands of warfare forced the army to fill senior command positions almost exclusively with officers who had general staff training or experience or both.[63] Hindenburg himself, the archetypal German commander, had attended and later taught at *Kriegsakademie* as well as holding various general staff jobs including as corps chief of staff. No fewer than twenty-two out of the twenty-five Army and corps commanders handling the defence against the 1917 spring offensive (88 per cent) had attended *Kriegsakademie* or served on the general staff or done both. One effect of this was that commanders understood staff work well. Ludwig von Falkenhausen claimed that as an Army commander he never forgot he had been a corps chief of staff and knew the other side of the coin. On several occasions when commanding a division and a corps, Otto von Moser helped out with staff work or even stood in for absent staff officers.[64]

Commanders and staff officers were therefore not separated by an unbridgeable gap. To an increasing extent they were the same officers fulfilling different roles or at different stages of their careers. In peacetime, there were only ten general staff posts above *Oberst* level, so to progress further most officers had to assume command functions.[65] It was not actually necessary even in 1917 to have *Kriegsakademie* or general staff qualifications to prosper in career terms. *Generalmajor* Arthur von Lindequist had neither, but commanded the prestigious 3rd Guard Infantry Division at Arras. Despite such examples, though, the trend was certainly towards commanders having general staff qualifications.

Individual cases both support and contradict Schulenburg's argument about the weaknesses of the commander cadre. *General der Infanterie* Karl

---

[62] Schulenburg, 'Erlebnisse', 97 and 256–7.

[63] Militärgeschichtliches Forschungsamt, ed., *Untersuchungen zur Geschichte des Offizierkorps: Anciennität und Beförderung nach Leistung* (Stuttgart: Deutsche Verlags-Anstalt, 1962), 166.

[64] Ludwig Freiherr von Falkenhausen, 'Erinnerungen aus dem Weltkrieg 1914–1918', unpublished manuscript in BArch, Falkenhausen Nachlass, N21/1, 85; Moser, *Feldzugsaufzeichnungen*, 103, 130, 293 and 338.

[65] Includes Bavarians and Saxons. For further details of general staff officers as senior commanders, see Daniel J. Hughes, *The King's Finest: A Social and Bureaucratic Profile of Prussia's General Officers, 1871–1914* (New York: Praeger, 1987), chapters 7 and 8. Bucholz suggests that the gap between commanders and staff officers was in fact growing: *Moltke, Schlieffen*, 190–1.

Freiherr von Plettenberg, who commanded the Guard Corps from 1913 till early 1917, exemplifies Schulenburg's concerns. Plettenberg was a *Kriegsakademie* graduate but from so far back – 1875–8 – that we may ask how relevant his attendance would have been during the war. Worries about his performance gradually increased from 1914 until he was sacked at the age of sixty-four in January 1917.[66] By contrast, Moser, who was seven years younger, was presumably the sort of commander Schulenburg wanted. After graduating from the *Kriegsakademie*, Moser alternated general staff and troop service up to the level of departmental head in the Great General Staff and regimental commander. He was an instructor at the *Kriegsakademie* and wrote several books and articles, including on mission command. In the war, he was successively a brigade, division and corps commander, winning the *Pour le Mérite*.[67]

One of Schulenburg's concerns, commanders lacking experience in all-arms co-operation, was especially serious given its central role in tactical success. Pre-war, there had been complaints about the predominance of infantry officers in senior positions.[68] By spring 1917, the proportion of divisional commanders from the infantry had fallen slightly compared with 1914 but was still overwhelming (Figure 2.1).

Moser's evidence adds a nuance to this. In early 1917, he established the first divisional command course, to train divisional commanders and their teams on the new defensive doctrine. He commented that though the doctrine made divisions the main combat unit, the majority of younger divisional commanders did not have the right background for this. The reason was that their previous posts commanding single-arm brigades tended to instil a certain narrowness of vision; they had then been suddenly and without appropriate training selected for divisional command, often recently.[69] This phenomenon arose from the personnel churn of the war years, itself the result of the great increase in formations and the attrition of the commander cadre caused by the length of the war. The number of divisions had increased from 50 in peacetime to 92 on mobilisation and was 228 by the opening of the Entente spring offensive; higher-level formations had expanded in parallel. The creation of all these new formations greatly increased the requirement for suitable commanders (and also of course for general and other staff officers).

---

[66] Lyncker to his wife, 13 January 1917, in Afflerbach, *Kaiser Wilhelm II. als Oberster Kriegsherr*, 466 and fn. 16.

[67] Chapter 4 examines Moser's career in more detail.

[68] Richard von Schubert, 'Auszug aus meinem Bericht über meine Theilnahme am Weltkrieg', unpublished manuscript in HSAS, Schubert Nachlass, M660/197 Bü 8, 83. Schubert, Seventh Army commander in 1916–17, was a field artilleryman by background.

[69] Moser, *Feldzugsaufzeichnungen*, 270.

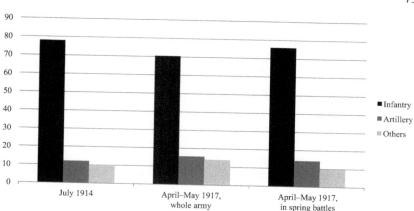

Figure 2.1 Divisional commanders by arm of service (percentage)

Some of this requirement was met by bringing back to active service officers who had left the army before the war – 're-employed inactive officers' in German parlance or 'dug-outs' in British. They occupied a relatively large proportion of formation commands. Over a third of divisional commanders on mobilisation were inactive officers; even in spring 1917 the figure was still nearly 25 per cent and the proportion of corps and Army commanders was similar. There is no doubt that some of these men were well thought of. At the top end was the respected *General der Infanterie* Franz Freiherr von Soden, whose 26th Reserve Division stopped the assault of five British divisions on 1 July 1916. He was later appointed a corps commander, was engaged against the Entente spring offensive, twice used as a fireman during crises at Verdun and awarded the *Pour le Mérite*.

Despite examples such as Soden, the re-employment of so many retired officers was a weakness in the commander cadre at division, corps and Army level. They had retired on average some three years before the outbreak of war. So theoretically their skills had not necessarily degenerated; and by spring 1917 these officers had had the same learning time and opportunities as their active colleagues. But the reality could be different. Gallwitz reported bluntly that older re-employed generals were not suited to command divisions in major battle since they often lacked understanding of modern combat, necessitating frequent intervention from above.[70] His comment clearly illustrates the problems of employing retired officers, as well as, once again, the linkage between mission command and skill levels.

[70] Gallwitz, *Erleben im Westen*, 119.

Much professional opinion after the war echoed Schulenburg in criti-
cising the appointment of royal personages to senior command positions,
on the basis that they had too little military knowledge for the role.
The most conspicuously placed royal commanders on the Western
Front in early 1917 were the three army group commanders: Crown
Prince Wilhelm, Crown Prince Rupprecht and Duke Albrecht, heirs
to the thrones of Germany and Prussia, Bavaria and Württemberg
respectively.[71] Wilhelm was a particular target of negative comment
owing to his dilettantism, not to mention security worries about his
French mistress.[72] Rupprecht himself expressed concern that people
would say nothing had been achieved on the Western Front because the
top commanders there were chosen only for dynastic reasons. Later
charges that dynastic interests had affected operational decision-making
in 1914, 1916 and 1918 justified his worry.[73] Well-founded or not, such
accusations were damaging to the dynasties concerned and efforts to
refute them formed a considerable part of the motivation, in Bavaria's
case at least, for the battle of the memoirs in the 1920s and 1930s.[74]

There were then undoubted disadvantages to royal commanders, but
Rupprecht noted two arguments in their favour. Not only were they
younger than other commanders, but also – and here Rupprecht claimed
to be quoting Schlieffen – their 'independent position' made them less
subject to 'the restraints of personal considerations'.[75] He presumably
meant that they did not have to consider their careers when taking decisions. At the time of this comment, he had recently been involved in
sacking Plettenberg and another corps commander, General der Infanterie
Dedo von Schenck. Gallwitz, their direct superior, believed they were
incompetent and should be removed; however, both were courtiers of
the Kaiser and Gallwitz was unwilling to take action against them.
Rupprecht, Gallwitz's own superior, therefore wrote the reports
disqualifying them from command.[76]

This suggests why royal commanders were not just figureheads.
Whatever their military competence, when push came to shove they
were too senior simply to brush aside: Rupprecht for instance played

---

[71] In addition Rupprecht's uncle, Generalfeldmarschall Prince Leopold of Bavaria, was
commander-in-chief on the Eastern Front [Oberbefehlshaber Ost].

[72] Gleich, Die alte Armee, 79; Epkenhans, Nicolai, 534–7.

[73] Rupprecht, Kriegstagebuch, 2:130 (5 April 1917). For the effect of dynastic interests on
operations, see Cowan, 'A Picture of German Unity?', 145–6.

[74] Pöhlmann, Kriegsgeschichte, 291–306.

[75] Rupprecht, Kriegstagebuch, 2:130 (5 April 1917).

[76] Rupprecht, unpublished diary, 4 December 1916; Kuhl, 'Kriegstagebuch',
14 June 1917.

a prominent part in the sacking of Falkenhayn in August 1916.[77] Their upbringing, education and political role also gave them a breadth of view that helped compensate for lack of the deep but narrow military knowledge taught at *Kriegsakademie*. Three other factors helped mitigate any professional deficiencies. First, all the royals had pre-war military training and experience, even if foreshortened and interrupted by other duties; this included attending parts of the *Kriegsakademie* course. Second, they had the same opportunities to learn during the war as re-employed inactive officers. Rupprecht's latest biographer comments that he was far from a figurehead, took his job seriously and by 1916 was almost the equal of his chief of staff. Duke Albrecht too was said to be well above average as a soldier, having thoroughly mastered his profession.[78] Third and linked to this, all three army group commanders were allocated as chiefs of staff some of the most experienced general staff officers in the army. This was in fact a two-edged sword as shown by Wilhelm's difficult relations with his first chief of staff, *Generalleutnant* Konstantin Schmidt von Knobelsdorf. But the general staff could not complain that royal commanders were not receiving professional advice.

Given the monarchy's role in Germany and the precedent of royal Army commanders in the Wars of Unification, what is surprising is not that there *were* royal personages in senior commands but how few there were. True, the highest ranks in the army lists were replete with royals, but almost all were in honorary positions. At the levels considered here, apart from the army group commanders, in early 1917 there were only three royal division commanders and one royal corps commander. The presence of these officers is conspicuous because it is apparently anachronistic and belies the notion of the German army as a progressive institution. But in the final analysis their military significance was limited.

The high average age of commanders to which Schulenburg referred had been a concern since at least the 1880s.[79] Reducing it was one reason for selecting divisional commanders from officers with general staff training: they enjoyed accelerated promotion and were therefore younger for their rank than non-staff officers.[80] But no progress was made between 1914 and 1917 in rejuvenating the cadre of senior commanders. The average age of all divisional, corps and Army commanders just before the war, on mobilisation and in spring 1917 was unchanging at fifty-eight to fifty-nine years. The oldest Army commander during the 1917 spring

[77] Boff, *Haig's Enemy*, 103–7.

[78] Ibid., 115 and 281–2; Anon., *Das alte Heer, von einem Stabsoffizier* (Charlottenburg: Verlag der Weltbühne, 1920), 103.

[79] Brose, *Kaiser's Army*, 48.

[80] Militärgeschichtliches Forschungsamt, *Anciennität und Beförderung nach Leistung*, 166.

battles was Falkenhausen, commanding Sixth Army at the age of seventy-two. Schulenburg, who had been his chief of staff some months before, thought well of Falkenhausen and described him as full of vigour and intellectual activity; but he also suffered the troubles of age. Less politely, the Army's operations officer considered him 'an elegant ruin' and, as we shall see, others were even ruder. Falkenhausen's age may not have mattered in quiet periods, but he was badly shaken by the defeat on 9 April and was posted to be Governor-General of Belgium when the position conveniently became available later in the month.[81]

General Staff Officers

Just at the time the balance of power was moving from commanders towards the staff, wartime strains complicated the selection, training and development of general staff officers. Before the war, they were selected by a rigorous process. After a tough entry exam, most had attended *Kriegsakademie* – or its Bavarian equivalent – for three years. At the end of the course, the best students were seconded to the general staff for a two-year trial period, after which the best of *them* were transferred substantively into the general staff, some fifteen to twenty per year or 1–2 per cent of the total officer intake. They then alternated between service on the staff and with troops.[82]

Both staff colleges closed on the outbreak of war and did not reopen, but nevertheless plenty of graduates were initially available. The earliest course attended by an officer who subsequently saw active service in the First World War began in 1871. Between then and 1914 over 5,500 officers attended the two colleges.[83] Even allowing for natural wastage and casualties, there was a large pool of officers with *Kriegsakademie* training, whether or not they had subsequently joined the general staff. However, by late 1916, OHL was concerned about the much greater demand for general staff officers and an emerging shortage. Posts in the new formations all needed filling, and in addition general staff officers were central to handling key issues such as improving all-arms

[81] Schulenburg, 'Erlebnisse', 122–3; Rudolf Ritter von Xylander, unpublished diary in KAM, R. Xylander Nachlass, Bd. 12, III, 29 August 1916.

[82] Details of staff officer selection and training in Bucholz, *Moltke, Schlieffen*, 72–6 and 185–7. See also Grawe, *Deutsche Feindaufklärung*, 34–5 and Korvetten-Kapitän Freiherr von Keyserlingk, 'Bericht des Korvetten-Kapitäns Freiherr von Keyserlingk über sein Kommando zum Großen Generalstabe im Oktober 1906', 1 November 1906, BArch, RM5/273, ff. 154–5.

[83] Calculated from figures for *Kriegsakademie* intake at different periods in Schwertfeger, *Großen Erzieher* and Othmar Hackl, *Die bayerische Kriegsakademie (1867–1914)* (Munich: C. H. Beck'sche Verlagsbuchhandlung, 1989).

co-operation and assimilating new tactical developments.[84] But for the first two years of the war, there were no formal staff courses, and new general staff officers received only ad hoc training.

There were particular concerns about the quality and size of the general staff component in divisions, now that they were the main combat unit. Moser asked rhetorically who would have thought that such important work would fall to young *Hauptleute*, the majority of whom were hardly thirty; his artillery commander had coined the term 'general staff kids' [*Generalstabsbüble*] for them.[85] Zwehl thought that because of the inadequacies of wartime general staff officers, corps and divisional commanders had to carry out many tasks which would normally have fallen to the staff.[86] A solution proposed in summer 1917 was to fill corps *Ia* posts with more junior officers, and to employ the experienced men thus freed up as divisional *Ia*s. But corps chiefs of staff rejected this, arguing that they needed an officer senior enough to substitute for them as necessary. Ludendorff, ever the micro-manager, also opposed the idea because the corps *Ia* had to supervise the divisional general staff officers.[87] This clearly suggests the limits on the greater autonomy accorded to divisions by the new defensive doctrine.

In peacetime, each division had one general staff officer. There had been doubts since Moltke the Elder's time whether this was enough, and indeed shortly after the war began it proved necessary to add a second post, *Ib*, to the most actively engaged divisions.[88] From late 1916, this became the focus for selecting and training new general staff officers. Initially, OHL decreed that officers would only be selected for permanent transfer into the general staff once they had demonstrated their suitability in two three-month postings as divisional *Ib* and in a higher-level staff; the *Ib* officers must have a minimum of eight years' commissioned service.[89] Throughout 1917, OHL issued increasingly rigorous instructions on selecting and training these officers. Following the spring fighting, it increased the length of preparatory postings before transfer to the general

---

[84] OHL circular to general staff officers, 'Kriegführung und Generalstab', M. J. Nr. 10000, 22 November 1916, KAM, HKR neue Nr. 378.

[85] Moser, *Feldzugsaufzeichnungen*, 262–3. [86] Zwehl, *Generalstabsdienst*, 31–2.

[87] OHL circular, M.J. No. 56600, 19 July 1917, HSAS, Soden Nachlass, M660/038 Bü 17, f. 58.

[88] Helmuth von Moltke, 'Memoire an Seine Majestät den König vom 25. Juli 1868 über die bei der Bearbeitung des Feldzuges 1866 hervorgetretenen Erfahrungen', in Großer Generalstab, ed., *Moltkes Militärische Werke*, vol. 2, pt 2, *Moltkes Taktisch-Strategische Aufsätze aus den Jahren 1857 bis 1871* (Berlin: E. S. Mittler, 1900), 81; Cron, *Geschichte des Deutschen Heeres*, 95. Chapter 6 covers changes to staffs during the war.

[89] OHL circulars, M.J. Nr. 7200 Zr., 12 October 1916 and M.J. Nr. 9276, 22 November 1916, both on HSAS, M33/2 Bü 423.

staff to six months as a divisional *Ib* and three months in a higher-level staff; the *Ib* posting was to include special training in the form of secondments to combat units.[90] Shortly after, a four-week course was set up in Sedan to train these new general staff officers, and later in 1917 satisfactory completion of the course became a precondition of transfer into the general staff.[91]

OHL's instructions make clear the difficulties of achieving both the short-term aim of producing officers who could become *Ia*s at the crucial divisional level, and the long-term aim of creating a competent general staff cadre. The problem was how to combine the training role which OHL envisaged for the *Ib* posts with the functioning of a division. Typically, divisions used *Ib* officers for burdensome logistical tasks rather than help their development by involving them in the tactical work of the *Ia*. In addition, the frequent short secondments to combat units disrupted both the divisional staff while the officer was absent and the receiving unit while he was present, particularly if he was commanding it. OHL issued orders to sort out the first problem, and stated that the second was a cost which must be accepted in the interest of producing future *Ia* officers; the key point of the six-month divisional secondments must be working closely with the *Ia*. Not surprisingly, senior commanders questioned whether excessive priority was being given to such training at the expense of actually doing the job.[92]

The pre-war custom of general staff officers rotating between staff and troop service was also disrupted. In peacetime, these officers ideally commanded a company or equivalent for at least two years, and a battalion for one; advantages of the rotation included developing the ability to assess the state of the troops. Although this task became increasingly important from late 1916, regular rotation between staff and troop service was no longer possible during the war, owing to the great demand for staff officers.[93] That does not mean the practice was abandoned. In the post-war army list, many staff officers recorded a troop command as their last active service job; and in early 1917, twenty-one generals who had previously held senior wartime staff positions were commanding divisions or higher-level formations. Nevertheless, there was resistance to moving from the staff to troop service. In May 1917, OHL referred to a feeling among general staff officers that being sent for service with the

[90] OHL circular, M.J. Nr. 55000, 22 June 1917, HSAS, M33/2 Bü 423.
[91] OHL circular, M.J. Nr. 68000, 22 December 1917, HSAS, M33/2 Bü 423.
[92] OHL circular, M.J. Nr. 60100, 8 September 1917, HSAS, M33/2 Bü 423; Zwehl, *Generalstabsdienst*, 33.
[93] Major von Stosch, 'Beiträge zum Wiederaufbau des deutschen Heeres', pt III, 2, *Militär-Wochenblatt*, vol. 103, no. 115 (1919), 2098.

troops was some sort of punishment. It denied this, and stressed that such service was an essential contribution to maintaining close links between staff and troops.[94] It was being disingenuous: some staff officers undoubtedly were being punished by transfer to troop command, however senior. Following OHL criticism of a minor loss of ground by his corps, Albrecht von Thaer expected to be made a scapegoat and moved from his chief of staff job to command a regiment; he described the prospect as being 'sent into the desert'.[95]

As we saw earlier, a shortage of general staff officers and frequent allocation of young officers to divisional staffs were said to be among the factors limiting mission command. Concerns about inexperienced general staff officers were clearly genuine, but were they justified? The divisional *Ia*s in post just before mobilisation in 1914 had an average commissioned service of twenty-one years; those whose ages are known averaged forty years old. Statistics for wartime *Ia*s are less comprehensive, but 166 can be identified who were in post in spring 1917 (70 per cent of the total). Their average commissioned service was seventeen years, implying an average age of thirty-six or thirty-seven. This certainly means they were younger and less experienced than their 1914 equivalents, but the decline was hardly catastrophic. Furthermore, as Figure 2.2 shows nearly all the 1917 *Ia*s had *Kriegsakademie* and/or subsequent general staff experience, either on probation or full transfer; only a very small minority had neither. These officers also had the experience gained in two and a half years of war. If there was a problem of age and experience, it was more likely to be with the *Ib*s: but even here the ninety-one officers who can be identified in the post in spring 1917 had an average commissioned service of nearly thirteen years.

There was, however, a downside to using officers with *Kriegsakademie* and pre-war general staff experience in *Ia* positions. Beginning with the *Kriegsakademie* intake and continuing into *Ia* posts, the preponderance of the infantry, though smaller than for commanders, was still overwhelming (Figure 2.3).[96] If anything, the proportion of infantry officers

[94] OHL circular, M.J. Nr. 53000, 20 May 1917, BArch, PH3/25, f. 005.
[95] Thaer, *Generalstabsdienst*, 83; he was not in fact moved. Cases of punishment in late 1916–early 1917 include Schmidt von Knobelsdorf and *Kriegsminister Generalleutnant* Adolf Wild von Hohenborn moved to corps command, and *Generalmajore* Nagel zu Aichberg and Tappen moved to divisional command. This had been a pre-war custom too as illustrated by Alfred Graf von Waldersee's forced move from Chief of the General Staff to corps command in 1891: Walter Görlitz, *Der Deutsche Generalstab: Geschichte und Gestalt 1657–1945* (Frankfurt: Verlag der Frankfurter Hefte, 1950), 160.
[96] Figure 2.3 shows all students at the Prussian and Bavarian *Kriegsakademien* in 1913–14, the last full year before the war. Statistics for these students and *Ia*s in 1914 are complete, but as explained are currently only available for 70 per cent of *Ia*s in the whole army in April–May 1917 (82 per cent in divisions facing the Entente spring offensive).

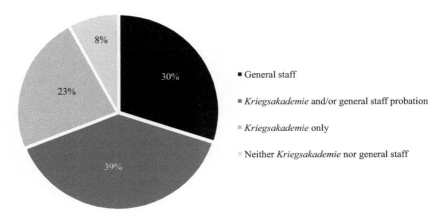

Figure 2.2 *Kriegsakademie* and general staff experience of divisional *Ia*s, April–May 1917

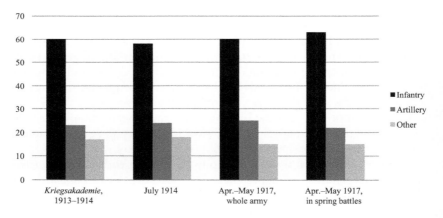

Figure 2.3 *Kriegsakademie* students and divisional *Ia*s by arm of service (percentage)

was slightly higher among *Ia*s in divisions facing the Entente spring offensive than for the whole army at the same period or for 1914. The limited information on *Ib*s indicates that their distribution by arm of service in the whole army was similar.

Concerns about the decreasing experience of general staff officers were genuine: we cannot simply dismiss them or Kuhl's statement that the inexperienced general staff officers at divisional level required more supervision from above than was usual in peacetime mission command practice. But the statistical evidence, though incomplete, suggests that despite problems of selection and training the German army had a relatively good supply of relatively experienced general staff officers. Certainly the British army would have thought so.[97] There is also evidence of a closed shop mentality towards general staff membership, illustrated by the post-war order that only officers who had been seconded or transferred to the general staff before the war were entitled to the honorific of wearing its uniform. As this snobbish treatment shows, war-trained officers in general staff posts were seen as second-class, not really general staff officers at all.[98]

Command Teams

Despite or perhaps because of the changing roles of commanders and general staff officers, the German army made considerable efforts to maintain the traditional commander–chief of staff relationship as a team. If such a team was to be successful, the characters of the commander and his chief of staff had to mesh. It was recognised that a strong chief might dominate his commander. Tact was therefore one of the requirements for selection as a general staff officer. This is reflected in some of the criticisms made of staff officers in their personal reports. Commenting on Sixth Army's *Ia*, *Major* Rudolf Ritter von Xylander, Rupprecht stressed his excellent qualities as a general staff officer but added that his marked self-confidence led to brusqueness, which caused resentment. After Xylander was sacked in April 1917 following the initial defeat at Arras, Kuhl's report on him again emphasised his good points and commented that he had made efforts to moderate his brusqueness. However, the events leading to his sacking proved him to be headstrong and unresponsive to guidance and the wishes of the troops. Kuhl concluded that despite his outstanding qualities he was not suited to be a corps chief of staff. Xylander went on to perfectly good jobs, but none were in the general staff.[99]

---

[97] For the British general staff, see Paul Harris, *The Men Who Planned the War: A Study of the Staff of the British Army on the Western Front, 1914–1918* (London: Routledge, 2016).

[98] Reichswehrministerium [Reich Ministry of Defence] letter to Major a.D. Rudolf Pattenhausen, Heeresleitung Personalamt I. Nr. 3900/8. 20.P.A., 14 September 1920, GLAK, E/8877. Adding insult to injury, Pattenhausen had been allowed to wear the general staff uniform during the war. See also Klaus-Jürgen Müller, *Generaloberst Ludwig Beck: Eine Biographie* (Paderborn: Schöningh, 2008), 25–6 on officers in the post-war *Reichsheer* forming cliques based on such differential treatment.

[99] Millotat, *Generalstabssystem*, 36; Schwertfeger, *Großen Erzieher*, 63; reports on Xylander, 11 March 1916 and 9 May 1917, KAM, OP 18705.

There is naturally evidence of both good and bad relationships within commander–chief of staff teams. Thaer's comments on the two corps commanders under whom he served in 1916 and 1917 show how a good relationship worked. The first, Boehn, left him a lot of autonomy but was very decisive in the areas he reserved for himself, including personnel matters and training; you knew where you were with him. The second, *Generalleutnant* Karl Dieffenbach, remained calm, sympathetic and friendly even under the great pressure of the opening defeat at Arras, and let the staff do its work without interference.[100] At divisional level, *Generalleutnant* Paul Ritter von Kneußl of 11th Bavarian Infantry Division found his *Ia* – the future *Generalfeldmarschall* Wilhelm Ritter von Leeb – difficult to get on with but had great respect for his ability: it was a hard blow when he left the division.[101]

Other relationships simply did not work or stopped working. *Generalleutnant* Emil Ilse, Fourth Army chief of staff, was said to get on the nerves of the Army commander, Duke Albrecht; but the latter could not summon up the ruthlessness to keep him within bounds. Not surprisingly, Albrecht did not take Ilse with him when he became army group commander in March 1917.[102] This was by no means the only case where a commander fell out with his chief staff officer, though we lack the information to assess how often it happened.[103] There could of course be other reasons why a commander–general staff officer team did not work. When 16th Infantry Division was accused of having failed in late 1916, its commander was judged to be not suitable for such a responsible position; the problem was compounded by the fact that the *Ia*, though capable and fit for his job, lacked experience of the Western Front to make up for the commander's inadequacies.[104] The *Ia* stayed, the commander was removed and not employed again on active service.

Commanders' complaints about the churn of general staff officers noted above would seem to suggest that creating a team, especially at divisional level, was difficult. Undoubtedly there could be problems: in the year from its formation, 107th Infantry Division had five substantive and acting *Ia* officers.[105] But statistical evidence indicates that *Ia*s may have remained in post longer than this implies. Precise dates of postings

---

[100] Thaer, *Generalstabsdienst*, 23, 99 and 111.
[101] Stachelbeck, *Militärische Effektivität*, 44.   [102] Anon., *Das alte Heer*, 103.
[103] The breakdown of relations between Schmidt von Knobelsdorf and Crown Prince Wilhelm is another example. Boff, *Haig's Enemy*, 91 describes how Rupprecht got rid of a chief of staff he fell out with.
[104] Boehn to AOK 1, 'Bericht über den Zustand der 16.I.D.', 25 October 1916, GLAK, F1/547.
[105] Calculated from Moser, *Feldzugsaufzeichnungen*; Moser was the division's first commander.

are available for half of all command teams in April 1917, and these commander–*Ia* partnerships lasted on average eleven months. Three-quarters were six months or longer; Kneußl and Leeb in 11th Bavarian Infantry Division were the longest partnership on the Western Front, at over two years. By the start of the Entente offensive, these partnerships had been in place for just over five months on average – a more than respectable figure given wartime circumstances.[106]

Whether the length of partnership actually mattered probably depended on other factors. 27th Infantry Division had only three commanders and three general staff officers in the entire war. It believed that this stability fostered mutual confidence and was a great blessing for the whole formation.[107] It was one of the best divisions in the army and we should take its comments seriously. As it happened, when the Entente spring offensive began the division's command team had been in place for only a month, but this did not prevent it stopping dead the British-Australian assault at Bullecourt. At the other end of the performance scale, 14th Bavarian Infantry Division's command team had come together just two weeks before the division collapsed under the British attack at Arras. Factors in the different performances are likely to have included the quality of the divisions. 27th Infantry Division was a high-grade peacetime active division, and 14th Bavarian Infantry Division a war-raised extemporisation still tired by a difficult stint on the Somme over winter, where concerns had been raised about its combat value.[108] In addition, the initial British assault at Arras was better conducted and heavier than the one at Bullecourt a few days later. But it cannot have helped that 14th Bavarian Infantry Division's *Ia* only arrived at the end of March, or that he was new to the Western Front.

The differing composition of the two command teams may also have affected these divisions' performance. 27th Infantry Division's commander was a field artillery officer, its *Ia* an infantryman; 14th Bavarian Infantry Division was commanded by an infantryman, the *Ia* was from the cavalry. Throughout the war, given the requirements of combined arms battle the most useful mix in a command team on the Western Front was infantry and artillery. The inquiry into the failure of 12th Infantry Division in November 1916 ascribed some of the blame to both

---

[106] The incomplete information on the precise dates of *Ia* postings necessitates the use of a sample here, hence the tentative conclusions. One partnership on the Eastern Front was longer than Kneußl-Leeb, at three years.

[107] Major a.D. Adolf Deutelmoser, *Die 27. Infanterie-Division im Weltkrieg 1914–18* (Stuttgart: Berger's Literarisches Büro und Verlagsanstalt, 1925), 107–9; Deutelmoser was the division's *Ia* from April 1916 till the end of the war.

[108] Doubts about 14th Bavarian Infantry Division: Sheldon, *Fighting the Somme*, 189–90; Lipp, *Meinungslenkung*, 235–7.

commander and *Ia* being field artillery officers who had not mastered the principles of the infantry battle.[109] OHL's views on the best balance in a command team are clear from the instructions for special training of general staff candidates recorded above. The lead item of this training was command of an infantry company or battalion as well as of a field and a heavy artillery battery. In these instructions OHL only mentioned infantry and artillery training by arm of service: acquiring knowledge of their methods was evidently the main goal of the special training.[110]

Statistical analysis shows why OHL was concerned. Because of the incomplete data on *Ia*s in 1917, Figure 2.4 is not comprehensive but does illustrate the problem. The preponderance of all-infantry teams is clear and in fact rose between 1914 and early 1917; just a quarter of command teams fitted the infantry-artillery model that was best suited for combined arms battle. Of course this does not mean that only command teams which fitted the model performed well: the successful 3rd Bavarian Infantry Division, for instance, was commanded during the battle of Arras by *Generalleutnant* Karl Ritter von Wenninger, a cavalry officer, with an infantryman as his *Ia*. But in contrast, the cavalry provenance of 14th Bavarian Infantry Division's *Ia* cannot have helped during the crisis of 9 April. There is also Moser's point above that many divisional commanders were relatively new to their jobs and had spent most of their

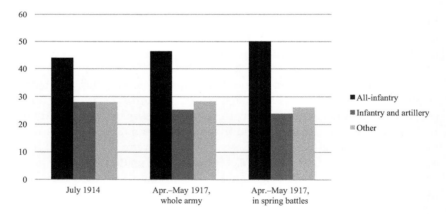

Figure 2.4 Composition of divisional command teams by arm of service (percentage)

---

[109] Generalleutnant Fuchs to HKR, XIV R.K. IIa 450 Pers., 16 November 1916, KAM, HKR neue Nr. 378, f. 21.
[110] OHL circular, M.J. Nr. 55000, 22 June 1917, HSAS, M33/2 Bü 423.

previous careers in a single-arms background. Overall, lack of the appropriate combined arms balance in command teams was one reason for persistent problems in all-arms co-operation during and after the Entente spring offensive.[111]

Such problems were less relevant at higher levels of command, but even in their larger staffs, combining the wrong personalities could have a poisonous effect as was alleged against Sixth Army's command team at the start of the battle of Arras. A corps chief of staff had the opportunity to observe the team at close quarters and years later wrote to the *Reichsarchiv* about its dysfunctionality. The Army commander, Falkenhausen, was obstinate, grotesquely vain and senile, probably good enough for the Eastern Front but not for his present very responsible position. After 10 April his will collapsed. His chief of staff, *Generalmajor* Karl Freiherr von Nagel zu Aichberg, was an excellent soldier and man but himself believed he was not up to his heavy responsibility. Also, he had to spend effort battling against his commander's characteristics. As a result, the dominant personality in Sixth Army headquarters was the operations officer, Xylander, against whose views no one could make any headway. Serious blame should be attached to the OHL department that created and sustained this combination.[112] As in other cases, we do not need to believe every word of these highly critical comments but the officer who wrote them clearly thought they would be plausible and acceptable to the *Reichsarchiv*.

The sub-optimal composition of Sixth Army headquarters was not unique, as we can see from the case of the neighbouring Fourth Army headquarters a couple of months later.[113] The Army had just been through the Messines battle and now faced a major British offensive at Ypres; the defence there would be the most important task on the Western Front, requiring the best officers to direct it. However, the Army's chief of staff, *Major* Max Stapff, though competent, was not asserting himself against his commander, *General der Infanterie* Friedrich Sixt von Armin; for his part, Sixt was seen as too old and not tough or sharp enough. It was not desirable to exchange Stapff with Fritz von Loßberg at Sixth Army: that would make it seem only Loßberg was any good, and also he might not fit in with Sixt. Swapping the Sixth and

---

[111] See Chapter 7.
[112] General von Kessel to the Kriegsgeschichtliche Forschungsanstalt des Heeres, 1 February 1939, BArch, RH61/1886.
[113] This and the following paragraph are based on Kuhl, 'Kriegstagebuch', 10–14 June 1917.

Fourth Army commanders only would give the impression Fourth Army had suffered a complete disaster at Messines.

It was therefore decided to exchange the commanders, chiefs of staff and some other officers of Sixth and Fourth Armies. However, the Kaiser then vetoed exchanging the commanders because he was becoming upset that the Bavarian Rupprecht had recently removed three Prussian generals (including Plettenberg and Schenck). In the end, Loßberg and Stapff alone changed places. At that point, Sixt asked if Rupprecht still had confidence in him following the move of his chief of staff; if not, he would be willing to serve anywhere as required. It was agreed to wait and see how Loßberg got on in Fourth Army before deciding whether to move Sixt.

Sorting out these problems took considerable effort, involving the Kaiser and the head of the Military Cabinet (in charge of personnel work); Hindenburg, Ludendorff and Georg Wetzell from OHL; Rupprecht and Kuhl from the army group; and Sixt, Stapff, Loßberg and Otto von Below from the Armies concerned. This effort demonstrates the value attached to creating the best possible command team given the circumstances, and also the constraints. Factors that had to be considered included the Kaiser, dynastic tensions, various personnel issues and the 'public relations' aspects of Messines. The prime movers were the senior general staff officers, but the role of Fourth Army commander in itself and as a member of a team had to be taken seriously.

Ironically, the importance of the commander-chief of staff team often becomes clear at the moment of failure. Even if the chief of staff alone was removed, this was still seen as lack of confidence in his commander, who bore ultimate responsibility for decisions, or as one Army commander described it, 'kicking the dog and meaning the master'.[114] The commander's standing was therefore damaged in the eyes of his subordinates and he might well offer or threaten to resign – 'even a dog has its pride'. Sixt von Armin's reaction to Stapff's removal was not unique at this period. Falkenhausen asked to resign when his chief of staff and operations officer (Nagel and Xylander) were sacked in April 1917: the request was rejected with expressions of confidence in his command, but as we saw when an opportunity to move him upstairs arose shortly after, it was exploited with some alacrity. In these

---

[114] Second Army commander Georg von der Marwitz writing in September 1918 when his chief of staff was removed against his wishes; he submitted his resignation but was transferred to another Army command instead. Tschischwitz, *Marwitz*, 318.

and other cases, none of the commanders who threatened to resign actually did so, but the threats were apparently treated as genuine.[115]

At least nine commanders were dismissed or replaced together with their chief general staff officers in late 1916–early 1917: in other words, the command team as a whole was seen to have failed or to be otherwise inadequate (Table 2.1). The 12th Infantry Division team was removed following the failure in November 1916 noted earlier; the next three pairs after the defeat at Verdun in December 1916, and the fifth in related command changes; the Seventh Army, XI Corps and Bavarian Ersatz Division teams were moved in preparation for the French offensive; and as noted, the Sixth Army trio were casualties of the initial debacle at Arras. Such clear-outs became a feature of Ludendorff's management style as pressure mounted in 1918. Corps command teams could also be changed less dramatically. Particularly after corps lost their organic link to divisions, it was possible to treat them merely as headquarters. If they failed in battle, they could easily be transferred to a quieter sector elsewhere. At least six were moved in this way in spring 1917.[116]

Table 2.1 *Joint removals of commanders and chief general staff officers, November 1916–April 1917*

Formation	Commander–chief general staff officer	Date
12th Infantry Division	Fouquet and Tempelhoff	Nov. 1916
Fifth Army	Lochow and Ledebur	Dec. 1916
VII Reserve Corps	Zwehl and Lösecke	Dec. 1916
39th Bavarian Reserve Division	Grüber and Pfistermeister	Dec. 1916
Army Detachment A	D'Elsa and Eulitz	Jan. 1917
Seventh Army	Schubert and Borries (plus the next two general staff officers and aviation commander)	Feb.–Mar. 1917
XI Corps (Gruppe Vailly)	Plüskow and Matthes	Mar. 1917
Bavarian Ersatz Division	Kiefhaber and Adam	Mar. 1917
Sixth Army	Falkenhausen and Nagel zu Aichberg (and the *Ia*, Xylander)	Apr. 1917

[115] Rupprecht, *Kriegstagebuch*, 1:495 (3 July 1916) on the damage done by removing chiefs of staff, and 2:141 and 149 (11 and 22 April 1917) on Falkenhausen.
[116] VI and XII Reserve Corps from Sixth Army in April before Arras; XV Bavarian Reserve Corps from Gruppe Sissonne and XIV Corps from Gruppe Prosnes in April, following

Conclusions

The traditional principles studied in this chapter – mission command and the partnership between a commander and his chief of staff – were part of the German army's mechanism for handling its first command task, co-ordinating a mass army. Proponents of the army's excellence see them as an important factor in its successes. But the realities of war on the Western Front in 1917 prevented their full application. Mission command could still play a significant role below the level of division. However, its use from division upwards was limited, and granting formations freedom of action was a risky procedure in Western Front conditions, as the failures at Arras and Messines proved. The army clearly placed value in creating effective commander–general staff officer teams. It was reasonably successful in terms of these teams' duration, less so in the vital all-arms balance required by modern battle.

The analysis in this chapter shows the complex interaction between the two principles. It was a given that mission command depended on well-trained commanders and general staff officers used to working together. Concerns about decreasing experience, particularly at divisional level, were one cause of greatly enhanced supervision from above. Statistical evidence suggests that some of these concerns were exaggerated, especially given the reality of personnel availability in wartime. Increased supervision may therefore have been more due to other factors such as risk aversion, the ability to intervene and the greater need for managerial control in battles of matériel. Commanders remained important but the expanded authority of general staff officers in trench warfare distorted the traditional relationship between them.

The first command task involved striking the right balance between decentralisation in the form of mission command and control. By 1917 the balance had moved towards more control. This of course contradicted the new tactical doctrine, which devolved direct handling of the battle to divisions. Many accounts of this period have accepted the doctrine as reality and downplayed the role of higher-level formations, especially corps.[117] But it was precisely divisions that were the object of concern about declining levels of experience and where there was therefore perceived to be a need for continued control from above. This is a reminder that principles and doctrine did not exist in a vacuum but, as the next two chapters demonstrate, depended on actual organisations and people to implement them.

---

problems during the French assault; LIV Corps (Generalkommando 54) from Gruppe Liesse in May; XIX Corps from Gruppe Wytschaete in June after Messines.
[117] See Chapter 3.

3   Organisation

> It is therefore of decisive importance that the Armies' operations are co-ordinated from the start.[1]

As the Introduction showed, German military thinkers believed that co-ordinating mass armies in modern battle required not only decentralisation in the form of mission command but also control. Control was therefore an essential part of the first command task, for both positive and negative reasons. The positive was the need to concentrate maximum resources at the decisive place. This is the well-known if often misunderstood principle of setting a *Schwerpunkt* or point of main effort for every operation.[2] The negative reason was to avoid chaos and was embodied in a less well known but, to the German army, equally fundamental principle: maintaining the chain of command. Both of these principles were implemented through the different elements of the higher-level military organisation – army groups, Armies, corps and divisions – which are the subject of this chapter. A *Schwerpunkt* was established by concentrating formations and other resources at the decisive point, and maintaining the chain of command by definition required a hierarchy on which to operate.

Understanding the role of the *Schwerpunkt* in early twentieth-century German military thought is complicated by modern doctrine, which stresses the importance of the concept while disagreeing on its meaning. The confusion stems from Clausewitz, who described various potential *Schwerpunkte* such as the enemy army, the capital city, the unity of an alliance, the paramount leader or public opinion. Whatever *Schwerpunkt* was selected, all action must be directed against it to achieve a decisive

---

[1] Kriegsministerium, *Grundzüge der höheren Truppenführung*, 12.

[2] Misunderstandings about the *Schwerpunkt* concept begin with varying translations such as 'centre of gravity', 'focal point' and 'point of main effort'; the last is the most suitable in a First World War context, as this chapter illustrates, but to avoid ambiguity the German term is used here.

result.[3] Although the *Schwerpunkt* concept does not feature prominently in German pre-war doctrinal manuals, it was a key part of German command by the 1870s.[4] It clearly had a more limited, battlefield focus than Clausewitz allowed. The 1910 doctrinal manual 'Essentials of High Command' stated that the *Schwerpunkt* depended on the overall operational intention, enemy dispositions and terrain. Forces should be deployed accordingly: they should be strongest where the decisive action was sought and economised elsewhere.[5] The *Schwerpunkt* was linked to the positioning of reserves, which could be used during the battle to shift the point of main effort if necessary. It was therefore unfortunate that pre-war organisation from corps to brigade was binary rather than triangular. Each level commanded two formations or units, so removing one to create a reserve automatically disrupted the chain of command and this in turn made setting a *Schwerpunkt* more difficult.[6]

Maintaining the chain of command is less familiar as a principle: after all, modern commentary on the German army through the ages often praises its organisational flexibility, particularly the ability to form ad hoc units for sudden tactical missions.[7] But in fact stress on maintaining the chain of command went back at least to Moltke the Elder. He believed that the greatest Prussian failure in the war of 1866 was making arbitrary changes to the army's organisation which prevented higher command exerting its influence once battle started. Orders could not be passed properly, direction from above often ceased and all-arms co-operation then failed. This would be a serious danger against a more competent enemy than the Austrians.[8] Such thinking fed directly into 'Essentials of High Command', which insisted that the order of battle should be strictly upheld. The situation might necessitate the creation of temporary formations but this must be reversed as soon as possible. Furthermore, orders must be transmitted through the chain of command: bypassing an intermediate headquarters paralysed it and should only occur in special circumstances.[9]

---

[3] Antulio J. Echevarria II, 'Clausewitz's Center of Gravity: It's Not What We Thought', *Naval War College Review*, vol. 61, no. 1 (winter 2003), 114.

[4] Samuels, *Command or Control?*, 8 citing a letter from the MGFA.

[5] Kriegsministerium, *Grundzüge der höheren Truppenführung*, 28.

[6] Friedrich von Bernhardi, *Deutschland und der nächste Krieg*, 6th ed. (Stuttgart: Cotta'sche Buchhandlung, 1913), 229–30.

[7] See, for example, John Buckley, *Monty's Men: The British Army and the Liberation of Europe, 1944–5* (New Haven, CT: Yale University Press, 2013), 209.

[8] Sigg, *Unterführer als Feldherr*, 130–43; Moltke, 'Memoire an Seine Majestät den König vom 25. Juli 1868', 74–5. Moltke backed up his argument with a quote from Clausewitz on the importance of maintaining the order of battle.

[9] Kriegsministerium, *Grundzüge der höheren Truppenführung*, 50 and 52.

Like other traditional principles, *Schwerpunkt* and maintaining the chain of command were developed to meet the requirements of the first command task in mobile, offensive operations, not the trench warfare which emerged on the Western Front. *Schwerpunkt* in particular seems to be an offensive concept, as suggested by Hindenburg's often-quoted – though badly referenced – remark that an attack without a *Schwerpunkt* was like a man without character; this was reflected in a 1918 manual on the offensive stressing that every attack should have its *Schwerpunkt*.[10] By contrast, the word *Schwerpunkt* itself does not appear in any of the three editions of the 'Defensive Battle' manual issued in 1916–17. So was the concept still relevant to the first command task in a situation where the German army had lost the initiative and was strategically on the defensive? It is easier to see why maintaining the chain of command remained important in this situation. Implementing the principle was, however, difficult. In the early crisis of the battle of the Somme, reinforcements were committed piecemeal and creating a proper organisation took weeks.[11] This was clearly not the best way to fulfil the first command task in a major defensive battle.

The secondary literature generally ignores issues of organisation, with the exception of changes to the respective roles of corps and divisions that, as will emerge, it often misunderstands. Table 3.1 sets out the organisation discussed in this chapter. Strict German usage distinguished the formation, e.g. *1.Armee* [First Army], and its headquarters, *Armee-Oberkommando 1*, usually contracted to AOK 1; the same applied at corps level. However, informal writing often paralleled British usage, in which 'First Army' might refer to either the formation or its headquarters, and the book adopts this practice.

Army Groups

On mobilisation, OHL commanded Armies directly. Early attempts to improve co-ordination by appointing the senior commander on a sector of the front to command two or more Armies led to friction: it was difficult for an Army engaged in battle to treat its neighbour objectively. The first permanent army group on the Western Front was set up in August 1915, but even that consisted of a strengthened Fifth Army headquarters also

---

[10] Herbert Rosinski, *The German Army*, ed. Gordon A. Craig (London: Pall Mall Press, 1966), 300–1; Chef des Generalstabes des Feldheeres, *Vorschriften für den Stellungskrieg für alle Waffen*, Teil 14, *Der Angriff im Stellungskriege: Vom 1. Januar 1918*, in Erich Ludendorff, ed., *Urkunden der Obersten Heeresleitung über ihre Tätigkeit 1916/18*, 2nd ed. (Berlin: E. S. Mittler, 1921), 641.

[11] AOK 1, 'Erfahrungen', 2.

Table 3.1 *German higher-level military organisation in 1917*

Formation	Translation	Headquarters	Composition in 1917
Heeresgruppe	Army group	*Oberkommando*	3–4 Armies or Army Detachments
Armee	Army	*Armee-Oberkommando* or AOK	3–7 corps or *Gruppen*
Korps	Corps	*Generalkommando*	2–4 divisions
Gruppe	Not translated	*Gruppenkommando*	2–5 divisions
Division	Division	*Divisionsstabsquartier*	1 infantry brigade of 3 regiments and 1 field artillery regiment

acting as headquarters of Army Group Crown Prince. This model was repeated when the provisional Army Group Gallwitz was established in July 1916, based on Second Army headquarters and commanding both Second and First Armies. As in 1914, friction and accusations of biased treatment quickly arose. In addition, the commander and chief of staff positions of both army group and Army were full-time jobs. In Army Group Crown Prince, Crown Prince Wilhelm and his staff commanded the army group in name only, because directing Fifth Army in the battle of Verdun took up all their time.[12]

Finally, in August 1916, OHL set up Army Group Rupprecht as a separate formation with its own headquarters and commanded by Crown Prince Rupprecht. This was also the model adopted when command at Verdun was reorganised in November 1916, and Army Group Crown Prince re-established as an entity separate from Fifth Army. The new organisation, though an improvement, did not cover the whole Western Front: for dynastic reasons, Fourth Army – commanded by Duke Albrecht of Württemberg – could not be placed under Rupprecht as the Crown Prince of Bavaria.[13] This problem was resolved in March 1917, when a third army group was established to cover the southern sector of the front, with Albrecht as its commander; Fourth Army was then subordinated to Army Group Rupprecht. The

---

[12] The joint army group/Army headquarters copied the model of the first permanent army group on the Eastern Front, Army Group Kiew, established in April 1915. Cron, *Geschichte des Deutschen Heeres*, 61–3 covers development of army groups. Friction: Gallwitz, *Erleben im Westen*, 77, 93 and 167. Impossibility of doing both jobs: Schulenburg, 'Erlebnisse', 128.

[13] Foley, 'The Other Side of the Wire', 157.

reorganisation was not completed till April, with further moves from
Army Group Crown Prince to Army Group Albrecht.[14]

A decisive factor in creating army groups as separate entities was the
need to relieve OHL of the work involved in the constant movement of
divisions on the Somme. It was also convenient to delegate control of the
battle at a time when OHL's attention was taken up by the threatening
situation on the Eastern Front. The order establishing Army Group
Rupprecht stated that its authority extended to all operational and tactical
matters, as well as related personnel affairs. It had complete autonomy
over moving units between Armies. It was not involved in logistics,
administration or legal matters, responsibility for which remained with
OHL and with the Armies.[15] In spring 1917, the role of the three army
groups was to prepare a co-ordinated defence against the expected enemy
offensive. Army Groups Rupprecht and Crown Prince, facing the most
serious threats, were given sufficient forces to maintain a major battle in
the first place from their own resources and if necessary could then draw
on OHL reserves behind their fronts; Army Group Albrecht was less
threatened and accordingly less well provided with forces. Although the
word was not used, these arrangements illustrate selection of defensive
Schwerpunkte.[16]

The main task of army groups was operational co-ordination of their
constituent Armies, especially the integrated handling of reserves and
defences. They ensured mutual support between Armies and sorted out
squabbles over boundaries.[17] Army groups provided reinforcement at
times of crisis and allocated Armies extra units on their own initiative or
at the latter's request.[18] They could also produce expert resources: with
the French offensive clearly imminent, in April 1917 Army Group Crown
Prince made its senior artillery adviser and his staff available to Seventh
Army.[19] They played a role in passing on intelligence, assessments and
resulting orders.[20] Sometimes they overrode the chain of command and
inspected corps and other sectors, intervening in detail down to regimental level at least. Such infringements of mission command could reach

[14] Reichsarchiv, Weltkrieg, 12:292. The titles of the three army groups varied slightly over
   time; the translated versions here have been adopted for clarity and conciseness.
[15] Reichsarchiv, Weltkrieg, 10:422, and 11:480; Rupprecht, Kriegstagebuch, 1:523
   (26 August 1916).
[16] Reichsarchiv, Weltkrieg, 12:75.
[17] AOK 6 to its Gruppen, 'Gegenseitige Unterstützung an den Armeegrenzen', Ia/Art.
   No. 92483, 2 March 1917, KAM, AOK 6 Bd. 369. Boundary squabbles: AOK 7 war
   diary, 1 February 1917, GLAK, F1/171.
[18] AOK 7 Army order [Armeebefehl], Ia No. 46/April 17, 6 April 1917, GLAK, F1/250.
[19] HDK telegram to AOK 7, Ia art nr 6694, 5 April 1917, GLAK, F1/250.
[20] HDK telegram to AOK 7, 1b nr 1726 geh., 7 April 1917, GLAK, F1/250.

absurd proportions, as when Army Group Crown Prince became involved in the movement of trench mortar companies.[21]

Handling of reserves had various aspects, including deployment, release for use in combat, replacement when fought out [*abgekämpft*] and training during rest periods. Deciding the deployment of reserves entailed complex calculations. In one example, a divisional relief in Army Group Rupprecht involved assessing the combat value of four divisions in three Armies, as well as balancing the interests of different command levels, including Army and OHL, and ensuring the correct relationship between formations at the front and in different forms of reserve.[22] In other cases, Armies' need for labour had to be set against the requirement to train reserves and keep them fresh for combat.[23] The complexity of the system for handling reserves arose from their scarcity, which, as we saw, was one of the constraints on mission command. Not surprisingly, during the Entente spring offensive army groups received daily updates on the state of reliefs. The volume of correspondence shows how much work was involved simply keeping this organisation going.[24]

In early 1917, OHL and army groups attempted to ensure that divisions all got three weeks' training.[25] Army Group Rupprecht initiated the divisional command courses which were established at Valenciennes and Sedan in its and Army Group Crown Prince's sectors. It kept an eye on the training of general staff officers who had not attended one or other of these courses, and issued instructions on selecting candidates for the general staff course at Sedan when this was set up in July 1917.[26] In addition to formal training, army groups aimed to raise the quality of formations by enforcing best practice. In March 1917, Friedrich Graf Schulenburg, chief of staff to Army Group Crown Prince, instructed Seventh Army on the principles to be used for defensive battle.[27] The army group later sent out questionnaires on the recent fighting and circulated lessons from it. There was a particular concern to find out what had caused poor performance after failures by some units in April.[28]

---

[21] HDK telegram to AOK 7, 1a 1688 rm 4. ang., 9 April 1917, GLAK, F1/250.

[22] HKR telegram to OHL, 13 October 1916, KAM, HKR alte Nr. 150. Cowan, 'Muddy Grave?', 466–71 analyses German handling of reserves on the Somme.

[23] AOK 7 telegram to HDK, 1a 66/apr. 17, 7 April 1917 and HDK reply, 1b nr 2196, 8 April 1917, both on GLAK, F1/250.

[24] See KAM, HKR alte Nr. 150 for Army Group Rupprecht, and GLAK, F1/249, 250 and 251 for Army Group Crown Prince.

[25] HKR to its AOKs, Iab No. 2064 geh., 21 January 1917, KAM, HKR neue Nr. 31.

[26] HKR to OHL, IIa No. 22131, 15 July 1917 and HKR telegram to its AOKs, 2a 23313, 25 July 1917, KAM, HKR alte Nr. 98.

[27] Gallwitz, *Erleben im Westen*, 93–4; AOK 7 war diary, 10 March 1917, GLAK, F1/171.

[28] HDK to its AOKs, Ic Nr. 2932, 8 June 1917, GLAK, F1/536; GLAK, F1/249, passim.

Army groups were of course subject to the authority of OHL and sometimes merely acted as its post-box. But as the next-highest level of command, staffed by some of the most senior and experienced officers in the army, they developed their own organisational interests and methods. Army Groups Rupprecht and Crown Prince faced different enemies in different terrain, had different experiences during the spring fighting and drew different lessons on further tactical development. This is reflected in their different approaches to the divisional command courses and even in terminology. For instance, the term 'Eingreifdivision' [intervention or counter-attack division] was introduced by Army Group Crown Prince in mid-April 1917. But even after its first appearance in official doctrine that June, Army Group Rupprecht often preferred to use other terms to describe divisions held in reserve such as 'Army battle reserve' [Armee-Kampfreserve] or 'shock division' [Stoßdivision].[29]

Army groups' differing interests could also cause tension between them. By June 1917, Army Group Rupprecht wanted to concentrate increasing resources in Flanders as the emerging defensive Schwerpunkt. Army Group Crown Prince's operations to improve local positions after the Nivelle offensive involved thirteen divisions up to mid-July, some of which at least could have been in Flanders. The army group also proposed larger-scale attacks to pre-empt renewal of the French offensive that it still expected despite the mutinies which had now broken out. Initially, OHL authorised it to continue planning and only gradually decided not to provide resources for attacks. Some officers saw such planning as usefully stimulating the offensive spirit; others, especially in Army Group Rupprecht, viewed it as a waste of effort and forces needed more urgently elsewhere. The ultimate arbiter was OHL, especially under Ludendorff, but overcoming the powerful interests represented by the army groups was not easy.[30]

Inevitably, relations between army groups and Armies were not always smooth, an example from Army Group Rupprecht being the withdrawal to the Hindenburg Line. The Armies concerned knew about this as a theoretical possibility but were only informed on 3 February 1917 that it was being seriously considered. Despite their objections, as Seventh Army recorded, 'the general impression was that this step, of such

---

[29] The earliest noted reference to Eingreifdivision is 11 April 1917, and two days later Seventh Army defined the term: XV.BRK war diary, 11 and 13 April 1917, KAM, XV. BRK 11. Armee-Kampfreserve: Reichsarchiv, Weltkrieg, 13:53. Stoßdivision: Otto von Below diary, 19 August 1917.

[30] Reichsarchiv, Weltkrieg, 12:556–9; Walther Obkircher, 'Bei Zwei Armee-Oberkommandos Generalstabsoffizier Ia: Januar 1917–August 1917', unpublished manuscript in BArch, Obkircher Nachlass, N2214/66, 3–4.

extraordinary consequence, was as good as already decided'. This was correct, and the decision to withdraw was announced the next day.[31] This sequence of events suggests that the army group had not properly consulted its Armies – unless it knew they would object and simply wanted to present them with a fait accompli ordered by OHL. In any case, there was no question of mission command here.

In this instance, dissent was overruled. Continuing dissent or non-compliance might be resolved by sacking. In spring 1917, Army Group Crown Prince instigated the removal of Seventh Army's commander, chief of staff, two senior general staff officers and aviation commander because of concern about the slow progress of defensive preparations. The new command team drove the work forward more satisfactorily.[32] As this and other cases examined earlier show, creating competent command teams was an important aspect of army group's work.

Army groups' grip on Armies evidently varied. Army Group Rupprecht displayed firm control in its handling of the decision on the Hindenburg Line withdrawal. When commanding Fifth Army, Gallwitz, an ex-army group commander himself, complained repeatedly about excessive dictation from Army Group Crown Prince.[33] But as the last chapter explained, the failure of army groups to impose their will on Armies was a significant cause of at least four heavy local defeats in 1917. After the first of these, at Arras on 9 April, Rupprecht himself recorded that one of the reasons was Sixth Army's failure to bring forward its reserves in time, contrary to the exhortations [Mahnungen] of the army group; he subsequently regretted not having ordered them to move the reserves.[34] Otto von Below, who took command of Sixth Army later in April, commented that 'the army group always shrank from giving definite orders but only ever made suggestions [Anregungen] as they called them. So they had to endure the painful experience of having these suggestions rejected.'[35] Perhaps Rupprecht was reacting to excessive OHL interference, which on occasion he saw as calling into question the purpose of having army groups.[36] These organisational relationships again demonstrate the problems of implementing mission command.

In early 1917, army groups generally succeeded in their main role of co-ordinating the overall conduct of the battle, particularly through using the forces at their disposal efficiently without calling for reinforcements.

---

[31] AOK 7 war diary, 3 February 1917, GLAK, F1/171.
[32] Schulenburg, 'Erlebnisse', 142; Kuhl, 'Kriegstagebuch', 6 March 1917.
[33] Gallwitz, Erleben im Westen, 160, 174, 209 and 234 (twice).
[34] Rupprecht, Kriegstagebuch, 2:135 (9 April 1917).
[35] Otto von Below diary, 6 July 1917.
[36] Rupprecht, Kriegstagebuch, 2:164 (12 May 1917).

Entente strategy was for the British attack to draw in German reserves before the main French assault. Chapter 8 shows how tight the army groups' reserves became, but at most one division was diverted from Army Group Crown Prince to Army Group Rupprecht.[37] The army group system therefore contributed to the defeat of the Entente offensive.

Armies

The Army level of command did not exist in peacetime and, as in 1866 and 1870–71, was created on mobilisation. The pre-war vision, especially under Schlieffen, was that individual Armies and their corps would conduct separate battles [*Teilschlachten*], which the supreme commander would weld together into the overall battle [*Gesamtschlacht*].[38] This concept of an Army's role continued into the trench warfare period, when one Army was often responsible for fighting a battle. Examples include Third Army in Champagne in late 1915, Fifth Army at Verdun, Sixth Army at Arras and Fourth Army at Messines and Ypres later in 1917. This was obviously the preferred solution, with all its advantages of integrated command. However, 'Defensive Battle' recognised that in principle Armies could only control four to six *Gruppen*: beyond that, it might be necessary to bring in extra Army headquarters.[39] The front threatened by the French on the Aisne was so wide that First Army headquarters was inserted to improve co-ordination. In all, two Armies and part of a third conducted the defence against the Nivelle offensive, an indication of its size. At Arras, a *Gruppe* involved in the fighting at Bullecourt was transferred from Second to Sixth Army even though the latter already had six *Gruppen*, illustrating the preference for one Army to control a battle if at all possible.

Armies were able to play this role because they combined operational and logistical functions. By 1917, they controlled directly some of the most important assets required for operations, including the Army's storm battalion [*Sturmbataillon*] and long-range air reconnaissance as well as, crucially, ammunition and the heaviest artillery. Although most of these assets were not permanently allocated, they were specifically Army troops [*Armeetruppen*]: Armies decided onward allocation to *Gruppen* and divisions.[40]

---

[37] 15th Reserve Division: 'Die Aisne-Champagne-Schlacht einschließlich der Vorbereitungskämpfe von Febr.–Ende Mai 1917', unpublished Reichsarchiv draft, BArch, RH61/1891, 27.

[38] Foley, *Schlieffen*, 185.   [39] '*Abwehrschlacht*', March 1917, 7.

[40] Kommandierender General der Luftstreitkräfte, *Weisungen für den Einsatz und die Verwendung von Fliegerverbänden innerhalb einer Armee* (GHQ: Druckerei des Chefs des Generalstabes des Feldheeres, 1917), 1.

Sixth Army headquarters' activities in early 1917 show how an Army prepared for and managed a defensive battle. Its detailed preparations were based on both its regular assessment of the situation and the relevant part of the 'Defensive Battle' manual.[41] The Army co-ordinated with its *Gruppen* employment of available current forces, what reinforcements they would need and how these would be used, again drawing on 'Defensive Battle'.[42] It then negotiated with Army Group Rupprecht for extra forces, generally receiving less than it requested, later than it wanted.[43] Its preparatory orders to *Gruppen* covered creation of reserves, logistics, labour, communications and medical arrangements.[44] Other work included co-ordinating development of defensive positions, both in forward areas and in the rearward *Wotan-Stellung*.[45]

Both before and during battle, Armies were expected to ensure effective and economical deployment of formations. 'Defensive Battle' described the 'solemn duty' of Armies and *Gruppen* to deploy the fewest possible divisions in the front line and the most possible in reserve.[46] Core to the system was the weekly reporting on the combat value of divisions instituted in November 1916. Part of Armies' work in this area was merely to forward *Gruppe* reports in their weekly assessments. But following the failure of at least one division on 9 April, OHL fretted that Armies lacked understanding of divisions' combat value and instructed them to visit formations themselves rather than just ask for reports.[47] Armies also controlled the parcelling out of reserves, requesting that they be placed at Army disposal by army group and in turn releasing them to *Gruppen* as appropriate. In Seventh Army, a corps headquarters was brought in to supervise training and movement of divisions in the rear area.[48]

One aspect of battle in which Armies regularly intervened was deciding how to react to loss of ground. If an immediate counter-attack failed, the three options were to launch a prepared counter-attack, do nothing or

---

[41] AOK 6 to its Gruppen and Etappen-Inspektion, 'Vorbereitungen für die Abwehrschlacht', Ia No. 97892 II.Ang., 26 March 1917, KAM, AOK 6 Bd. 369. AOK 7's preparations against the French paralleled these measures: see, for example, GLAK, F1/250, passim.

[42] AOK 6 to its Gruppen, 'Vorbereitungen gegen einen feindlichen Angriff', Ia No. 84117, [n.d.], KAM, AOK 6 Bd. 369.

[43] HKR army group order [*Heeresbefehl*], Iab No. 2660 geh., 2 April 1917, KAM, AOK 6 Bd. 409.

[44] AOK 6 circular, 'Vorbereitungen gegen einen fdlen. Angriff', Ia No. 99547, 30 March 1917, KAM, AOK 6 Bd. 369.

[45] AOK 6 to its Gruppen and Etappen-Inspektion, 'Stellungsbau', Ia No. 530 g., 7 March 1917, KAM, AOK 6 Bd. 369.

[46] '*Abwehrschlacht*', March 1917, 8.

[47] OHL to CGS AOK 7, Ia No. 2812 geh. op., 12 April 1917, GLAK, F1/374.

[48] HDK telegram to AOKs 3 and 7, 1b 1781 geh., 21 April 1917, GLAK, F1/251.

withdraw to more favourable terrain. Sixth Army provides examples of all three. On 3 May 1917, the British captured the village of Fresnoy and repulsed a counter-attack. Sixth Army removed the division responsible, which it believed had failed, and forbade further immediate counter-attacks. However, the ground was tactically important and the Army therefore ordered a planned counter-attack four days later, which succeeded.[49] Later in the month, a similar situation arose when the village of Roeux was lost, recaptured and lost again. Sixth Army at first ordered it to be retaken, because of the danger to neighbouring positions. Further assessment suggested this danger was not acute and the attack was cancelled, with the advantage of saving troops and ammunition for the impending battle in Flanders.[50] The third option, withdrawal, was less in the Army's independent control. The decision to withdraw after the defeat of 9 April, although theoretically taken by the Army commander, was heavily influenced by events and Army Group Rupprecht, as well as being subject to OHL approval. The voluntary evacuation of a local salient in June was a Sixth Army initiative. The aim, saving on one division in the front line, accorded well with the 'Defensive Battle' principle.[51]

Armies' second function, logistics, was as important as the operational function, and their major logistical apparatus did not exist at other levels of command. An Army's area was divided into an operations zone [*Operationsgebiet*] and a communications zone [*Etappengebiet*]. The latter extended from the rear boundary of the operations zone to the forward boundary of the General Government, in the case of Belgium, or to the border with Germany [*Heimatgebiet*]. Work in this zone was controlled by the Army's lines of communication commander [*Etappen-Inspekteur*], a senior officer with the status of a divisional commander. He co-ordinated logistical work with the *Oberquartiermeister* [Senior Quartermaster, usu-ally not translated], the third-ranking officer on the Army's staff. Reflecting the importance of the Army's logistical role, this post did not exist in most army groups or corps.[52] The work was, literally, big business: Sixth Army claimed that by June 1917 economic exploitation of the land had already produced value considerably exceeding the 1870–71 war reparations.[53]

---

[49] Otto von Below diary, 3–8 May 1917. Orders and after-action reports are on KAM, AOK 6 Bd. 409 and Bd. 419.

[50] Otto von Below diary, 12 to 24 May 1917.   [51] Ibid., 3 and 21 June 1917.

[52] For details of the logistics organisation, see Cron, *Geschichte des Deutschen Heeres*, 72–3 and especially 267–75.

[53] Otto von Below diary, 9 June 1917.

The German army in different ages has been criticised for ignoring logistics, and indeed Schlieffen showed an alarming lack of interest in the subject.[54] But this was not the case in trench warfare, where Armies' logistical work increased, if anything. As an illustration, the administrative part of First Army's report on its Somme experiences was not much shorter than the operational.[55] Generally during the spring fighting, Armies were able to fulfil all logistical requirements despite production difficulties in Germany. Supply problems occurred nearer the front, where shelling and bombing could make transportation of matériel almost impossible, but were never significant enough to have a fundamental effect on operations. The exception was artillery ammunition. 'Defensive Battle' called for offensive handling of artillery, and in spring 1917 this consumed vast quantities of ammunition. By early May expenditure far outstripped production and reserves were rapidly disappearing.[56] One field artillery regiment's highest use of ammunition in the whole war was in June 1917: tellingly, this was during small-scale fighting after the main offensive and when the French mutinies were in full swing.[57] As noted earlier, OHL's serious concerns over ammunition supply and frequent orders to economise limited Armies' ability to conduct independent operations.

Armies' experience in fighting major battles and the seniority of their command teams enhanced their authority: First Army's Somme report was important enough to circulate to the whole army as semi-doctrine. Not surprisingly, Armies evolved their own procedures. First Army, for instance, issued orders for *Gruppen* to play a larger role in the handling of artillery than envisaged in 'Defensive Battle'.[58] Nevertheless, Armies were components of an army group, and much of what they did reflected the army group's activities. Indeed, it is sometimes difficult to tell where the authority of one ended and the other began. In February 1917, Sixth Army forwarded to *Gruppen* Army Group Rupprecht's comments on their defensive plans. Towards the end of March, army group officers toured units and made further recommendations for improvement, which the Army then discussed with its *Gruppen* and divisions.[59] In these cases, one might have expected the Army to be in charge. In other cases though,

[54] Groß, *Mythos und Wirklichkeit*, 95.
[55] AOK 1, 'Erfahrungen der 1. Armee in der Sommeschlacht 1916, II. Teil: Verwaltungs- und Wirtschafts-Erfahrungen', HSAS, Soden Nachlass, M660/038 Bü 80.
[56] Reichsarchiv, *Weltkrieg*, 12:408–9.   [57] Heidrich, *Feldartillerie-Regiment Nr. 79*, 102.
[58] AOK 1 Army order, 'Gliederung und Kampf der Artillerie', Ia Nr. 2121 geheim, 24 January 1917, KAM, HKR neue Nr. 31.
[59] CGS AOK 6 to Gruppen and divisions, Ia No. 98751, 26 March 1917, KAM, AOK 6 Bd. 369.

army group intervention was perfectly reasonable, for instance in ensuring proper artillery support on Army boundaries.[60]

As with army groups and Armies, relations between Armies and their *Gruppen* varied. The issue of mission command potentially limited an Army's control of its *Gruppen*. Gallwitz, who clearly believed in his right to command, nevertheless did not insist on one of his *Gruppen* evacuating the front line when obviously faced with a French attack at Verdun; nor did he intervene to prevent what he saw as its imperfect handling of counter-attacks. On the other hand, Seventh Army gave detailed orders to Gruppe Sissonne on the quartering of a reserve division in the *Gruppe* area, down to naming the individual villages and the location of the divisional headquarters.[61] Unspecified frictions between Boehn at Seventh Army and *General der Artillerie* Maximilian Ritter von Höhn, commanding Gruppe Sissonne, led to the removal of the latter's corps headquarters soon after the French offensive opened.[62] Sixth Army's relations with Gruppe Arras (IX Reserve Corps) were also troublesome at first. Things improved when the Army's own command changed in April, but deteriorated again when the headquarters of XIV Reserve Corps took over the *Gruppe*: as we will see, there were growing doubts about Otto von Moser, the new *Gruppe* commander.[63]

Corps and *Gruppen*

In peacetime, corps were the highest level formations in the army and intended to be the basic unit of manoeuvre in a war of movement.[64] Their main component was two infantry divisions but their tactical importance was increased by a battalion of heavy artillery and an aviation wing for reconnaissance. Most corps were regionally based and had strong local identities.[65] Their commanders ranked among the most senior generals in the army: corporately they were one of the four pillars of German military control, alongside the Ministry of War, Military Cabinet and General Staff. They were subordinate to the Kaiser alone and they had the right of direct access to him [*Immediatrecht*]. They were in charge of all

---

[60] AOK 6, 'Gegenseitige Unterstützung an den Armeegrenzen'.
[61] Gallwitz, *Erleben im Westen*, 219 and 224; AOK 7 telegram to Gruppe Sissonne, 1a nr 110/april 17, 11 April 1917, GLAK, F1/250.
[62] Bavarian Militärbevollmächtigter [Military Plenipotentiary] at GHQ to Crown Prince Rupprecht, 19 April 1917, HAM, Rupprecht Nachlass Nr. 614.
[63] Xylander diary, 3 April 1917; Thaer, *Generalstabsdienst*, 108 and 111.
[64] Foley, *Schlieffen*, xxiv. Bernhardi, *Deutschland und der nächste Krieg*, 239 stated explicitly that the corps was the tactical and operational unit.
[65] Generaloberst Karl von Einem, *Erinnerungen eines Soldaten 1853–1933* (Leipzig: K. F. Koehler, 1933), 165.

aspects of their corps and corps areas; in particular they played a pivotal role in training.[66] They outranked the most senior civilian authority in their areas and on declaration of a state of emergency, executive power over public affairs passed to them.[67]

On mobilisation, corps were replaced by Armies as the highest-level formations but their other peacetime characteristics continued. Their regional links remained strong and there was no decline in the seniority of their commanders. Throughout 1914–15 attempts were made to maintain the tactical unity of corps, with varying success. There were examples in the opening campaigns on both Western and Eastern Fronts of corps giving up or acquiring divisions, but this was temporary: divisions returned to their parent corps in due course, in accordance with the principle of maintaining the chain of command. More significant was the decision not to incorporate divisions formed from early 1915 permanently into corps.[68] Despite these variations on the traditional pattern, when the battle of Verdun opened in February 1916 many peacetime characteristics survived. Of the forty infantry corps that existed on mobilisation, the original commanders of nineteen were still in place, including all eight of Fifth Army's corps commanders. During the battle, it proved possible to maintain the corps system by temporarily allocating extra units as required.[69]

However, the intensification of the war of attrition during 1916 led to three major changes: the replacement of the organisationally integrated corps by *Gruppen* that controlled a varying number of divisions; the arrival of many new commanders; and the devolution to divisions of responsibility for direct conduct of the battle. Like the British, the Germans found that handling corps as fixed tactical units was no longer possible. The principal reason was that divisional infantry, which suffered the heaviest casualties, needed to be relieved sooner than artillery and other arms. Requirement for divisions was also uneven, because more were needed in

---

[66] Paul Schneider, *Die Organisation des Heeres* (Berlin: E. S. Mittler, 1931), 65–7; Mombauer, *Moltke*, 24–5; Hermann Frobenius, ed., *Militär-Lexikon: Handwörterbuch der Militärwissenschaften* (Berlin: Martin Oldenbourg, 1901), entry for *Generalkommando*.

[67] Wilhelm Deist, 'Aufgaben und Kompetenzen der Militärbefehlshaber', in Wilhelm Deist, ed., *Militär und Innenpolitik im Weltkrieg 1914–1918* (Düsseldorf: Droste Verlag, 1970), 1: xliv; Roger Chickering, *Imperial Germany and the Great War, 1914–1918* (Cambridge: Cambridge University Press, 2004), 33.

[68] Otto von Moser, *Ernsthafte Plaudereien über den Weltkrieg* (Stuttgart: Chr. Belser, 1925), 51. Bruce I. Gudmundsson, 'Learning from the Front: Tactical Innovation in France and Flanders, 1914–1918', unpublished D.Phil. thesis, University of Oxford, 2009, chapter 5 argues that on the Western Front, adding an extra division to corps was a longer-lasting and revolutionary change.

[69] For example, Conrad von Goßler, *Erinnerungen an den Großen Krieg dem VI. Reservekorps gewidmet* (Breslau: Korn, 1919), 74.

hot spots than in quieter sectors. Under the two-division structure, a corps commander could only create a reserve by disrupting one or both divisions. Finally, if a complete corps and its headquarters were pulled out of the line, there was no element of continuity in its sector; long-term and sector-wide issues suffered, an obvious example being defensive works.[70]

In the new system, instead of commanding an integrated tactical formation, a corps headquarters managed a *Gruppe* controlling a sector. Corps headquarters never became completely static but did remain in place for substantial periods; meanwhile divisions moved in and out of *Gruppen* as required.[71] This change dramatically affected the composition of corps/*Gruppen*. A peacetime corps comprised about 40,000 men; in April 1917, IX Reserve Corps, acting as headquarters for Gruppe Arras, had about 140,000 men under command, a colossal management task by comparison. From April to December 1917, it commanded some seventy different divisions; at any one time it typically had under command the infantry of twelve to fifteen divisions, including all those in the front line, acting as counter-attack divisions and on the move. Moser – whose *Gruppe* commanded a mere thirty divisions from spring 1917 to spring 1918 – commented that it was like a madhouse with all the unknown divisions moving in and out.[72] The dislocation to divisions was similar. 27th Infantry Division was with its parent corps throughout 1916 and into March 1917; from then till the end of the year it belonged to or moved through ten *Gruppen* and two Armies.[73]

The rupture of the traditional corps relationship with divisions was much disliked. Senior commanders worried that the establishment of so many independent divisions damaged training and created too many command units with a concomitant demand for experienced officers; it also greatly increased the effort needed to get commanders and staffs to work together, including for the all-important combined arms battle. More than one senior officer thought a better solution would have been to expand corps to three or four permanently allocated divisions. Consciously or unconsciously, this echoed pre-war military thinking on three-division corps, one big advantage being to facilitate creation of a reserve.[74] Against this background, in January 1917 OHL raised the

[70] Cron, *Geschichte des Deutschen Heeres*, 86.   [71] Reichsarchiv, *Weltkrieg*, 11:106.
[72] Thaer, *Generalstabsdienst*, 10, 114 and 154; Moser, *Ernsthafte Plaudereien*, 51.
[73] From the divisional *Findbuch* [catalogue], HSAS, M39.
[74] Moser, *Ernsthafte Plaudereien*, 50–2; Gallwitz, *Erleben im Westen*, 98; Bernhardi, *Deutschland und der nächste Krieg*, 239–40. Gudmundsson, 'Learning from the Front', 140–5 has more on the pre-war debate. The British official history commented that the Germans later saw making the division the tactical unit rather than the corps as a mistake:

question whether divisions could be reattached to corps, in order to create a tighter-knit command. Some respondents favoured this, but overall recognised that because divisions needed to be moved frequently, it was impossible to restore the corps link.[75] In addition, the desirability of divisions fighting under familiar corps commanders was trumped by the need for continuity in control of the battle: this could only be secured by having static *Gruppe* headquarters.[76]

As with so many changes, the shift from fixed corps to *Gruppen* took time to penetrate the whole army. IX Reserve Corps did not lose its divisions till mid-April 1917, by which time it had been a *Gruppe* for months; VII Corps only lost its divisions in May. The introduction of geographical designations for *Gruppen* (Gruppe Arras and so on) emphasised their static nature and control of specific sectors, though even by June 1917 this system only extended to the left flank of Third Army in the Argonne. Formations from there to the Swiss border were still listed as corps though they had all lost their original divisions.[77] Various questions about subordination arose. *Gruppe* commanders could obviously give tactical orders to divisions, but what about training, personnel matters, justice, discipline, logistics and labour? And what about non-Prussian divisions coming under Prussian corps or Prussian divisions under non-Prussian corps? It took from September 1916 till July 1917 fully to resolve such questions.[78]

The change to *Gruppen* shattered corps' local links and the cohort of corps commanders also saw extensive change. When Hindenburg and Ludendorff formed the Third OHL in August 1916, only one of the nineteen original corps commanders just mentioned had departed. But in the seven months from then till the opening of the Entente spring offensive, a further twelve went and another was sidelined in a quiet sector (and forced into retirement shortly after). We cannot tell if the new

one could hope to find 50 or more good generals to command corps, but not over 200 good divisional commanders (Brigadier-General Sir James E. Edmonds and Lieutenant-Colonel R. Maxwell-Hyslop, *Military Operations: France and Belgium 1918*, vol. 5, *26th September–11th November: The Advance to Victory* (London: HMSO, 1947), 611). I am grateful to Professor Stephen Badsey for this reference.

[75] AOK 7 to HKR, Ia Nr. 160/Jan.17, 28 January 1917 and HKR to its AOKs, 'Unterstellung von selbstständigen Divisionen unter Gen. Kdos.', Iab No. 8940, 2 February 1917, both on GLAK, F1/374. This idea was again considered and abandoned as impractical in spring 1918: Reichsarchiv, *Weltkrieg*, 14:41.

[76] AOK 1, 'Erfahrungen', 8.

[77] Thaer, *Generalstabsdienst*, 112; Gallwitz, *Erleben im Westen*, 185. Reichsarchiv, *Weltkrieg*, 13: Beilage 2a shows one *Gruppe* in the whole southern sector, Gruppe Metz.

[78] OHL circular, Ic Nr. 35638 op., 17 October 1916, BArch, PH1/9, ff. 271–3, which refers to a September document on the same subject and was eventually replaced by OHL circular, Ic Nr. 58966 op., 3 July 1917, HSAS, Soden Nachlass, M660/038 Bü 17, f. 49.

brooms were deliberately at work here, but the transfer of so many of the original corps commanders was certainly convenient in terms of breaking any resistance to the organisational and tactical changes taking place over the same period. And it is surely no coincidence that four of the five remaining original commanders were Bavarian or Saxon, who could not automatically be removed by the Prussian-dominated central authorities.[79]

Devolution of tactical control of the battle from corps to division had been proceeding *de facto* from autumn 1916 and was codified in 'Defensive Battle'. Moser, in charge of training divisional command teams on the new doctrine, considered that this devolution was its most significant innovation.[80] Wynne and his disciples therefore assume that corps now played only a supporting role, and even that there was no longer a chain of command in the traditional sense.[81] But this is to misunderstand both the theory and reality behind the changes.

In terms of theory, the German army clarified the roles of corps/ *Gruppen* and divisions as they had evolved by late 1916. This fits with some pre-war thinking about command, especially attempts to define battle in the three levels of *Kampf*, *Gefecht* and *Schlacht*, with different units corresponding to them. *Schlacht* was the top level, and the smallest formation believed capable of engaging in it was the division.[82] Conceptually therefore we can see the 1917 changes as moving the division out of the *Schlacht* category and into one below. There is supporting evidence for this from the earliest post-war German doctrinal manual, 'Combined Arms Command and Combat' [*Führung und Gefecht der verbundenen Waffen*, known as the *F.u.G.*], which divided command into three levels: higher, comprising formations down to and including corps; middle, the division; and lower, all units below division. Divisions were now formations that conducted *Gefecht*, the level of battle below *Schlacht*.[83]

Whether or not such theorising affected events in 1917, reality on the ground shows that *Gruppen* continued to play a central role. 'Defensive Battle' stated that divisions were to be accorded sufficient autonomy but

---

[79] On Bavarian and Saxon control of senior postings, see Cowan, 'A Picture of German Unity?', 146–7.

[80] Moser, *Feldzugsaufzeichnungen*, 267.

[81] Wynne, *If Germany Attacks*, 85; Samuels, *Command or Control?*, 177 and 183; Lupfer, *Dynamics of Doctrine*, 20.

[82] Georg von Alten, *Handbuch für Heer und Flotte: Enzyklopädie der Kriegswissenschaften und verwandte Gebiete* (Berlin: Deutsches Verlagshaus Bong, 1911), 3: entry for *Einheit*.

[83] Reichswehrministerium, *Führung und Gefecht der verbundenen Waffen (F.u.G.): Vom 1. September 1921* (Berlin: Offene Worte, Charlottenburg, 1921), 2 and 4.

Gruppen were responsible for organising a close-knit defence.[84] This loose formulation concealed the importance of the *Gruppe* function. Having assessed which points in their sector were vulnerable, *Gruppen* decided divisional frontages, allocated the forces available, positioned reserves and issued orders for work on fixed defences. They instructed the divisions under their command in the general manner in which to conduct the battle, and such orders might go into considerable detail about the formations to be adopted and tactics to be used. Orders on artillery work – which in principle had been devolved to division – could be very prescriptive.[85] Once battle began, *Gruppen* initiated and co-ordinated the bigger counter-attacks. They controlled the flow of reserves and supplies to the most threatened areas, and they ensured mutual co-operation between divisions. Even in raids and similar small operations they expected to check all divisional arrangements beforehand in detail.[86] To quote Moser, the *Gruppe* was the highest combat authority on its front, and intellectually the tactical link that co-ordinated the battle.[87]

Gruppen provided integrated command in space (their sectors) and time (continuity of the defensive effort). Two aspects of their work demonstrate their role here: training and development of fixed defences. *Gruppen* were responsible for training and assessing the combat value of formations in their area, including divisions in OHL reserve.[88] Training was a traditional corps responsibility, and its retention in 1917 gave *Gruppe* commanders some opportunity to act like old-style corps commanders. Maximilian von Höhn was a strong supporter – possibly the originator – of the controversial tactic of large-scale counter-attack from the rear, incorporated it into the defensive plan of his Gruppe Sissonne and trained his divisions on it. His orders on training were issued down to company commander level.[89] Training was regarded as a crucial aspect of combat value, so it is not surprising that *Gruppen* were responsible for both.

Fixed defences were an integral part of the new tactics. As chief custodians of continuity in their sectors, *Gruppen* co-ordinated construction

---

[84] '*Abwehrschlacht*', March 1917, 2 and 7.
[85] XV.BRK to its divisions, 'Gegenstoß aus der Tiefe', Abt. I Nr. 195/4, 10 April 1917 and 'Einteilung, Bezeichnung u. Verteilung der artilleristischen Zielräume u. Zielstreifen u. der in ihnen zu lösenden Gefechtsaufgaben', Abt. I/Art. Nr. 100, 26 March 1917, KAM, XV.BRK 171.
[86] 'Einleitender Vortrag des Kursleiters', 7–8; Chef des Generalstabes des Feldheeres, *Anlage kleiner Angriffs-Unternehmungen bei Gruppe Vailly*, 4.
[87] Moser, *Feldzugsaufzeichnungen*, 305.
[88] HDK circular, Ia Nr. 1949, 17 March 1917, GLAK, F1/374.
[89] XV.BRK circular, 'Gefechtausbildung der Infanterie', Abt. Ia Nr. 15/2, 2 February 1917, KAM, XV.BRK 185.

and maintenance of the defences. How this worked in practice varied. In March 1917, Gruppe Vimy laid down general principles, pointed out the enemy's likely assault methods and indicated eight locations that therefore needed special attention; it left details to the divisions. Gruppe Sissonne went into specifics about what it required.[90] Of course, reality might differ from intent. In May, First Army complained that its *Gruppen* had not developed firm plans, organisation or supervision to improve rearward positions. Also in May, Paul von Kneußl of 11th Bavarian Infantry Division found some of Seventh Army's rearward defences in a deplorable condition.[91]

After the spring fighting, Army Group Crown Prince recognised that during battle, front divisions concentrated their labour almost exclusively on maintaining the defences of the first (most forward) position. It recommended that development of rearward positions, roads and anything demanding long-term attention should be transferred from divisions to *Gruppen*; labour troops should be distributed accordingly. At about the same time, creation of senior engineer posts in *Gruppe* headquarters strengthened their ability to control this work.[92] All this of course emphasises the continuing importance of *Gruppen*, given the nature of modern battle.

Divisions

By the opening of the Entente spring offensive, two-thirds of the army's 228 infantry divisions were on the Western Front. The division of early 1917 was very different from the pre-war one.[93] The new tactics' aim of substituting machines for manpower continued a trend begun in 1915–16 with the removal of one brigade headquarters and one infantry regiment from each division. At the same time divisions' organic infantry firepower increased, and much greater support was allocated to help carry out their combat tasks; this was either placed directly, if temporarily, under their control or made available at the discretion of higher command.

[90] I.BRK to its divisions, 'Vorbereitungen für die Abwehrschlacht', Ia No. 13720, 21 March 1917, KAM, AOK 6 Bd. 409; Gruppe H. [later Sissonne], 'Ausbau und Verteidigung des Abschnitts der Gruppe H.', Ia Nr. 740/3, 31 March 1917, KAM, XV.BRK 185.

[91] AOK 1 to its Gruppen, Ia Nr. 407 geheim, 22 May 1917, HSAS, Glück Nachlass, M660/091 Bü 16; Paul von Kneußl, unpublished diary, 4 May 1917, KAM, Kneußl Nachlass, Bd. 13.

[92] HDK to OHL, army groups and its AOKs, 'Zusammenstellung einiger Lehren aus der Doppelschlacht Aisne-Champagne', Ic Nr. 2880, 8 June 1917, GLAK, F1/523, 14; Cron, *Geschichte des Deutschen Heeres*, 169.

[93] Reichsarchiv, *Weltkrieg*, 12:5–6 summarises the changes.

A regiment in 5th Guard Infantry Division (Gruppe Liesse) illustrates the firepower that a division's infantry now possessed. In March 1917 it had twenty-four medium and thirty-six light machine guns, eighteen mortars and eighteen grenade throwers.[94] Tactically, the principal new weapon was the light machine gun. The British and French armies were a year ahead of the Germans in the general issue of these weapons. The German type, the MG 08/15, was not universally popular because of various technical compromises between mobility, reliability and effectiveness, but it did substantially raise infantry firepower. The initial plan was to give each company three guns, or thirty-six per regiment. This firepower was explicitly intended to substitute for manpower: once companies had their three guns, battalion strength would be cut.[95] The Guards regiment above was lucky to have its full complement. In early May 1917, only three divisions out of some twenty in Seventh Army had light machine guns. The Army commented that the gun had proved its usefulness and asked to be given priority in allocation. It was told that it would receive all new guns available but supply had stopped because of production difficulties.[96]

Front divisions were also allocated important extra assets, particularly artillery and aviation, to help them take control of the battle as mandated in the new doctrine. Gruppe Liesse's 20th Infantry Division permanently possessed thirty-six field guns and howitzers. As a front division in April and May 1917, it was given an extra seventy-two field and sixty-two heavy guns. It also took command of an air wing and a protective fighter squadron; a further eighteen medium machine guns and thirty-two mortars; one *Landsturm* and one labour battalion for security and construction purposes; and various communications units.[97] It could if necessary be allocated further resources controlled by *Gruppe* or Army, such as the Army's storm battalion. None of these extra assets became part of the division: they were all designated as Army troops and were in principle static [*bodenständig*], remaining in the *Gruppe* or at least Army area when the division was relieved. Given their importance, it would be almost as true to say that infantry divisions were allocated to them as that they were allocated to divisions. Orders of battle show that divisions' main contribution was their staffs, infantry regiments and machine guns.

---

[94] Oberstleutnant a.D. Paul Doerstling, ed., *Kriegsgeschichte des Königlich Preußischen Infanterie-Regiments Graf Tauentzien v. Wittenberg (3. Brandenb.) Nr. 20* (Zeulenroda: Bernhard Sporn, 1933), 722.

[95] Kriegsministerium circular, M.J. 7863/17.A.1, 12 March 1917, GLAK, F1/374.

[96] AOK 7 telegram to HDK, 1a nr. 24/mai 17, 3 May 1917 and HDK reply, 1d 2550, 4 May 1917, both on GLAK, F1/249.

[97] Gruppe Liesse order of battle, 4 May 1917, HSAS, Schall Nachlass, M660/037 Bü 71. The *Landsturm* mainly comprised older men fit for military service but not for combat; the term is usually not translated.

The official line was that the greatly increased firepower now available more than compensated for the decrease in manpower caused by the removal of one of the division's original four regiments and a cut in size of battalions; smaller divisions enabled the creation of more divisions, seen as operationally and psychologically advantageous; and they were easier to transport.[98] The disadvantages were less often mentioned. More divisions, especially independent of corps, meant a greater requirement for good commanders and staff officers, who were at a premium.[99] Above all, battles of matériel proved that increased firepower did not in fact compensate for decreased manpower. To some extent it aggravated the problem, since crews for support weapons such as machine guns largely came from the infantry of the unit concerned. Personnel for other tasks, whether permanent such as communications or temporary such as carrying parties, were also drawn mainly from the infantry. All these deductions from rifle strength and the inevitable casualties caused by battle reduced the infantry's ability to carry out their core tasks of holding ground and making counter-attacks.[100]

The result was a constant need to reinforce the front divisions piecemeal during a battle. This could only be achieved by drawing on the counter-attack divisions held behind the front, and the process could reach extreme proportions. In May 1917, 11th Bavarian Infantry Division was a counter-attack division in Gruppe Liesse. Kneußl recorded that of its three infantry and one field artillery regiments, all except one artillery detachment [*Abteilung*] were in Army or *Gruppe* reserve, or at the disposal of one of the front divisions; then his final detachment was taken for *Gruppe* reserve too.[101] There were examples of counter-attacks in regimental strength or more during the Entente spring offensive, but Wynne's picture of counter-attack divisions ready for action as a single formation on the issuing of a codeword is exaggerated. The term *Eingreifdivision*, in the spring battles at least, was a misnomer: other terms used at this period, such as relief division [*Ablösungsdivision*], reinforcement division [*Verstärkungsdivision*] and Army battle reserve, were in many ways more accurate.[102]

---

[98] Curt von Morgen, *Meiner Truppen Heldenkämpfe* (Berlin: E. S. Mittler, 1920), 142; Tappen, 'Kriegserinnerungen', f. 35.

[99] Gallwitz, *Erleben im Westen*, 98.

[100] Morgen, *Meiner Truppen Heldenkämpfe*, 141; Stachelbeck, *Militärische Effektivität*, 210.

[101] Kneußl diary, 5 May 1917. In this context, an *Abteilung* was a battalion-level unit in the field artillery.

[102] Wynne, *If Germany Attacks*, 128 and 150; 'Einleitender Vortrag des Kursleiters', lecture to a divisional command course in Sedan, [n.d. but probably early April 1917], HSAS, Urach Nachlass, GU117 Bü 362, 9; Reichsarchiv, *Weltkrieg*, 13:53.

It is undoubtedly true that divisions gained in independence at this time, as well as being strengthened by measures such as the allocation of a staff to command the engineer units.[103] But there were definite limits to this independence. Most obviously, divisions were still operating under the command of *Gruppen*. Indeed, a division might be subject to more than one authority at the same time: on 9 April 1917, 26th Infantry Division came under Sixth Army for tactical matters, Gruppe A for quartering and supply and its parent XIII Corps for remaining issues.[104] Second, there were some formal restrictions on divisions' tactical authority. In particular, as we saw decisions to evacuate positions were to be taken by the Army or *Gruppe* except in emergency.[105] Finally, even a division's ability to intervene in the battle was limited, not least by communications problems. Infantry regimental histories make clear the extent to which fighting, especially in the front line, was a matter of companies or at most battalions. Recognition of this reality lay behind the introduction of new arrangements for forward control of the battle whereby one officer, usually a battalion commander, took responsibility for all aspects of his sector as combat troop commander [*Kampftruppenkommandeur*, KTK].[106]

Case Study

A description of German command preparations for the battle against the French will show how the principles of the *Schwerpunkt* and maintaining the chain of command contributed to fulfilling the first command task in 1917. These preparations were guided by intelligence and military judgement on what the French were planning. Once OHL had formed an assessment of the nature and extent of the coming French assault, including where the French *Schwerpunkt* was, it began a major programme to strengthen the threatened sector by improving command arrangements, bringing up reinforcements and developing fixed defences.

At the highest level, Seventh Army moved into Army Group Crown Prince and Army Detachment C moved out to the new Army Group Albrecht. This gave Army Group Crown Prince control of the whole threatened sector and by removing some subsidiary areas allowed it to focus on the coming battle. OHL decided that command arrangements on the Aisne needed further strengthening by deploying First Army's headquarters, freed up by the withdrawal to the Hindenburg Line, to

[103] Kriegsministerium circular, 'Pionierformationen', Nr. 105/17.g.A6, 24 January 1917, BArch, PH2/500, ff. 111–16.
[104] 26.ID war diary, 9 April 1917, HSAS, Urach Nachlass, GU117 Bü 376.
[105] '*Abwehrschlacht*', March 1917, 6.   [106] Wynne, *If Germany Attacks*, 84.

take over part of the sector. The official history gives the reason as the great length of the threatened front, but this may be disingenuous.[107] First Army was inserted between Seventh and Third Armies and took over three of their *Gruppen*. Seventh Army still had a central role in the impending battle, but Third Army's involvement was now limited to part of one *Gruppe* only: this raises the question whether OHL was deliberately sidelining it.

Whatever the truth of this, if an extra Army headquarters was needed there were good reasons to choose First Army. Its command team comprised *General der Infanterie* Fritz von Below and Fritz von Loßberg, who had fought the battle of the Somme together and had the most up-to-date experience of a defensive battle. Boehn, commanding Seventh Army on their right, had served under them on the Somme as a corps commander; his chief of staff, *Oberstleutnant* Walther Reinhardt, had worked for Loßberg in the first months of the war (and had the added advantage of being an expert on the French army).[108] Loßberg had been chief of staff to *Generaloberst* Karl von Einem of Third Army, the left-hand neighbour, during the Champagne battle of autumn 1915: he knew both the area and Einem well. This would have been a strong team but the plan was disrupted in the panic after the initial defeat at Arras. OHL considered whether the headquarters of Sixth Army, controlling the battle there, was reliable or should be replaced by First Army. In the event a half-measure was adopted: Sixth Army's chief of staff was replaced by Loßberg, and Below went on down to the Aisne with First Army. Loßberg insisted on taking with him his operations officer (the *Ia*), meaning that First Army was deprived of two of its top general staff officers just before engagement in a major battle in a new area.[109]

Nor did the disruption stop there. First Army's removal from Army Group Rupprecht entailed redistributing its subordinate *Gruppen* to the neighbouring Armies. By then two other *Gruppe* headquarters in the army group had been replaced, apparently because of concerns about their competence.[110] Adding to the disruption, Seventh Army only moved fully into Army Group Crown Prince on 12 April, and First Army did not take over command of its new sector until 16 April – respectively four days before and the actual day of the French assault. To make matters worse, one of First Army's *Gruppen*, Gruppe Aisne, was newly created to ensure integrated command in a crucial area of the front,

---

[107] Reichsarchiv, *Weltkrieg*, 12:292.   [108] Grawe, *Deutsche Feindaufklärung*, 185.
[109] Kuhl, 'Kriegstagebuch', 11 April 1917; Fritz von Loßberg, *Meine Tätigkeit im Weltkriege 1914–1918* (Berlin: E. S. Mittler, 1939), 281.
[110] Reichsarchiv, *Weltkrieg*, 12:195; Xylander diary, 12 January and 19 March 1917.

only taking over its sector on 17 April.[111] Summing up these complex moves, in the two weeks leading up to and including the British and French assaults, command reorganisations disrupted all three army groups, six Armies or Army Detachments and ten *Gruppen* in the front line – and by bad luck, some of this was going on during full-scale battle.

Lower down the chain of command, as of early February there were twelve German divisions in the Aisne-western Champagne sector, organised in four *Gruppen*; by mid-April the total, including formations still arriving, was forty-three divisions in eight *Gruppen*. Artillery and aviation assets had increased in parallel. These forces were deployed on the basis of the assessed French *Schwerpunkt*, with heavier concentrations in areas judged particularly favourable to a French advance – part of the Gruppe Vailly area covering the hinge of the German line at Condé and offering the shortest route to Laon (a centre for headquarters, quartering troops, logistics and transport); the flat land of Gruppe Sissonne where the French were expected to deploy tanks for the first time; and parts of the neighbouring Gruppe Brimont where captured documents revealed the French assault plan in detail.[112]

This case study shows the application of the *Schwerpunkt* concept in a 1917 defensive context, even though the word itself was little used. It also shows the importance accorded by the German army to creating the best possible chain of command, despite the disruption entailed, and how this linked to the defensive *Schwerpunkt*. The resulting concentration of forces and effective command arrangements contributed to the rapid defeat of the French breakthrough attempt.

Conclusions

Schwerpunkt and maintaining the chain of command were traditional principles evolved to meet the requirement for control in the first command task, co-ordinating a mass army, in mobile war when the Germans expected to take the offensive. They proved equally relevant in the static warfare of 1917, in which the German army stood on the defensive. However, the organisation through which they were implemented had greatly changed. Of the four command levels covered by this book, the army group system reached maturity from autumn 1916 and contributed to the defeat of the Entente spring offensive. Armies were probably the level least changed by the war and wherever possible retained

---

[111] Reichsarchiv, *Weltkrieg*, 12:292.
[112] AOK 7 telegram to HDK, Ia nr. 17/April 17, [n.d.], GLAK, F1/250; Reichsarchiv, *Weltkrieg*, 12:291 and 295.

responsibility for fighting individual battles. Corps and divisions were both radically altered, though the effects have often been misunderstood in the secondary literature: despite devolution of tactical control to divisions, corps/*Gruppen* remained central to the conduct of battle.

Some of these changes and the problems underlying them had been discussed pre-war. There had been debate since the days of Moltke the Elder on whether the corps or division should be the main unit of battle.[113] Schlieffen was concerned about how to co-ordinate Armies, fearing their commanders would engage in a 'wild chase after the *Pour le Mérite*' at the expense of the overall plan.[114] This vividly expresses the difficulty of striking the right balance between the two elements of the first command task, decentralisation and control. It is no coincidence that most of the organisational changes in this chapter took place in 1916–17, reflecting the problems of fulfilling the first command task in battles of matériel. The British and French armies were forced to adopt similar expedients, particularly changes to the role of corps, and for the same reasons.

The areas of authority of different levels in the chain of command were not always clearly delineated, partly because of the sheer number of headquarters in a restricted area. The factors limiting mission command described earlier also had an effect, especially the ease with which superior commanders and staff could intervene. In addition, the actual as opposed to 'constitutional' authority of any particular formation was contingent on both events and personalities. First Army under Fritz von Below and Loßberg was a more influential formation than, say, Sixth Army under Falkenhausen and Nagel zu Aichberg. The crisis of 9 April greatly raised the importance of Sixth Army. It also led to the arrival of Loßberg and Otto von Below in command, which in turn boosted the influence of the Army – until the next crisis saw the removal of Loßberg to Fourth Army in Flanders, now the epicentre of the Western Front, and the creation of a new locus of power. These shifts reflect moves of the defensive *Schwerpunkt* too.

The actual authority of a particular formation strengthened what can be called its robber baron instincts. The tendency of army groups to develop and follow their own interests occurred throughout the army. As we will see later, such departmentalism [*Ressortegoismus* or *Ressortpartikularismus*] could lead to insistence, justified or not, on doing things 'our way' and reluctance to accept external ideas as 'not invented

---

[113] Moltke, 'Memoire an Seine Majestät den König vom 25. Juli 1868', 155–9.
[114] Görlitz, *Deutsche Generalstab*, 221.

here'.[115] It was an old problem. Clausewitz remarked that commanders often assumed ownership of their troops and resisted giving up any part of them even for a short time. The conflict between the Great General Staff and Ministry of War is well known; the different arms of service feuded about new technology and tactics; and as noted above corps commanders were supreme in their own realms.[116] These tensions continued into the war. Chapter 7 records vituperative remarks by Kneußl, an infantryman, against the artillery. Fritz von Below and Loßberg were so influential that First Army's Somme report was treated as semi-doctrinal even though in some aspects it contradicted actual doctrine. Höhn was a senior general and had played a central role in developing the new defensive doctrine. This is why as a *Gruppe* commander he was able to adopt the controversial tactic of large-scale counterattack from the rear, even though experience since 1915 had proved it was highly likely to fail.

***

The first command task – co-ordinating a mass army – involved the old problem of striking the right balance between decentralisation and control. Under 1917 conditions the dial was moving towards greater control. The German army fulfilled this command task well against the French through timely concentration of forces and effective command arrangements. It was less successful at Arras, where for reasons explained in Chapter 5 the defensive concentration was not complete when the British attacked. A further cause of the initial defeat there – as later at Messines – was Army Group Rupprecht's failure to impose its will on the local Army: in other words it struck the wrong balance between decentralisation and control. As these different results suggest, the outcome of the first command task was subject to a complex interplay of principles, formal responsibilities, events and in particular personal influence, which fundamentally affected it.

---

[115] I am grateful to Major General (retd) Mungo Melvin for his advice on the German terms in this paragraph and elsewhere.

[116] Clausewitz, *On War*, book 5, chapter 5, 294; Mombauer, *Moltke*, 41; Brose, *Kaiser's Army*, 5–6.

4   Personality

> You don't need to be an eminent historian to understand the impact of personality upon history, but it is a, perhaps the, key element of command.[1]

German military thinkers had long recognised the influence of the personal factor on command. Moltke the Elder stressed that although in peacetime the moral element seldom came into play, 'in war the qualities of the character are more important than those of the intellect'. He adapted his orders to the personality of the recipient: the less he trusted the commander to act correctly on his own initiative, the more binding the order.[2] Nor was it just a question of the individual officer, as good personal relationships were recognised to be essential for the efficient working of a headquarters.[3] One of the general staff's top military historians, *Oberstleutnant* (later *General der Infanterie*) Hugo Freiherr von Freytag-Loringhoven, had published a book on the power of personality shortly before the war to draw together Clausewitz's thoughts on the subject.[4]

The second command task, selecting the right men, was therefore important in itself and closely linked to the first. The loss of Fresnoy described in the previous chapter shows how failure to fulfil the second task had a direct effect on the battlefield, even in a war of masses and matériel. Sixth Army believed that the formation responsible, 15th Reserve Division, had made serious mistakes. Its commander, *Generalleutnant* Leo Limbourg, was a heavy artillery [*Fußartillerie*] officer

---

[1] General Sir John McColl, 'Modern Campaigning: From a Practitioner's Perspective', in Jonathan Bailey, Richard Iron and Hew Strachan, eds., *British Generals in Blair's Wars* (Farnham: Ashgate, 2013), 110.

[2] Helmuth von Moltke, 'Verordnungen für die höheren Truppenführer vom 24. Juni 1869', in Großer Generalstab, ed., *Moltkes Militärische Werke*, vol. 2, pt 2, 171; Hughes, *Moltke*, 12.

[3] Otto von Moser, *Die Führung des Armeekorps im Feldkriege* (Berlin: E. S. Mittler, 1910), 15–16.

[4] Oberstleutnant Hugo Freiherr von Freytag-Loringhoven, *Die Macht der Persönlichkeit im Kriege: Studien nach Clausewitz* (Berlin: E. S. Mittler, 1905).

who was well-regarded but new to divisional command. He had not been properly supported during the battle by his general staff officer, who had collapsed under the pressure. In addition the infantry brigade commander, *Generalmajor* Justus Roeder, was a retired officer, re-employed after the outbreak of war in home service, recently arrived and in action for the first time. Roeder and his adjutant, a reserve cavalry officer, had not exercised proper control over the brigade. To cap everything, a regimental and a battalion commander had failed in action. The end result was that the battalion ordered to make an immediate counter-attack did not move forward. The counter-attack which was eventually mounted was overhasty, badly prepared and unsuccessful. At this point the Army took control, as recounted in the previous chapter.[5]

Clearly personnel selection of commanders and staff officers at Fresnoy had been poor. Historians have been divided about the German army's handling of the second command task, reflecting the argument outlined in the Introduction as to whether it was a thinking institution. For Martin Kitchen, the army's constant attempts to avoid becoming more liberal or democratic distorted its officer selection policies. In contrast, David T. Zabecki believes that there was a traditional command principle in which function overrode rank: the most suitable officer could be put into any post regardless of his rank and automatically assumed the authority of the post.[6] What was the reality of the selection system?

Personnel Selection: Seniority Tempered by Merit

Selection of officers for posts was a major aspect of overall command, stemming from the top. Indeed, personal appointments were the crucial point of the Kaiser's power.[7] He exercised this power through the Military Cabinet, which was very much part of his personal fiefdom as illustrated by its wartime title 'The Military Cabinet of His Majesty the Kaiser and King'.[8] It was originally part of the Ministry of War but became independent in 1883. Under Wilhelm II, it was the subject of increasing political controversy as part of his attempts to extend his absolutist right of command [*Kommandogewalt*] outside parliamentary scrutiny. Its

---

[5] Otto von Below diary, 3 and 4 May 1917; AOK 6 memorandum, 'Meldung über Fahrt mit Oberbefehlshaber zur Gruppe Vimy, 15.R.D. und Gruppe Arras am 4.5.17', 6 May 1917, KAM, AOK 6 Bd. 369.

[6] Kitchen, *German Officer Corps*, 30–1; Zabecki, *Chief of Staff*, 1:12.

[7] Holger Afflerbach, 'Wilhelm II as Supreme Warlord in the First World War', *War in History*, vol. 5, no. 4 (1998), 448.

[8] Oberst a.D. von Rodenberg, 'Militär-Kabinett', in General der Infanterie a.D. Ernst von Eisenhart Rothe, ed., *Ehrendenkmal der deutschen Armee und Marine 1871–1918* (Berlin: Deutscher National-Verlag, 1926), 52.

head – from 1908 Moriz von Lyncker – was the senior General Adjutant to the Kaiser and ranked as a corps commander, with all the status that implied. One *Reichstag* [parliament] deputy described him as the most powerful man in the Empire.[9] This was an exaggeration, but the head of the cabinet was undoubtedly influential, not least because almost every family of high standing in Germany had one or more members in the military and the cabinet's decisions therefore affected them all. Promotion at higher levels was very competitive and even one mistake at manoeuvres could be grounds for dismissal. In such an atmosphere, it is not hard to see why the Military Cabinet was feared and resented.[10]

Nevertheless, the cabinet's power was limited by four structural factors. First, it was small. Before the war, it had some nine officers and thirty-eight military officials.[11] It was divided into two departments, with one handling appointments, promotions and so on, and the other the award of decorations and military ceremonies. This organisation had long been thought inadequate to the growing workload, but the *Reichstag* had refused a proposal to add a third department, ostensibly on cost grounds. Even by 1917, and faced with the burden of a world war and hugely expanded army, the cabinet had only eleven officers and sixteen officials serving at GHQ, with another section in Berlin.[12]

As senior General Adjutant and head of the Military Cabinet, Lyncker was in effect private secretary to the Kaiser. This role took up so much time that he had to delegate most of the personnel work to his deputy, reserving to himself the right to propose the most senior appointments. As this delegation increased during the war, the deputy, *Oberst* Ulrich Freiherr von Marschall gen. Greiff, was given the title 'Head of the Personnel Office in the Military Cabinet' [*Chef des Personalamts im Militärkabinett*].[13] This change also made sense in personality terms:

[9] Rudolf Schmidt-Bückeburg, *Das Militärkabinett der preußischen Könige und deutschen Kaiser: Seine geschichtliche Entwicklung und staatsrechtliche Stellung 1787–1918* (Berlin: E. S. Mittler, 1933), 238.

[10] Afflerbach, *Kaiser Wilhelm II. als Oberster Kriegsherr*, 70–1.

[11] Königliches Ministerium des Innern [Royal Ministry of the Interior], *Adreß-Kalender für die Königl. Haupt- und Residenzstädte Berlin und Potsdam sowie Charlottenburg auf das Jahr 1914* (Berlin: Carl Heymanns Verlag, 1914), 40–1. In the German army, many staff dealing with matters such as administration, logistics, finance and justice were military officials rather than officers or soldiers.

[12] GHQ Telegraphendirektion, 'Verzeichnis der Fernsprechteilnehmer im Grossen Hauptquartier. Stand Mai 1917', BArch, PH3/4, 25. No information on the Berlin section has come to light. GHQ [*Großes Hauptquartier*] was the Kaiser's General Headquarters. Its main component was OHL, and by 1917 other departments included the Military, Naval and Civil Cabinets, together with representatives of the Ministry of War, the Foreign Office, allies and Bavaria, Saxony and Württemberg: Cron, *Geschichte des Deutschen Heeres*, 3–7.

[13] GHQ Telegraphendirektion, 'Verzeichnis der Fernsprechteilnehmer', 25.

Marschall was widely seen as industrious, well-informed, shrewd and possibly more intellectually able than Lyncker, whom he replaced in July 1918.[14]

The second structural factor was the actual system for personnel selection, seniority tempered by merit. The Military Cabinet was in charge of this but it was by no means the only player. Its basic management tool was the confidential report. The cabinet managed but did not write these reports. That was the task of the subject officer's chain of command, which was outside the cabinet's control. The cabinet's role in selection was to propose appointments to the Kaiser, who then made the decision. In most cases, of course, he simply accepted the proposal, but where he had a personal interest in the post concerned, for instance command of the Guard Corps, whatever the cabinet said, he insisted on having men he liked appointed.[15]

The third constraint was that the general staff handled the personnel affairs of its officers, and the Military Cabinet only had broad oversight.[16] The organisation responsible was OHL's Central Department [Zentralabteilung], which was directly subordinate to the Chief of the General Staff. By May 1917, the department numbered four officers and seventeen officials.[17] Like the Military Cabinet, it had a huge workload, dealing not just with the selection and hasty training of the large numbers of new general staff officers required, but also with a wide range of non-personnel affairs. The examples quoted in this chapter show that the department operated similar policies and mechanisms to the Military Cabinet. It may have placed slightly more weight on merit than seniority, but it certainly did not ignore seniority and was subject to the same external influences as the Military Cabinet. Indeed, its first wartime head was criticised for favouring noble or Guards officers, one of the main complaints made against the Military Cabinet.[18]

The final structural constraint on the power of the Military Cabinet was the federal nature of the German *Reich,* in particular the Bavarian and Saxon contingents' right to handle their own personnel affairs. The available evidence suggests they used much the same procedures as the Prussians, but this was nevertheless a limitation on the Military Cabinet's powers and of course on the free appointment of officers across the army. With rare exceptions, only Bavarian and Saxon officers held command and general staff positions in their respective corps and

[14] Afflerbach, *Kaiser Wilhelm II. als Oberster Kriegsherr,* 77.
[15] Schmidt-Bückeburg, *Militärkabinett,* 230.   [16] Rodenberg, 'Militär-Kabinett', 62.
[17] GHQ Telegraphendirektion, 'Verzeichnis der Fernsprechteilnehmer', 12.
[18] Epkenhans, *Nicolai,* 233. For criticism of the Military Cabinet's favouring nobles and rebuttal, see Rodenberg, 'Militär-Kabinett', 61–3.

divisions.[19] Nor could broader federal issues be ignored. The Military Cabinet selected *Oberstleutnant* (later *General der Infanterie*) Martin Chales de Beaulieu to command the infantry regiment based in the capital of the federal Duchy of Sachsen-Meiningen because he had been the Hereditary Prince's adjutant and would be well received there. Such local issues mattered even during the war: *Major* Walther Obkircher believed he had been selected as operations officer in XV Corps because the commander, *General der Infanterie* Berthold von Deimling, was notoriously difficult and the fact that both were from Baden might ease the relationship.[20]

The reorganisation of the Fourth Army command team after the defeat at Messines described in Chapter 2 illustrates the interplay between these structural issues and non-structural ones. To recap, factors that had to be considered included the Kaiser's refusal to sack the Army commander, dynastic tensions, various personality issues relating to creating the best team and the 'public relations' aspects of Messines. The prime reason for the reorganisation was the external fact of the battle, and the end result was a compromise between the various interests involved, including the Kaiser, the Military Cabinet, OHL and the individual officers concerned, many of whom were senior and influential figures who could not simply be deployed willy-nilly. One side effect of such changes was often a chain of personnel moves, avoided in this case as Fritz von Loßberg and Max Stapff simply swapped jobs as Fourth and Sixth Army chiefs of staff. But when *Generaloberst* Richard von Schubert was sacked from the command of Seventh Army, the resulting chain reached down to brigade level at least.

The German army had adopted seniority tempered by merit as its principle for appointing and promoting officers in the early nineteenth century.[21] It is easy to condemn seniority as a primary criterion in personnel selection. As the British Admiral Sir John Fisher put it, 'Going by seniority saves so much trouble. "Buggins's turn" has been our ruin and will be disastrous hereafter!'[22] However, selection by seniority did have

---

[19] Discussed fully in Cowan, 'A Picture of German Unity?'; see also Gavin Wiens, 'Guardians and Go-betweens: Germany's Military Plenipotentiaries during the First World War', *Journal of Military History*, vol. 86, no. 2 (April 2022), 369.

[20] Martin Chales de Beaulieu, 'Erinnerungen aus meinem Leben', unpublished manuscript in BArch, Chales de Beaulieu Nachlass, N187/2, 91 and N187/3, 166; Walther Obkircher, 'Achtzehn Monate Generalstabsoffizier Ia/XV. Armeekorps', unpublished manuscript in BArch, Obkircher Nachlass, N2214/65, 16.

[21] Militärgeschichtliches Forschungsamt, *Ancienniät und Beförderung nach Leistung*, 131–9 describes development of the personnel reporting and selection system from 1808 to 1918.

[22] Admiral Sir John Fisher to the Earl of Selborne, 13 January 1901, in Arthur J. Marder, ed., *Fear God and Dread Nought: The Correspondence of Admiral of the Fleet Lord Fisher of*

advantages, including clarity and simplicity; also, it could be key in determining the chain of command if two officers were of equal rank. Its impersonality was a defence against possibly arbitrary selection methods and especially against favouritism. It emphasised the importance of experience too.[23] As we have seen, under wartime conditions, lack of experience became a growing concern. But the army had long recognised that though experience was a necessary precondition of successful command, it was not sufficient. Or as Frederick the Great put it, 'If experience were all a great general needs, the greatest would be Prince Eugene's mules.'[24]

Seniority clearly had to be tempered with merit, which should be measured as objectively as possible, again to avoid favouritism. The problem was how to define merit. Attempts to do so, as in the regulations for confidential reports, tended to throw in everything but the kitchen sink:

There must be a clear statement about which of the many characteristics requisite for success are possessed to a particularly high degree by the individual officers. These include a firm will, thirst for action, the courage to take responsibility, self-confidence, prudence, imagination, judgement of character, self-denial and many others in addition to knowledge and ability as well as good health.[25]

A central difficulty in looking for merit was assessing how officers would react under the pressures of war, almost impossible to test in peacetime. Moltke the Elder's point that in war character is more important than intellect hints at the problem. People who are good in peacetime function well in hierarchies, those who are good in war, in chaos; the two types have been aptly called regulators and ratcatchers.[26]

As in many armies, the confidential personal report [*Qualifikationsbericht*] was the mechanism used by the Military Cabinet to assess merit and the

Kilverstone, vol. 1, *The Making of an Admiral 1854–1904* (London: Jonathan Cape, 1952), 181.

[23] Aimée Fox, 'The Secret of Efficiency? Social Relations and Patronage in the British Army in the Era of the First World War', *English Historical Review*, vol. 135, no. 577 (December 2020), 1535 and 1537.

[24] Karl Demeter, *The German Officer-Corps in Society and State 1650–1945*, trans. Angus Malcolm (London: Weidenfeld and Nicolson, 1965), 68.

[25] Kriegsministerium, *D.V.E. Nr.291. Bestimmungen über Personal- und Qualifikations-Berichte (P. u. Q. Best.) vom 19. Juni 1902* (Berlin: Reichsdruckerei, 1902), Anlage 1a (hereafter '*Qualifikations-Berichte*'). This annex is a memorandum from the Kaiser dated 2 January 1912.

[26] John Bourne, 'Hiring and Firing in the BEF on the Western Front, 1914–1918', paper to the military history seminar of the Institute of Historical Research, 6 October 2009; Andrew Gordon, 'Ratcatchers and Regulators at the Battle of Jutland', in Gary Sheffield and Geoffrey Till, eds., *The Challenges of High Command: The British Experience* (Basingstoke: Palgrave Macmillan, 2003), 26–33. Gordon got the idea of 'ratcatchers' from a quote by Admiral Sir Walter Cowan (no relation, sadly).

basis for all its personnel selection.[27] Regulations laid down that without being unnecessarily critical, reports were to describe an officer concisely and objectively. They must then reach clear conclusions about his performance and suitability for promotion. How well the reporting officer carried out this task was itself a significant indicator for his own report; in fact, one often learned more from a report about the reporting officer than the subject. Officers further up the chain of command were to add comments, or in modern terms, to countersign. The subject of a report did not see its contents, though he could be informed orally of them. In principle, reports were submitted every two years. However, officers falling into certain categories were to be registered on one or more of seventeen lists and to be reported on yearly. These included officers under consideration for accelerated promotion or special employment such as the general staff, 'higher adjutancy' and Ministry of War; and also officers not fit for active service, not doing their job properly or not suitable for promotion. Every four years, a report containing an officer's personal details [*Personal-Bericht*] was also to be submitted. Reports were kept for six years, and forwarded to the officer's new unit if he moved.[28]

This carefully structured system was evidently taken seriously and conscientious reporting officers agonised over the process for weeks.[29] But the system was by no means perfect. Following Moltke the Elder's views quoted earlier, the regulations strongly emphasised character over intellect. They omitted expertise in technology and all-arms co-operation, both crucial to modern operations. It was necessary to have a reason for submitting different comments from the preceding reporting officer, so some officers either followed the previous report or wrote nothing meaningful – an incentive to groupthink.[30] *Generalmajor* Gerold von Gleich thought that reports hardly distinguished between officers and tended to praise more than criticise:

Almost every battalion commander was a 'talented, extremely zealous officer, who trained his battalion very conscientiously and successfully, was an excellent influence on his officers, possessed good tactical understanding, did his job well and was suitable for promotion'.[31]

---

[27] 'Qualifikations-Berichte', 1.

[28] 'Qualifikations-Berichte', 2–4, 9, 12–14, 18 and 20–1; Schoenaich, *Mein Damaskus*, 61. The higher adjutancy covered adjutant posts from brigade level upwards.

[29] Otto von Below, 'Lebenserinnerungen. Bd. 8: Brigadezeit', unpublished manuscript in BArch, Otto von Below Nachlass, N87/44, 633–4.

[30] 'Qualifikations-Berichte', 11 (which listed competencies to be demonstrated by officers at different levels) and 20a; Schoenaich, *Mein Damaskus*, 107–8.

[31] Gleich, *Die alte Armee*, 81–2.

Such superficiality aroused official concern, and in 1912 a new annex to the regulations ordered reporting officers to make improvements in this area. But whatever was in the written report, the reporting officer could always add criticism orally. Countersigning officers did not necessarily know the subject of the report well enough to assess the original judgements.[32]

As the product of a human organisation, the reporting and selection system was of course also influenced by various non-objective factors. For a start, the reporting officer or subject might use any influence they had in the Military Cabinet to affect the result of the report. Cavalry officer Paul Freiherr von Schoenaich was convinced that he had Fritz von Below, whom he knew well, to thank for a favourable report which qualified him for the higher adjutancy; and his brigade and regimental commanders for a subsequent even more favourable qualification for the Ministry of War. This in turn secured him a greatly accelerated promotion to *Major*.[33] Senior commanders might insist on particular officers being allocated to their staffs, a clear case being Max von Gallwitz and *Oberst* Bernhard Bronsart von Schellendorff at Fifth Army in late 1916, discussed later in this chapter.

The confidential reporting system remained the basis for personnel decisions during wartime and indeed was tightened up. From 1915, reports were called for every year and could also be specially requested [*außerterminlich*]. Increasingly, they became a precondition for personnel moves. In May 1917, *Generalleutnants* Fritz von Unger and Leopold von Stocken were in the frame for selection as corps commanders, but this could not happen unless reports based on the recent fighting clearly showed their suitability.[34] Doubts whether senior officers were up to their jobs were to be stated unconditionally in their reports, since this was the only way in which the Military Cabinet could propose to the Kaiser the removal of inadequate officers. Ludendorff particularly disliked the habit of describing officers as suitable for a quiet sector, because anywhere could rapidly become an attack front. Officers were to be described as doing their jobs properly in all respects or not.[35]

Reporting was also linked more closely to tactical requirements. As explained in Chapter 2, during the 1917 spring fighting corps and Armies were ordered to assess the combat performance of each division, its

---

[32] Gleich, *Die alte Armee*, 82–3; '*Qualifikations-Berichte*', Anlage 1a.

[33] Schoenaich, *Mein Damaskus*, 50–1.

[34] Oberstleutnant Max Holland (Württemberg representative in the Military Cabinet) to Duke Albrecht, 29 May 1917, AHW, Herzog Albrecht Nachlass, G331/549 and 8 September 1918, AHW, G331/548.

[35] OHL circular, II Nr. 70131 op., 14 November 1917, KAM, HKR neue Nr. 382.

commander and its *Ia*; if the division had performed poorly, the reports should suggest remedial action. Separate assessments were to be submitted on general staff officers who had distinguished themselves or shown that they were not fit for their jobs. Ability in conducting combined arms battle became a topic of reporting: one reason given for removing *Generalmajor* Guido Sontag from command of 111th Infantry Division during the battle of Arras was that he was not properly integrating action by all elements of the division. Indeed, OHL stressed the need for general staff officers to have a good knowledge of the different arms of service and technical means. As we have seen, it backed this up with improved training of new general staff officers in these areas.[36]

Reporting officers continued to take their duties seriously. When Gallwitz was rushed down to Verdun in December 1916, he made sure he finished the confidential reports before going.[37] Nevertheless the results of the system were mixed. Gallwitz and Crown Prince Rupprecht both thought that the size of the army and rapid turnover of divisions made reporting based on detailed knowledge of subordinates increasingly difficult.[38] There was a concern that too much weight was given to negative reports hastily written while still under the psychological effects of battle.[39] However, Gleich, an infantry brigade commander at Arras, took precisely the opposite view. He believed that the weaknesses he had mentioned were even more prominent in wartime. Reports increasingly became a collection of superlatives, especially as it was more difficult for countersigning and other officers to check them.[40] Many surviving examples support this view. In a typical case, *Hauptmann* Kurt Spemann, *Ia* of 5th Infantry Division, was described as energetic, industrious, unassuming, popular, with outstanding strategic and tactical flair as well as thorough knowledge of all arms. He was an excellent general staff officer and support for his divisional commander (who wrote the report); the final sentence was the formal statement that he did his job satisfactorily and was fit for promotion.[41]

Ludendorff found that many oral criticisms of senior commanders were not subsequently backed up in written reports, making changes in command more difficult to implement.[42] Also, despite his strictures, reports

---

[36] OHL Zentralabteilung to HKR, M.J. Nr. 53635, 5 June 1917; AOK 6 to Chef des Militär-Kabinetts, IIa. Nr. 129 g., 19 April 1917; OHL circular, 'Kriegführung und Generalstab'; all on KAM, HKR neue Nr. 378.
[37] Gallwitz, *Erleben im Westen*, 147.
[38] Ibid., 202; Rupprecht, unpublished diary, 2 November 1916.
[39] Rodenberg, 'Militär-Kabinett', 59.   [40] Gleich, *Die alte Armee*, 83–4.
[41] 'Qualifikationsbericht zum Dezember 16 über den K.W. Hauptmann Kurt Spemann im Gen. Stab der 5. Inf. Div.', n.d., HSAS, M430/2 Bü 2044. The M430 series of personal files contains many similar confidential reports.
[42] OHL circular, Nr. 2376 persönlich, [n.d.] September 1917, KAM, HKR neue Nr. 378.

continued to recommend officers as fit for service on quiet fronts even if not for major battle. When Schubert was removed from command of Seventh Army in March 1917, Rupprecht reported him as not able to withstand the pressures of a major defensive battle but suitable to be an Army commander on a quiet front. Friedrich Graf Schulenburg believed that the German army was not ruthless enough in getting rid of such officers, who often re-emerged in positions of command, only to fail again; the British and French were much better at dealing with this problem.[43]

The Military Cabinet's work during the war was the subject of bitter complaint within the army. Ludendorff criticised it for sticking too closely to its peacetime templates for personnel selection, a contributory factor being that its chiefs did not have active service experience.[44] Freytag-Loringhoven agreed, adding that too many senior generals emerged from the 1st Foot Guard Regiment. Some were competent to do their jobs, but many had been chosen instead of better-qualified officers. (This was rich coming from someone who admitted he himself had benefitted from his Guards provenance.)[45] *Oberst* Max Bauer, the influential wartime head of Second Section in OHL's Operations Department, accused Lyncker of opposing almost all improvements to the promotion system, which as a result was unbelievably ossified. It was almost impossible to reward capable officers by accelerated promotion, or to get rid of overaged and reactionary generals.[46] Echoing Schulenburg's complaints about the superannuated commander cadre, Albrecht von Thaer thought there should be no question in such times of sticking to seniority and dates of promotion warrants. There were many 'clever dogs' [*fixe Hunde*] in regiments and rather than letting them be killed off, they should replace the 'good old generals' who were out of date and no longer up to their jobs.[47]

Former members of the Military Cabinet naturally rebutted many of these criticisms, and at least one important outsider also defended it – Hindenburg, an old friend of Lyncker. He claimed that Lyncker had done everything possible to fit personnel selection to the demands of the war. His only other yardstick for appointments was an unbending fairness. In both peace and war, personnel decisions were based on the proposals of the next higher level of command, and all senior positions were staffed in

[43] Kuhl, 'Kriegstagebuch', 1 March 1917; Schulenburg, 'Erlebnisse', 250.

[44] Ludendorff, *My War Memories*, 262.

[45] General der Infanterie a.D. Hugo Freiherr von Freytag-Loringhoven, *Menschen und Dinge wie ich sie in meinem Leben sah* (Berlin: E. S. Mittler, 1923), 74 and 275–6.

[46] Oberst Max Bauer, *Der große Krieg in Feld und Heimat*, 3rd ed. (Tübingen: Osiander'sche Buchhandlung, 1922), 78.

[47] Thaer, *Generalstabsdienst*, 30. Note the similarity of Thaer's phrase to 'ratcatchers' earlier.

agreement with OHL.[48] Indeed, it was said after the war that the Kaiser could not even appoint a divisional commander against OHL's will.[49]

One of the major criticisms of the Military Cabinet's personnel policies during the war was that it placed too much emphasis on maintaining the existing rank structures and lists for when peace was restored. Both Lyncker and Marschall were personally accused of excessive conservatism in this area, including out of concern for maintaining the homogeneity of the officer corps as a class.[50] In the first place, such thinking assumed that there would be a rapid victorious peace and return to normality. But even in 1917–18 when this optimism had dissipated, many organisations were planning for peace. Walter Nicolai held meetings to examine arrangements for the intelligence and press services in peacetime, and subsequently briefed the navy and Ludendorff on the outcome. The Ministry of War worked up plans for demobilisation, remobilisation in the event of another war and even a Victory Museum. And as late as 2 November 1918, the Bavarian army was drafting arguments against creating a centralised military administration in peacetime.[51] So the Military Cabinet was not alone in its mistaken planning for peace, a reminder of the easily forgotten truth that we know Germany would lose the war but the Germans at the time did not.[52]

Personnel Selection: The Role of Sacking

The need to remove officers such as Schubert could be seen either as a failure of the personnel system that had retained them, or more positively as an essential precondition to getting the right men into the right jobs. It was in fact a design feature of seniority tempered by merit, which relied on sifting out officers no longer doing their jobs properly as well as developing promising ones [*Aussiebung/Auslese*].[53] We think of this as sacking, but often things were not so straightforward. Officers were indeed sometimes outright relieved of their command, a clear example being the three generals removed after the December 1916 defeat at Verdun. This was such an open-and-shut case that it was described in

---

[48] Afflerbach, *Kaiser Wilhelm II. als Oberster Kriegsherr*, 79.
[49] Schmidt-Bückeburg, *Militärkabinett*, 245.
[50] Afflerbach, *Kaiser Wilhelm II. als Oberster Kriegsherr*, 74; Schoenaich, *Mein Damaskus*, 57.
[51] Epkenhans, *Nicolai*, 386, 396–7 and 399–400; Schoenaich, *Mein Damaskus*, 140–1; Wiens, 'In the Service of Kaiser and King', 344.
[52] In 1942, the *Wehrmacht*'s Personnel Office [*Personalamt*] was equally concerned about the effect of rapid promotion on the structure of the future peacetime officer corps: MacGregor Knox, *Common Destiny: Dictatorship, Foreign Policy, and War in Fascist Italy and Nazi Germany* (Cambridge: Cambridge University Press, 2000), 216.
[53] Militärgeschichtliches Forschungsamt, *Anciennität und Beförderung nach Leistung*, 131.

the official history, which was never keen to wash dirty linen in public. But defeat did not always lead to dismissal. The commander and *Ia* of 39th Bavarian Reserve Division at Verdun were both removed; their opposite numbers in 14th Bavarian Infantry Division at Arras were not.

Sacking might or might not mean the end of an officer's active service career. Within two months of being dismissed as Sixth Army chief of staff, Nagel zu Aichberg was appointed to command a division. This was a less influential position, but entirely appropriate to his rank. In contrast, Schubert and Plettenberg were forced into retirement. In both cases, the blow was softened by the award of high Prussian decorations. This technique was frequently employed, and could be supplemented by posting to jobs in the huge military apparatus in Germany or the occupied territories. Some of the latter jobs, such as regional governorships outside Germany, counted as active service and carried the added sweetener of active service pay. Guido Sontag for instance became military governor of Kalisch in Poland.

Another way of removing officers was sidelining them, and if necessary their entire headquarters, to a quiet sector. Removal of headquarters was covered in Chapter 2. As an example of sidelining an individual, *Generalleutnant* Theodor Melior moved from commanding 5th to 6th Reserve Division on the Eastern Front in April 1917 just before the former was deployed to the west. When 6th Reserve Division was also despatched westwards soon after, he moved to the low-grade 92nd Infantry Division, a semi-*Landwehr* formation that stayed in the east for the rest of the war. Various factors may have told against Melior: he had neither attended *Kriegsakademie* nor had general staff experience; he had retired some years before the war and been re-employed on its outbreak; and in 1917 he was sixty-four. He was evidently thought inadequate to the demands of the Western Front in 1917, but adequate to command a division in the east. Ludendorff's insistence on assessing officers according to uniform criteria made sense in terms of producing standardised command teams for deployment anywhere. But assessing officers as adequate for quiet fronts also made sense in terms of best exploiting the experience and talent actually available. In the real world of 1917, it was rational to select lower-quality officers for the many less pressurised positions away from the Western Front.

It will be obvious that the number of possible permutations complicates assessment of who was actually removed from post. An important clue is what happened next. A move to a lower-level or low-grade unit, transfer to quiet sectors, no further active service job or, in the case of a general staff officer, no further general staff employment – all indicate something had gone wrong. Even then only in a few cases do sources confirm that the officer was in fact sacked. Removal could be for reasons other than poor performance, such as ill health. In some cases we simply do not know. In April 1917 *Generalleutnant* Hermann von Bertrab left command of 39th Infantry Division just before its engagement in battle. He became head of the general staff's survey department [*Chef der Landesaufnahme*]. Much of his career had been in survey, he was the last holder of this post before it was abolished on mobilisation, it was now being re-established and he was a natural choice. But his expertise itself suggests he was not a man expected to take on major operational responsibilities and he may have been a poor choice as divisional commander. His return to survey therefore looks like he was being sidelined before the enemy offensive. In fact, 39th Infantry Division had been criticised for its performance at Verdun in December 1916 and he was probably lucky to escape sacking then.[54]

Putting all this together, Table 4.1 sets out statistics for removals during the period November 1916–July 1917. The 'known sacked' column covers cases where there is evidence that officers were removed for poor performance and similar reasons. 'Moved unexpectedly ... ' includes these officers and all whose postings suggest they were removed or sidelined for whatever reason (principally poor performance, ill health or age), including removal of their headquarters from major battle fronts. 'Moved unexpectedly ... ' can be seen as a maximum number for

Table 4.1 *Senior officers removed from post, 15 November 1916–16 July 1917*

Formation	Post	Moved unexpectedly, sidelined or sacked	Of which, known to have been sacked
Army group	Commanders	0	0
	Chiefs of staff	1	1
Army	Commanders	6	5
	Chiefs of staff	8	5
Corps	Commanders	15	9
	Chiefs of staff	11	2
Division	Commanders	35	9
	Ias	9	6
Total	Commanders	56	23
	Chiefs of staff/*Ias*	29	14
Grand total		85	37

[54] Reichsarchiv, *Weltkrieg*, 11:171; Ulrich Trumpener, Review of *The King's Finest: A Social and Bureaucratic Profile of Prussia's General Officers, 1871–1914* by Daniel J. Hughes, *International History Review*, vol. 10, no. 4 (November 1988), 646.

removals, and 'known sacked' as a minimum. But both probably under-state the reality because of lack of information, especially for divisional *Ia*s. Nor do they include removals of other senior officers outside the two categories covered.

These statistics are therefore not conclusive but do illustrate three points. First, the German army made continuous efforts to weed out unsuitable or unfit officers by one or other of the methods available to it. Second, only ten of the entries relate purely to the Eastern Front. The overwhelming majority of removals listed – over 90 per cent of known sacked – took place on the Western Front, followed service there or immediately preceded a move of the formation concerned to the west. The priority given to the Western Front in 1917 and the higher standards prevailing there are clear. Third, the number of commanders 'moved unexpectedly' is striking, involving some 15 per cent of divisions, 22 per cent of corps and 32 per cent of Armies and equivalent. Not all of these were sacked or sidelined but enough were to rebut the argument that after setbacks general staff officers rather than commanders were removed.[55] These figures also reinforce the point in Chapter 2 that despite the swing towards the general staff, commanders remained important: if they were not, why bother removing the inadequate?

The widespread removals in the period of November 1916–July 1917 suggest a concerted policy by the Third OHL to refresh the leadership of field formations. To some extent events made this necessary, especially the December 1916 and April 1917 defeats at Verdun and Arras. But most of the changes were deliberate choices, as also emerges from two collective changes of personnel at this period. The first is the removal of Seventh Army's commander and several other officers mentioned earlier, based on OHL concerns that defensive preparations before the Entente spring offensive were not proceeding fast enough. The second case involved the Bavarian Ersatz Division, holding a critical point on Seventh Army's front. Shortly before the offensive opened, the division and infantry brigade commanders were replaced by younger and more active officers. The *Ia* was exchanged for an officer more able to cope with the challenges of the coming battle. In contrast to sensitivities about personal feelings described later in this chapter, the new *Ia* had shortly before been the subordinate of the officer being replaced.[56]

The speed and thoroughness of these changes demonstrate a determination to get the right men into the right jobs, as well as the

---

[55] Rosinski, *German Army*, 146. Army 'equivalent' means the Army Detachments and Headquarters of Coastal Defence [*Oberkommando der Küstenverteidigung*].

[56] Bavarian Kriegsministerium to the king, 'Stellenbesetzungen', Num. 57173 P, 10 April 1917, KAM, Kriegsministerium 2211.

attention paid to command teams. There was, however, a downside. Rudolf von Xylander criticised the large-scale and rapid change of Seventh Army's staff, which he thought should have started sooner and been more gradual. Falkenhausen, writing about the removal of his chief of staff and *Ia* (Xylander) in April, considered that such sackings had become almost a rule whereas previously they had been exceptions; they damaged the confidence and creativity of commanders. Falkenhausen was of course *parti pris*, but others agreed. *Generalleutnant* Hans von Below, Otto's brother and a divisional commander at Arras, believed that Ludendorff's increasingly frequent dismissal of general staff officers inhibited independent thinking which varied from the prevailing, over-optimistic line and thereby encouraged distorted reporting.[57]

Function Did Not Automatically Override Rank

David T. Zabecki has suggested that the German army 'routinely appointed officers to command and staff positions far above their actual rank. Once in the position, however, the officer functioned with the full authority of the position, regardless of the nominal ranks and pay grades of his functional subordinates.' Zabecki sums this practice up as 'function overrode rank' and he sees it as one of the traditional principles that lent flexibility to the German command system.[58] If he is right, merit in effect trumped seniority in the personnel selection process. Such appointments certainly did happen during the war. Indeed, on mobilisation the Kaiser declared that he had often had to depart from the seniority lists in filling posts, and this would continue.[59] Illustrating that it did, when Fritz von Below was appointed to command Second Army in April 1915, he jumped over seven active and many other re-employed retired corps commanders senior to him. And in 1918, Ludendorff commented that seniority was not the decisive factor in appointing an Army commander; in war, not being selected for command or being subordinated to a junior were not reasons for resignation.[60]

---

[57] Xylander diary, 12 March 1917; Falkenhausen, 'Erinnerungen', 118–19; Oberst Friedrich Immanuel, *Siege und Niederlagen im Weltkriege: Kritische Betrachtungen* (Berlin: E. S. Mittler, 1919), 164; Generalleutnant Hans von Below memorandum, 'Meine Ansichten zu vorstehenden Auseinandersetzungen', 27 February 1919, unpublished manuscript in BArch, Otto von Below Nachlass, N87/2, 5. Chapter 6 covers distorted reporting.

[58] Zabecki, *Chief of Staff*, 1:12.

[59] The Kaiser to the Kriegsminister, 1 August 1914, BArch, PH1/3, f. 8.

[60] Hanns Möller, *Fritz v. Below, General der Infanterie: Ein Lebensbild* (Berlin: Bernard & Graefe, 1939), 45–6; Jan Hoffmann, 'Die sächsische Armee im Deutschen Reich 1871 bis 1918', unpublished PhD thesis, University of Dresden, 2007, 336.

Nevertheless the situation was more complex than Zabecki claims. To begin with, there were not two elements in the German grading system but three: rank, post (Zabecki's 'function') and what is here called 'status' (in German *Dienstgrad, Stelle* or *Dienststelle,* and *Rang*). Each substantive rank – *Generalleutnant* and so on – was normally allocated by warrant [*Patent*], which accorded seniority [*Dienstalter*] in the army list. An officer could be 'appointed' to a rank or promoted 'without warrant' [*ernannt/ ohne Patent*], which gave him the rank but not the seniority; or he could be given brevet rank [*charakterisiert*], which accorded the rank but not the pay and was often honorific. Substantive rank decided the officer's basic pay and some allowances.

Holding a post included carrying out the main role – for instance tactical command of a division – and also exercising authority over issues such as military justice. Posts could be held either substantively or provisionally. In the latter case, an officer in charge of a unit was called a 'leader' rather than a 'commander' [*Führer/Kommandeur*]; he or an officer handling a staff or similar function was said to be 'commissioned to exercise the command of' or 'commissioned to exercise the business of' the function [*mit Wahrnehmung der Führung/Geschäfte des ... beauftragt*], and did not receive the pay associated with the post. Finally, in establishment terms posts were graded at a certain level and officers holding the posts substantively were given the appropriate status. This was typically expressed in terms of 'status as' a certain level of post-holder such as regimental commander together with the associated pay and allowances.[61]

Some examples will show how the system worked in practice. As Sixth Army *Ia* in early 1917, though only a *Major* Xylander was accorded the status and pay of a regimental commander. He was allowed to retain these when he was sacked; the extra pay in particular – nearly 4,000 marks a year or 40 per cent – would have been important to him as he was in debt and had to give up his Munich flat to save money.[62] Justus Roeder had retired in 1912 as an *Oberst* with brevet rank as *Generalmajor*. He was re-employed in November 1914 to command a home service brigade. On the Kaiser's

---

[61] Kriegsministerium, *D. V.E. Nr. 101. Kriegs-Besoldungs-Vorschrift (K. Besold. V.) Vom 29. Dezember 1887: Neuabdruck 1914* (Berlin: Reichsdruckerei, 1914), sections 3, 10 and 25; Kriegsministerium, *D. V.E. Nr. 102. Gebührnisnachweisungen (Beiheft zur Kriegsbesoldungsvorschrift vom 29. Dezember 1887): Vom 6. Januar 1912* (Berlin: Reichsdruckerei, 1912), Vorbermerkungen, I-II; Kriegsministerium, *D. V.E. Nr. 219a. Stärkenachweisungen der Behörden und Truppen in der Kriegsformation. (St. N.) (Beiheft zum Mobilmachungsplan vom 1. Juli 1907.) Neuabdruck vom 1. Juni 1911* (Berlin: Reichsdruckerei, 1911), Vorbemerkungen, 1.

[62] Bavarian Kriegsministerium to the king, 'Stellenbesetzungen', Num. 62186 P, 19 April 1917, KAM, Kriegsministerium 2211; 'Nachweisung über die Bezüge der Offiziere, Unteroffiziere und Gemeinen im Frieden und Krieg', June 1916, HSAS, M1/ 6 Bü 1116, ff. 151–2; Xylander diary, 1 January 1917.

birthday in 1915, he received his warrant as *Generalmajor*, and this was his rank when commanding the brigade responsible for the loss of Fresnoy. He was sacked shortly after and spent the rest of the war as an inspector of prison camps; he even received a promotion in this post.[63] *Generalleutnant* Richard Wellmann, who commanded 20th Infantry Division on the Aisne, was appointed a corps commander later in the year. For technical reasons his title was 'leader' of the corps and he took good care to check that he was in fact the substantive commanding general 'with all the powers, allowances, pension rights and so on' which went with it.[64]

Where officers were appointed to posts theoretically above their rank, the third element of the system, status, accorded the requisite authority. Pre-war establishment regulations and some wartime staff lists published the status of posts. A December 1916 Fifth Army headquarters list records *Oberst* Bronsart von Schellendorff as the chief of staff, adding in brackets 'divisional commander'; the next general staff officer, the *Oberquartiermeister*, was given status as a brigade commander and the *Ia* as a regimental commander. This made their authority plain to everyone.[65] The linkages with reward and punishment are also clear, given the connection of post and status with pay. This could be significant as the Xylander case shows. Active service pay had a similar effect. Roeder received one-third more pay on active service compared with home service and lost the extra money when he was sacked. Appointment to or removal from different posts therefore had a substantial effect on officers' income. Such factors would surely have weighed on their minds, and this is presumably what Rupprecht meant about the independent position of royal commanders and their consequent freedom from 'the restraints of personal considerations'.

The system undoubtedly did allow posting officers of different rank to do the same job. Indeed this was nothing new, as the absolute link between particular posts and ranks had been broken in the mid-nineteenth century.[66] One result was that the rank of post-holders fell during the war as illustrated by Table 4.2, comparing the chiefs of staff of the seven Armies on the Western Front in August 1914 with their successors in April 1917.

However, this does not in itself prove that 'function overrode rank'. First, these officers would have had enhanced status as divisional commanders or similar, as in the case of Bronsart von Schellendorff at Fifth

---

[63] Roeder personal file, GLAK, E/9729.

[64] Generalleutnant a.D. Richard Wellmann, *Mit der Hannoverschen 20. Infanterie-Division in Ost und West: Oktober 1916 bis Dezember 1917* (Hannover: Edler & Krische, 1923), 153.

[65] *Gebührnisnachweisungen*, Vorbermerkungen, II; AOK 5, 'Dienstanweisung für das Oberkommando der 5. Armee', IIa Nr. 11304, 21 December 1916, BArch, Gallwitz Nachlass, N710/60a.

[66] Militärgeschichtliches Forschungsamt, *Anciennität und Beförderung nach Leistung*, 123.

Table 4.2 *Army chiefs of staff on the Western Front, August 1914 and April 1917*

Army	2 Aug. 1914	9 Apr. 1917
First	*Generalmajor* von Kuhl	*Oberst* von Loßberg
Second	*Generalleutnant* von Lauenstein	*Oberst* Wild
Third	*Generalmajor* von Hoeppner	*Oberst* Freiherr von Oldershausen
Fourth	*Generalleutnant* Freiherr von Lüttwitz	*Generalleutnant* Ilse
Fifth	*Generalleutnant* Schmidt von Knobelsdorf	*Oberst* Bronsart von Schellendorff
Sixth	*Generalmajor* Krafft von Dellmensingen	*Generalmajor* Freiherr von Nagel zu Aichberg
Seventh	*Generalleutnant* von Hänisch	*Oberstleutnant* Reinhardt

Army. Second, like the divisional *Ia*s described in Chapter 2, the lower-ranking Army chiefs of staff of 1917 were experienced officers. The *Obersten* and *Oberstleutnant* in Table 4.2 had an average age in April 1917 of forty-nine and length of service of twenty-nine years. Over the war as a whole, 68 officers served as Army or equivalent chiefs of staff, in a total of 126 postings.[67] Only six of these officers were as junior as *Major* on appointment, and these had between them only ten postings as Army chiefs of staff; of the six, three were subsequently promoted. All other Army chiefs of staff were *Oberstleutnants* or higher. And in any case, the *Majore* too were experienced officers: Max Stapff, who held three of the ten postings, was aged forty-six with nearly twenty-seven years' experience when he took up the first.

As the example of Army chiefs of staff suggests, there were restrictions on which officers could hold which posts, and seniority did count. In April 1917, *Generalleutnant* Eberhard von Hofacker was awarded the *Pour le Mérite* for his performance in the battle of Arras and recommended for corps command. This was turned down, the first reason being that two officers senior to him had not yet received corps commands.[68] With one exception, all substantive divisional commanders during the war were *Generalmajore* or higher. The exception, which proves the rule, was the Kaiser's second son, *Oberst* Prince Eitel Friedrich, who commanded 1st Guard Infantry Division in 1915–18 (and he was promoted *Generalmajor* in 1918). Similarly, there is no evidence of an officer lower than *Hauptmann* serving as substantive *Ia* of a division. Cynics would claim that this showed the conservatism of the Military Cabinet. One could

---

[67] 'Posting' means one officer's period of holding one post.
[68] Holland to Duke Albrecht, 29 May 1917, AHW, Herzog Albrecht Nachlass, G331/549.

equally say that experience was needed in such jobs, and this could only be accumulated with time and hence seniority. The lack of experience in 1917 of some divisional commanders and general staff officers was a real concern, as we saw in Chapter 2.

There is a wealth of evidence that attempts to implement function overriding rank did not work as smoothly as Zabecki suggests. When control of artillery was devolved to divisions, senior artillery officers at army group, Army and corps level became advisers subordinate to the chief of staff; the Ministry of War stressed that in general these officers should be junior to him.[69] At divisional level, problems arose because the *Ia* would certainly be junior to the artillery and engineer commanders. It was recognised that he would need considerable tact to deal with them, and similarly they were recommended not to insist on their seniority. A possible solution to this problem would be appointing *Majore* to be divisional *Ia*s, which could in principle be achieved by swapping corps and divisional *Ia*s.[70] But, as noted earlier, this proposal was dropped following almost unanimous objections from corps. One reason was that the seniority problem would simply re-emerge at corps level: junior general staff officers there would have increased problems exerting their authority precisely because they lacked seniority.[71]

The question of relative seniority occurred frequently enough that instructions had to be issued on how to deal with it. Attempting to sort out the chain of command between front and counter-attack divisions, Army Group Crown Prince stated that in general the commander of the front division should have control over both divisions regardless of rank; this had to be repeated more formally in the September 1917 edition of the 'Defensive Battle' manual.[72] In other words, the relative rank of the commanders *was* an issue and resolving it did not happen automatically. The instructions for divisional command courses included how to handle cases where students or the commander of the training division might outrank the course leader.[73] Nor were such problems confined to senior commanders. When in April 1917 a new *Ia* arrived in 6th Bavarian Landwehr Division who was junior to the *Ib*, the latter was moved.[74]

[69] Kriegsministerium circular, Nr. 445/17.g.A4, 16 February 1917, BArch, PH1/10, f. 145.
[70] 'Organisation des Divisionsstabes in der Abwehrschlacht', 4.
[71] CGS Gruppe Dixmude to AOK 4, Nr. 70949/566 Pers., 25 June 1917, GLAK, F6/72.
[72] HDK to AOKs, Ia/Ic Nr. 2381, 19 April 1917, GLAK, F1/374; Chef des Generalstabes des Feldheeres, *Vorschriften für den Stellungskrieg für alle Waffen*, Teil 8, *Grundsätze für die Führung der Abwehrschlacht im Stellungskriege. Vom 1. September 1917* (Berlin: Reichsdruckerei, 1917), 10 (hereafter, '*Abwehrschlacht*', September 1917).
[73] HKR army group order, Ic 1998 geh., 13 January 1917, KAM, HKR neue Nr. 31.
[74] Bavarian Kriegsministerium to the king, 'Stellenbesetzungen', Num. 68233 P, 28 April 1917, KAM, Kriegsministerium 2211.

It is clear then that function did not automatically override rank: merit did not trump seniority. Placing an officer above one of higher rank could be done, especially as he could be bolstered by the authority of the enhanced status of the post. However, such appointments might well cause trouble, particularly when senior officers were involved. It is true that the ranks held by officers in most posts dropped between 1914 and 1918, but given the army's expansion and losses, this was natural during a long total war. The lower ranks were a correction of pre-war over-engineering and not a sign that officers could be freely placed wherever they were needed regardless of rank.

The German army failed to recognise that it had in fact two possible methods available to resolve the conundrum of function and rank, one of which was in full view across No Man's Land. Faced with the problem of staffing a vastly increased officer establishment at all levels, the British army made extensive and effective use of temporary rank. Thus Cecil Lothian Nicholson was a substantive Colonel and Temporary Major-General while commanding 34th Division. By according the rank appropriate to any post, this system averted arguments over seniority. It also facilitated trialling officers in ranks and posts, and removing them if they failed. In effect it tested, exploited and rewarded merit. Finally it allowed for the problem of reduced post-war establishments, admittedly at the personal cost of officers who reverted to lower substantive ranks.[75]

During the Second World War, the German army increasingly adopted the second method, promoting officers by merit rather than seniority. To achieve this, it made regular use of predating commissions and accelerated promotion. As a result, in comparison to the First World War, infantry officers reached *Hauptmann* on average three years earlier, *Major* ten years earlier, *Oberstleutnant* eleven years earlier and *Oberst* six years earlier. Some of this change arose from the Nazi policy of 'advancement of leadership personalities'.[76] But it is fair to assume that some was pushed through by senior officers who had served in the First World War and seen that the solutions adopted then had not produced ideal results.

---

[75] I am grateful to Professor John Bourne for his ideas on the British use of temporary rank.

[76] Militärgeschichtliches Forschungsamt, *Anciennität und Beförderung nach Leistung*, 175–6 and 202–6; Militärgeschichtliches Forschungsamt, ed., *Germany and the Second World War*, vol. 5, *Organization and Mobilization of the German Sphere of Power*, pt I, *Wartime Administration, Economy, and Manpower Resources 1939–1941* (Oxford: Clarendon Press, 2000), 1030–2.

The Importance of Personal Factors and Relationships

> A military body, such as a Staff, is after all only an assembly of human beings, and the fact that it is composed of men who have all won their way by hard competition, who all have careers and ambitions, does not tend to attenuate the more obvious defects of human nature.[77]

Zabecki's theory that function overrode rank exemplifies the tendency to stress the professionalism of the German officer corps in the sense of 'the cultivation of particular skills and competence in a specialized area, requiring appropriate training'.[78] But the sensitivities over pay and seniority described in this chapter show that officers were also professional in the other sense of the word, pursuing their careers and earning their livelihoods in the army. As such, they were naturally motivated not just by patriotism but also human feelings such as ambition, reputation, jealousy and personal relationships; and by 1917 they were increasingly subject to the strains of a long war in which the German army was no longer confident it had the upper hand.

A lecturer at one of the divisional command courses explicitly linked the army's and individuals' interests: everyone was working for 'the great common cause' but it was only human to want some advantage for oneself as well. More than one senior officer recorded personal considerations in his diary while adding that 'the cause' was what really mattered. In December 1916, Gerhard Tappen was removed from his post as chief of staff in Army Group Mackensen on the Eastern Front and transferred to command a low-grade division there. Tappen commented that his name had been in all the papers when he was Mackensen's chief of staff, but it would now disappear; there were no laurels to be won with his new division. He added piously that what counted was to serve the Fatherland and do his duty.[79]

Personnel records suggest obsessive attention to the standing of each officer, both by the system – because of the importance of seniority – and no doubt by the officer himself. Officers' rank warrants carried a date but this was not enough to show who was senior to whom, particularly if many officers were promoted on the same date. On 1 October 1913, in the infantry alone, over 576 officers were promoted to *Hauptmann*.[80] Letters

---

[77] Spears, *Prelude to Victory*, 27, writing about Joffre's staff when it became clear he was about to be removed.

[78] Ian F. W. Beckett, *A British Profession of Arms: The Politics of Command in the Late Victorian Army* (Norman, OK: University of Oklahoma Press, 2018), 4.

[79] 'Organisation des Divisionsstabes in der Abwehrschlacht', 1; Tappen, 'Kriegserinnerungen', f. 162.

[80] 'Over 576' because these figures are calculated from the 1917 *Dienstalters-Liste* [seniority list], the first since 1912; they therefore do not allow for casualties, likely to have been heavy in the infantry at this level.

and numbers were therefore added after the warrants to distinguish between them, and to enable comparison of seniority between officers of the different arms of service promoted on the same day. The 1 October 1913 *Hauptmann* promotion went round the alphabet fifty-five times, ending at A56a. These apparently minute differences mattered: Walther Obkircher believed that a contemporary with a warrant of the same date as his was awarded a coveted corps chief of staff post because he was one letter higher in seniority.[81]

This system continued in wartime and in addition units ran 'war rank lists' [*Kriegsranglisten*] recording in great detail information on every officer. A particular feature of these lists was the attention devoted to the actions an officer had taken part in, carefully defined by the organisation responsible for battle nomenclature, and to his decorations. Hermann von Kuhl's record lists nineteen actions from the outbreak of war to the battle of Messines in June 1917, and eighteen awards over the same period. Such detail risked descending into farce, in effect equating his *Pour le Mérite* with his Lippe War Service Cross. As this suggests, the existence of the federal German states with their individual award systems greatly aided officers chasing decorations.[82]

Standing and reputation as displayed by service records and decorations mattered because of their effect on an officer's prospects – in other words, on the merit element of selection – and also on his feelings about his career progress and his honour. Martin Kitchen focuses on honour as an essential condition for the continued existence of the officer corps as a special caste, and on the army's alleged use of it to suppress internal criticism.[83] But honour also played a wider role, both positively and negatively. Positively, it limited the extent to which obedience could be required of an officer and in doing so guaranteed a certain independence in the form of personal responsibility. Also, it was seen as a necessity if trust and confidence were to exist within a community.[84] In this way, honour played a role in mission command, which relied crucially on mutual trust between superior and subordinate.

On the negative side, individual conceptions of reputation and honour clearly affected operations. The most serious example in early 1917

[81] Obkircher, 'Achtzehn Monate Generalstabsoffizier Ia/XV. Armeekorps', 2.

[82] Details of Kuhl's record from the Heeresgruppe Rupprecht *Kriegsrangliste*, www .ancestry.co.uk (accessed 18 June 2022). Federal awards and decoration-hunters: Arndt von Kirchbach, *Pietate et Armis: Erinnerungen aus dem Leben von Arndt v. Kirchbach*, ed. Esther von Kirchbach and Ernst Kähler, vol. 2, *1914–1918: Der Erste Weltkrieg* (Göppingen-Jebenhausen: self-publication, 1987), 173. The Principality of Lippe was one of the smallest federal states that together constituted the German *Reich*.

[83] Kitchen, *German Officer Corps*, 49 and 59–63.

[84] Oetting, *Auftragstaktik*, 86; Echevarria, *After Clausewitz*, 78–9.

relates to the defeat at Messines: one reason for Fourth Army's refusal to pre-empt the British attack by evacuating the salient was that the newly arrived commander, Sixt von Armin, did not want to begin his command with a withdrawal.[85] Criticism of operational performance on the battlefield could produce thick files of claim and counter-claim by those involved. Falkenhausen made a formal complaint about Hindenburg during the battle of Arras, following an OHL letter circulated at a senior level throughout the army that effectively blamed Sixth Army for the defeat of 9 April. In parallel, there was an extensive exchange of correspondence in which Army Group Rupprecht and Sixth Army accused each other of responsibility for the defeat.[86]

Apart from aspiring to higher – and therefore more responsible – posts, officers' best hopes for fulfilling their career ambitions were either by promotion or by decoration. Prospects for promotion were not particularly good even during the war. This was because of the Military Cabinet's conservative policy on establishments described earlier, which ruled out an acceleration of substantive promotion. As a result, the time taken to reach various ranks changed little during the war: an infantry officer became *Major* after twenty-two years on average, only three years quicker than in peacetime. After a mass advancement to *Oberleutnant* and *Hauptmann* in August–September 1914, promotion remained largely by seniority. Some exceptional or exceptionally privileged officers – including Tappen, Loßberg and Schulenburg – were given accelerated promotion during the war as a mark of distinction, so for them merit was favoured over seniority. But in general, fewer officers than in peacetime received accelerated promotion.[87]

With a few exceptions, then, above-average performance was rewarded with decorations rather than promotion.[88] Analysis of awards is complicated by the profusion of decorations: the Prussian Order of the Red Eagle [*Roter Adler-Orden*] alone had ninety-three different grades and variants.[89] Decorations were distributed lavishly after the defeat of the Entente spring offensive, and nineteen *Pour le Mérite*s or its oak leaves were awarded to commanders and general staff officers from division to army group level. Some of the recipients deserved their awards, including

[85] Kuhl, 'Kriegstagebuch', 7 June 1917.   [86] Falkenhausen, 'Erinnerungen', 122–8.

[87] Militärgeschichtliches Forschungsamt, *Anciennität und Beförderung nach Leistung*, 163 and 169–70.

[88] Ibid., 168.

[89] Calculated from Willi Geile, *Die im 'Militär-Wochenblatt' und im 'Marineverordnungsblatt' veröffentlichten preußischen und fremdstaatlichen (deutschen und außerdeutschen) Ordensverleihungen an Offiziere der preußischen Armee und der kaiserlichen Marine von 1914 bis 1918* (Konstanz: Autengruber, 1997), 3–32. Anon., *Das alte Heer*, 128, aiming to ridicule the system, only found thirty-eight grades and variants.

Boehn and Reinhardt at Seventh Army, and Loßberg at Sixth Army. But the reason for the award to *Oberst* Martin von Oldershausen, Third Army chief of staff and only peripherally involved in the battle, is less obvious: he was a Saxon officer, so was it for political purposes? And *Generalleutnant* Hermann Schubert's advancement in the Order of the Red Eagle is inexplicable, given that OHL deliberately decided not to deploy his 22nd Reserve Division in the spring fighting, owing to doubts about its combat value. This may have been an instance of not wanting to leave an officer out when his peers were receiving decorations.[90]

Turning to personal relationships, despite the size of the German army, many officers knew each other from peacetime or, increasingly, wartime service together. Otto von Below had not previously served on the Western Front when he took over Sixth Army in April 1917, but already knew three of his seven *Gruppe* commanders, two of the chiefs of staff, four division commanders and a number of other officers. The peacetime acquaintanceships arose in a variety of ways, including from serving as superior and subordinate in the same unit, serving in neighbouring units or working together on manoeuvres; in one case, he had served with the officer's father. He also knew officers from shared wartime experience. The depth of these relationships is often unclear, but they were meaningful enough to record, and some were more than that. Below's pre-war divisional adjutant, *Oberstleutnant* Oskar Schwerk, was badly wounded at the beginning of the battle of Arras as a regimental commander. Below visited Schwerk in hospital nine times and secured the oak leaves to the *Pour le Mérite* for him, even though he himself had not been in France at the time of the action: an example of the practical effect of patronage.[91]

Of course, knowing someone did not necessarily mean liking them, and even general staff officers – often idealised as technocrats of war – were not above personal animosities.[92] Diaries and memoirs show that officers frequently saw each other as rivals. Tappen was convinced that Hindenburg and Ludendorff had removed him from his job in Army Group Mackensen out of malevolence, based on personal motives.[93] Kuhl too ascribed personal motives to what may have at least begun as professional differences, as the second case study at the end of this chapter recounts. Even Thaer, generally balanced in his comments, was annoyed when an ex-subordinate was appointed an Army chief of staff,

---

[90] Kuhl, 'Kriegstagebuch', 3 August 1917 records a Fourth Army request for a *Gruppe* commander to receive the *Pour le Mérite* so that he would not be the only one without it, even though the Army also wanted him removed.
[91] Otto von Below diary, 29 April–20 June 1917; Hanns Möller, ed., *Geschichte der Ritter des Ordens 'pour le mérite' im Weltkrieg* (Berlin: Bernard & Graefe, 1935), 2:320.
[92] Pöhlmann, *Kriegsgeschichte*, 250–1.   [93] Tappen, 'Kriegserinnerungen', f. 158.

a level he himself aspired to. The man was able enough but Thaer felt himself in no way inferior; however, 'the cause' overrode all such considerations.[94]

Relationships could develop into networks and cliques that influenced the way business was actually handled in the army. On arrival in 90th Fusilier Regiment, a unit from the Grand Duchy of Mecklenburg, *Leutnant* (later *General der Infanterie*) Curt Liebmann found an uncomradely atmosphere in a disunited officer corps riven by cliques between aristocrats and bourgeois, rich and poor and Mecklenburgers and Prussians.[95] Friendships formed by young officers studying in the same class [*Hörsaal*] at *Kriegsakademie* or serving in the same regiment could have a long-lasting effect.[96] Regiments also offered networking opportunities with senior officers who remained in honorific positions after moving away or retiring and who were expected to act as unofficial mentors to their juniors.[97] For instance, as a retired *General der Infanterie*, Hindenburg was still carried on the books '*à la suite*' to the 3rd Foot Guard Regiment, which he had served in as a young officer. This connection remained important to him much later as president of the Weimar Republic and clearly benefitted the careers of ex-officers of the regiment.[98]

Fritz von Loßberg exemplifies how networking affected careers. He knew Erich von Falkenhayn from before the war in various service situations; more personally, he had helped Frau von Falkenhayn when her husband was serving in China. Loßberg's career break came in September 1915 when he was appointed chief of staff to Third Army during a moment of crisis. Falkenhayn played a key role in this appointment and their relationship may well have contributed to the selection.[99] Loßberg was also close to another senior officer at OHL, Quartermaster-General Freytag-Loringhoven, having served in the same foot guard company. By the time Falkenhayn and Freytag-Loringhoven left OHL in summer 1916, Loßberg had already established himself as a defensive expert. But in terms of personal contacts, he retained an ace up his sleeve – his relationship with Lyncker, the head of the Military Cabinet. Loßberg had served as Lyncker's divisional *Ia* before the war, explicitly described

[94] Thaer, *Generalstabsdienst*, 165.   [95] Liebmann, 'Lebenserinnerungen', 19.

[96] Pöhlmann, *Kriegsgeschichte*, 249–50.

[97] Mungo Melvin, *Manstein: Hitler's Greatest General* (London: Weidenfeld & Nicolson, 2010), 17.

[98] Waldemar Erfurth, *Die Geschichte des deutschen Generalstabes von 1918 bis 1945* (Göttingen: Musterschmidt-Verlag, 1957), 105 and 113. Generals Kurt von Schleicher and Kurt Freiherr von Hammerstein-Equord, respectively chancellor and head of the army under Hindenburg, were two beneficiaries of service in 3rd Foot Guards.

[99] Meyer, 'Operational Art', 361 suggests that Loßberg knew his proposals in September 1915 accorded with Falkenhayn's views and was in effect lobbying for a job.

him as 'my old patron' [*Gönner*] and took the opportunity of having long conversations when he could.[100] Loßberg clearly was an able officer, but these relationships would certainly not have harmed his career, including two rapid promotions.

In some instances, the relationship was a family one. Gleich commented that whereas in peacetime it was forbidden for a son to serve in his father's regiment or on his staff, in war examples of close relatives serving in higher staffs continually increased.[101] The Bavarian Kneußl went even further. He thought there was hardly a Prussian staff without the son of some prominent family on it, usually the commander's. In May 1917, he criticised the performance of the commander (Richard Wellmann) and *Ia* of 20th Infantry Division, which his division was due to relieve. The *Ia* was Hindenburg's son, *Hauptmann* Oskar von Hindenburg, and Kneußl suspected this showed Prussian patronage at work; no doubt this feeling was strengthened shortly afterwards when Oskar received a distinguished award. The following month Kneußl discovered that Max von Boehn's son-in-law was serving in Seventh Army headquarters and wrote furiously that such patronage was simply shameless, asking himself rhetorically to what extent this sort of mismanagement was responsible for Germany's current plight.[102]

Kneußl could have extended this rant to include the predominance in the Prussian army of its Guards mafia.[103] Boehn's son-in-law, *Major* Kurt Freiherr von Wangenheim, and Oskar von Hindenburg had both served in the 3rd Foot Guard Regiment; as mentioned the field marshal had too, which no doubt eased Oskar's entry; so had one of his adjutants, *Hauptmann* Kurd von Bismarck; and Boehn had been its second-in-command. In all, nine of the ten Prussian officers named in this and the previous two paragraphs had served in the Guards.[104] Nor is this particularly unusual. Indeed, Gleich commented that the Guards undeniably benefited from outright preferential treatment and that the majority of corps commanders in the army emerged from them.[105] He was right: nearly two-thirds of Prussian corps commanders in July 1914 were Guards officers, and even by spring 1917 this had only dropped to 50 per cent. Guards officers also occupied many other top jobs in the

---

[100] Loßberg, *Meine Tätigkeit*, 126, 185 and 291.   [101] Gleich, *Die alte Armee*, 83.
[102] Kneußl diary, 7 May 1917; Stachelbeck, *Militärische Effektivität*, 46.
[103] 'Guards' here means Prussian Guard units of any arm of service; 'Guards officers' are defined as having served at least five years in a Guard unit or having held a command position in a Guard unit or formation from battalion up.
[104] Bismarck, Boehn, Falkenhayn, Freytag-Loringhoven, both Hindenburgs, Loßberg, Lyncker and Wangenheim had all served in the Guards. The Prussian exception is Wellmann; Gleich was a Württemberger and Kneußl Bavarian.
[105] Gleich, *Die alte Armee*, 77.

army. All chiefs of the general staff from the late 1880s up to the end of the First World War were from the Guards (or had served with them), so were the three heads of the Military Cabinet until mid-1918 as well as one third of Military Cabinet officers over the same period. For good measure, the two wartime heads of OHL's Central Department, in charge of general staff personnel work, were also Guards officers.[106]

The preponderance of Guards officers in important jobs was one of the most persistent complaints against the Military Cabinet, as we saw. It was a source of annoyance and concern to contemporaries, both military and civilian, but was perhaps inevitable given the nature of the German regime. The Guards were not only its ultimate defender, but also the 'favourite child' of the Kaiser and his court, many of whose members were from Guards regiments. The Kaiser and Lyncker – between them in overall charge of officers' careers and postings – had both served in the 1st Foot Guard Regiment, the army's premier unit. Continuing the personal bonds, by the outbreak of war the Kaiser's second son Prince Eitel Friedrich was commanding the regiment and Lyncker's eldest was serving in it. Lyncker and *Generaloberst* Hans von Plessen, First Commandant of GHQ, were both *à la suite* to the regiment. As the editor of their papers comments, it was this mixture of personal interest and social ties that led to the preferential treatment of Guards officers.[107]

However, there were mitigating factors. Chief among them was that the existence of cliques such as the Guards did not necessarily result in incompetence. A British army parallel helps explain this, since even within a notorious clique such as the Wolseley Ring, merit, skill and talent were preconditions for career progress.[108] In the German case, one-eighth of the Prussian *Kriegsakademie* students in 1913–14 were from Guards regiments. This is particularly significant, since entrance exams to the *Kriegsakademie* were now anonymous, in order to prevent precisely the sort of preferential treatment received by Guards officers.[109] Seven of the students were from the 1st Foot Guards, suggesting that it was good form in such regiments to attend the *Kriegsakademie*. As Gleich admitted, the Guards officer corps was selected for performance and talent as well as on social grounds. Schoenaich – a particularly valuable witness here as he became a pacifist after the war – thought that the 1st Foot Guards were

---

[106] The corps statistics exclude those commanded by non-Prussian officers who could not serve in the Prussian Guards.
[107] Afflerbach, *Kaiser Wilhelm II. als Oberster Kriegsherr*, 80.
[108] Fox, 'The Secret of Efficiency?', 1530.
[109] Rodenberg, 'Militär-Kabinett', 63. Saxon and Württemberg officers attended the *Kriegsakademie*, but Prussian officers naturally comprised by far the largest part of the student body (88 per cent).

militarily excellent, and even the royal princes serving in the regiment were treated strictly. These positive views are supported by the examples of exceptionally able Guards officers such as Loßberg; and, in a later generation, *Generalfeldmarschall* Erich von Manstein, who had joined the 3rd Foot Guards because Hindenburg was his uncle.[110]

Confirming the need for competence, Guards provenance did not protect senior officers from dismissal. In the period covered by this book, four Army and five corps commanders who had served as Guards officers were sacked or sidelined. One of the most prominent was Plettenberg, who had commanded the 1st Foot Guards as well as the Guard Corps; in addition he was a General Adjutant to the Kaiser. This combination of personal circumstances may have insulated him when concerns about his performance originally arose in 1914 but could not ultimately save him in January 1917. At about the same time, *Oberst* Wilhelm von Hahnke was removed from his post as *Oberquartiermeister* in Seventh Army even though he was not only a former 1st Foot Guards officer but had been Schlieffen's adjutant and son-in-law.

The final personal factor to note is the continually increasing physical and nervous strain of service on the Western Front. A historian of the Military Cabinet believed that the German army had underestimated the strain inflicted on all levels of command by the war, and that this was one of the most important reasons for the failure of officers who had seemed well qualified for their posts.[111] In early July 1917, Kneußl wrote of his officers' nerves being worn down, leading to extremely unpleasant results on the battlefield; and his 11th Bavarian Infantry Division had not even been engaged in the worst parts of the spring offensive. Shortly afterwards, he himself was criticised as having lost his energy and offensive spirit due to physical illness.[112] This sort of problem was cumulative and Kneußl was certainly not the only senior officer affected. The great psychological burden on the Kaiser and his entourage caused and exacerbated frequent physical illnesses at GHQ.[113] Health and mental state were factors in the dismissal of Plettenberg and two other corps commanders in early 1917. One of these, *General der Infanterie* Otto von Plüskow, was removed from command of Gruppe Vailly facing the French offensive expressly because he was no longer considered adequate for Western Front conditions. He was sent to command a corps on the Eastern Front, but even there his nerves were thought not good enough

---

[110] Rodenberg, 'Militär-Kabinett', 65; Gleich, *Die alte Armee*, 77; Schoenaich, *Mein Damaskus*, 58–9; Melvin, *Manstein*, 16.
[111] Rodenberg, 'Militär-Kabinett', 61.
[112] Stachelbeck, *Militärische Effektivität*, 47 and 298.
[113] Afflerbach, *Kaiser Wilhelm II. als Oberster Kriegsherr*, 86.

and shortly after arrival he retired.[114] Ludendorff, Kuhl and Loßberg were others clearly suffering from strain at this period.[115]

An ever-present element of the strain, beginning as soon as the war's heavy casualties became clear in August 1914, was concern for sons and other loved ones, and grief if the worst happened. The officers in this book, particularly senior commanders, often seem to us unsympathetic characters, but they are at their most human when struggling to cope with such personal feelings. Many had sons and relatives serving at the front and therefore in danger, including Loßberg, Lyncker and Plettenberg. Falkenhayn was 'out of action' for twenty-four hours when his son went missing (he survived). Ludendorff lost two stepsons; the death of the second in particular had a deep emotional impact on him.[116]

Walter Nicolai, himself very upset when his brother went missing in May 1917, thought the effect of such 'human emergencies' on senior commanders was so severe that they should not have to endure this test. He did not quite say so but he meant that their sons should not be put at risk. This was of course completely impractical and would have raised the most serious 'us and them' issues, a problem which Nicolai himself half-realised. So as Thaer wrote during the battle of Arras when he was grappling with decisions about his son's joining the army: 'Any father who knows war as well as I do will be more than serious in such considerations'.[117]

Case Studies

Two case studies will flesh out the realities of the second command task. The first, on the Württemberger Otto von Moser, describes a typical career, including how it was reflected in and affected by the confidential reporting system; it also shows the effects of prolonged strain on senior officers.[118] He was well thought of, reached *Major* some four years ahead of the average and was ennobled in 1908. In September 1914, aged fifty-four, he was severely wounded when commanding a brigade in the west.

---

[114] Holland to Duke Albrecht, 18 March 1917, AHW, Herzog Albrecht Nachlass, G331/549; Möller, *Pour le Mérite*, 2:142.

[115] Ludendorff: Kuhl, 'Kriegstagebuch', 2 July 1917. Kuhl: Rupprecht, unpublished diary, 25 December 1916. Loßberg: Thaer, *Generalstabsdienst*, 124.

[116] Epkenhans, *Nicolai*, 156; Watson, *Ring of Steel*, 532.

[117] Epkenhans, *Nicolai*, 384–5; Thaer, *Generalstabsdienst*, 119–20. Nicolai's brother was subsequently reported wounded and captured.

[118] Main sources for this section are Gerhard Hümmelchen, 'Otto von Moser: Ein württembergischer General', *Wehrwissenschaftliche Rundschau*, vol. 31, no. 6 (1982), 196–202, and Moser, *Feldzugsaufzeichnungen*, both passim.

After recovering, he formed and led a division on the Eastern Front. In 1916, he moved back west and commanded one of the best formations in the army, the Württemberg 27th Infantry Division, during the battle of the Somme. He established and ran the first divisional command course in early 1917, after which he took over XIV Reserve Corps and fought in the battles of Arras and Cambrai as a *Gruppe* commander. In early 1918, he was removed from his post and in July retired with the award of a high Württemberg decoration.

Moser's appointment to XIV Reserve Corps illustrates the working of seniority tempered by merit, as well as the role of serendipity. Any move like this depended both on there being a vacancy and on the candidate being available. In this case, the dismissal of Richard von Schubert created a gap at Seventh Army, which was filled by transferring Max von Boehn from Army Detachment C. The resulting vacancy there was filled by the commander of XIV Reserve Corps. Moser was available to take over the corps because his divisional command courses had been paused during the withdrawal to the Hindenburg Line, and he was geographically nearby.

Corps commanders were either Generals (*Generale der Infanterie* and so on) or, increasingly, *Generalleutnants*. So as a *Generalleutnant* with nearly two years seniority, Moser was in the frame, and indeed two officers junior to him had been appointed corps commanders in January 1917; no doubt coincidentally, both were Guards officers. At fifty-seven, he was four years younger than the average for corps commanders at the time, a positive factor given the effort to rejuvenate the cadre of senior officers. In terms of merit, he had a good mix of general staff and unit experience in peacetime. His stint as instructor at the *Kriegsakademie* and his pre-war publications proved his intellectual capacity for high command. His brigade and divisional commands in wartime gave him the practical experience, capped by successfully leading a high-quality division on the Somme. Finally, his establishment and running of the divisional command courses had brought him up-to-date with the latest tactical thinking. These appointments show the regard in which he was held, further demonstrated by award of the *Pour le Mérite* for his performance at the Somme and Arras.

In bureaucratic terms, Moser's performance in both peace and war was reflected in his confidential reports. These were unanimously positive until summer 1917. However, in June that year Otto von Below recorded in his diary that Moser – whose corps headquarters was then running Gruppe Quéant in Sixth Army – was less optimistic than his predecessor, always shouting for help and sometimes needing to be encouraged in a rather sharp tone. He described Moser to Kuhl as intelligent but hopping about all over the place and pessimistic. He asked if Moser could be moved, though nothing came of this.[119]

Below's report on Moser the next month was positive overall and indeed said he was suitable for promotion. However, introducing a negative element for the first time in these reports, Below added that Moser's intellectual agility could easily lead to unsteadiness and an adverse effect on the troops. In December, Moser's new Army commander, Georg von der Marwitz, agreed about the unsteadiness and its possible adverse effect, which entailed the need to monitor Moser's orders. As part of a pre-offensive assessment of all senior officers, in January 1918 Marwitz reported that Moser would probably not meet the coming demands, should be replaced by a calmer officer and then reassigned to a similar post on a quiet front. Rupprecht, countersigning, concurred, and Moser was removed.

Were this final report and Moser's dismissal justified? Factors in the negative report may have included differences of character and possibly regional origin between Marwitz, a Prussian cavalry officer of the old-school, and the self-confident, intelligent Württemberger Moser.[120] Both positive and negative remarks in the reports use similar language, displaying groupthink and reflecting Gleich's criticisms of the system. Moser undoubtedly performed well at Arras in spring and Cambrai in November, as Marwitz recognised. Moser himself, of course, bitterly resented Marwitz's final report. He challenged it first with a formal complaint, questioning its facts and language, and later with a written submission to the Kaiser; both failed.[121] He may well have been right on points of detail. The Württemberg Minister of War and Moser's ex-corps commander certainly disagreed with the decision to remove him but could not overturn the report, especially as the countersigning officer concurred with the reporting officer.

Bringing in the question of strain, however, throws a completely different light on Moser's removal. On the Somme in August 1916, during and perhaps because of what he described as physically and psychologically one of the most difficult nights of the war, he endured 'an absolutely appalling bout of dysentery with the worst vomiting etc.'. But the fundamental problem was that pain from his wound affected him throughout the war. As a *Gruppe* commander in May 1917, he recorded that after a month's fighting he and his staff were all exhausted, 'but luckily my nerves are holding out despite the increasing neuralgia and pain from my

[119] Otto von Below diary, 17 June 1917; Kuhl, 'Kriegstagebuch', 17 June 1917.
[120] Hümmelchen, 'Moser', 200.
[121] The formal complaint and submission to the Kaiser are on HSAS, Moser Nachlass, M660/031 Bü 6.

scars caused by the continuous strain'. Moser was proud of his performance at Cambrai, but suffered great nervous stress and physical pain; he
could hardly hold a pen to deal with the mass of paperwork. A row with
Marwitz proved the final straw. By now he was deeply agitated and
suffering from a pounding heart, sleeplessness and enormous fatigue.
Three weeks' leave at the turn of the year failed to restore his nerves
sufficiently, especially not for the major task of preparing for the spring
offensive. Aggravating factors were that he no longer had complete trust
in part of his staff, who he believed were going behind his back; and his
adjutant, to whom he was close, was posted away from the corps.[122]

From Moser's own account therefore, his removal in early 1918 looks
justified. The Württemberg representative to the Military Cabinet commented that his downfall was due to his temperament, which was still
affected by his wound.[123] This could well have been behind the unsteadiness that both Below and Marwitz noticed. Marwitz may have got some
details in his report wrong but his overall conclusion was correct. He was
also fair in recognising Moser's achievements (as was Below), and his
proposed solution of a posting at the same level to a quiet front was
sensible. In the event it was not taken up, possibly because people were
annoyed by Moser's self-justifying and indeed self-pitying appeal to the
Kaiser in the run-up to the spring 1918 offensive. The effect of strain is
clear. Moser was obviously already worried about his psychological ability
to cope with the spring 1917 fighting and was relieved to find his nerves
held out then, but by the year's end he could not continue.

The second case study, from Army Group Rupprecht, illustrates the
interaction between personal relationships and operations, as well as the
subsequent effect on the historiography. The protagonists were Otto von
Below, Stapff (chief of staff to Fourth and later Sixth Armies) and Wetzell
(head of the First Section in OHL's Operations Department) on one side;
and Kuhl and to a lesser extent Rupprecht on the other. The story begins
after the disaster at Messines in early June 1917 with the debate about
improving the Fourth Army command team described in Chapter 2.
A main point at issue was whether Stapff could handle 'the most demanding post we have'.[124] Kuhl in particular had doubts and was a driving
force in Stapff's move from Fourth Army, in the army group's view now
the defensive *Schwerpunkt* on the Western Front, to Sixth Army where the
battle of Arras appeared to be over. This was the same level of job and

---

[122] Moser, *Feldzugsaufzeichnungen*, 246, 302, 355, 358 and 360–1.
[123] Holland to Duke Albrecht, 25 February 1918, AHW, Herzog Albrecht Nachlass,
G331/549.
[124] Kuhl, 'Kriegstagebuch', 10 June 1917.

Stapff kept the same status and pay, but in reputational terms he would naturally feel aggrieved.

Kuhl began to record in his diary a series of criticisms of Sixth Army, Stapff and Wetzell; these were reciprocated by Otto von Below in *his* diary. Some of these mutual criticisms reflected genuine and strongly held differences of opinion on two military issues. First was disagreement whether Sixth Army faced renewed attack and should therefore be reinforced. Below, Stapff and Wetzell believed in the threat. Kuhl assessed that the principal British effort would be aimed at Fourth Army in Flanders; any attack on Sixth Army would be purely diversionary, and sending reinforcements there would play into British hands. This argument continued for a month until on 15 July OHL finally agreed that reinforcements should go purely to Fourth Army. The second and slightly later disagreement was whether Sixth Army should make a flank attack on the British in Flanders. Below, Stapff and Wetzell were for this; Army Group Rupprecht, including Kuhl, was against, on the grounds that the attack would itself be vulnerable to flank attack. OHL allowed preparations to go ahead, but in the end the attack did not take place.

As Kuhl saw it, Wetzell unduly favoured Sixth Army because he and Stapff were friends. The two were in frequent phone contact, giving Stapff the opportunity to press the Army's case that it still faced a major threat and should be reinforced. As a result, OHL deployed an extra division to Sixth Army. Kuhl also thought (wrongly) that Wetzell was responsible for allowing Seventh Army to fight a series of actions after the failure of the Nivelle offensive, which cumulatively used up formations better deployed in Flanders. From what he had heard, a strong stream of opinion in OHL believed that Wetzell was inadequate and that he himself was the only person in a position to persuade Ludendorff to deal with this problem. He shared the negative opinion of Wetzell but was unwilling to intervene. Wetzell had Ludendorff's support and was a dangerous enemy who could do much damage behind one's back. Kuhl believed that Wetzell continually made difficulties for Army Group Rupprecht, intrigued against him personally and also denigrated Loßberg. The cause of all this trouble was the original decision to replace Wetzell's friend Stapff with Loßberg.[125]

For their part, Below and no doubt Stapff believed that Kuhl lacked offensive spirit; he was a 'safety inspector', and Sixth Army headquarters nicknamed him 'the Self-Preserver' [*Selbstretter*] from his habit of suggesting a withdrawal before an attack so that if anything went wrong he could

---

[125] Ibid., passim, June–September 1917. Reichsarchiv, *Weltkrieg*, 13:39 shows that Wetzell in fact regarded Seventh Army's actions as highly unwelcome, but they were authorised within limits by Ludendorff (see also Chapter 8).

say 'I told you so'. The nickname had been circulating in Sixth Army for months and survived the change of commander, chief of staff and *Ia* in April, an example of the corporate mentality adopted by organisations.[126] Did it arise originally from Kuhl's actions at the Marne? As First Army chief of staff and in the absence of his Army commander, he had accepted the fateful order to withdraw from an OHL emissary who may or may not have had the proper authority.[127] Long after the war, Wetzell – who had been *Ia* in one of First Army's corps during the Marne – wrote to Otto von Below that this was when Kuhl first appeared as 'Massenbach', a deadly insult alluding to General Christian von Massenbach and his disastrous role in the 1806 Jena campaign. He was regarded as the worst type of theoretical soldier, whose failings included indecisiveness, mistaken assessments and covering his back with his superiors; he subsequently attempted to justify his performance in innumerable writings.[128]

How well did this criticism fit Kuhl? He was clearly a capable general staff officer, valued by Schlieffen and Moltke. During the war, he and Rupprecht formed an effective command team.[129] However, almost all his pre-war service was on the staff, and indeed under the regulations he would have had to retire if special arrangements had not been made for him to command a brigade temporarily. Most unusually, he had gained a PhD before joining the army. Subordinates both before and during the war found him over-controlling and pedantic – or, to quote what may have been a *Reichsarchiv* euphemism, he was 'an enthusiastic writer'. His personal like or dislike of officers was said to play a major role in how he treated them, and he was a snob who was greatly impressed by subordinates who were noble, Guards officers or rich. Little of this criticism became public, and Gallwitz's example shows why. Gallwitz actually regarded 'the gentle Kuhl' as a dangerous man and a pussyfooter. But his publisher was a friend of Kuhl, so in his books Gallwitz described Kuhl as very competent. He admitted privately that this was a mere courtesy.[130]

[126] This pun cannot be fully translated. A *Selbstretter* was a breathing apparatus for use in emergencies (e.g. for miners escaping from gas); the pun presumably had an element of running away from danger too. Xylander diary, 12 April 1917; Otto von Below diary, 27 June and 26 August 1917.

[127] Reichsarchiv, *Weltkrieg*, vol. 4, *Der Marne-Feldzug: Die Schlacht* (Berlin: E. S. Mittler, 1926), 220–8 and 255–67. For a modern account, see Holger H. Herwig, *The Marne, 1914: The Opening of World War I and the Battle that Changed the World* (New York: Random House, 2009), 281–3.

[128] Wetzell letter to Below, 15 December 1937, BArch, Otto von Below Nachlass, N87/68; Bayerische Akademie der Wissenschaften, *Neue Deutsche Biographie*, Massenbach entry, http://daten.digitale-sammlungen.de/bsb00016334/image_370 (accessed 18 June 2022).

[129] Boff, *Haig's Enemy*, 91.

[130] Möller-Witten, *Hermann von Kuhl*, 4 and 17; Pöhlmann, *Kriegsgeschichte*, 192; Liebmann, 'Lebenserinnerungen', 41–2; Obkircher, 'Bei Zwei Armee-Oberkommandos

Whether we agree with such comments or not, it is easy to see how Kuhl, the eternal staff officer, the pen-pusher with the doctorate, the pedant, the snob and the 'Self-Preserver' attracted such criticism. In late 1916–early 1917, some officers in Army Group Rupprecht headquarters certainly had concerns about him. Rupprecht believed that strain and age were taking their toll on Kuhl, and he was not the man he had been before the Somme. The army group *Ia* called him a doubt-spreader, an old man who should be pensioned off as soon as possible. The next year, Leeb commented that Kuhl was fussy, schoolmasterly, very intelligent but with no strength of character: 'it's not for nothing that he has the nickname "Self-Preserver"'.[131] There may have been a generation gap here: Kuhl was sixty, Rupprecht forty-seven, the *Ia* forty-four and Leeb forty.

Below and Stapff undoubtedly did use their relationship with Wetzell to further their plans for an attack on the British. Below and Wetzell had served together shortly before the war as commander and *Ia* of a division: Below explicitly saw this as creating a link to Wetzell in 1917. The basis for the friendship between Stapff and Wetzell is less clear, but they were contemporaries at *Kriegsakademie*; they stood next to each other in the general staff rank list; and they served at Verdun at the same time in early 1916. These relationships allowed Below and Stapff to approach Wetzell directly and not, as the chain of command required, through the army group. They would have found Wetzell a ready listener for their offensive plan as he was a consistent proponent of attacking somewhere.[132] He made the case for an attack to Ludendorff, but in the end it never happened and Kuhl had the last laugh. As recounted earlier, from mid-July, OHL accepted that priority should be given to Fourth rather than Sixth Army. Seventh Army's local operations on the Aisne eventually provoked the French attack at Malmaison. Kuhl saw the serious defeat there as a devastating verdict on Seventh Army's and OHL's policies.

Kuhl's and Below's vitriolic remarks illustrate the influence of personality and personal relationships on command. Whether or not their individual judgements were correct, the pattern they depict was part of the reality of the German army. This is particularly clear in Kuhl's case.

Generalstabsoffizier Ia.', 3–4; Jakob Jung, *Max von Gallwitz (1852–1937): General und Politiker* (Osnabrück: Biblio Verlag, 1995), 1–2, 79 and 109.

[131] Rupprecht, unpublished diary, 25 December 1916 and 21 February 1917; Georg Meyer, ed., *Generalfeldmarschall Wilhelm Ritter von Leeb: Tagebuchaufzeichnungen und Lagebeurteilungen aus zwei Weltkriegen* (Stuttgart: Deutsche Verlags-Anstalt, 1976), 21 and 113. Leeb had moved from 11th Bavarian Infantry Division to Army Group Rupprecht headquarters.

[132] On Wetzell's desire to take the offensive in 1917, see, for example, Reichsarchiv, *Weltkrieg*, 12:69–70.

Unlike Below, he sent his diary to the *Reichsarchiv*. As the Introduction suggested, his intention was to influence the historiography of the war. He must therefore generally have regarded his commentary, including on personalities and motivation, as important, plausible and acceptable to the *Reichsarchiv*. They would have been willing allies: by the time he submitted the diary in or after August 1932, they and Kuhl among others had long been engaged in an historiographical battle with Wetzell over the interpretation of the war.[133]

On the policy issues, although Kuhl was right that from June onwards Fourth and not Sixth Army faced the main threat, British diversionary operations at Arras and the delay in mounting the Flanders offensive complicated the assessment. Handling the aftermath of the Nivelle offensive was also not easy, as Chapter 8 will show. We do not therefore need to assume that personal motivation lay behind Wetzell's decisions. Similarly, though other sources lend weight to Below's – exaggerated – claims about Kuhl's caution, the Germans had insufficient means for Sixth Army to mount an attack. In opposing this operation, Kuhl was being realistic rather than lacking offensive spirit. He was of course also right to suspect that Below and Stapff were using their personal connection with Wetzell to promote Sixth Army's agenda. Markus Pöhlmann explains how networks furthered the issues in which their members were interested, and were in turn strengthened by being on the same side of the argument: the network described here is a good example of this. Kuhl's subsequent co-operation with the *Reichsarchiv* would have had the same reciprocal effect.[134]

As for Stapff's performance, there is evidence both for and against him. He was well reported on by Gallwitz as Second Army's *Ia* in 1916.[135] He was then a *Gruppe* chief of staff for five months, including during the Nivelle offensive. When he became Fourth Army chief of staff in late May 1917 he was an experienced officer, but not at this level. In fact he was thrown in at the deep end, arriving two weeks before the battle of Messines. He was from the heavy artillery, and as with Limbourg at Fresnoy, this was possibly too specialised a background. The army appears to have thought so anyway: Stapff was one of only three heavy artillery officers to serve as Army chief of staff during the war. Wetzell maintained that he was treated unfairly, but others shared Kuhl's doubts about him. As a *Gruppe* chief of staff in Fourth Army, Albrecht von Thaer found Stapff agitated, nervous and unsure what to do; he recognised

[133] For an introduction to the dispute, see Pöhlmann, *Kriegsgeschichte*, 314–21.
[134] Ibid., 248–50.
[135] Gallwitz comment on Stapff's *Qualifikationsbericht*, 2 June 1916, BArch, Gallwitz Nachlass, N710/61.

Stapff's intelligence but was one of those proposing his replacement by Loßberg.[136]

Events proved that Stapff was not the right man for the Fourth Army job. Exchanging him with Loßberg, the German army's chief defensive expert, was sensible, and ideally would have happened earlier. But apart from the factors complicating creation of the best Fourth Army command team mentioned in Chapter 2, this would have required certainty that the battle of Arras was over. Also, as Wetzell implied Stapff may have become a scapegoat for the defeat at Messines. Kuhl's admission that the defeat could have been avoided if Army Group Rupprecht had simply ordered evacuation of the threatened position shows that he himself bore a large share of responsibility, and may have been glad to find someone else to blame: the 'Self-Preserver' at work perhaps.

Following further criticism from Kuhl, Stapff was moved twice over the next few months. He was initially sent to be Second Army's chief of staff, in a quiet sector till the battle of Cambrai flared up there in November. He was awarded the *Pour le Mérite* for his performance then, but this did not save him from a negative assessment of his fitness for the March 1918 offensives as part of the same review that led to Moser's removal. He was transferred to be chief of staff of an army on the secondary Eastern Front.[137] As in the Moser case, strain may have played a role. Stapff's Army commander, Marwitz, wrote in January 1918 that he would shortly be returning from leave which he had really needed. He had looked pretty bad in the opening phase of Cambrai, recovered a bit during the successful German counter-attack and got noticeably better when awarded the *Pour le Mérite*.[138] But perhaps doubts about his mental robustness, already evident in the aftermath of Messines, swung the balance against him.

Conclusions

Both before and during the war, the German army stressed the influence of the personal factor and therefore the importance of the second command task, selecting the right men. It operated the seniority tempered by merit principle for appointing and promoting officers, based on a carefully structured though flawed confidential reporting system. During the war, it made continuous, but not always successful, efforts to select good and weed out unsuitable commanders and general staff

[136] 'Die Abwehrschlacht zwischen Ancre und Oise 8.-12.8.1918. I. Lage vor der Schlacht', unpublished Reichsarchiv research paper, BArch, Obkircher Nachlass, N2214/3; Thaer, *Generalstabsdienst*, 125–6.

[137] Kuhl, 'Kriegstagebuch', 2 December 1917 and 23 February 1918.

[138] Tschischwitz, *Marwitz*, 275.

officers. There were, however, limits on its ability to post officers freely, especially because of the constraints on and conservatism of the Military Cabinet. Suggestions that function automatically overrode rank are at best oversimplified. There was always the possibility of friction in such cases, illustrating the effect of personal motivations such as reputation, honour, ambition, pay and strain. Personal relationships, sometimes developing into networks and cliques, interacted with objective professional considerations and influenced the conduct of operations as well as the subsequent historiography.

The German army was not unique in its approach to the second command task, and there are for instance similarities with the British army, despite their very different natures. The British too operated a selection policy of seniority tempered by merit. They too struggled to get officers to report honestly on subordinates, without which it was impossible to remove incompetents. British officers too were motivated by a sense of duty and service towards sovereign and country – and by a desire for honours and glory, as well as financial necessity. One commander-in-chief about to assume office was warned, 'There are so many cross currents. So many cliques to reckon with. So many people to keep in good humour. The Court, Parliament, Society, the Army itself, with all its subdivisions.'[139] Above all perhaps, the effect of strain was the same. The commander of the main British formation fighting the battle of Arras, General Sir Edmund Allenby, was obsessed by the safety of his only son and used to ask the casualty reports office when he was in action, 'Have you any news of my little boy today?' Later on, when his son was killed, Allenby was stricken by grief but soldiered stoically on – holding out.[140]

The previous chapter showed how the actual authority of a formation depended on both events and personalities. Personal authority also fluctuated as Gallwitz's career in 1916–17 demonstrates. He had most influence when called in at moments of crisis – at Verdun in March 1916, as army group commander on the Somme in July–August and most obviously as commander of Fifth Army at Verdun after the disaster of December 1916. In between and after the Verdun defeat of August 1917, his influence waned. A clear indicator is whether he could secure Bronsart von Schellendorff as his chief of staff. Whereas Gallwitz valued Bronsart, others – particularly Kuhl – distrusted him. When Gallwitz's influence was low in autumn 1916, Bronsart was removed as his chief of staff. Gallwitz successfully insisted on Bronsart as chief of staff

---

[139] Beckett, *British Profession of Arms*, 9, 19–37, 57 and 248.
[140] Justin Fantauzzo, 'Dead Sea fruit: Edmund Allenby, the First World War and the Politics of Personal Loss', *First World War Studies*, vol. 7, no. 3 (2016), 292.

when he took over Fifth Army at the height of the December 1916 panic, but lost him again after the August 1917 defeat.[141] Throughout this period, though Gallwitz's jobs and influence changed, his actual rank of *General der Artillerie* did not.

The analysis here of the second command task both supports and contradicts Michael Geyer's thesis that the Third OHL had a cult of mechanisation and efficiency, sidelining Wilhelmine aristocratic culture and emphasising performance rather than personality.[142] The increased importance of the confidential report as the basis for personnel selection, serious attempts to rejuvenate and develop the skills of higher-level command teams and Ludendorff's desire to achieve a uniform standard of assessment across the whole army support the argument. Against it, the reporting system remained imperfect, Schulenburg's criticisms show that command was not properly rejuvenated, the Guards clique retained its grip on senior positions, and reports at all levels persisted in distinguishing between officers who were up to Western Front pressures and those who were not. Above all, human realities of personality and personal relationships played a much greater role in the exercise of command than a cult of mechanisation and efficiency would allow. At the end of the day, '[a]n army ... is a combination of individuals, and not a weight obeying the laws of physics'.[143]

---

[141] Kuhl, 'Kriegstagebuch', 15 September and 4 October 1916; Gallwitz, *Erleben im Westen*, 133–4, 146 and 235–6.
[142] Michael Geyer, *Deutsche Rüstungspolitik 1860–1980* (Frankfurt: Suhrkamp Verlag, 1984), 98–102.
[143] Strachan, *First World War*, 1:178.

5   Intelligence

> At the moment of battle, information about the strength of the enemy is usually uncertain, and the estimate of one's own is usually unrealistic.[1]

We saw earlier that the German army traditionally viewed war as the realm of constant uncertainty which created problems but also offered opportunities. Reducing the uncertainty to an acceptable level, where the opportunities could be exploited, was the third command task. As the quotation from Clausewitz suggests, the uncertainty involved both one's own forces and the enemy. Various means were available to cope with it. Achieving superiority by establishing a *Schwerpunkt* and taking the initiative transferred the burden of uncertainty to the enemy. Doctrine, training and accurate assessment of the quality of one's own forces created greater certainty about their combat value. However, the two principal means of reducing uncertainty were intelligence and communication in the sense of handling information. The German army's use of the word *Nachrichten* for both concepts shows the links between them. Nevertheless as a recent study of British army communications on the Western Front argues, they are different: roughly speaking, intelligence relates to the enemy and information to one's own troops.[2] Both were essential to fulfilling the third command task, but they are treated here as separate. Accordingly, this chapter covers intelligence and the next communication.

German military theory saw intelligence as an important aspect of command. Clausewitz wrote, 'By "intelligence" we mean every sort of

---

[1] Clausewitz, *On War*, book 4, chapter 4, 233. This quotation is a starting point for John Robert Ferris' chapter 'Intelligence, Uncertainty and the Art of Command in Military Operations' in his *Intelligence and Strategy: Selected Essays* (Abingdon: Routledge, 2005). The chapter comments usefully on the role, methodology and problems of intelligence.

[2] Brian N. Hall, *Communications and British Operations on the Western Front, 1914–1918* (Cambridge: Cambridge University Press, 2017), 13. Lukas Grawe uses *Feindaufklärung* (literally, 'enemy reconnaissance') to cover the collection, analysis, assessment and circulation of intelligence, while admitting it is anachronistic: *Deutsche Feindaufklärung*, 19–20.

information about the enemy and his country – the basis, in short, of our own plans and operations.' He stressed the difficulty of obtaining accurate intelligence: 'Many intelligence reports in war are contradictory; even more are false and most are uncertain.' This was 'one of the most serious sources of friction in war'.[3] By the end of the nineteenth century, the German general staff was devoting major resources to acquiring and analysing a vast volume of material on potential enemies and allies.[4] Many prominent officers were involved in this work: Hermann von Kuhl, for example, served for over sixteen years in the Third Department of the Great General Staff (covering France and Britain), including seven as its chief.[5] By 1914, regulations emphasised the importance of intelligence to operations. In a three-step command process, the initial assessment phase should first set out the mission then intelligence on the enemy. One military theorist commented that assessments must be free of preconceptions, which had often had a fatal effect: a famous example was Napoleon's conviction that Blücher could not intervene at Waterloo. When orders were issued, intelligence on the enemy was the first point to make.[6]

Despite this apparent emphasis on the importance of intelligence, the German army has the reputation historically of underplaying it. Indeed, Robert M. Citino comments that German intelligence has been 'among the worst in European military history'.[7] This is certainly exaggerated, but German intelligence before the First World War was flawed in three major ways. First, the army expected to fight a mobile, offensive war in which it would have superiority and the initiative, so it would constantly force the enemy to react under pressure. Knowledge of the enemy's intentions and reducing uncertainty were therefore secondary to operations.[8] Second, assessments frequently interpreted information in the light of existing German doctrine, the Russo-Japanese War being an example. Schlieffen wrote that high commanders often rejected as completely false any information which contradicted the picture they had created for themselves. Cultural stereotyping – shared by many ordinary Germans – was common. The French, for instance, were regarded as typical of the Latin race – intelligent, versatile, resourceful and patriotic,

[3] Clausewitz, *On War*, book 1, chapter 6, 117.
[4] Grawe, *Deutsche Feindaufklärung*, 42 and 47.   [5] Möller-Witten, *Hermann von Kuhl*, 9.
[6] Hauptmann Friedrich Immanuel, *Handbuch der Taktik* (Berlin: E. S. Mittler, 1905), 37–8, 41 and 44.
[7] Citino, *German Way of War*, xiv–xv.
[8] Hilmar-Detlef Brückner, 'Die deutsche Heeres-Fernmeldeaufklärung im Ersten Weltkrieg an der Westfront', in Jürgen W. Schmidt, ed., *Geheimdienst, Militär und Politik in Deutschland* (Ludwigsfelde: Ludwigsfelder Verlagshaus, 2008), 205 and 238. This is a succinct account of German wireless intelligence on the Western Front.

but also inconstant, disorganised and badly disciplined. Such preconceptions distorted objective assessment based on observations from manoeuvres and open source reporting. This led to contradictory judgements, such as seeing the French army both as one of the best in the world but also as riven by weaknesses and therefore inferior to the German army.[9]

Finally, the general staff believed any conflict would be a continental European war on two fronts. Military intelligence, including Section IIIb as the organisation responsible for collecting secret intelligence, therefore concentrated on possible war with France and Russia, and only on the opening phases at that. Its main interest was the strengths, deployment and intentions of the opposing forces, together with tactical developments once hostilities began. The intelligence system was basically set up for a short, victorious war and it therefore made few preparations to maintain its peacetime intelligence inputs under wartime conditions. It paid only rudimentary attention to likely enemies' economic and financial preparations, or longer-term aspects such as economic potential.[10] It did not differ from the general staffs of other powers here: like all bureaucracies, German intelligence had finite resources and pragmatically had to focus on the most pressing issues. But these weaknesses were compounded by lack of a central organisation to co-ordinate grand strategic or strategic military, naval and political intelligence requirements and assessments. It has been aptly said that in the years before the First World War, Germany had established an intelligence system but not an intelligence culture.[11]

In effect, there were two attitudes to intelligence in the German army before and at the start of the First World War: theory, which stressed its importance to good decision-making in the chaotic circumstances of mobile war; and practice, which suggested that German superiority made intelligence secondary and focused it on narrow requirements. However, the war which developed on the Western Front from autumn 1914 was not mobile, and from some time in 1916 the German army had neither superiority nor the initiative. It was clear too by then that the duration and total nature of the war meant previously ignored long-term issues must be addressed.

How should we assess the effectiveness of German intelligence as it faced this new situation? Commentators on intelligence are often happier

---

[9] Grawe, *Deutsche Feindaufklärung*, 17, 23–4, 118 and fn. 66, 183, 198, 221, 340, 464 and 468.

[10] Ibid., 462.

[11] Markus Pöhlmann, 'The Evolution of the Military Intelligence System in Germany, 1890–1918', in Simon Ball, Philipp Gassert, Andreas Gestrich and Sönke Neitzel, eds., *Cultures of Intelligence in the Era of the World Wars* (Oxford: Oxford University Press, 2020), 145–65.

talking about organisation or specific operations than about results.[12] But clearly an account of intelligence must evaluate its effect. Markus Pöhlmann has proposed three possible measures: results compared with the means available; how the intelligence service learned and improved over time; or comparing the performance of different services.[13] This approach has merits but needs development. The key measure is surely the impact of intelligence on the real world. We can break this down further into questions such as how accurate was the intelligence? What was the reputation of the intelligence service with its own high command – how well did it fare in the struggle for bureaucratic survival? How well integrated was intelligence with planning and operations? However, for the purposes of this book, the crucial question is simply, how well did intelligence help the German army carry out its missions?

Intelligence Sources and Structures

In peacetime, the chief German intelligence sources were military attaché reporting, probably the most highly valued information reaching the general staff;[14] open source material from professional and other journals; more or less clandestine trips by officers to areas of interest; and a relatively small amount of espionage, mainly handled by IIIb. All incoming intelligence was assessed by the relevant Great General Staff department, for example intelligence on France by the Third Department. In the event of war, IIIb would send agents through the front to gain intelligence, for both operational and tactical purposes; and cavalry would perform its usual reconnaissance roles. So the pre-war expectation was of traditional intelligence-gathering. Two new techniques were emerging: air reconnaissance was producing promising results on manoeuvres, and experiments to intercept Russian wireless traffic had begun.[15]

---

[12] This was, for instance, a feature of 'German Intelligence History from Bismarck to the Present', the 17th Annual Conference of the International Intelligence History Association in 2011.

[13] Pöhlmann, 'German Intelligence at War', 26.

[14] On military attachés, see Heinrich Otto Meisner, *Militärattachés und Militärbevollmächtigte in Preußen und im Deutschen Reich: Ein Beitrag zur Geschichte der Militärdiplomatie* (Berlin: Rütten & Loening, 1957).

[15] Pöhlmann, 'German Intelligence at War', 33–4, 40 and 47; Foley, 'Easy Target or Invincible Enemy?', 3–4 and 19. Russian wireless traffic: Generalmajor a.D. Friedrich Gempp, 'Geheimer Nachrichtendienst und Spionageabwehr des Heeres', 15 vols., NARA, Publication Number T77L, Rolls 1439–1440 and 1507–1509, II. Teil, 'Im Weltkrieg, 1914–1918', Abschnitt 6, 'Der Nachrichtendienst im Osten, insbesondere im Gebiet des Oberbefehlshabers Ost, vom Mai 1915 bis zum Ende des Jahres 1916', 341

The advent of war radically changed this picture. Following the 1870 model, an Intelligence Department [*Nachrichtenabteilung*] was established in OHL to integrate assessment of intelligence from all sources; its two wartime chiefs were the last head and deputy head of the old Third Department. Wartime conditions greatly reduced the attachés' access and the usefulness of open source information, previously the two main sources of intelligence. As we shall see, several of IIIb's clandestine contacts also collapsed at this point, illustrating the lack of preparation mentioned earlier. In the west at least, the onset of trench warfare eliminated cavalry reconnaissance and agent work through the front. A IIIb list from 1916 (Table 5.1) shows that in these circumstances, non-traditional sources either emerged for the first time or became more important.[16]

In their diaries, senior officers frequently refer to two types of intelligence – prisoner statements and agent reports. This is perhaps because both came as narratives that generalist officers could understand immediately; by contrast, intelligence from air reconnaissance and interception would need interpretation. Prisoner and deserter interrogation covered more than just questioning captives. It included producing intelligence by eavesdropping on prisoners or using agents posing as fellow prisoners, and acquiring documents from prisoners, dead bodies or captured positions. By January 1917, prisoner interrogation was seen as one of the two surest ways of gaining intelligence

Table 5.1 *Intelligence sources*

Deserter statements
Prisoner statements
Agent reports
Air reconnaissance reports
Interception of trench communications
Unit observation
Interception and decryption of wireless messages

(this is the Gempp Report; hereafter, Gempp, Abschnitt 6 etc.). For an assessment of German military intelligence's pre-war performance, see Grawe, *Deutsche Feindaufklärung*; also his 'German Secret Services before and during the First World War – A Survey of Literature and Recent Research', *Journal of Intelligence History*, vol. 18, no. 2 (2019), 199–219.

[16] Gempp, Abschnitt 6, Anlage 33. This list, from the Eastern Front in summer 1916, presumably includes captured documents in deserter and prisoner statements; it omits liaison and technical artillery information from sound-ranging and flash-spotting, increasingly important in the west. The reason for the list order is unclear.

on the enemy. Army Group Crown Prince commented that knowledge of the enemy's order of battle was vital and could only be maintained by frequent small-scale operations to take prisoners.[17] Days before the French assault in April 1917, one German *Gruppe* captured men who identified or confirmed the presence of five French divisions opposite.[18] The volume of prisoner interrogation reports surviving on file demonstrates the extent of this activity, as do statistics. In the first half of 1917, IIIb produced an average 200 reports per day from mail to and from prisoner of war camps, and 32,000 reports from these camps overall.[19]

Pöhlmann suggests that the advent of trench warfare raised the importance of prisoner and technical intelligence at the expense of IIIb's agent reporting.[20] In relative terms and in view of the sheer volume of reports, this may be so. But agent reporting was clearly still taken seriously in early 1917, to judge from its frequent mention in senior officers' diaries and its regular appearance in compilations of intelligence circulated down to divisional level.[21] However, like any form of intelligence, this reporting could be problematic and contradictory. It was often doubted or seen as stating the obvious, and Hindenburg even commented that the agent-running service produced derisory results.[22] Summing up this conflicting evidence, Pöhlmann believes that the Germans did not manage to place a single top source in an enemy decision-making body or military staff (but nor did the Entente), and that in general terms IIIb's agent reporting was at best of medium quality.[23]

This judgement may be too harsh though. The Germans were certainly aware of the need for high-level intelligence and, as we shall see, made considerable attempts to acquire it, with some success. They appear to

---

[17] HDK, 'Wochenübersicht 18.II. – 24.II.1917', Ia Nr. 1596 geh., 25 February 1917, GLAK, F1/246.

[18] Gruppe Sissonne, 'Gruppen-Nachbefehl', Ia No. 240/4, 13 April 1917, KAM, XV. BRK 89.

[19] Gempp, Abschnitt 7, 'Gesamtorganisation des Nachrichtendienstes und ihre Durchführung auf dem westlichen Kriegsschauplatz und in Deutschland vom Mai 1915 bis Ende 1916', 126–7, and Abschnitt 9, 'Die mobile Abteilung IIIb beim Chef des Generalstabes des Feldheeres im Jahre 1917', 86, both NARA, Publication Number T77L, Roll 1440.

[20] Markus Pöhlmann, 'Towards a New History of German Military Intelligence in the Era of the Great War: Approaches and Sources', *Journal of Intelligence History*, vol. 5, no. 2 (winter 2005), vi.

[21] For example, Rupprecht, *Kriegstagebuch*, 2:85–6 (18 January 1917); Xylander diary, 29 January 1917; Major Georg Hans Reinhardt, Hauptmann a.D. Fritz Hauptmann, Hauptmann Rudolf Hartmann et al., eds., *Das kgl. Sächs. 8. Infanterie-Regiment 'Prinz Johann Georg' Nr. 107 während des Weltkrieges 1914–1918* (Dresden: Baensch Stiftung, 1928), 341.

[22] Gempp, Abschnitt 6, 82; Hindenburg, *Out of My Life*, 315.

[23] Pöhlmann, 'German Intelligence at War', 38.

have had one or more human sources able to report, at least occasionally, on Entente military decision-making. According to a trusted agent in late April 1917, if attacks at Arras did not succeed, in fourteen days' time the British would launch an attack on the Yser in Flanders; the details were wrong, but at this time British offensive intentions were indeed shifting from Arras to Flanders. Shortly after, Crown Prince Rupprecht noted an agent report on the Anglo-French conference in early May which decided military policy for the next months. '*Weltkrieg*' correctly pointed out that apart from a minor error about the date, the report accurately summarised what the conference had agreed.[24]

Technical means included two forms of interception. In late 1915, the Germans introduced so-called Arendt stations to intercept trench telephone conversations. This source mainly produced order of battle intelligence, but on occasion provided higher-level information. A well-known intercept early on the morning of 1 July 1916 forewarned of the imminent British assault.[25] In January 1917, Arendt interception was thought as productive as prisoner interrogation in gaining reliable intelligence on the enemy.[26] However, the technique had its weaknesses. First, it was of limited range and covered front-line units rather than reserves. Second, over time Arendt became less productive. The British and French learned of it soon after its introduction and gradually tightened speech security in the forward areas. During 1917, the value of Arendt reporting therefore decreased, particularly on the British.[27] Nevertheless, in volume terms, it remained a significant source as shown by the existence of 10 stations in the Seventh Army area in May 1917, and a total of 292 in all theatres as late as March 1918.[28]

The other form of interception was wireless intelligence. This term covers decrypting enemy wireless messages as well as locating transmitters and identifying their parent formations from analysis of their traffic. German operational success based on intercepting Russian communications is well known. Wireless intelligence was slower to get going on the

---

[24] Rupprecht, *Kriegstagebuch*, 2:155 and 165 (29 April and 13 May 1917); Reichsarchiv, *Weltkrieg*, 12:256 and 547. David Stevenson, *With Our Backs to the Wall: Victory and Defeat in 1918* (London: Allen Lane, 2011), 146 says that in 1918 the Bulgarians had an agent in the Allied Supreme War Council; no further detail is available.

[25] Christopher Duffy, *Through German Eyes: The British and the Somme 1916* (London: Weidenfeld, 2006), 131. Arendt was the name of the interception technique's inventor.

[26] AOK 3 Nachrichtenoffizier [Intelligence Officer], 'Armeebefehl', Nr. 6003, 27 January 1917, BArch, PH5-II/370.

[27] Nachrichten-Abteilung (Sekt. West) memorandum, 8 February 1916, BArch, PH3/602, f. 67; Gempp, Abschnitt 9, 55.

[28] F. E. Station 14, 'Bericht über den funkentechnischen Beobachtungsdienst im Bereiche der 7. Armee (1.5.17–31.5.17)', Br. No. 651, 1 June 1917, GLAK, F108/188; Cron, *Geschichte des Deutschen Heeres*, 234–5.

Western Front. From November 1914, each Army was supposed to have one wireless station for interception, and a year later two direction-finding sections as well. But as so often reality differed from theory. By July 1916, only Sixth Army had direction-finding sections; and even as late as December, only four of the ten Armies and Army Detachments on the Western Front had received their interception stations.[29] Despite such delays, the organisation for handling wireless intelligence developed steadily. In spring 1916, OHL set up a section for integrated processing of cryptanalytical results. As the importance of signals and wireless intelligence rose, so too did the rank of their commanders at each level. By mid-1917, the OHL sections responsible for wireless intelligence and Arendt had become departments [Abteilungen], meaning that their heads were the same level as the chiefs of OHL's Intelligence Department and IIIb.[30]

The increasing status and independence of wireless intelligence are a clear sign of its value. The Germans may have achieved good results at this period against British ciphers at least. During the battle of Arras, British General Headquarters recorded evidence that the Germans had decrypted messages in the standard field cipher. As John Ferris comments, this security failure could have compromised British preparations for the battle; and the need to introduce new signals regulations during operations would surely have hindered efficient communication. Despite these countermeasures, the British later assessed that in July 1917 German wireless intelligence identified the plan for a landing on the Belgian coast. Ferris suggests that because of weak British security practices, throughout 1917 and 1918 'extraordinary opportunities' were open to German traffic analysts. It may also have been significant that Sixth Army, the formation fighting the battle of Arras, had the most experienced wireless intelligence experts on the Western Front, and in fact received intercepted traffic from the whole front for decryption.[31]

In February 1917, OHL stated that air reconnaissance was especially useful for early warning of the enemy's assault preparations.[32] German aviation distinguished between different types of reconnaissance. Close reconnaissance [Nahaufklärung] extended to a depth of nine kilometres behind the enemy front; on Sixth Army's front, this would include the city

---

[29] Cron, *Geschichte des Deutschen Heeres*, 225; Brückner, 'Deutsche Heeres-Fernmeldeaufklärung', 214 and 220.
[30] Brückner, 'Deutsche Heeres-Fernmeldeaufklärung', 222–3.
[31] John Ferris, ed., *The British Army and Signals Intelligence during the First World War* (Stroud: Alan Sutton, 1992), 115–17 and 132; Brückner, 'Deutsche Heeres-Fernmeldeaufklärung', 214.
[32] OHL circular, II Nr. 48626 op./Nachr.Abtlg., 28 February 1917, HSAS, Soden Nachlass, M660/038 Bü 17, f. 19.

of Arras. Long-range reconnaissance [*Fernaufklärung*] covered from there to about thirty kilometres beyond the front; this would take in British First and Third Army headquarters. Beyond that again, the zone of operational reconnaissance [*operative Fernerkundung*] stretched to the coast.[33] The role of the two longer-range forms of reconnaissance, carried out by Army or *Gruppe*, was to watch enemy rail transport, establishment of major camps, new aerodromes, ammunition dumps and unloading points: this contributed to locating the enemy's operational reserves.[34] Close reconnaissance was the task of the aviation allocated to divisions. This covered the enemy's defensive construction, shelters, assembly points for assault troops, battery positions and extension of the light railway system. It was therefore seen as the best means of understanding the enemy's intentions.[35]

From mid-1915 air reconnaissance increasingly meant photographic reconnaissance. The German air force made continuous improvements to photographic equipment, organisation and arrangements to exploit air photography for intelligence, mapping and artillery targeting.[36] A precondition for any form of air reconnaissance was preventing the enemy achieving air superiority, so reconnaissance and fighter operations were closely linked.[37] In early 1917, the Germans were greatly aided by their technical superiority over both British and French aircraft. However, though technology was important, it was not everything. Other factors in the success or failure of air reconnaissance included the weather, production, organisation, policy, tactics, training and familiarity of crew and ground staff with aircraft. Individuals too made a difference: when German fighter ace *Rittmeister* Manfred Freiherr von Richthofen went on leave at the beginning of May, the British noticed an immediate drop in pressure against them.[38]

Both British and Germans agreed that even with air superiority it was not possible to completely prevent enemy reconnaissance.[39] Given the complex interaction of the factors above, it is not surprising that both sides claimed success in their air reconnaissance during the battle of Arras, with the

---

[33] 'Die Luftwaffe der 6. Armee von Ende Januar 1917 bis zum Beginn der Frühjahrsoffensive bei Arras am 9. April 1917', unpublished Reichsarchiv research paper, BArch, RH61/737, 2 and 9 (hereafter, 'Luftwaffe der 6. Armee').

[34] Kommandeur der Flieger 6, 'Befehl für die Fernaufklärung', Nr. 25100, 1 April 1917, KAM, AOK 6 Bd. 409; '*Abwehrschlacht*', March 1917, 33.

[35] '*Abwehrschlacht*', March 1917, 34.

[36] On the development of photo reconnaissance, see Helmut Jäger, *Erkundung mit der Kamera: Die Entwicklung der Photographie zur Waffe und ihr Einsatz im 1. Weltkrieg* (Munich: Venorion, 2007).

[37] '*Abwehrschlacht*', March 1917, 32 and 36.   [38] Jones, *War in the Air*, 3:370.

[39] '*Abwehrschlacht*', March 1917, 37; Jones, *War in the Air*, 3:340–1.

Germans having the upper hand in April and the British in May.[40] The French, however, were initially caught in a dilemma. Their new assault methods depended crucially on surprise. They knew that concentrating fighter forces in a particular sector was a sure sign of an attack and they therefore initially held back most of their fighter squadrons from the front. But this enabled German aviation to carry out much successful reconnaissance and to seriously impede the work of French spotter planes.[41] However, by mid-May, French fighter reinforcements with improved aircraft types secured air superiority and made German reconnaissance much more difficult.[42]

A big part of overall intelligence coverage came from information on enemy activity routinely compiled by front-line units. This was incorporated in the regular situation reports [*Beurteilungen der Lage*] sent up through the chain of command. By the time these reports reached Army or army group level, they generally covered enemy artillery, infantry and aviation activity. Changes in this activity were possible indicators of enemy intentions, and this could be measured statistically. In a typical weekly 'Intelligence on the Enemy' [*Nachrichten über den Feind*] report, Sixth Army compared the number of enemy infantry raids and identified battery positions and calibres of guns firing with the previous week.[43] From autumn 1915, an increasingly important contribution to these reports came from technical methods such as flash-spotting and sound-ranging intelligence on the enemy's artillery.[44]

Integration of the Intelligence System

So by early 1917, 'intelligence meant more than simply reading newspapers and sending out cavalry patrols'.[45] The dense network of traditional and new sources that had now been created inevitably led to problems of integration. Indeed, one of the measures of effectiveness proposed at the beginning of the chapter was how well intelligence was

[40] Jones, *War in the Air*, 3:370–1.
[41] Groupe d'armées de réserve, 'Rapport sur les conditions dans lesquelles s'est effectuée la préparation d'artillerie pour l'attaque du 16 avril', 7 May 1917, AFGG, V/1: Annexe 1883; General der Kavallerie Ernst von Hoeppner, *Deutschlands Krieg in der Luft: Ein Rückblick auf die Entwicklung und die Leistungen unserer Heeres-Luftstreitkräfte im Weltkriege* (Leipzig: K. F. Koehler, 1921), 106. On French aviation in the Nivelle offensive, see Denis Rolland, 'Un ciel allemand?', in Offenstadt, *Chemin des Dames*, 121–36.
[42] Reichsarchiv, *Weltkrieg*, 12:379.
[43] AOK 6 circular, 'Nachrichten über den Feind in der Zeit vom 3.3 bis einschließlich 9.3.17', Ia/M.S.O. No. 95672, 10 March 1917, KAM, AOK 6 Bd. 369.
[44] For their development, see Cron, *Geschichte des Deutschen Heeres*, 164–7, and Otto Schwab, 'Meßtrupps', in Kaiser, *Ehrenbuch der Deutschen Schweren Artillerie*, 70–2.
[45] Pöhlmann, 'German Intelligence at War', 54.

integrated with planning and operations, meaning particularly integration of the producing organisations and integration of the product into an all-source intelligence picture.

On the organisational side (Figure 5.1), different parts of the system were integrated but the whole was not. At the beginning of the war, the only agency specialising in intelligence production was IIIb. In terms of bureaucratic survival, it had certain strengths. Modern research suggests it performed competently in providing intelligence before and at the outbreak of war.[46] Its network of intelligence sections attached to every Army and later army group – which developed into what became known as the 'Front Intelligence Service' [*Frontnachrichtendienst*] – initially placed it in a strong position to co-ordinate production of intelligence from all sources. Falkenhayn praised its achievements in 1915 and 1916. This led directly to its elevation from a section to a department of OHL, putting it on a bureaucratic par with OHL's Operations and Intelligence Departments and so increasing its prestige within the staff; its chief, Walter Nicolai, now gained the right of direct access to Falkenhayn.[47] In 1917, Ludendorff thanked him for the contribution his officers made to subverting the Russian army.[48] IIIb largely controlled the important prisoner interrogation resource and it was given wide-ranging new non-intelligence tasks, including censorship and propaganda. These raised its status, and Nicolai's flexibility in delegating responsibility for different activities spread the burden.

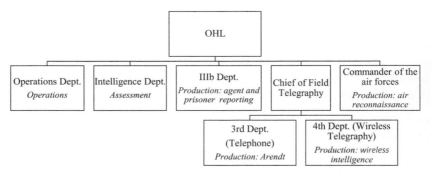

Figure 5.1 OHL departments involved in intelligence, early 1917

[46] Foley, 'Easy Target or Invincible Enemy?'; Trumpener, 'War Premeditated?'
[47] Gempp, Abschnitt 7, 1 and 35; Epkenhans, *Nicolai*, 30 and 181.
[48] Epkenhans, *Nicolai*, 410.

Nevertheless, IIIb was more and more distracted from its core role of intelligence gathering.[49]

IIIb's aspiration to a monopoly of intelligence production was increasingly challenged by the air force and the signal troops, in charge of air reconnaissance and both forms of interception respectively. The air force became a separate arm of service in late 1916, the signal troops a year later. Both were huge organisations – the signal troops eventually numbered almost 200,000 – whose heads had status as corps commanders. No reliable details are available for IIIb's wartime strength, but an incomplete list from March 1917 has an officer head count of under 150 including those at OHL, in the Front Intelligence Service and at various stations. The list does not include staff in support and other functions, but compared with the air force and signal troops, IIIb was clearly a minnow. Nicolai was acutely aware too that his relatively junior rank as *Major* made his job more difficult.[50] So it is not surprising that throughout the war it proved impossible to establish an integrated intelligence organisation. There was no way that the air force and signals giants would hand over their intelligence producers to IIIb or anyone else.

A further hindrance to integration was that the air force and signal troops were operational organisations. Their raw intelligence together with reporting from front-line units was fed into the general staff *Ic* officers at divisional and *Gruppe* level (Figure 5.2).[51] The general staff – including Max Bauer in OHL's Operations Department – fiercely resisted IIIb's attempts to co-ordinate any of this intelligence as interference in operational matters. This may seem odd given that IIIb was originally part of the Great General Staff. The poor relationship between Bauer and Nicolai, including occasional open clashes, must have had an effect here.[52] Another factor may well have been fall-out from the traditional general staff emphasis on operations rather than intelligence. In addition, although senior IIIb staff such as Nicolai were general staff officers, most wartime personnel were not. There were thirteen IIIb chief intelligence officers in Army and army group headquarters on the Western Front in spring 1917. Four had attended *Kriegsakademie* but only two had

[49] Ibid., 60–2, 251 and 453; Pöhlmann, 'Evolution of the Military Intelligence System in Germany', 157.

[50] Cron, *Geschichte des Deutschen Heeres*, 231; Major Ammon a.D., 'Das Nachrichtenwesen', in Max Schwarte, ed., *Die Technik im Weltkriege* (Berlin: E. S. Mittler, 1920), 245; 'Rangliste der mob. III b.', 1 March 1917, Gempp, Abschnitt 9, Anlage 8; Epkenhans, *Nicolai*, 482. Nicolai was promoted *Oberstleutnant* in 1918.

[51] VII.RK, 'Geschäftsordnung der Generalstabsabteilungen', IIa Nr. 2221, 23 April 1917, HSAS, Soden Nachlass, M660/038 Bü 18.

[52] Epkenhans, *Nicolai*, 178–80.

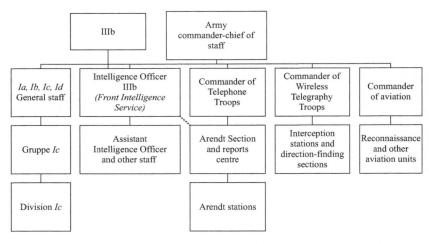

Figure 5.2 Organisation of intelligence in an Army, early 1917

subsequently been seconded to and none permanently transferred into the general staff before the war. They were in effect seen as inferior, an impression strengthened by OHL's rejection of Nicolai's wartime request to transfer them all into the general staff.[53]

Finally the Front Intelligence Service's dual subordination to IIIb and to parent Armies and army groups regularly caused friction. In late 1916 and early 1917 there was a fight over prisoner interrogation, and IIIb was forced partially to cede control to *Gruppen* and divisions. Also in early 1917, there was a clash over handling Arendt stations and their product; this time IIIb lost out to the signal troops.[54] Theoretically, an OHL order in March 1917 sorted out these various problems. It included instructions for the IIIb front intelligence officers to report directly to OHL intelligence from all sources within their Army or army group. This was clear enough, but equally clearly it did not work: within a month Army Group Rupprecht's chief intelligence officer requested an OHL order that he and his IIIb colleagues should have absolute priority in prisoner interrogation and should be given all intelligence on the enemy by the fastest means. As in so many other areas, much depended on the personalities and relationships of those involved.[55] Internal IIIb orders for sections to report

[53] Ibid., 233.
[54] Gempp, Abschnitt 7, 57–61 and Abschnitt 9, 20–6; Brückner, 'Deutsche Heeres-Fernmeldeaufklärung', 226.
[55] Gempp, Abschnitt 7, 155–6 and Abschnitt 9, Anlage 5. See also Pöhlmann, 'German Intelligence at War', 38–9.

fortnightly on use of their material in OHL-issued intelligence briefing suggest a general feeling of insecurity at this time.[56]

These tensions were not unique to IIIb. In late 1916, Army Group Rupprecht argued that Arendt stations should not evaluate their own product, a task it claimed only the general staff could undertake. In this case, the general staff lost out. By mid-1917, OHL's Chief of Field Telegraphy controlled all Arendt reporting, the central school for training Arendt interpreters and evaluating stations' reporting, all knowledge of enemy codes and ciphers and all cryptanalysis. Later in the year, he established evaluation offices [Auswertungsstellen] at Army and Gruppe level to integrate analysis of Arendt and wireless intelligence material.[57] His control of these assets, which collectively produced and analysed some of the most reliable material available, can only have increased his influence in the intelligence world.

Lack of organisational integration did not necessarily preclude sensible co-operation. IIIb provided support to Arendt stations and the interpreters school; from late 1916, it was tasked to acquire enemy cipher material for the signal troops. Conversely, wireless intelligence analysts could draw on information from prisoners and captured documents as well as all forms of intercept to improve their product.[58] OHL's wireless intelligence department had a section covering diplomatic traffic, including Italian reporting from Russia and transmissions from the Spanish and Turkish embassies in Berlin among others. The section's support for the German Foreign Office [Auswärtiges Amt] included testing and improving its codes.[59]

IIIb's relations with the Foreign Office were generally not good, but this did not prevent effective collaboration in arranging Lenin's fateful return to Russia in April 1917.[60] The legation in The Hague provided cover for four different counter-intelligence organisations from IIIb, Fourth Army, the navy and the police.[61] Military attachés, who came under embassy auspices, were not IIIb officers or in the IIIb chain of command. Relations with them varied, but it was possible in at least some cases to co-operate

[56] Gempp, Abschnitt 9, 11–12.
[57] Brückner, 'Deutsche Heeres-Fernmeldeaufklärung', 226 and 231–2.
[58] Gempp, Abschnitt 7, Anlage 6 and Abschnitt 9, 53; Franz Benöhr letter to Peter Liddle, 5 March 1973, University of Leeds Special Collections, LIDDLE/WW1/GE/29/05. Benöhr worked on wireless intelligence at OHL in 1917–18. I am grateful to Dr Jim Beach for this reference.
[59] Hermann Stützel, 'Geheimschrift und Entzifferung im Ersten Weltkrieg', Truppenpraxis, July 1969, 543. Stützel headed the diplomatic section.
[60] Werner Hahlweg, 'Lenins Reise durch Deutschland im April 1917', Vierteljahrshefte für Zeitgeschichte, vol. 5, no. 4 (1957), 307–33.
[61] Admiralstab der Marine Abteilung G, No. G.1790 I³, 3 February 1917, BArch, RM120/66.

well. *Major* Busso von Bismarck in Berne was the most productive attaché, both acquiring secret intelligence and supporting IIIb's agent work. Indeed, he was so active that IIIb sent him an assistant and arranged other support; it also had to rein him in for fear he would endanger his position in Switzerland.[62]

IIIb's links with naval intelligence were described as 'loose' – probably a euphemism for bad – but this too did not prevent some important co-operation. IIIb reached joint arrangements with the navy on agent-running practicalities, and on one occasion it handed over an intelligence station to the Admiralty.[63] In the wireless intelligence field, army units successfully attacked British naval ciphers from 1915. By 1917, the navy received thousands of these messages every month, and it obviously valued the product. In May that year, a joint meeting of all those with wireless intelligence interests agreed to share cryptanalytical results and reporting.[64]

A further aspect of intelligence integration was liaison with Austro-Hungarian, Bulgarian and Turkish counterparts. IIIb had liaison stations with all three. The most long-standing of these relationships, with Austria-Hungary, was also the most productive, particularly in the counter-intelligence and wireless intelligence fields. Indeed, the Austro-Hungarians were several years ahead of the Germans in exploiting wireless intelligence and seem to have maintained this lead during the war, at least on Russia and Italy. From December 1915, they could read Italian traffic between Rome and the embassy in Petrograd. The Italian ambassador's reports yielded a stream of useful intelligence on Russia's political and military situation, including pressure on Rumania in 1916 to enter the war and, the next year, growing Entente disappointment with the results of the Russian Revolution. More significantly for this book, as the case study later in this chapter shows, the reports also gave the first concrete evidence of Entente plans for the spring offensive. Later on, they and intercepted Russian messages warned of preparations for the Kerensky offensive. This intelligence could not avoid

[62] Gempp, Abschnitt 8A, 'Die Ergebnisse des Nachrichtendienstes der mobilen Abteilung IIIb im Westen vom Frühjahr 1915 bis Ende 1916. A: Vom Frühjahr bis Ende 1915', 145 and 165–70, and Abschnitt 8B, 'Die Ergebnisse des Nachrichtendienstes der mobilen Abteilung IIIb im Westen vom Frühjahr 1915 bis Ende 1916. B: Im Jahre 1916', 120, both NARA, Publication Number T77L, Roll 1440. See also Bismarck's account of his work in Oberstleutnant a.D. Busso von Bismarck, 'Der Militärattaché im Nachrichtendienst', in Generalmajor von Lettow-Vorbeck, ed., *Die Weltkriegsspionage* (Munich: Verlag Justin Moser, 1931), 104–10.

[63] Pöhlmann, 'German Intelligence at War', 28; Gempp, Abschnitt 8A, 55.

[64] Hilmar-Detlef Brückner, 'Germany's First Cryptanalysis on the Western Front: Decrypting British and French Naval Ciphers in World War I', *Cryptologia*, vol. 29, no. 1 (January 2005), 1–22; Gempp, Abschnitt 9, 46.

a severe initial defeat, but did enable the Central Powers to prepare a counter-offensive even before the Russian assault began.[65]

One final and perhaps surprising area of integration is the extensive employment of civilians. The clearest example here is wireless intelligence, where by summer 1917 200–300 civilians were working on deciphering and analysis in OHL alone. They were chiefly recruited from men with a university degree or similar level of education who had a knowledge of foreign languages and the ability to think logically. They included at least two professors.[66] A third, classical philologist Ludwig Deubner, played a prominent role in Germany's early wireless intelligence successes against the Russians and later in developing the system on the Eastern Front.[67]

IIIb too called in civilians to help in unfamiliar areas, including chemists to develop aids such as secret inks and mathematicians to develop cipher systems and carry out deciphering work. Remarkably, it employed a woman PhD graduate, Elisabeth Schragmüller, as a case officer on one of its stations.[68] Many lawyers were given jobs in counter-intelligence, counter-subversion and censorship. IIIb's counter-intelligence section was headed by a senior judge assisted by a lecturer in jurisprudence at the University of Straßburg, with an active general staff *Hauptmann* covering purely military aspects of the work.[69] Revealingly, the two civilians both held *Hauptmann* rank in the *Landwehr*, following the usual military service as young men. Many civilian recruits held such ranks, which together with their previous military experience would certainly have eased their assimilation into the wartime army and acceptance by the chain of command.

Such integration speaks well of German intelligence's flexibility, particularly compared with operations where the general staff in effect maintained a closed shop to which only professional military officers gained

---

[65] Albert Pethö, *Agenten für den Doppeladler: Österreich-Ungarns Geheimer Dienst im Weltkrieg* (Graz: Leopold Stocker Verlag, 1998), 149–50, 158, 176 and 223–30. Grawe, *Deutsche Feindaufklärung*, 99–104 gives more detail of pre-war German intelligence liaison with Austria-Hungary.

[66] Benöhr letter to Liddle.

[67] Christian Deubner, 'Ludwig Deubner: A Professor from Königsberg and the Birth of German Signal Intelligence in WWI', *Journal of Intelligence History*, vol. 18, no. 2 (2019), 164–98.

[68] Epkenhans, *Nicolai*, 271; Hanne Hieber, '"Mademoiselle Docteur": The Life and Service of Imperial Germany's Only Female Intelligence Officer', *Journal of Intelligence History*, vol. 5, no. 2 (winter 2005), 91–108.

[69] Epkenhans, *Nicolai*, 315–16. On German counter-intelligence and security work in occupied France and Belgium, see Élise Rezsöhazy, 'De la protection du secret militaire à l'occupation des populations civiles: Les polices secrètes allemandes derrière le front Ouest (1914–1918)', unpublished PhD thesis, Université catholique de Louvain, 2020.

access. This suggests that one reason why intelligence could employ civilians was precisely its perceived secondary role to operations. The lowly ranks attained by many of the civilians support this. For instance, one of the professors in OHL wireless intelligence was a sergeant. He was promoted lieutenant for deciphering a British diplomatic code, a rare honour.[70]

The other side of integration, producing intelligence assessments from all available sources, was well handled. OHL's Intelligence Department (renamed Foreign Armies Department [*Abteilung Fremde Heere*] in May 1917) was the only organisation able to generate authoritative, all-source intelligence analysis. This unique position, especially from within OHL, meant that the highest-level intelligence product was integrated by default. The department briefed Ludendorff on the overall intelligence picture [*Gesamtbild*].[71] Its frequently issued and detailed 'Briefing Notes' [*Vortragsnotizen*] on the different theatres were widely circulated and contributed to decision-making by OHL, army groups and Armies. The case study later in this chapter, on German foreknowledge of the Nivelle offensive, gives the example of an Intelligence Department assessment that formed the basis for Ludendorff's own appreciation and all the subsequent defensive preparations. The department also provided the analysis of enemy strengths and intentions for the 'Assessments of the Situation', which OHL began issuing in early 1917. It compiled lists of enemy commanders, nicknamed the 'Rogues' Gallery' [*Verbrecher-Album*], though apparently not the personality reports that were a feature of peacetime intelligence work.[72] And it produced much other background material, British examples from early 1917 including reports on manpower reserves and the effect of the Irish question on them.[73]

By spring 1917, the department had twenty-one officers and seven military officials (mainly cartographers). They were supported by person-nel in the Deputy General Staff [*Stellvertretender Generalstab*] in Berlin, but this was still a tiny number to handle the workload.[74] The OHL

---

[70] Benöhr letter to Liddle.

[71] Oberst a.D. Leopold von Rauch, 'Der Deutsche Nachrichtendienst im Weltkriege', *Deutscher Offizier-Bund*, vol. 6, no. 20 (1927), 848–50. Most air reconnaissance and wireless intercept reporting went first to OHL's Operations Department.

[72] Reichsarchiv, *Weltkrieg*, 12:76; Grawe, *Deutsche Feindaufklärung*, 44.

[73] OHL Nachrichtenabteilung, 'Der englische Ersatz', Nr. 2567a, 11 January 1917, and 'Die irische Frage in ihrer Bedeutung für den englischen Heeresersatz', Nr. 2802a, 27 January 1917, both on HSAD, 11250–056. For a negative view of the department, see Afflerbach, *Auf Messers Schneide*, 189–90; note, however, that he elides IIIb and the Intelligence/Foreign Armies Department into one and believes, for instance, that Nicolai was responsible for assessment.

[74] On mobilisation, the department had five officers and two officials: Gempp, Abschnitt 9, 85. Spring 1917 figures from GHQ Telegraphendirektion, 'Verzeichnis der

department had grown four-fold since mobilisation, indicating the increasing value placed on intelligence. We know little about its work but can tell something from its composition in early 1917. First, nearly 90 per cent of its officers senior enough to have attended *Kriegsakademie* before the war had done so. This implies that, unlike the IIIb posts described in this chapter, the department was seen as doing proper general staff work. However, none of its officers were specialised intelligence analysts, though the four who had served in the general staff before the war, on transfer or secondment, probably had relevant experience. Second, almost one-third of the officers had previously been more or less seriously wounded or invalided for health reasons. These are the ones we know about, so the real proportion may have been higher. Posting such officers to non-combatant roles reflected the army's continuing efforts to comb out men fit for active service. Finally, six of the officers – over a quarter – were from the Guards.

One of the Guards officers was the departmental head from late 1914 to the end of the war, *Major* Leopold von Rauch. Like the rest of his department, but unlike his colleague Nicolai, he has left little trace in the historiography – surprisingly so, as he was extremely well connected. He was the grandson of a Prussian Minister of War, the son of a *General der Infanterie* and the nephew of a *General der Kavallerie*. His father had served in the 1st Foot Guard Regiment. In due course, he and his elder brother both joined the regiment, the brother cementing his status by serving as military governor to the royal princes. Rauch probably met his wife, a Bismarck, through one of her cousins who was serving in the regiment. Usefully, Hindenburg's adjutant, Kurd von Bismarck, was her brother. When Nicolai discovered that his wife had met Frau von Rauch, he encouraged her to pursue the relationship, a good piece of networking with his colleague Rauch and the influential adjutant.[75]

Total War and New Tasks

The emergence of total war led to two important new tasks: evaluating the quality of enemy divisions and acquiring economic and political intelligence. Evaluating enemy divisions mattered at both strategic and tactical

Fernsprechteilnehmer', 13–14. In August 1914, part of the peacetime Great General Staff became OHL, and part remained in Berlin as the Deputy General Staff: for details of the latter's organisation and development, see BArch, PH3/310. From late 1915, intelligence analysis work was carried out in its Second Department. A 1916 organigram lists thirty-seven officers and four civilians in the department, but does not say which were engaged on intelligence: see 'Chef des Stellvertretenden Generalstabes der Armee', 5 May 1916, BArch, Eberhardt Nachlass, N12/88.
[75] Epkenhans, *Nicolai*, 386. Sadly for Nicolai's networking efforts, the late Chancellor Otto von Bismarck was from a different branch of the family.

levels. Strategically, a concentration of highly rated divisions indicated an offensive; tactically, German formations needed to know what they would be facing. Military attachés had reported on the quality of their host state's forces during peacetime, and German intelligence had assessed enemy formations on the Western Front since at least July 1915. Every enemy unit now had an entry on a card index. Such records were essential for assessing two factors, the intrinsic combat value of enemy divisions and their combat value at any given time.[76] The difficulty of making the latter assessment was well-known, because of the need to discount exaggerations by prisoners who were psychologically exhausted or desperate to please.[77]

Throughout 1917, the German army refined its methods for making these judgements. By summer, the Intelligence Department was issuing formal assessments of every enemy division. These covered the division's original status, where its men came from, participation in major battle, judgement of intrinsic combat value [*Beurteilung*] and finally current combat value [*Augenblicklicher Gefechtswert*], the latter to include combat strength and casualties. Based on such categories, the Germans divided British formations into particularly good or good assault divisions, average and mediocre. The good and particularly good assault divisions comprised some of the regular divisions and a majority of those whose men came from Scotland, London, Canada, Australia and New Zealand.[78] In the French army, over one-third of combat divisions were viewed as good assault troops, particularly formations from the pre-war border corps, some colonial divisions and those with regiments from the north and centre of France. Men from the south of the country were less highly regarded, and it was noted that they were usually mixed with troops from other areas. Among the colonial divisions, units from West Africa were considered poor, those from North Africa good.[79]

---

[76] Meisner, *Militärattachés*, 52; Gempp, Abschnitt 7, 5 and Abschnitt 8B, 145–6. Chapter 8 defines the two types of combat value.

[77] Gempp, Abschnitt 6, 101–2.

[78] HKR Nachrichtenoffizier, 'Gliederung des Feindes vor Heeresgruppe Kronprinz Rupprecht vom 16. bis 22. März 1917', 22 March 1917, HAM, Rupprecht Nachlass Nr. 506; AOK 6 Nachrichtenoffizier, 'Beurteilung der vor der Front der 6. Armee stehenden britischen Divisionen', B. Nr. 11186 Geheim, 13 August 1917, KAM, ID (WK) 7168–2; OHL Abteilung Fremde Heere circular, 'Mitteilung über die britische Armee Nr. 4. Kampfwert des britischen Heeres', Nr. 4610, 1 January 1918, HSAS, M33/ 2 Bü 536. Inexplicably, the Germans rated 34th Division mediocre.

[79] Chef des Generalstabes des Feldheeres Nachrichtenabteilung, *Kurze Zusammenstellung über die französische Armee*, 4th ed. (Hauptquartier Mézières-Charleville: Druckerei des Chefs des Generalstabes des Feldheeres, 1917), 24 and 27–8; OHL Abteilung Fremde Heere circular, 'Divisionsliste. Bewertung der französischen Divisionen', Nr. 5660a, 5 September 1917, GLAK, F3/650. See also Gregory Martin, 'German and French

The Intelligence Department commented that the particularly good and good assault divisions of both armies were often used in special actions; their identification at the front was therefore a significant indication of enemy intentions. There was of course a risk that such assessments could degenerate into the stereotypes described earlier. In summer 1917, the German view of the French as prone to rapidly changing moods [*Wankelmütigkeit*] contributed to uncertainty about French national and military morale during the mutinies.[80] Similarly, as we shall see, German beliefs about the British character may have coloured their judgement of British military capabilities. But the evaluation of British formations was not simple prejudice, since it drew on reports from German units about British performance in battle. Chapter 8 shows that German commanders used the same sort of methods to assess their own troops: so too did the British and French, some of whom would have agreed with German opinions of their formations.[81]

Organisationally, the German system was badly prepared for the second new task, acquiring intelligence on high-level economic and political affairs. These areas had been covered in pre-war reporting only to the extent they affected the military strength and intentions of potential enemies and other nations of interest. But they had never been the focus of attention – surprisingly, perhaps, given both Moltkes' belief that a future war might be long and economic potential therefore important.[82] The sources for such reporting, mainly military attachés and the press, had anyway largely dried up on the outbreak of war. Replacing this coverage immediately would have required large means and years of detailed preparation in peacetime, which had been precluded by over-concentration on battlefield intelligence.[83] A further complication was that Britain had always been of greater concern to German naval intelligence than military. In IIIb's eyes, only France and Russia had really counted as enemies. Work against Britain in peacetime was therefore secondary, and the section's scarce resources prevented assigning it a higher priority. One consequence after war broke out was difficulty

---

Perceptions of the French North and West African Contingents, 1910–1918', *Militärgeschichtliche Mitteilungen*, vol. 56, no. 1 (1997), 31–68.

[80] OHL Abteilung Fremde Heere, 'Die Stimmung im französischen Heere und Volk', Nr. 4824a, 30 June 1917, HSAS, M635/2 Bd. 111.

[81] Positive British views of Australian and Canadian formations: BOH 1918, 5:178–9. Negative French views on troops from the south: Nicolas Offenstadt, 'La Grande Guerre des régions', *Le Monde*, 12 May 2014, www.lemonde.fr/centenaire-14-18/article/2014/05/12/la-grande-guerre-des-regions_4415168_3448834.html (accessed 18 June 2022).

[82] Grawe, *Deutsche Feindaufklärung*, 462.

[83] Pöhlmann, 'German Intelligence at War', 38; Gert Buchheit, *Der deutsche Geheimdienst: Geschichte der militärischen Abwehr* (Munich: Paul List, 1966), 30.

assessing the size and quality of the new citizen army which Britain was raising.[84]

Realistically, from the range of sources available, the only ones that could contribute to the new high-level tasking were prisoners and agents, both under the control of IIIb. Interrogators were instructed not to limit themselves to purely military information but to explore economic and political issues too. Such reports, especially when well written, were warmly welcomed by senior officers.[85] In the British case, subjects of interest included conditions at home as well as political tensions in Ireland and India. Christopher Duffy has praised the breadth of vision and skill with which German intelligence officers extracted such information.[86] But with a few exceptions it is difficult to see how prisoners would have had particularly useful knowledge of these topics.

The burden of reporting on the new economic and political requirements therefore fell on IIIb's human intelligence assets. Overall, the department was not well-placed here. Nicolai claimed that various clandestine contacts with officers and officials in France and Russia had functioned well until the outbreak of war, when they suddenly collapsed. Just a few high-level contacts remained, and of these Nicolai named only the most long-standing, August Schluga Freiherr von Rastenfeld or Baron Schluga, codenamed 'Agent 17'. He had worked for the Germans since the 1860s and in 1914–16 they undoubtedly continued to value his reporting: Nicolai handled Schluga himself and on at least one occasion introduced him to Rauch.[87] However, modern research suggests that by this time Schluga may have been a French double agent, and in any case his production tailed off in 1916. Later in the year, it became clear that he was fabricating intelligence; he was moved to house-arrest in Brussels and died shortly after.[88]

Adding to IIIb's woes at this period, the stream of so-called 'Kleist reports' dried up in spring 1916. Ewald Freiherr von Kleist, a retired Guards officer and *Rittmeister*, was a major industrialist living in Switzerland. From early 1915, he used his professional connections to provide IIIb with intelligence on high-level French, British and Russian economic developments. Despite some concerns, his reports were so valued that Falkenhayn read them in raw form. Why this flow of intelligence came to an end in 1916 is not clear, but it suffered from various problems. Nicolai handled Kleist personally, and since he was already overburdened with other work he could not devote to the case the detailed

---

[84] Epkenhans, *Nicolai*, 11 and 165.   [85] Gempp, Abschnitt 7, Anlage 7.
[86] Duffy, *Through German Eyes*, 43–5.   [87] Epkenhans, *Nicolai*, 97–8, 166, 221–3.
[88] Hilmar-Detlef Brückner, 'Schluga von Rastenfeld', *Newsletter of the International Intelligence History Study Group*, vol. 6, no. 2 (winter 1998), 1–5.

attention it needed. This was particularly serious since Kleist himself lacked any training in intelligence work. Worse, he contacted his main sub-sources through a shady middleman. Indeed the reliability of the reporting may have been compromised from the start; if so, the end of the case in spring 1916 may not have been such a loss to IIIb as it believed at the time.[89]

The urgent need to acquire new high-level sources and the difficulty of doing so form the background to IIIb's most famous case, Mata Hari (Agent H 17). She offered her services to German intelligence in 1915, planning to exploit previous love affairs with leading French figures such as Adolphe Messimy, a former minister of war and currently a colonel commanding an elite brigade. Nicolai at first turned her approach down, but was persuaded by his subordinates, including Elisabeth Schragmüller, to try her out. Having insisted on meeting her personally, he claimed to find her uneducated and stupid and to have rejected her attempts to seduce him. Nevertheless, in March 1916 he reluctantly agreed that she should be recruited. He later commented that her reporting was useless. Her case officer, however, stated after the war that opinions about her performance varied. He himself thought that she was one of the most intelligent women he had ever met and that she was observant and reported accurately.[90] Whichever view is correct, French intelligence had penetrated German cipher systems and discovered her espionage activities. She was arrested in February 1917 and shot later that year. This disastrous ending does not mean that IIIb was wrong to recruit her: in different circumstances, her access to well-placed French sources might indeed have produced valuable intelligence.[91]

Other attempts to recruit high-level Russian and French sources at this period merged with subversion and confidential contacts relating to peace initiatives conducted by IIIb and various German foreign policy organisations. In Russia, the Germans provided funding and logistical support to Lenin and the Bolsheviks throughout 1917, including Lenin's transport to Russia in the sealed train. He was not an agent in the sense that the Germans controlled him, but his actions certainly suited their interests and his value to them was clear.[92] In particular, he took Russia out of the

---

[89] Summary of the case at Gempp, Abschnitt 8A, 171–84, 229–30 and 8B, 98–101 and Anlage 10; details of Kleist from the family genealogical site at www.v-kleist.com/FG/fgn093.htm (accessed 18 June 2022).

[90] Epkenhans, *Nicolai*, 223–5; Gempp, Abschnitt 8B, Anlage 8.

[91] For an overview of the Mata Hari case, see Gerhard Hirschfeld, 'Mata Hari: die größte Spionin des 20. Jahrhunderts?', in Wolfgang Krieger, ed., *Geheimdienste in der Weltgeschichte: Von der Antike bis heute* (Cologne: Anaconda Verlag, 2007), 179–202.

[92] Sean McMeekin, 'Was Lenin a German Agent?', *The New York Times*, 19 June 2017; Stevenson, *1917*, 368–9.

war and thus ended the two-front nightmare that Germany had been facing since the days of Moltke the Elder.

In 1917 and early 1918, French authorities charged a series of senior figures, including ex-premier Joseph Caillaux, minister of the interior Louis Malvy, a high-ranking police officer (Malvy's former *chef de cabinet*), a parliamentary deputy and several journalists, with various offences relating to treason or contact with the enemy.[93] The arrests took place in the febrile political atmosphere following the army mutinies and general collapse of confidence, and once calm returned after the war many of the sentences imposed – including on Caillaux and Malvy – were overturned as unfounded or unjust. But the Germans had actually recruited two prominent journalists to spread defeatist propaganda and act as conduits to politicians such as Caillaux and Malvy. They had also recruited not one but two politicians who sat on the Chamber of Deputies' military commission, Léon Accambray and Louis Turmel. One or the other of them might even have been the source of the accurate intelligence on the Anglo-French meeting in May referred to earlier. In the absence of hard evidence, this must remain speculation, but Busso von Bismarck, who met Turmel at least once in Berne, claimed that he produced much important information on French armaments and intentions.[94]

In a further attempt to fulfil the new tasking, Nicolai set up the Home Intelligence Service [*Inlandsnachrichtendienst*] in 1916. Its task was to exploit senior German and visiting foreign personalities, particularly in the industrial, banking, trade and press sectors, to gain intelligence on economic and political matters. It could use confidential agents [*Vertrauensleute*] to approach people of interest but was not to engage in actual espionage. The first station dealing with this work was established in Düsseldorf in January 1916, and following initial success there Nicolai expanded the network to Berlin, Dresden, Frankfurt, Hamburg, Munich and Stuttgart. By July 1917, he was writing that this service had become one of the most important sources of intelligence for OHL.[95]

Gempp described the effort to produce intelligence on the new high-level requirements, the agents recruited and the reports subsequently circulated.[96] But despite his and Nicolai's positive statements, there is

---

[93] Jacques Bariéty, 'L'Allemagne et les problèmes de la paix pendant la première guerre mondiale à propos d'une publication récente', *Revue Historique*, vol. 233, no. 2 (1965), 369–92; Fabienne Bock, 'Le secret est-il compatible avec le régime parlementaire? L'exemple de la Grande Guerre', *Matériaux pour l'histoire de notre temps*, vol. 58 (2000), 40–4.

[94] Bismarck, 'Der Militärattaché', 108.

[95] Epkenhans, *Nicolai*, 212–15; Gempp, Abschnitt 7, Anlage 5; IIIb letter to the Kriegsministerium, Nr. 12344 geheim, 28 July 1917, HSAS, M1/4 Bü 1543.

[96] For example, Gempp, Abschnitt 8B, 9–10, 12 and 28.

no convincing evidence from customers of the accuracy of this reporting or the value they placed on it. Part of the problem was that the Intelligence Department had no specialist unit for processing economic and political reporting. So it was left to IIIb, unusually, to arrange for assessment of this material. Nicolai was aware that few intelligence officers possessed the intellectual training to understand reporting on these issues. He therefore looked for officers with the qualifications to recruit suitable sources and critically analyse their reports. He also considered establishing a central assessment section in the Deputy General Staff in Berlin, to be headed by a professor of political science.[97] Despite this further attempt to exploit non-military expertise, Ludendorff for one was unhappy with the results.[98]

German military intelligence cannot be said to have performed adequately on these new high-level requirements. But nor did German naval intelligence do any better in early 1917, especially on the crucial question of the prospects for unrestricted submarine warfare. Given that the resulting U-boat campaign was a major factor in US entry into the war, the deeply flawed naval assessment was a catastrophic intelligence failure – compounded by a further failure to realise that in anything but the short term the United States would have a decisive effect on the outcome of the war.[99]

Case Study: German Intelligence on the Entente Spring Offensive

Briefly to recap Entente plans, in November 1916, an inter-allied conference agreed to launch synchronised offensives from early February 1917 on the Eastern Front, in Italy and on the Western Front. In its final version, the Western Front offensive would comprise four attacks. In order of implementation, these were a powerful but subsidiary British assault at Arras; a French attack on the Oise river; the main element of the offensive, the French attack on the Aisne northwest of Reims; and closely linked with that,

---

[97] Epkenhans, *Nicolai*, 213 and 255.
[98] Walter Nicolai, *Nachrichtendienst, Presse und Volksstimmung im Weltkrieg* (Berlin: E. S. Mittler, 1920), 16–17.
[99] Holger H. Herwig, *'Luxury' Fleet: The Imperial German Navy 1888–1918* (London: Allen & Unwin, 1980), 197–8 lists the mistakes in the German assessment. Note that it was based on work by civilian experts, illustrating that employing civilians might show flexibility but did not guarantee good performance. Thomas Boghardt, *Spies of the Kaiser: German Covert Operations in Great Britain during the First World War Era* (Basingstoke: Palgrave Macmillan, 2004) also damns German naval intelligence's overall failure to produce significant reporting.

a smaller but still important attack in Champagne to the east of Reims. There would also be a deception operation in Alsace.

The Germans expected an all-out Entente offensive in spring 1917. They did not have enough resources permanently to provide every area with forces and fixed defences sufficient for a long battle. On the Western Front, they aimed to make sectors safe against sudden or local attacks, which would by definition be comparatively limited. They would then strengthen any sector threatened by a full-scale offensive.[100] Crucial to success therefore was identifying the date and place of the offensive in sufficient time to deploy extra forces and complete defensive preparations. The 'Defensive Battle' manual gave guidance on what to look for, the first two points including arrival in the sector of enemy formations known to be of high quality and the strengthening of the enemy air force to prevent German reconnaissance.[101]

The Germans were initially uncertain where the Entente would make their offensive. In early January 1917, Army Group Rupprecht's chief intelligence officer summarised intelligence on possible French attacks in the Somme, Champagne, Verdun, Nancy and Alsace sectors.[102] Later in January, Rupprecht recorded what he regarded as two important agent reports. The first stated that there would soon be a French offensive in the Verdun-Belfort sector. The second covered French plans to attack in February in Alsace and Lorraine as well as at Verdun; the Russians and Italians would launch offensives in support as soon as the weather allowed; the British would mount operations against Zeebrugge and the Flanders coast, and probably also a ground attack in the Ypres sector. The first report may reflect a French deception operation planned in January to cover the actual offensive; the second missed detail of the spring offensive on the Western Front but was broadly accurate on overall Entente intentions, including Haig's desire to attack in Flanders.[103]

In early February, Ludendorff was expecting an Allied attack in Italy, then in Alsace and at three other points of the Western Front; and somewhat later in Rumania and elsewhere on the Eastern Front. The battle would be in full swing in March. By 'three other points' on the Western Front, Ludendorff probably meant the Arras-Somme front, the French sector at Reims and possibly also the coastal area where a British

---

[100] AOK 6 to its Gruppen and Etappen-Inspektion, 'Vorbereitungen für die Abwehrschlacht', Ia No. 97892 II.Ang., 26 March 1917, KAM, AOK 6 Bd. 369.
[101] '*Abwehrschlacht*', March 1917, 3.
[102] HKR Nachrichtenoffizier, 'Feststellungen nach Aussagen von Gefangenen, Agentenmeldungen und Truppenbeobachtungen über Angriffsabsichten der Franzosen', 5 January 1917, HAM, Rupprecht Nachlass Nr. 516.
[103] Rupprecht, *Kriegstagebuch*, 2:85–6 (18 January 1917).

landing had long been expected.[104] This is all pretty scatter-gun and again perhaps reflects the influence of Nivelle's deception operations. In particular, the French army made convincing preparations to attack in Alsace; the still-influential Konstantin Schmidt von Knobelsdorf, now commanding a corps there, clearly believed this deception and secured reinforcements against it.[105]

Two intelligence developments in February helped clarify the situation. First, the Austro-Hungarians passed the Germans intercepted reporting from the Italian representatives to the inter-allied conference in Petrograd, which was co-ordinating the Eastern Front offensive. Although this intercept did not cover the whole conference, OHL's Intelligence Department was able to quote Allied thinking on overall strategy for early 1917 directly. This included the primacy of the Western Front, the general size and extent of the offensive there and the supporting attacks to be launched by the Italians and Russians. Importantly, the Department now knew that the British and French intended to begin their offensive at the beginning of April, but that the Russians would not be ready till the end of April at the earliest.[106]

Second, on 15 February the Germans made a local attack on French I Corps in Champagne. Part of the intelligence haul was the French manual on conducting the coming assault, 'Instruction on the Objective and Conditions for a General Offensive'. Prisoners and an order captured at the same time showed that the corps, which the Germans rated highly, was being moved to the Reims area to take part in a major attack.[107] The next day, the Germans tasked air reconnaissance to follow up. This produced evidence of new construction strongly suggesting an attack near Reims. Wireless intelligence's contribution was limited by the late allocation of an interception station to Seventh Army, and by changes in French signals procedure. But it did reveal that many French reinforcements

[104] Reichsarchiv, *Weltkrieg*, 12:64–6.

[105] AFGG, V/1:312–22; Wellmann, *20. Infanterie-Division*, 34.

[106] OHL Nachrichtenabteilung, 'Die Petersburger Konferenz und ihr militärisches Ergebnis für Rußland', Nr. 3204a, 27 February 1917, BArch, R43/2466i; Reichsarchiv, *Weltkrieg*, 11:495, and 12:65.

[107] Reichsarchiv, *Weltkrieg*, 12:279–80; HKR, 'Lage am 20.2. vorm.', Abtlg. Ic., 20 February 1917, GLAK, F1/246. AFGG, V/1, 174–9 describes the document, 'Instruction visant le but et les conditions d'une action offensive d'ensemble', and its origin. The German summary is in Chef des Generalstabes des Feldheeres, *Das französische Angriffsverfahren nach der unter dem 16. Dezember 1916 von der franz. O.H.L. herausgegebenen 'Anweisung über Ziel und Vorbedingungen für eine allgemeine Offensive'* (GHQ: Druckerei des Chefs des Generalstabes des Feldheeres, 1917).

were moving into the potential attack area. Frequent trench raids helped identify French units.[108]

On 20 February, OHL's Intelligence Department circulated a memo on Entente intentions. Based on both intelligence and what made sense militarily for the Entente, the memo assessed that the French would launch their main offensive in the Aubérive-Reims-Vailly area, and the British a linked attack either on the Somme front or at Arras; there would also be subsidiary operations to pin German forces, probably including in Alsace.[109] On 26 February, Ludendorff issued a circular assessing Entente plans in the light of this memo, the reserves the enemy were believed to have available and their likely employment as described in the captured manual. He concluded that the French would attack on both sides of Reims and on the Oise. Subsidiary operations were also possible, including in Alsace. The main British attack would probably be on the Somme, with limited attacks in other areas, especially the Messines salient and Vimy.[110]

So by the end of February the Germans had correctly identified the area of the principal French effort on the Aisne, and the subsidiary operation on the Oise. They still thought the French would attack in Alsace, and were not particularly clear about British intentions. The withdrawal to the Hindenburg Line disrupted the intelligence picture, not least because it forced the Entente to change their plans, including scaling down the Oise offensive and substituting a big attack in Champagne. The Germans initially assessed that no major attacks would take place in Champagne, though local operations could not be ruled out.[111]

April brought further useful intelligence. On 4 April, a raid captured a document setting out the assault orders for a battalion in French VII Corps on the right of the Aisne attack and containing other information on neighbouring units. The Germans considered this corps particularly capable and had seen its move in early March from a quiet sector to the Aisne as a significant sign of an attack there. They now knew the likely direction of the main attack, the objectives for VII Corps and its neighbour, as well as much detail on how the attack would be carried out in this sector. They could also fix with certainty the right-hand limit of this attack. By now too they had a good understanding of the French order of battle; they expected an attack between St Quentin and the Oise; and they realised that after the opening of the assault on the Aisne, the French

---

[108] F. E. Station 14, 'Bericht über die bisherige Tätigkeit der Funkenempfangs-Station 14', Br. No. 545, 23 May 1917, GLAK, F108/188; 'Die Aisne-Champagne-Schlacht einschließlich der Vorbereitungskämpfe von Febr.-Ende Mai 1917', unpublished Reichsarchiv draft, BArch, RH61/1891, 3–4.
[109] Reichsarchiv, *Weltkrieg*, 12:76–8.   [110] Ibid., 79–81.   [111] Ibid., 286–7.

would probably also attack in western Champagne.[112] At the tactical level, they had good intelligence on French plans to use tanks for the first time.[113]

Shortly after this, the start of the French preliminary bombardment confirmed the frontage of the attack. It was obvious too that the infantry assault was imminent: prisoner statements suggested 16 April. The Germans continued to acquire valuable intelligence. On 10 April, Gruppe Sissonne – in the central part of the Aisne front – captured a prisoner with a sketch showing details of his regimental attack plan. On 15 April, OHL circulated an agent report that the infantry assault would begin next morning; this was clearly taken seriously. Finally, Gruppe Sissonne reported shortly before midnight on 15 April that prisoner statements and Arendt interception confirmed the enemy trenches were filling with assault troops. The infantry attack followed early next day.[114]

What action was taken on this intelligence? The Germans repeatedly took steps to confirm and supplement intelligence from one source by other means. They used air reconnaissance to check the original prisoner- and document-based intelligence pointing to the Aisne as the main attack front. They backed this up with orders for raids to produce more intelligence where French intentions were not clear.[115] When the picture clarified in late February, they took energetic steps to strengthen the previously quiet Aisne sector with major reinforcements and defensive construction. Nevertheless, OHL worried that preparations were not moving fast enough and, as recounted in Chapter 4, made wide-ranging changes in Seventh Army headquarters as well as lower down the chain of command. Once the French assault manual captured in February was translated and circulated, the divisional command courses concentrated on how to defeat the new French tactics.[116] Lower down, preparations

[112] Rupprecht, *Kriegstagebuch*, 2:111 (8 March 1917); HKR Nachrichtenoffizier memorandum, 'Wichtigstes', 6 April 1917, HAM, Rupprecht Nachlass Nr. 506; Reichsarchiv, *Weltkrieg*, 12:288–9. The captured French order is in AFGG, V/1: Annexe 1011 and the full German translation, issued by the Seventh Army intelligence officer on 7 April 1917, in General der Infanterie Magnus von Eberhardt, *Kriegserinnerungen* ([Neudamm]: Verlag J. Neumann-Neudamm, 1938), 184–8; Eberhardt commanded the *Gruppe* that captured the order.

[113] Tony Cowan, 'The Basis of Our Own Plans and Operations? German Intelligence on the Western Front, 1917', paper to the military history seminar of the Institute of Historical Research, 26 February 2013.

[114] AOK 7, 'Planmaterial der 7. Armee', n.d.; 5.BRD, 'Gefechtsbericht der 5. bay. Reserve Division über ihren Einsatz in der Schlacht an der Aisne', n.d., both on KAM, XV. BRK 89.

[115] Reichsarchiv, *Weltkrieg*, 12:284.

[116] Generalleutnant Karl Ritter von Wenninger, 'Französisches Durchbruchs-Verfahren', lecture to the fourth divisional command course in Valenciennes, 28 March–3 April 1917, HSAS, Urach Nachlass, GU117 Bü 362, 7.

included training and equipping units to deal with tanks. Finally, when intelligence arrived that the French assault was imminent, *Gruppen* and divisions ordered a bombardment of the enemy trenches and support positions.[117]

Summing up, good intelligence enabled the establishment of a strong defence which defeated the French breakthrough attempt on the first day, inflicting heavy casualties and knocking out many tanks. The French official board of inquiry on the failure of the offensive assessed that poor French security had played a role in German foreknowledge of it. The board criticised Nivelle and the high command for giving out too much information too soon, with the result that by the end of January 1917, both front and rear of the French army knew much about the offensive, including its location. Worse, officers of all ranks had the deplorable habit of passing on secrets to friends, parliamentarians and journalists.[118] Accounts of Nivelle's indiscretions, particularly as vividly recorded in Edward L. Spears's *Prelude to Victory*, have appeared in much subsequent historiography, with the implication that lack of security contributed directly to the defeat.[119] But, oddly perhaps, there is in fact no evidence that any of this reached German eyes or ears, including through their parliamentary agents Turmel and Accambray, who were still active at this period.

At Arras, things had gone less well for German intelligence. Part of the reason was the withdrawal to the Hindenburg Line. This large and difficult operation absorbed much command attention, especially in Army Group Rupprecht, until it was completed successfully on 18 March. Even then, the army group was preoccupied dealing with the advancing enemy. The withdrawal had various consequences for German intelligence on the impending battle and preparations for it. The army group was unable to focus properly on whatever the British might be planning in the Arras sector. As we have seen, OHL was anyway less sure about British than French intentions. In addition, loss of contact with the enemy during the withdrawal temporarily disabled the two most reliable sources on order of battle, prisoners and Arendt; by the end of March the Germans had lost track of sixteen to eighteen British divisions. Finally, OHL wrongly

---

[117] Cowan, 'The Basis of Our Own Plans and Operations?'; 'Gefechtsbericht der 5. bay. Reserve Division'.

[118] 'Rapport de la Commission d'Enquête instituée par Lettre Ministérielle N° 18.194, du 14 Juillet 1917', SHD, GR/5/N/255, 18–19 (hereafter, Brugère Report).

[119] Spears, *Prelude to Victory*, 41; Doughty, *Pyrrhic Victory*, 345. During the Nivelle offensive, Spears (then known as Spiers) was British liaison officer to French Army Group North and Tenth Army.

assessed that the withdrawal would force the Entente to delay their offensive, possibly by as much as two months.[120]

By 22 March, Army Group Rupprecht had accurately identified the British and Canadian divisions in the front line both sides of Arras; they included nine divisions assessed as particularly good on the basis of their regular, Scottish and London provenance. But apart from one division identified by wireless intelligence, nothing was known of reserves in front of Sixth Army.[121] As late as 29 March, the army group was not certain that the British planned to break through.

Sixth Army was just as unsure. Even on 7 April – after the British bombardment had started and two days before the infantry assault – it displayed considerable ignorance of British intentions. The British were clearly about to launch a major attack, but its size and date were uncertain. The Army ruled out the possibility of an attack in the northern half of its sector. Observation of the area of heaviest bombardment and intelligence on British divisional sectors suggested that the British would attack from Vimy to the south-east of Arras. This was too narrow for a breakthrough. If the British extended the front to enable a breakthrough, the most likely area was north of Arras. But they were not currently concentrated there. South of the city, they had closed up to the Hindenburg Line but were not ready to attack. The Army therefore expected the British first to capture Vimy Ridge, which would create favourable conditions for a later breakthrough attempt. Against this, however, British activity south of Arras was obviously more than just a demonstration. The assessment ended with the plaintive statement that the intentions of the enemy were still unclear, especially as on 7 April enemy combat activity along the whole attack front had decreased.[122]

This assessment by Sixth Army was both accurate and inaccurate. It was right that an attack was impending, that Vimy Ridge was a primary objective and that the British would not attack in the northern half of Sixth Army's area. It was wrong that the British might extend their attack northwards, and it failed to recognise the intention to attack in the southern sector. Nor did it realise that the British were in fact trying to break through, and it misappreciated both the imminence and especially the weight of the British attack. It is striking that just two days before the attack, the Germans were in so much uncertainty about the enemy's

---

[120] Reichsarchiv, *Weltkrieg*, 12:84 fn. 1 and 149–50.
[121] HKR Nachrichtenoffizier, 'Gliederung des Feindes vor Heeresgruppe Kronprinz Rupprecht vom 16. bis 22. März 1917'.
[122] AOK 6, 'Beurteilung der Lage', Ia No. 1500, 7 April 1917, KAM, AOK 6 Bd. 369.

Table 5.2 *German and British data on British forces at Arras, 7–9 April 1917*

Source	Sector covered	In the front	In the rear	Total
German intelligence assessment	South of the La Bassée canal (i.e. broader than the attack front)	19	–	19
Actual British deployment	Souchez-Croisilles (i.e. the attack front)	15	8 infantry and 3 cavalry	23 infantry and 3 cavalry

intentions. This illustrates how even in Western Front conditions it was possible to achieve tactical surprise with important results.

There are various reasons why the Germans may have made these mistakes. First, they appear to have rather underestimated the British forces facing them, especially in reserve (Table 5.2).[123]

Second, cultural assumptions dating back long before the war led to persistent underestimation of the British army. Traditional German grand strategic thinking saw Britain as important because of its navy rather than its army. In the early 1900s, German military intelligence regarded the British army as a 'negligible quantity', based on its poor performance at the start of the Anglo-Boer War of 1899–1902 and its small size in continental terms. However, the Haldane reforms and the increasing likelihood that Britain would intervene on the side of France in any war with Germany led to a reassessment. In 1911, the military attaché in London reported that though the commanders of any British expeditionary force would show no great operational talent, the troops would fight excellently and would be fully equal to any enemy of the same strength.[124] An assessment the following year passed by Moltke to the German Foreign Office echoed this. But it added that the small size of the army, which could not easily be increased, and concerns for homeland and imperial security would limit British operations on the continent. Other belligerents would be fighting

---

[123] Ibid.; BOH 1917, 1: Sketch 7 'Arras, 1917: Zero, 9th April'. British and German information on location of divisions covers different lengths of front, preventing direct comparison between German intelligence estimates and the reality.

[124] Major Roland Ostertag report, 25 February 1911, in Johannes Lepsius, Albrecht Mendelssohn Bartholdy and Friedrich Thimme, eds., *Die Große Politik der Europäischen Kabinette 1871–1914: Sammlung der Diplomatischen Akten des Auswärtigen Amtes* (Berlin: Deutsche Verlagsgesellschaft für Politik und Geschichte, 1927), 29: Nr. 10520, fn. **.

for their existence with their mass armies, but Britain would just be fighting a 'cabinet war' with its 'mercenary army'.[125]

Citing such evidence, Lukas Grawe refers to 'massive underestimation' of the British army before the war. This is going too far, but as with other intelligence assessments there was undoubtedly an 'on the one hand . . . on the other hand' ambivalence about the British. Moltke reflected this, telling the Foreign Office in 1913 that it would be possible to deal with the British Expeditionary Force quickly.[126] Even in August 1914 when he learned that the British had landed in France, in an echo of Bismarck's well-known words from fifty years before, he sneered, 'We'll arrest them.'[127]

Such negative attitudes towards British military capability were widespread and lasting. Gerold von Gleich commented that German military writers, from the time of the Boer War till just before the collapse in 1918, consistently reported that the British lacked all understanding of command. This was part of a general wish to believe news unfavourable to the enemy and, especially as expressed by superior officers, too easily led to distorted reporting.[128] Throughout 1917, the Germans looked on the British as tough but operationally clumsy and tactically rigid. Such assessments fitted well with national stereotypes about 'the blinkered mental uniformity of the British' and 'beefy British ignoramuses' obsessed by sport.[129] The assessments were right when it came to semi-mobile and mobile war, as we shall see, but overlooked the fact that the British had learned from the Somme and had greatly increased their striking power. A possible factor in these flawed judgements may have been the preconceptions warned against by military theorists, in two ways. First, the Germans viewed mobile war as the 'correct image of war' with the implication that trench warfare was therefore inferior and less worthy of study; and second, in assessing whether the British intended to break through, they may have projected their own methods onto the enemy.[130]

---

[125] Grawe, *Deutsche Feindaufklärung*, 313–14.   [126] Ibid., 3, 195–6, 314 and 463.

[127] Lukas Grawe, 'Albion an Holsteins Küsten? Der preußische Generalstab und die Furcht vor einer britischen Landung in Norddeutschland und Dänemark, 1905–1914', *Militärgeschichtliche Zeitschrift*, vol. 79, no. 1 (May 2020), 42. During the war with Denmark in 1864, a British diplomat asked Chancellor Otto von Bismarck how he would react to a British landing in Schleswig-Holstein. Bismarck replied, 'Then I would order a policeman to arrest them.'

[128] Gleich, *Die alte Armee*, 96; Gempp, Abschnitt 6, 118. Cf. Crown Prince Rupprecht's comment that only wanting to believe good news caused the Germans to underestimate each enemy in turn: *Kriegstagebuch*, 2:199–200 (16 June 1917).

[129] Wetzell memorandum, 12 December 1917, in Reichsarchiv, *Weltkrieg*, 14:64; Duffy, *Through German Eyes*, 31 and 51.

[130] More on the ideal German image of war in the concluding chapter.

Whatever the reason, it was only in late March that Army Group Rupprecht and Sixth Army calculated what forces were needed for a full-scale defensive battle and submitted their final requests for reinforcements to OHL – a month later than in the French sector, even though the British attacked earlier.[131] Reinforcements did arrive and more were on the way, but it was impossible to make up for lost time. Also, failure to identify properly the southern limit of the British offensive led to a lack of emphasis on reinforcement and defensive construction there, with serious consequences at the start of the battle. On 9 April, Sixth Army suffered a heavy defeat.[132]

Conclusions

> The aim of intelligence is to minimise uncertainty about the enemy and to maximise the efficiency of the use of one's own resources.[133]

Before and at the start of the war, German theory stressed the importance of intelligence to the decision-making process. But despite the resources devoted to it in peacetime, practice accorded it an inferior role to operations. By 1917, however, reducing uncertainty about enemy intentions was essential to compensate for loss of the initiative and to deploy scarce resources to best effect.[134] A dense network of intelligence sources, both traditional and new, had emerged. Lack of integration caused organisational friction, but this did not preclude effective ad hoc co-operation. OHL's small Intelligence Department produced all-source intelligence assessments used extensively by decision-makers. Total war led to new tasking: German intelligence performed well on the assessment of enemy divisions, which was similar to its traditional work, but despite serious efforts poorly on high-level economic and political issues.

The German army's success in fulfilling the intelligence part of the third command task during the Entente spring offensive was mixed. Good intelligence on French intentions enabled timely concentration of

---

[131] AOK 6 to HKR, 'Berechnung des Bedarfs an Formationen für die Abwehrschlacht zwischen la Bassée und Arras', Anlage zu Ia No. 97892, 25 March 1917; AOK 6 to its Gruppen and Etappen-Inspektion, 'Vorbereitungen für die Abwehrschlacht', Ia No. 99775, 31 March 1917, both on KAM, AOK 6 Bd. 369.

[132] 'Luftwaffe der 6. Armee', 27. Albrecht von Thaer, chief of staff to the corps which took over Gruppe Arras in early April, complained bitterly about Sixth Army's and the preceding corps' derelictions in the southern sector: Thaer, *Generalstabsdienst*, 111 and 113.

[133] Ferris, *The British Army and Signals Intelligence*, 1.

[134] In an interesting parallel, British commanders most valued intelligence when they had lost the initiative and were on the defensive in early 1918: Beach, *Haig's Intelligence*, 302 and 327.

forces – in other words, creation of a defensive *Schwerpunkt* – and thus played a central role in the resulting German victory; but considerable and lasting uncertainty about British plans was a major factor in delaying defensive preparations, leading to the initial defeat at Arras. These positive and negative examples clearly illustrate the close links between the first and third command tasks.

The case study of the Entente spring offensive also shows that reducing or removing uncertainty about the enemy was necessary to success in 1917, but it was not sufficient. Intelligence was valueless unless effective operational action could be taken on it, a point brought out clearly by the French mutinies. Accusations that the German army failed to understand the severity of the mutinies and so lost an opportunity to do fatal damage to the French army are wide of the mark: Pöhlmann is surely right that whatever the state of intelligence on the mutinies, lack of resources and operational freedom prevented the German army from exploiting them in any decisive way.[135] Ironically, the mutinies had been sparked by the bloody failure of the Nivelle offensive, caused in no small measure by competent German action taken on good intelligence. Given that the mutinies weakened the French army for a prolonged period, this also explains how operational and tactical level intelligence could have a strategic effect – an example of the way in which the different levels of war mutually interacted.

---

[135] Markus Pöhlmann, 'Une occasion manquée? Les mutineries de 1917 dans la stratégie et l'historiographie allemandes', in Loez and Mariot, *Obéir/désobéir*, 392.

6 Communication

Without communication, command cannot function; it can neither receive information, nor get out its orders.[1]

As the last chapter showed, the German army believed that the constant uncertainty of war arose from faulty knowledge of its own forces as well as the enemy's. The injunction quoted in the Introduction, that in the midst of this uncertainty one's own decision at least must be certain, stemmed from an insight of Moltke the Elder. He believed: 'Everything depends on seeing clearly the actual circumstances of each situation, shrouded as they are in the fog of uncertainty, to appreciate the right thing to do, to estimate the unknown, to make a quick decision and then to carry it out strongly and unwaveringly.'[2]

This aspect of reducing uncertainty, the third command task, was the role of communication. Moltke wrote that continuity of communication was indispensable to achieving the army's mission and even to effective control; this was repeated almost verbatim in the 1910 instructions for senior commanders. Indeed, we should see good communication as central to German command methods.[3] The essence was speedy transmission of reports upwards and orders downwards, which not only reduced uncertainty but also enabled its exploitation by creating a higher tempo than the enemy could achieve. A modern British doctrinal manual defines tempo as 'the rhythm or rate of activity of operations relative to an adversary's. The side which consistently decides and acts fastest should gain and hold an advantage ... the primary goal should be to maintain the initiative.' This is to get inside the enemy's decision cycle,

---

[1] From the British army's 1932 Kirke Report on lessons of the First World War, quoted in Hall, *Communications and British Operations*, 1.
[2] Kriegsministerium, *Grundzüge der höheren Truppenführung*, 3; Helmuth von Moltke, 'Ueber Strategie', in Großer Generalstab, ed., *Moltkes Militärische Werke*, vol. 2, pt 2, 292.
[3] Moltke, 'Verordnungen für die höheren Truppenführer', 179; Kriegsministerium, *Grundzüge der höheren Truppenführung*, 51; Sigg, *Unterführer als Feldherr*, 136–8.

and ideally cause it to collapse, leading to increasing operational and tactical mistakes.[4] The German army believed that its superior communication techniques gave it an edge in this area.

Pre-war Principles and Wartime Developments

In his study of British army communications on the Western Front, Brian N. Hall defines communications as 'the provision and passing of information and instructions which enable ... [an] organisation to function efficiently and employees to be properly informed about developments. It covers information of all kinds which can be provided; the channels along which it' passes; and the means of passing it.' To be useful, information must be gathered, processed, stored and disseminated. Hall therefore defines a complete communications system as 'the combination of equipment, methods, procedures and personnel, organised to accomplish the conveyance of information'. Technology is an important part of an army's communications system, but not the only one. Others include the general staff and its information handling procedures, doctrine and less structured methods such as conferences, visits and personal exchanges.[5]

The German army used two terms for communication – *Nachrichten* and *Verbindung*. The former in particular included both the contents of what was communicated and the means of communication, especially in the sense of signals. As the previous chapter explained, it was also the main term used for intelligence. This triple meaning did highlight the links between the concepts but also led to confusion of nomenclature, not sorted out till 1917.[6] In outline, the German army saw communication as the upward flow of reports carrying information to commanders and the downward flow of orders based on the information.[7] Once information had arrived, the commander and his staff made an assessment of the situation [*Beurteilung der Lage*]; this acted as the basis for the commander to take his decision and issue orders.[8]

Running this system depended on a mixture of organisation, technical communications and personal involvement. The backbone of the system was efficient staff work implemented through the chain of command,

---

[4] Ministry of Defence, *Army Doctrine Publication: Operations* (London: Ministry of Defence, 2010), 5–24; Antulio J. Echevarria II, 'Optimizing Chaos on the Nonlinear Battlefield', *Military Review*, vol. 77, no. 5 (September/October 1997).
[5] Hall, *Communications and British Operations*, especially the Introduction. Hall drew his definition of communications from Tim Hannagan, *Management: Concepts and Practices*, 4th ed. (London: FT Prentice Hall, 2005).
[6] Pöhlmann, 'Towards a New History of German Military Intelligence', vii.
[7] Moltke, 'Verordnungen für die höheren Truppenführer', 179.
[8] Immanuel, *Handbuch der Taktik*, 37–46.

which Chapter 3 showed was seen as vital to the issuing of orders. In addition, the Great General Staff had introduced standardised procedures, both in the field and in the office.[9] The allocation of work to individual officers in a staff dated back to 1828 and by the 1870s had settled into a pattern that continued throughout the First World War.[10] German staffs were traditionally small in size, often seen as conferring important benefits for management and decision-making. The standard text on staff work commented that small staffs eased the task of finding suitably qualified officers. In contrast, large staffs reduced the number of officers available for troop service; in the field, increased the difficulty of quartering to the detriment of other units and thereby exacerbated dislike of the staff; and above all, the devil found work for idle hands.[11]

Of the technical communications means available, the telephone was seen as key since it was the fastest way of passing orders and also enabled commanders to exchange information personally. Such hope was placed in it that before the war the army signals service converted from telegraph to telephone operation, dropping the use of teleprinters.[12] The army also believed that the newer technology of wireless telegraphy would permit good communication between the highest-level commanders. Senior officers, including Schlieffen and Falkenhayn, were in two minds about modern communications: when they worked they were very effective, but they did not always work.[13] Regulations carefully considered the pros and cons of each means. Since any one might fail, several should be used together to ensure that messages were passed.[14]

At a less technical level, information-handling technology such as typewriters and duplicators [*Umdruckpressen*] to copy orders was available down to at least divisional headquarters. Duplication was the main method of producing written orders, with carbon copies as a back-up. Some divisional clerks could take shorthand, speeding up the production of orders and recording of important phone conversations. Otto von Moser advocated employing a form to indicate quickly and for the record how orders were to be circulated to sub-units, as well as confirming despatch. All units held forms for simplifying and standardising

[9] Bucholz, *Moltke, Schlieffen*, 101 and 171–2.
[10] Major Bronsart von Schellendorff, *Der Dienst des Generalstabes*, 4th ed. (Berlin: E. S. Mittler, 1905), 40–1 and 221–9 for composition and duties of staffs in the field from Army to division.
[11] Bucholz, *Moltke, Schlieffen*, 102; Bronsart von Schellendorff, *Dienst des Generalstabes*, 216–17.
[12] Ammon, 'Nachrichtenwesen', 248–9.
[13] Strachan, *First World War*, 1:233–4; Cowan, 'German Army Command and Control', 17–18.
[14] Kriegsministerium, *Grundzüge der höheren Truppenführung*, 51.

messages, and every officer was equipped with a pad for submitting immediate reports [*Meldekarten*].[15]

Personal involvement was also seen as essential to communication. A commander needed to make his own direct assessment of the situation, and also of the state of his subordinate commanders and troops. Indeed, leading from the front and dialogue between different levels of command were central elements of German command style from the Wars of Unification on.[16] However, in the years before 1914, location of headquarters and especially the commander became increasingly problematic. Going forward enabled him to make his own assessment but also exposed him to modern firepower and deprived him of the support of modern communications. How was this circle to be squared? Pre-war regulations stated that a divisional or corps commander in major battle must be located further back than had previously been the case: only in this way would he have available the communications necessary to gain a clear picture of the overall situation, as well as remaining in contact with his superiors and colleagues. He should use all possible communications means and, in case under the stress of combat subordinate headquarters forgot their duty to report upwards and sideways, he should send out liaison officers to discover their situation and intentions.[17]

Early experience in the war showed that the optimists' faith in modern technology was ill-founded. Inadequate communications were an important factor in the failure of the initial German offensive in the west.[18] The transition to trench warfare enabled the establishment of a comprehensive communications network there, but the advent of the war of matériel by the end of 1916 created a series of interlocking problems. The growing complexity of the war necessitated larger staffs and more bureaucracy. By 1917, the bureaucratic burden contributed to the reduced scope of mission command, as described in Chapter 2; in fact, OHL worried that the information-handling system was buckling under the strain. Second, the increasing depth of battle brought about by long-range artillery, air attack and new defensive tactics forced headquarters to the rear. This impeded personal contact between senior commanders and their units at the most critical moments. It also created a greater need for communications between headquarters and units, but it was precisely these – especially phone lines forward of division – which were most vulnerable to the

[15] Großer Generalstab, *Anhaltspunkte für den Generalstabsdienst* (Berlin: Reichsdruckerei, 1914), 39 and 88; Moser, *Führung des Armeekorps*, 11–12; Frobenius, *Militär-Lexikon*, entry for *Meldekarte*.
[16] Sigg, *Unterführer als Feldherr*, 138–43 and 462.
[17] Kriegsministerium, *Grundzüge der höheren Truppenführung*, 17, 54 and 60.
[18] Mombauer, *Moltke*, 253–4.

firepower which had driven back headquarters. The resulting communications problems were likely to prevent or at least drastically slow the movement of information.

Size of Staffs and Location of Headquarters

The number and size of headquarters steadily expanded during the war. Numbers rose with the creation of army groups and the establishment of new formations; size grew with the increasing tasks, especially managerial and technical, for which headquarters became responsible. Table 6.1 illustrates the process in a typical corps/*Gruppe* headquarters.[19]

These headquarters were substantial units. Even at the start of the war a divisional staff numbered 111. This was later increased by at least 10, including a second general staff officer, an intelligence officer and 2 assistants for the central divisional staff. But the number of officers and especially clerks was still seen as inadequate to deal with the headquarters' tasks in modern battle.[20] On mobilisation, a corps headquarters totalled 311, of which 66 were officers and officials.[21] A strength return for Fifth Army headquarters in December 1916 gives 384 officers, officials, NCOs and men; this is, however, not the total and certainly excludes drivers and cyclists. In April 1917, the ration strength of Army Group Rupprecht's headquarters was 735, the largest component being a signals detachment. By the end of the year, the headquarters had grown to 1,036, the signals detachment having been strengthened and – a sign of the times – anti-aircraft and searchlight troops added.[22] Such staffs, especially from corps upwards, were too big to go into action or to be quartered together. They were therefore often split into two echelons [*Staffeln*]. In principle, the first echelon – also known as the 'closer staff' [*engerer Stab*], the innermost ring of the concentric circles mentioned earlier – included those involved in daily operational work. At corps level and above, it typically comprised the chief of staff, general staff officers, adjutants and their assistants.[23]

Early in the war, corps and divisional headquarters often positioned themselves quite far forward, in defiance of doctrine. They believed that the advantages – rapid communication with subordinate units and the boost to troops' morale from seeing their commanders on the battlefield – greatly

---

[19] Cron, *Geschichte des Deutschen Heeres*, 92–3.
[20] Ibid., 95–6; 'Organisation des Divisionsstabes in der Abwehrschlacht', 11–12.
[21] Cron, *Geschichte des Deutschen Heeres*, 92.
[22] AOK: AOK 5, 'Dienstanweisung für das Oberkommando der 5. Armee', IIa Nr. 11304, 21 December 1916, BArch, Gallwitz Nachlass, N710/60a. Army Group Rupprecht: HKR, 'Nachweisung der Gesamtverpflegungsstärke', IIb No. 13210, 3 April 1917 and IIb Nr. 37080, 3 January 1918, both on KAM, HKR neue Nr. 113.
[23] Moser, *Führung des Armeekorps*, 14–15; Loßberg, *Meine Tätigkeit*, 232.

Table 6.1 *Additions to corps/*Gruppe *headquarters, 1914–late 1917*

Date	Post
Not long after mobilisation	OHL intelligence officer [later removed]
Not long after mobilisation	Ammunition officer [*Munitions-Referent*]
Not long after mobilisation	Reports collection officer [*Meldesammeloffizier*]
Not long after mobilisation	Sanitary adviser [*beratender Hygieniker*]
Not long after mobilisation	Pharmacist officer [*Stabsapotheker*]
May 1915	Commander of ammunition columns and trains [*Kommandeur der Munitionskolonnen und Trains, Komut.* Replaced two separate commanders; moved to Army in December 1916]
Oct. 1915	Map officer [*Kartenoffizier*]
Dec. 1916	Telephone commander [*Gruppen-Fernsprech-Kommandeur, Grukofern*]
Dec. 1916	Wireless telegraphy commander [*Gruppen-Funker-Kommandeur, Grukofunk*]
Dec. 1916	Aviation commander [*Gruppenführer der Flieger, Grufl*]
?	Air photography officer [*Gruppen-Bildoffizier*]
Jan. 1917	Anti-aircraft commander [*Gruppen-Kommandeur der Flugabwehrkanonen, Flakgruko*]
Feb. 1917	Staff officer for field artillery
Feb. 1917	Staff officer for heavy artillery
May 1917	Staff officer for engineers [replaced original commander of the corps engineer battalion]
Spring 1917	Map officer post expanded to map section [*Gruppen-Kartenstelle*]
Mid-1917	Salvage officer [*Gruppen-Sammeloffizier*]
Mid-1917	Machine gun adviser [*beratender Maschinengewehr-Offizier*]
Sept. 1917	Signals commander [*Gruppen-Nachrichten-Kommandeur, Grukonach.* Replaced *Gruppe* telephone and wireless telegraphy commanders]

outweighed the disadvantage that the headquarters were occasionally shelled.[24] However, as a divisional commander on the Somme in summer 1916, Moser found this no longer possible. He and his closer staff originally used an advanced battle headquarters [*Gefechtsstand*] in a village seven kilometres from the front. But continuous shelling so disrupted both work and rest that they had to withdraw to the main headquarters six kilometres further back.[25]

Based on such experiences, First Army's Somme report advised against long-term use of battle headquarters; as a rule divisional commanders and

[24] Loßberg, *Meine Tätigkeit*, 13, 16 and 22; Schulenburg, 'Erlebnisse', 80.
[25] Moser, *Feldzugsaufzeichnungen*, 229–41.

staffs should operate from their main headquarters. The manual 'Defensive Battle' agreed. It added that the headquarters of *Gruppen* and divisions must be far enough back not to be forced to move by long-range enemy artillery fire at the start of the battle or by minor enemy advances; this meant ten to fifteen kilometres or more from the front line. Lecturing to a divisional command course in March 1917, Moser's old *Ia* drew on his Somme experience to support 'Defensive Battle' on these points. In particular, it was not possible for a division to deal with the great volume of business, especially paperwork, in the confines of an advanced battle headquarters under fire.[26]

This guidance was not necessarily followed in the spring fighting. Particularly in the Aisne sector, hilly terrain allowed the construction of battle headquarters close to the front. The first echelons of 16th Reserve, 20th Infantry and 11th Bavarian Infantry Divisions successively occupied such a headquarters about seven kilometres from the Chemin des Dames, with the second echelon remaining in Laon, another seven kilometres back. The battle headquarters was well protected against shellfire by a hill in front, and screened from air observation by trees.[27] But other head-quarters were not so fortunate and tended to move further away from the front. After the French had begun their pre-assault bombardment in April, Seventh Army issued a sharp order reminding subordinate forma-tions of the rules. Staffs up to and including brigade were not to let themselves be shelled to the rear. In order to maintain contact with higher staffs and to ensure re-supply, divisional headquarters should establish themselves outside the range of 'normal enemy fire', but not further back than the furthest range of the enemy's heaviest guns. *Gruppe* headquarters must be as secure from enemy fire as possible.[28]

As so often, arguments could be made both for and against this order. Higher-level headquarters undoubtedly needed to be further back in order to carry out their intensive and complex work free from enemy fire. But equally the rules would reinforce the 'us and them' attitude between staff and fighting troops, while also making visits by the former to the front more difficult. Nor was it necessarily sensible for brigade headquarters to be located in the main fire zone. After the spring fighting, 45th Reserve Division reported that its infantry brigade headquarters had originally been located some five kilometres behind the front. Enemy fire caused almost continual failure of communications forward and

---

[26] AOK 1, 'Erfahrungen', 112; '*Abwehrschlacht*', March 1917, 10; 'Die Einrichtung des Divisions-Gefechtsstandes', lecture to the fourth divisional command course in Valenciennes, 28 March–3 April 1917, HSAS, Urach Nachlass, GU117 Bü 362.

[27] Wellmann, *20. Infanterie-Division*, 48–9; Kneußl diary, 8 May 1917.

[28] AOK 7 Army order, Ia Nr. 160/April 1917, 14 April 1917, GLAK, F1/251.

rearward, putting the headquarters out of action. Divisional headquarters then had to take on parts of the brigade's role, an unwelcome additional burden.[29] Even Army headquarters were not immune from risk, as illustrated by a British attempt to bomb Sixth Army headquarters in May.[30]

The physical circumstances of headquarters varied. The 16th Reserve Division battle headquarters consisted of a long line of wooden huts dug into a hillside and linked up by a track; they were protected on the open side by an earth wall and had a shelter underneath. They were said to be well set up but cramped and noisy.[31] Other divisional headquarters were modest houses. But as with the British and French armies, larger staffs had to be located where sufficient accommodation and good communications – both road access and phone or telegraphic connections – were available. So the main building used was often a chateau or manor house in a village or town. As a corps commander in early 1917, Moser's headquarters was located successively in three magnificent chateaux. The first of these was almost ideal as it was big enough to house him, the general staff and much of the rest of the closer staff.[32] In 1916–17, First Army was established in Bourlon near Cambrai because of its good road connections to the Army's front. The Army commander and closer staff occupied the chateau, with the rest of the staff in the village. When the Army moved to the Aisne in spring 1917, Rethel – thirty kilometres behind the front – was chosen as its new location because it was the meeting point of several roads.[33]

The Burden of Bureaucracy

> If I attempt to answer the mass of futile correspondence that surrounds me I should be debarred from the serious business of campaigning.[34]

Previous chapters have described the growing burden of bureaucracy, its causes and its effects in both limiting mission command and aggravating the strain on commanders. It can be seen as a perversion of the need to reduce uncertainty – what happened when the desire for certainty got out of hand. The British and French armies also suffered from this: indeed,

---

[29] 45.RD, 'Erfahrungen aus den Kämpfen in der Doppelschlacht Aisne-Champagne (am Chemin des Dames bei Braye)', Tgb. No. 2236 Ia.geh., 23 May 1917, GLAK, F1/523.
[30] Otto von Below diary, 2 May 1917.
[31] Wellmann, 20. Infanterie-Division, 48–9; Kneußl diary, 8 May 1917.
[32] Moser, Feldzugsaufzeichnungen, 232, 282–3, 306 and 315.
[33] Loßberg, Meine Tätigkeit, 231–2 and 280.
[34] The Duke of Wellington to the Secretary of State for War in 1810, quoted by General Sir Claude Auchinleck, British Commander-in-Chief Middle East, in a May 1942 circular on reducing bureaucracy: Philip Warner, Auchinleck: The Lonely Soldier (London: Cassell, 2001), 140–1. I am grateful to Dr William Fletcher for the 1810 date.

the Wellington quote shows that it plagued the former over two centuries. In the German army, it had first arisen in peacetime, but we can see from statistics that by 1917 had become common at all levels of command.[35]

The general staff section of 5th Reserve Division logged some 1,700 letter references in 1916 when it was on the Eastern Front; in early 1917, the division moved west and the number reached 5,000. The reason for the increase was that *Gruppen* asked for a report on everything – in one case when a regiment moved one machine gun. Arriving in a new sector, the division's *Ia* inherited a stack of files over a metre high.[36] Some divisions had to keep sixty or more maps up to date, and their artillery commanders a further thirteen; there were cases of divisions making eight to ten reports a day and the artillery up to four more. Higher up the chain of command, a large Army headquarters might send and transmit well over 10,000 telegrams per day during major battle. To deal with this flood of paper, one headquarters was said to employ thirty-six clerks instead of the four on its establishment.[37]

Complaints about what was called 'the paper bombardment from the rear' or 'fruitfulness from above' were vociferous.[38] The worst culprits were said to be the Ministry of War and departments responsible for logistics, which was not surprising in a war of matériel. Identifying the problem was simple, but solving it was not – especially as some would-be solutions actually made it worse. In March 1917, OHL circulated instructions on the need to cut paperwork. It set out sensible suggestions such as omitting levels of command from correspondence if they were only acting as post-boxes, and including short summaries of previous correspondence rather than simply references that had to be looked up. The circular was already the third piece of OHL paper issued in 1917 on cutting paperwork, and Table 6.2 shows how it was handled.[39] This is undoubtedly not the full chain of events but it does indicate the delay and extra work caused even by well-meaning attempts to reduce bureaucracy.

Various solutions were adopted to deal with the problem. At the conceptual level, the German army issued updated doctrine to give officers an integrated intellectual framework for decision-making. The more procedures were a 'common property' of all officers, as the German

[35] See Bucholz, *Moltke, Schlieffen*, 194–5 for a peacetime example.

[36] Major Hugold von Behr, *Bei der fünften Reserve-Division im Weltkriege* (Berlin: E. S. Mittler, 1919), 212–13.

[37] OHL circular, II No. 47869 op., 20 February 1917, GLAK, F1/374; Ammon, 'Nachrichtenwesen', 255.

[38] OHL circular, II Nr. 59707 op., 11 July 1917, HSAS, Soden Nachlass, M660/038 Bü 17; Gallwitz, *Erleben im Westen*, 209.

[39] OHL circular, II Nr. 49020 op., 3 March 1917, HSAS, Soden Nachlass, M660/038 Bü 17.

Table 6.2 *Circulation of a document on cutting paperwork, March 1917*

Originator	Action	Date
OHL	Issues original	3 Mar.
Army Group Crown Prince	Forwards, adding two references, one to a document only it had received, with no summary	14 Mar.
Third Army	Forwards with no summary or comment	15 Mar.
Gruppe Reims	Retypes, duplicates and circulates forty-one copies internally and to its divisions	17 Mar.

phrase went, the less would have to be communicated as specific information and orders: there is an obvious link to mission command. A key
role was played by the series 'Regulations for Trench Warfare for All
Arms'. This was backed up by the divisional command courses, and less
formally through lectures by highly regarded officers such as
Generalleutnant von Wenninger and the circulation of the texts used for
them.[40] On the Aisne, First Army revived its 1916 practice of issuing
basic orders [*grundlegende Befehle*] on how the battle was to be fought.
These were given reference numbers, formed part of an indexed collection and could be individually replaced by updates.[41]

The army also took practical steps to overcome the burden of paperwork.
In a direct attempt to cut the volume of written business, Ludendorff
encouraged greater use of the phone. The divisional command courses
advised on best practice in organising staff work in headquarters. Divisions
were given a second clerk and personnel to prepare maps and sketches, and
detailed orders were issued on the rapid updating and distribution of
maps.[42] Attempts were made to reduce the volume of information by
substituting maps for text, but this could still lead to excessive effort.
Reports on enemy activity and on combat value were combined with the
regular situation reports.[43] Questionnaires were increasingly used to simplify surveys, especially of combat experience and knowledge of enemy
activities. Orders for the drafting of after-action reports stressed the need to

---

[40] On the link between doctrine and information, see Hall, *Communications and British Operations*, introduction.

[41] The *Armeebefehl* [Army order] in the next footnote is an example of these orders. There is a good collection on HSAS, Soden Nachlass, M660/038 Bü 21.

[42] 'Organisation des Divisionsstabes in der Abwehrschlacht', 11–12; AOK 1, 'Armeebefehl für die Bearbeitung des Kartenwesens', Ia/Ib Nr. 227 geheim, 30 April 1917, HSAS, Glück Nachlass, M660/091 Bü 16.

[43] AOK 6 Army order, 'Eingaben über Beurteilung der Lage', Ia/Ib No. 6371, 23 April 1917, KAM, AOK 6 Bd. 369.

keep them short: formations were to submit conclusions rather than detailed descriptions of the fighting. One aim here was to prevent units being overwhelmed by theoretical material.[44]

Many of these were sensible measures, but it remained difficult to find the correct balance between keeping people informed and not swamping them with information; and also between circulating information promptly and ensuring security. A typical Seventh Army situation report in April 1917 had twenty addressees, excluding internal circulation within its own headquarters and spare copies; no doubt it was distributed further by the addressees.[45] And the provision of two clerks at division level was still seen as completely inadequate. As one reflection of the overall problem, whenever an officer changed job, his details were painstakingly copied by hand into his new unit's war rank list.[46]

One surprising omission in the steps taken by the German army to overcome the burden of paperwork is automation of information-handling in the office. In contrast, the British army adopted automation with enthusiasm according to their Director of Army Printing and Stationery Services in March 1916:

The duplicator and typewriter have eliminated altogether the group of 'copyists'; the Sunprinting Apparatus has reduced the number of draughtsmen; the 'Addressograph' has cut down the 'Despatch Room' by 90%; the 'Dictaphone' has replaced the shorthand writer; and the Calculator and Comptometer have revolutionised the Counting House.

The director added that every unit seeking to optimise office administration must strike the balance between the human and the mechanical.[47] Use of modern information-handling equipment and techniques became increasingly widespread in the British army. In the important area of analysing German casualties and manpower, the army used the most advanced equipment available, the Prudential Assurance Company's new punch card tabulating machines.[48]

The German army made extensive use of the duplicator and typewriter, as we have seen, but apparently had none of the other machines

---

[44] AOK 6 circular, 'Berichte über Erfahrungen in der Arrasschlacht', Ia/Ib. Nr. 21581, 8 June 1917, KAM, AOK 6 Bd. 419; OHL circular, II Nr. 57804 op., 16 June 1917, HSAS, Soden Nachlass, M660/038 Bü 17.

[45] AOK 7, 'Ereignisse und Beurteilung der Lage vom 7.–13. IV. 17', Ia No. 156/April 17, 14 April 1917, GLAK, F1/251.

[46] Examples in the Bavarian *Kriegsranglisten*, available at www.ancestry.co.uk.

[47] Brian N. Hall, 'The British Army, Information Management and the First World War Revolution in Military Affairs', *Journal of Strategic Studies*, vol. 41, no. 7 (2018), 1014.

[48] Aimée Fox, *Learning to Fight: Military Innovation and Change in the British Army, 1914–1918* (Cambridge: Cambridge University Press, 2018), 196–9; Beach, *Haig's Intelligence*, 176.

listed.[49] At first sight, this is surprising. Germany was technologically at least as advanced as Britain, and the civilian sector was using this equipment before the war. Also, the army was in principle no enemy of technological innovation, as wartime developments in aircraft, artillery and communications showed. Possible explanations include that the equipment was too expensive for an army fighting a 'poor man's war' compared with the Entente – even typewriters were costly and scarce.[50] There may also have been cultural resistance. As head of the German army in the 1920s, *General der Infanterie* Hans von Seeckt viewed the typewriter and duplicator as equipment suited for trench warfare, a lower form than the ideal, mobile war. This echoes OHL's 1916 views about mobile war as the 'correct image of war' discussed in the final chapter, and, as we shall see, even then the aspiration was to return to this ideal.[51]

It is also possible that military innovation flourished in areas with a strong civilian involvement. For example, Wilhelm Ohnesorge, the head of GHQ's telegraphic directorate, had studied maths and physics at university before the war. He then became a communications expert in the German post office, where he made various useful innovations. During the war, one of his inventions enabled the first telephone connections between the Western Front and Constantinople.[52] As shown in the previous chapter, wireless intelligence also developed rapidly through the employment of large numbers of civilians; indeed, the work was only possible using the civilian skills of linguists and mathematicians. By contrast, the long-service military officials and soldiers handling administration, where advanced office equipment could have been used, may have been more conservative: an example of the 'not invented here' syndrome or even the dichotomy between tradition and modernity discussed in the Introduction.

The Importance of Personal Contact and Impediments to It

Only through constant and intimate contact with the troops does one learn to 'take their pulse'.[53]

---

[49] Personal communications from Drs Markus Pöhlmann and Christian Stachelbeck.
[50] Paddy Griffith, *Battle Tactics of the Western Front: The British Army's Art of Attack 1916–18* (New Haven, CT: Yale University Press, 1994), 180.
[51] Citino, *German Way of War*, 242.
[52] Bayerische Akademie der Wissenschaften, *Neue Deutsche Biographie*, Ohnesorge entry, http://daten.digitale-sammlungen.de/bsb00016337/image_508 (accessed 4 January 2022).
[53] 'Einrichtung des Divisions-Gefechtsstandes', quoting pre-war remarks by *General der Kavallerie* Moritz Freiherr von Bissing.

Although technical means were indispensable, personal contact remained a vital element of communication. First Army's Somme report commented that meetings produced the best basis for decision-making, and were definitely preferable to phone calls: they were particularly important to co-ordination of the battle and all-arms co-operation. Commanders clearly agreed with this. In the two months from 29 April to 30 June 1917, Otto von Below made thirty visits to *Gruppen* and forty to divisions in Sixth Army, in many cases with his chief of staff, Loßberg; he also visited various other facilities and locations. Other senior officers followed the same pattern. Franz von Soden, now commanding Gruppe Reims, visited units or was otherwise out on the ground on all but three days in April and May 1917. From the other side, in ten days in May Paul von Kneußl of 11th Bavarian Infantry Division received two visits from his Army commander, two from his *Gruppe* commander and one from a senior general staff officer.[54]

These visits could be rather formal. Ludwig von Falkenhausen, Below's predecessor at Sixth Army, issued orders that when he visited a division, the commander, general staff officer and commanders of artillery, heavy artillery and engineers should be present; the *Gruppe* commander or a representative might also attend; twenty specified maps, currently marked up, were to be available.[55] His visits were known colloquially as 'oral exams' [*Abhören*]. Perhaps the vocabulary used to describe a visit reflected its nature: in some cases, a visiting commander 'had himself briefed' [*liess sich Vortrag halten*]; in others there was a conference [*Besprechung*]; and sometimes, the visitor merely held 'consultations' [*Rücksprachen*] with the receiving units.[56] What happened during visits also varied. When Below and Loßberg travelled together, they left the operations officer, the *Ia*, at headquarters. This meant they could phone through orders to implement immediately what they agreed with the formation they were visiting. On occasion, Below also took action on the spot. During his visit to Gruppe Quéant on 5 May, the commander, Moser, proposed a withdrawal. Below did not agree with this, but before deciding drove to one of the *Gruppe's* divisions, received a positive impression of the situation, drove back and ordered not just that

---

[54] AOK 1, 'Erfahrungen', 12; Otto von Below diary, April–June 1917; Gruppe Reims war diary, April–May 1917, HSAS, Soden Nachlass, M660/038 Bü 33; Kneußl diary, 4–14 May 1917.

[55] AOK 6 Army order, 'Besprechung des Herrn Oberbefehlshabers mit den Divisionen', Ia No. 5019, 21 April 1917, KAM, AOK 6 Bd. 369.

[56] Moser, *Feldzugsaufzeichnungen*, 295; Gruppe Reims war diary, 1 and 3 April and 17 May 1917, HSAS, Soden Nachlass, M660/038 Bü 33.

the position should be held but that a counter-attack should be made to recover lost ground.[57]

A crucial purpose of visits was to assess the mood of the command teams. In April 1917, Moser accompanied Falkenhausen and Loßberg on a visit to the three front-line divisions of his *Gruppe*. The commanders made short presentations, which showed clearly who was a pessimist, who a realist and who an optimist. Ironically, a couple of months later the new Army commander, Otto von Below, made the comments about Moser's pessimism and other negative characteristics noted in Chapter 4. But on that occasion, Moser got off lightly. Later in the summer, Below had a conference with *Generalleutnant* Theodor von Wundt of 18th Reserve Division. The record gives the impression of a lacklustre presentation by the division, and Wundt was replaced a few days later; he was not actively employed again.[58]

Headquarters also saw inward visits as an important way of keeping up to date with developments both below and above their level. Officers who had taken part in major battle were invited to discuss lessons learned.[59] Higher-level headquarters benefited from a flow of well-informed visitors: Army Group Crown Prince hosted a *Reichstag* delegation, Chancellor Bethmann Hollweg and the Austro-Hungarian foreign minister among others. Such visits enabled Crown Prince Wilhelm and Schulenburg to hear the latest political and diplomatic news.[60] Senior military visitors afforded an update on matters of more direct interest. Gallwitz discussed problems of the home organisation and formation of new divisions with *Oberst* (later *Generalmajor*) Ernst von Wrisberg, director of the General War Department in the Ministry of War.[61] Some visitors, however, must have been less welcome: while still fire-fighting the crisis caused by the initial British attack at Arras, Xylander at Sixth Army had to brief three Turkish officers who had come for a week-long visit.[62]

The dense webs of senior officers' personal contacts facilitated informal exchange of information. The relationship between Stapff and Wetzell is one example. Kuhl greatly valued the judgement of his close friend corps commander *Generalleutnant* Georg Fuchs, and in January 1917 was much influenced by Fuchs' view that withdrawal to the Hindenburg Line was urgently necessary.[63] Duke Wilhelm of Urach, a Württemberg division and then corps commander, regularly exchanged news with his good

[57] Otto von Below diary, 5 and 11 May 1917.

[58] Moser, *Feldzugsaufzeichnungen*, 295; AOK 6 memorandum, 'Notizen zur Besprechung des Herrn O.B. bei der 18.R.D.', 21 August 1917, KAM, AOK 6 Bd. 369.

[59] Kuhl, *Generalstab*, 191.   [60] Schulenburg, 'Erlebnisse', 148–52.

[61] Gallwitz, *Erleben im Westen*, 164.   [62] Xylander diary, 11 April 1917.

[63] Kuhl, 'Kriegstagebuch', 21 January 1917.

friend the Württemberg Minister of War *General der Infanterie* Otto von Marchtaler. This gave him the opportunity to pass on his views on a range of subjects, including tactical concerns, organisational changes and other officers. Urach was not only a senior officer but also a member of the Württemberg royal family. Officers who could claim acquaintanceship therefore took the trouble to maintain the contact by corresponding with him. *Hauptmann* Heinrich Höring, who had served as a staff officer under Urach, exchanged letters with him at least four times in early 1917. Höring's division was rushed to Messines after the defeat there, and he gave Urach an informal view of what had gone wrong. Such relationships were clearly a good way to supplement official information and to pass personal views directly to senior officers, bypassing the chain of command.[64]

Despite the importance of personal contact, the pressure of work on commanders and staff often prevented it. Periods of severe fighting kept officers tied to their desks for days. OHL believed that one of the reasons for the defeat on 9 April 1917 was failure to assess the state of the troops accurately and that this was caused by staff officers not visiting troops enough, in turn due to excessive preoccupation with paperwork. Army groups and Armies were to ensure that *Gruppe* and divisional staff officers visited units as often as possible.[65] But this was easier said than done, especially during battle. A report from Gruppe Sissonne two days after the initial French assault explained why it could not submit the usual casualty reports; part of the reason was that all the higher-level staffs had been too busy running the battle and handling the flow of information.[66]

Conditions on the ground also prevented much visiting by staff officers during battle: certainly there is little evidence of such visits in archival material or regimental histories. It was sometimes possible for officers further forward to reach the advanced positions. On 4 May 1917, a regiment in Wellmann's 20th Infantry Division sent its orderly officer to check the condition of a battalion that had suffered heavy losses and claimed it could no longer hold out.[67] But this was in response to a critical situation and may not have happened often. Throughout the year, OHL continued to worry that higher commands did not have an accurate picture of the state of the troops.

---

[64] The Marchtaler correspondence is on HSAS, Urach Nachlass, GU117 Bü 1025, and the Höring correspondence on Bü 1076.

[65] OHL circular, M.J. Nr. 50631, 22 April 1917, BArch, PH3/25.

[66] XV.BRK to AOK 7, 'Zeitangaben', Abt. IIb Nr. 1701, 18 April 1917, GLAK, F1/639.

[67] Oberleutnant a.D. Helmut Viereck, *Das Heideregiment. Königlich Preußisches 2. Hannoversches Infanterie-Regiment Nr. 77 im Weltkriege 1914–1918* (Celle: August Pohl, 1934), 381.

Technical Means and Organisation

> When these inventions of the devil work, then what they achieve is more than amazing; when they do not work, then they achieve less than nothing.[68]

In these circumstances, commanders and staffs were forced to rely more and more on technical means of communication. Even if attempts to cut bureaucracy had succeeded, the army would still have needed to quickly transmit large quantities of information at all levels of command from OHL to the battlefield. Achieving this required constant technical and organisational change. Given the nature of battle in 1917, communications from OHL down to division involved different problems to those between division and the front line. At the higher level, the chief issue was the volume of information to be moved. At the lower level, volume was also a consideration, but the principal difficulty was the vulnerability of communications to enemy fire. Information from the front was the basis for most action further up the chain of command, so the performance of the lower level of communications affected the higher.

At the higher level, the two main communications systems were the phone and teleprinter. Technical developments allowed much more intense use of phone lines, improved security and longer range. Reversing the pre-war decision, the introduction of teleprinters lessened the burden on the phone system and greatly increased the ability to handle text. Initial models doubled the rate of morse transmission. The later Siemens high-speed teleprinter [*Schnellfernschreiber*] was even faster and the paper tapes used for transmission could be re-used for forwarding traffic, eliminating the need to retype messages. Some of these developments seem, to the non-specialist at least, astonishingly modern. The German army was able to fax maps and photographs by land-line and, experimentally, artillery target information by wireless from aircraft. Teleprinters were still using Siemens-type tapes into the 1980s and later.[69]

The hardware and labour involved in establishing these communications systems were enormous. An Army headquarters might have between 300 and 600 telephone extensions. Many 'special networks' [*Sondernetze*] were created: apart from the general and tactical networks,

---

[68] Falkenhayn's comments on a 1912 exercise involving modern communications means, quoted in Strachan, *First World War*, 1:233.

[69] Chef IIIb circular, Nr. 8202, 19 October 1915, BArch, PH3/602; Ammon, 'Nachrichtenwesen', 249–60; Jonathan Coopersmith, *Faxed: The Rise and Fall of the Fax Machine* (Baltimore, MD: John Hopkins University Press, 2015), 69; personal knowledge.

there were others for the artillery and ancillaries such as sound-ranging and flash-spotting, and for aviation and anti-aircraft troops. By May 1917, 515,000 kilometres of phone cabling had been laid on the Western Front alone. Not surprisingly there was a shortage of some of the raw materials involved, especially copper, and this itself was one incentive for developing wireless telegraphy for tactical use.[70]

At the lower level, both 'Defensive Battle' and instructors lecturing on it stressed that the phone was the main means of communication between divisional headquarters and the front line, for two reasons. In the long run, it was essential to controlling the battle and could not be replaced by other means; and, echoing the pre-war view, it best enabled the commander to exert his personality even though he was physically distant from the front. The problem of course was that phone lines were very vulnerable to enemy fire and would almost certainly break in battle, leading to an information vacuum [*Nachrichtenleere*]. To get over this, divisions were continually to repair breaks; and they were to set up a comprehensive communications system so that if one means failed, messages could still be transmitted by others.[71]

If the main phone network did indeed fail, the next step was to use the artillery special network. If that too collapsed, divisions had available to them a variety of other communications possibilities. Technical means included light signalling, heliographs, flares, wireless, earth telegraphy ('power buzzers' to the British) and message-throwers (in effect small mortars). These were supplemented by animals – pigeons and dogs – and men – runners, riders, cyclists, motorcyclists, recce troops and if all else failed, officers taking reports to headquarters in person. Observation posts and balloons to the rear, as well as infantry liaison aircraft overhead ('contact aeroplanes' to the British), were also important. 'Defensive Battle' regarded aircraft as especially valuable: other communications means could only pass on details, but aircraft were the fastest way for commanders to obtain an overview of the situation on the battlefield.[72]

Some of these communications methods had been covered in pre-war regulations, but the overall system now required new organisation, doctrine and training. By early 1917, all of the means mentioned here, except the balloons and infantry liaison aircraft, had been brought under a new divisional signals section [*Divisions-Nachrichtenmittel-Abteilung*]. No post

---

[70] Generalleutnant William Balck, *Entwickelung der Taktik im Weltkriege*, 2nd ed. (Berlin: R. Eisenschmidt, 1922), 179; Ammon, 'Nachrichtenwesen', 253–4.
[71] '*Abwehrschlacht*', March 1917, 20; 'Vortrag [über das Nachrichtenwesen] bei der Übungs-Division', lecture to the fourth divisional command course in Valenciennes, 28 March–3 April 1917, HSAS, Urach Nachlass, GU117 Bü 362, 3–4 and 6.
[72] 'Einrichtung des Divisions-Gefechtsstandes'; '*Abwehrschlacht*', March 1917, 20.

had yet been established for its commander, who was usually the officer in charge of the divisional telephone section. The division's *Ib* was responsible for co-ordinating the whole communications system. Higher up, separate posts for phone and wireless telegraphy commanders were created at *Gruppe* and Army level, army groups were given a signals adviser and three overall theatre commanders of signals [*Generale der Telegraphentruppen*] were appointed.[73]

To underpin all this change, OHL issued and updated doctrine on communications, and training was pushed forward in various courses. A 1916 manual on communications equipment was among the earliest to be issued in the 'Regulations for Trench Warfare for All Arms' series. Its second edition in December that year was the version in use during the 1917 spring fighting. Other manuals published over the same period on topics such as aircraft and balloons included instructions on air–ground communications.[74] At least some divisions had trained on communications before the spring fighting and reaped the benefit during it. 14th Infantry Division had frequently exercised air–ground communications; its infantry were thoroughly confident in the method and were happy to use it. 45th Reserve Division stressed the great value of co-ordinating all signals means within the divisional signals section. Preconditions for success included careful selection and continuity of personnel, a clear organisation and, again, frequent exercises.[75]

Communication during and after the Entente Spring Offensive

No comms, no bombs. No data, no crater.[76]

Communication at the higher level of command between OHL and division worked effectively during the spring 1917 fighting. The German army drew initial lessons from the British attack on 9 April and applied them before the French assault a week later. Seventh Army had received the first lessons learned and passed them on to its *Gruppen*

[73] Cron, *Geschichte des Deutschen Heeres*, 227–8; 'Vortrag [über das Nachrichtenwesen] bei der Übungs-Division', 2–6.
[74] The main communications manual is *Vorschriften für den Stellungskrieg für alle Waffen*, Teil 9, *Nachrichtenmittel und deren Verwendung*, summer 1916; second edition 15 December 1916. For the full list of doctrinal manuals at this period, see Chapter 7.
[75] 14.ID, 'Erfahrungen während der Kämpfe an der Aisne bei Gruppe Liesse vom 2.– 14.5.1917', I 2482, 23 May 1917, GLAK, F1/523; 45.RD, 'Erfahrungen'.
[76] 'Combat Boot' tweet repeating modern signals aphorisms, 5 June 2019, https://twitter .com/combat_boot/status/1136388540919701506 (accessed 18 June 2022).

together with corresponding orders by the end of 9 April, and OHL followed up with a more considered assessment three days later.[77]

The French attacked at 0700 (German summer time) on 16 April and the first report reached Seventh Army's *Gruppe* Sissonne at 0740. The *Gruppe's* logs record a regular flow of information from its divisions and other sources such as balloon troops, observation posts and neighbouring formations. Despite some confusion about precisely how far the French had advanced, the *Gruppe* had a sufficiently accurate and timely picture to keep Seventh Army informed. In this area, the French made good progress and the *Gruppe* asked Seventh Army to release two divisions in Army reserve to its control. However, an air raid had now severed all phone communications and the request originally failed to get through. When it finally arrived at 0950, Seventh Army immediately released the divisions and twenty minutes later the *Gruppe* ordered them to counter-attack.[78] This sequence of events demonstrates a competent information-handling and decision-making process in action, despite the strains and uncertainties of battle.

At the lower level of communications between divisions and the front line, experience in the two army groups engaged against the offensive varied, largely based on differing terrain. In particular, hilly terrain in the Army Group Crown Prince sector facilitated light signalling and in some cases even the maintenance of phone connections forward of division during much of the fighting.[79] For most divisions, however, sooner or later phone communications to their units in the front failed and they then resorted to the other means available to them. After-action reports show that none used all these means, but all used several of them; in doing so they were following both pre-war and wartime doctrine.[80] What worked varied from division to division, and no particular communications means emerged clearly as the best. The key was, if one or more failed, to be able to turn to others.

The reports suggest that despite problems, especially breaks and delays in the passing of information, communications performance at the lower level was good enough. There are probably two reasons for this. First, with a few exceptions the difficulties of mobility and logistics generally

---

[77] AOK 7 telegram to its Gruppen, [no ref.], 9 April 1917, GLAK, F1/250; Reichsarchiv, *Weltkrieg*, 12:291.

[78] XV.BRK war diary, 16 April 1917, KAM, XV.BRK Bd. 11, and XV.BRK, 'Außerzeitige Lagemeldungen, Ferngespräche usw.', 16 April 1917, KAM, XV.BRK 89.

[79] 44.RD, 'Erfahrungen der 44. Reserve-Division in der Abwehrschlacht Aisne-Champagne', Ia Nr. 163/V, 23 May 1917, GLAK, F1/523.

[80] Kriegsministerium, *Grundzüge der höheren Truppenführung*, 51; '*Abwehrschlacht*', March 1917, 20. The after-action reports are on KAM, AOK 6 Bd. 419 for Arras and GLAK, F1/523 for the Nivelle offensive.

prevented the Entente attackers attaining a tempo that would have got inside the German decision cycle. Adding to their problems was the Western Front reality that communications usually favoured the defence rather than the offence.[81] Second, the German army mitigated some of its tactical communications problems by good organisational and information-handling techniques. The main problem involved infantry–artillery co-operation. Devolving control of artillery to the division and control of the forward infantry battle to a local commander (the KTK) lessened the need for detailed communication. The best way of securing infantry–artillery co-operation was to co-locate headquarters down to regimental level at least. This was a firm recommendation in 'Defensive Battle', and though not practised everywhere in spring 1917, where it *was* it certainly helped obtain good co-operation. Ironing out difficulties beforehand through conferences also reduced the need for detailed communication during combat. Finally some divisions used effectively the pre-war idea of establishing report centres [*Meldesammelstellen*] just behind the front. Ernst Jünger, in 111th Infantry Division, commanded one such centre during the battle of Arras.[82]

Despite the generally satisfactory or better performance, there was room for improvement in both information handling and the organisation of communications. Some of the worst lapses of communication occurred during German offensive rather than defensive actions, illustrating the point that Western Front communications generally favoured the defence. When 11th Bavarian Infantry Division made a local attack on the morning of 11 May, Kneußl received nothing but delayed and confused reports till the commander of the assault troops himself came to divisional headquarters that afternoon.[83] Such uncertainties were an unwelcome but expected consequence of the nature of war. More culpable was the failure to allow enough time for orders to reach all units involved in an attack, not least to ensure good all-arms co-operation. Army Group Crown Prince called this an 'obvious old rule' that had been repeatedly breached in the spring fighting, with serious

---

[81] More on Entente difficulties in Chapter 8. Sheldon, *Vimy Ridge*, 286 quotes an example on 9 April when despite good communications the German decision cycle could not cope with the tempo of a Canadian attack.

[82] '*Abwehrschlacht*', March 1917, 27; 206.ID, 'Erfahrungen über Nachrichtenwesen der 206.I.D. während ihres Einsatzes in der Aisne-Schlacht vom 5. Mai-12. Juni in der Gegend Pargny-Filain', Anlage 5 to Ib 220/7. Geheim, 1 July 1917, GLAK, F1/523; Ernst Jünger, *Kriegstagebuch 1914–1918*, ed. Helmuth Kiesel (Stuttgart: Klett-Cotta, 2010), 235–50. See also Markus Pöhlmann, 'A Portrait of the Soldier as a Young Man: Ernst Jünger at Fresnoy, April 1917', *Journal of Military and Strategic Studies*, vol. 18, no. 2 (2017), 105–17.

[83] Kneußl diary, 11 May 1917.

consequences. In Army Group Rupprecht, the carefully planned counter-attack at Fresnoy nearly failed when the difficulty of establishing the location of the German front line prevented full artillery preparation till the evening before.[84]

Aggravating these problems, the burden of bureaucracy evidently worsened at this period and further attempts to reduce it assumed an air of desperation. After its experience at Arras, 35th Infantry Division stated that ever-increasing paperwork was becoming a tactical danger: on days of battle it was no longer possible to distinguish the important from the trivial.[85] The perceived tactical danger from excessive paperwork was either already common currency or the division's use of the phrase struck a chord with higher levels of command. The first formal doctrinal instructions issued after the spring fighting also referred to the tactical danger caused by the immense increase of paperwork which chained officers as junior as company commanders in their offices, as well as limiting their independence.[86] In July, Ludendorff developed this thought: paperwork was an ever-increasing tactical danger which was impairing to a greater and greater degree independence, initiative, interest in the service and, in the final analysis, reliability and honesty.[87]

A document issued by OHL to all general staff officers on the same day in July clarifies the reference to reliability and honesty. There were frequent complaints, including from officers of sound judgement, that reports from units were no longer reliable. This 'extremely unwelcome' phenomenon was caused by excessive interference and bureaucratic demands from above coupled with a decline in personal contact between higher-level headquarters and units. Out of resentment or fear of further paperwork, some officers were either keeping quiet against their better conscience or fudging [frisieren] their reports.[88]

Ludendorff clearly accepted that there was at least a core of truth to these complaints but he was oversimplifying the causes. Chapter 8 describes pressure from above to adjust assessment of divisions' fitness for battle to current operational needs, and this could take a very personal form. The army saw willpower as the deciding factor in war, expected officers to be optimistic and frowned on anything suggesting pessimism.

---

[84] HDK, 'Zusammenstellung einiger Lehren aus der Doppelschlacht Aisne-Champagne', 2.

[85] 35.ID, 'Erfahrungen aus der Schlacht bei Arras', Ia Nr. 1345 geh., 29 April 1917, KAM, AOK 6 Bd. 419, f. 126.

[86] Chef des Generalstabes des Feldheeres, *Sonderheft zum Sammelheft der Vorschriften für den Stellungskrieg: Vom 10. Juni 1917* (GHQ: Druckerei des Chefs des Generalstabes des Feldheeres, 1917), 26 (hereafter, '*Sonderheft*').

[87] OHL circular, II Nr. 59707 op., 11 July 1917, HSAS, Soden Nachlass, M660/038 Bü 17.

[88] OHL to all general staff officers, M.J. Nr. 55555, 11 July 1917, BArch, PH3/25.

In an exaggerated form, this 'can-do' attitude threatened the free flow of information. Although the army prided itself as a self-critical organisation willing to learn from mistakes, even in peacetime parts of it suffered from falsified reporting and, as we saw in the Introduction, a fear of disagreeing with senior officers.[89]

During the war, officers could be sacked for pessimism.[90] When Max von Boehn wrote his memorandum on the deteriorating quality of the army, he felt it necessary, even as a senior general, to state that he was not shrinking from expressing such views because he believed he was 'above the suspicion of pessimism or untimely weakness'. Discussing the impossibility of maintaining the position on the Somme in January 1917, Georg Fuchs wrote, 'Acknowledging this takes courage. No one wants to admit it to anyone else, and the higher one goes the rosier the colour of the reports.'[91] Ironically, apprehension of Ludendorff's own overbearing manner was one reason why even senior officers were unwilling to speak truth to power.[92]

The charge is not of course that all or even most reports were doctored. Handling of after-action reports is evidence of a basic honesty in the system. If a higher level of command disagreed with a report, the practice was not to suppress it but to forward it with an explanation of why it was wrong. An example is a report from 17th Infantry Division quoted in Chapter 7. Forwarding it to Sixth Army, the *Gruppe* commander commented that it was largely inaccurate and that its sharp criticism of the *Gruppe* came as a complete surprise to him; in fact, it displayed a regrettable misunderstanding of the purpose of such reports. But he forwarded it nevertheless.[93] In addition, some anecdotes of falsified reporting possibly originated from embittered commanders who had been sacked.[94] However, Ludendorff's admission, together with the number of references to falsified reporting made both during and after the war by officers at different levels, proves that it was a genuine problem at least as early as 1917. Over the next year, it continued to get worse and by late 1918 the increasing punishment of dissent and stifling of open

[89] Gleich, *Die alte Armee*, 86 and 94–5.
[90] Hans von Below memorandum, 'Meine Ansichten zu vorstehenden Auseinandersetzungen', 5.
[91] Kuhl, 'Kriegstagebuch', 21 January 1917.
[92] Steltzer, *Sechzig Jahre Zeitgenosse*, 53–4; Steltzer was quoting from his time as a *Hauptmann* in OHL.
[93] Boff, *Haig's Enemy*, 159–61 presents a more negative view of German after-action reporting following the initial defeat at Arras.
[94] For example, *General der Kavallerie* Ludwig Freiherr von Gebsattel: Boff, *Winning and Losing*, 240–1.

debate contributed in no small measure to the German army's eventual defeat.[95]

If OHL failed to take effective action on these intractable issues, it did tackle the second area where 1917 experience showed improvement was necessary: the organisation of communications. The increasing importance of communications, the complexity of the means now available and the huge expansion of the signal troops all demonstrated that the current organisation was insufficiently integrated.[96] In September 1917, signals was therefore established as an arm of service. Previously separate phone and wireless posts were combined into Army and *Gruppe* commanders of communications, the *Akonach* and *Grukonach*. The post of divisional communications commander, *Divkonach*, was also established in order to ensure 'a particularly firm control'.[97] In addition, OHL pushed through doctrinal change. The questionnaires steering after-action reports in spring 1917 did not call for comment on communications performance, but many divisions nevertheless went into some detail about it. This experience fed as usual into the drafting of new doctrine. The manual on communications was updated for the second time in December 1917; other manuals were also issued and updated on signals and related subjects such as air–ground communications.

Conclusions

Prior to 1914, the German army had recognised the importance of communication to the third command task, reducing uncertainty, and had evolved a mixture of organisational, personal and technical means to handle it. The realities of battle in 1917 confirmed some pre-war ideas and disproved others. Headquarters expanded in size and were generally forced to the rear by firepower. The bureaucratic burden continually increased despite attempts to rein it in and partly because of failure to adopt modern methods of information handling within the office. Personal contact remained essential to command, though 1917 conditions, including bureaucracy, made it more difficult. The same conditions led to ever-greater reliance on technical communications means and organisations, which the German army continually strove to develop.

---

[95] Ibid., 240–2 and 247. Hermann Geyer, 'Einige Gedanken über Verteidigung, Ausweichen und dergleichen', *Militärwissenschaftliche Mitteilungen*, vol. 1 (November 1921), 4 mentions cases of falsified reporting from September 1914.

[96] Signal troops increased from about 26,000 on mobilisation to an establishment in 1918 (never actually reached) of over 190,000 – and even that did not include the thousands of unit signallers: Ammon, 'Nachrichtenwesen', 245.

[97] Cron, *Geschichte des Deutschen Heeres*, 231–3.

The performance of the communications system in the spring fighting was at least adequate, a contributory factor being the slow tempo achieved by the Entente attackers. But the unstoppable growth of bureaucracy and the linked problem of falsified reporting were danger signals that the urge to reduce uncertainty had got out of hand.

Links between communication and the concepts discussed in earlier chapters such as mission command and personality are clear. Moltke the Elder stressed that orders must be tailored to the recipient, depending on whether they could be trusted to implement mission command properly. A modern US military manual pointed out that 'the need of commanders to balance reduction of uncertainty with tempo is the essence of the C2 [command and control] challenge'.[98] This idea would have been familiar to the German army, which saw communication in the form of reports and orders as a principal way of reducing uncertainty to an acceptable level, and mission command as a technique to exploit it. Chapter 2 described a further, ironic link: the greater capacity and demand for technical communications was both a cause and an effect of the limited application of mission command on the Western Front at this period.

Many of the challenges and experiences in this chapter were common to all armies on the Western Front. Just to take one example, the 'obvious old rule' of allowing enough time for orders to reach all units involved in an attack elicited similar responses from both the British and German armies. German First Army found on the Somme that an order could take eight to ten hours to get from division to the front line. British doctrine issued after the Somme recommended allowing twenty-four hours between the order for an attack leaving divisional headquarters and the time of the assault.[99] There were other striking similarities between the two armies in the area of communication – organisational and control issues; information overload and the need to improve information-handling techniques to cope with relentlessly mounting bureaucracy; the weaknesses of the means of communication on the battlefield and the need to develop a system with redundancy as one of its core features; and finally the difficulty of personal contact in the heat of battle and the debates concerning the location and proximity of headquarters.[100]

***

---

[98] Headquarters, Department of the Army, *Field Manual No. 6–0: Mission Command: Command and Control of Army Forces* (Washington, DC: Department of the Army, 2003), 1–54.

[99] AOK 1, 'Erfahrungen', 14; General Staff, *S.S. 135: Instructions for the Training of Divisions for Offensive Action* (London: Harrison, 1916), 1:7.

[100] Personal communication from Dr Brian N. Hall.

The primary means of meeting the third command task, reducing uncertainty, were intelligence on the enemy and communication of information about German troops. Intelligence performance before the Entente spring offensive was mixed – good on the French, considerably poorer on the British. Despite the increasing bureaucratic burden, the communication system functioned well enough: French and British inability to achieve a high tempo except in isolated instances helped here. During the spring fighting, the German army can therefore be judged to have completed the third command task at least adequately.

7 Learning

It takes 15,000 casualties to train a Major-General.[1]

A popular image of the Western Front is one of stagnation coupled with failure to foresee or solve the problems of modern warfare. In contrast, many scholars argue that armies effectively faced up to and overcame these problems by means of a continuous learning curve or process.[2] Whether we accept this argument or not, it is clear that the opposing armies constantly strove for tactical, technological and organisational advantage. Ironically, it was their attempts to break the deadlock which confirmed it.[3] This was the dynamic equilibrium of the Western Front, or war as a continuous interaction of opposites as Clausewitz called it:

> Today armies are so much alike in weapons, training and equipment that there is little difference in such matters between the best and the worst of them . . . what it usually comes down to is that one side invents improvements and first puts them to use, and the other side promptly copies them.[4]

In modern terms, armies on the Western Front were 'symmetrical'.[5] The 1917 Entente spring offensive illustrates how tactical advantage could change sides in a startlingly short time. The British attack at Arras on 9 April was of unprecedented weight. The Germans drew and applied initial lessons from the battle before the French assault began on 16 April, contributing to its defeat. One of the methods they used was large-scale counter-attack by reserves brought up close behind the front. Within a week the French had found an antidote by using heavier barrages

---

[1] Attributed to Ferdinand Foch: Robert Debs Heinl, Jr, *Dictionary of Military and Naval Quotations* (Annapolis, MD: United States Naval Institute, 1966), 128.

[2] For a recent overview of the learning curve debate, see Christopher Newton, 'An Anatomy of British Adaptation on the Western Front: British Third Army and the Battles of the Scarpe, April–June 1917', unpublished PhD thesis, King's College London, 2019, 9–13.

[3] Hew Strachan, *The First World War: A New Illustrated History* (London: Pocket Books, 2006), 169.

[4] Clausewitz, *On War*, book 2, chapter 2, 136 and book 5, chapter 3, 282.

[5] Hew Strachan, 'Clausewitz and the First World War', *Journal of Military History*, vol. 75, no. 2 (April 2011), 377.

to prevent the movement of reserves, and the Germans in turn began working on a counter-antidote.[6]

Understanding and adapting to this rapidly changing environment was the German army's fourth command task. This chapter examines both how and what the army learned. Recent research by Robert T. Foley and Aimée Fox is important to the 'how' question. Following on from earlier commentary on the German army as an example of institutionalised innovation and on tactical development during the Somme, Foley has compared learning in the British and German armies. He argues that both learned effectively but in different ways, the Germans making extensive use of formal learning processes to create and transfer knowledge upwards and downwards throughout the system, the British non-formal. In the German learning process, after-action reports played a greater role than doctrine in tactical innovation, and the success of this system was based on the culture of learning that permeated the officer corps.[7]

In her groundbreaking book about British army learning in the First World War, *Learning to Fight*, Fox stresses 'the complexity and messiness associated with learning' and the difficulties of learning in a 'desperate and lethally competitive environment'. To explain this complexity, she proposes that learning should be viewed as a network including liberal, horizontal, vertical and external approaches. 'Liberal' here means informal learning based on individual interactions and social networks; 'horizontal' covers lateral exchanges of experiences, mainly between groups; 'vertical' is largely a top-down dissemination of doctrine and instruction, but in an effective system draws extensively on freely offered bottom-up experience; and finally 'external' involves learning from enemies, allies and other outside sources, especially civilians. At the centre of this network are the individual and human factors, together with the army's organisational culture and ethos.[8]

Even more important than how the German army learned is what it learned, meaning both the content of learning and the extent to which it was absorbed. After all, an army at war is not learning for its own sake or in a vacuum but for a purpose, to improve performance in the battle it actually faces. The measure of effective learning therefore has to be performance. Fox considers that no direct link can be drawn between

---

[6] HDK telegram to AOK 7, 1a 2431, 24 April 1917, GLAK, F1/249.

[7] Robert T. Foley, 'Horizontal Military Innovation', 815–16, and 'Dumb Donkeys or Cunning Foxes? Learning in the British and German Armies during the Great War', *International Affairs*, vol. 90, no. 2 (March 2014), 280 and 287–90. See also his 'Learning War's Lessons', 504 and 'Institutionalized Innovation', passim.

[8] Fox, *Learning to Fight*, 3–4 and 53–72.

learning and performance, because the outcome of battle depended on multiple issues such as terrain, weather and the enemy.[9] She is right about the difficulty, but nevertheless the effort must be made.

The key to tactical success, and therefore our focus in attempting to measure how German learning affected performance, was combined arms battle. The different arms of service could not work together without a common understanding of procedures. Combined arms battle was the core element of doctrinal change in 1916–17 and so illuminates how and what the army learned. Combined arms traditionally meant infantry, cavalry and artillery; but by this period the cavalry had effectively dropped out on the Western Front and aviation, engineers, signals and transport had assumed increasing importance. The analysis here covers what really decided battle at a tactical level, the indispensable trio infantry, artillery and aviation.

From Pre-war to Late 1916

By 1914, German doctrine incorporated the insight of military theorists that combined arms tactics were essential to solving the problem of modern defensive firepower.[10] Implementing doctrine was another matter. Hindenburg thought that before the war only the infantry's tactics were common property throughout the army; knowledge of the technical arms was seen as unimportant and to be handled by a few specialists.[11] *Generalleutnant* William Balck – an infantry officer, well-known writer on tactics and wartime divisional commander – wrote that although both artillery and infantry regulations called for co-operation between the two arms, there had not been enough practice for this to work properly. The pre-war emphasis on a battle of annihilation had instilled in German infantry training a 'mad rush to attack' [*Angriffshetze*], which had prevented fully effective infantry–artillery co-operation.[12] In a serious omission, there were no regulations on combined arms battle.[13]

Organisational issues compounded the problem. Below divisional level, the army was largely organised in single-arm units and, as Otto von Moser suggested, this tended to instil a certain narrowness of vision. Friedrich Graf Schulenburg wrote that before 1914 few officers got the

---

[9] Fox, *Learning to Fight*, 9.

[10] Echevarria, *After Clausewitz*, 217; Raths, *Vom Massensturm zur Stoßtrupptaktik*, 50–1, 55–7, 80, 87 and 208. For an overview of combined arms battle, see Jonathan M. House, *Combined Arms Warfare in the Twentieth Century* (Lawrence, KS: University Press of Kansas, 2001).

[11] OHL circular, 'Kriegführung und Generalstab'.

[12] Balck, *Entwickelung der Taktik*, 32 and 39.   [13] Strachan, *First World War*, 1:238.

chance to command a formation of all arms.[14] As noted earlier, officers' confidential reports did not assess performance in combined arms work, a significant gap. The infantry were regarded as the main arm and the statistics in Chapter 2 back up complaints that they occupied a disproportionate number of higher posts: in 1914, over three-quarters of divisional commanders and nearly half of divisional command teams were from the infantry. Attempts to compensate for such imbalances by secondments of *Kriegsakademie* students and other officers to different arms were worthwhile but clearly insufficient to overcome the single-arm bias.

In 1914, aviation was joining the traditional infantry–artillery–cavalry combined arms mix. Air reconnaissance produced promising results in manoeuvres, and Schlieffen believed aircraft would eventually replace cavalry in this role.[15] Thought was given to other ways in which aircraft could co-operate with ground troops, including artillery observation, bombing, close air support, transport and liaison. However, such conceptual thinking had not become reality by the outbreak of war. Despite some experimentation, practical co-operation between aircraft and artillery was almost unknown in Germany; the French were ahead in this area.[16]

The opening campaigns of the war saw a mixed German tactical performance. Some units were skilled in combined arms tactics; others adopted dense formations without adequate artillery support.[17] Even Terence Zuber, a proponent of German military excellence, accepts that there were widespread problems of artillery–infantry co-operation during the battle of the Frontiers.[18] The fighting in 1915 proved that success could only be achieved through close co-operation between the two arms.[19] A semi-official German history of Verdun commented that the artillery had far less effect than expected; co-ordination between the arms often failed, and the infantry were then faced with an impossible task.[20]

The initial phases of the battle of the Somme showed just how far the Germans had fallen behind in combined arms tactics. Effective Entente

---

[14] Schulenburg, 'Erlebnisse', 256.   [15] Bucholz, *Moltke, Schlieffen*, 212.

[16] Echevarria, *After Clausewitz*, 169; Major a.D. Georg Paul Neumann, ed., *Die deutschen Luftstreitkräfte im Weltkriege* (Berlin: E. S. Mittler, 1920), 59 and 397.

[17] Strachan, *First World War*, 1:237.

[18] Terence Zuber, *The Mons Myth: A Reassessment of the Battle* (Stroud: History Press, 2010), 44–5.

[19] OHL circular, 'Gesichtspunkte für den Stellungskrieg', Nr. 7563 r, October 1915, BArch, PH3/1901, 20.

[20] Ludwig Gold and Alexander Schwencke, *Die Tragödie von Verdun 1916*, Schlachten des Weltkrieges 13–15, vol. 1, *Die deutsche Offensivschlacht* (Oldenburg: Gerhard Stalling, 1926), 254.

artillery–air co-operation caused heavy casualties and control of the air-space over the battlefield became a precondition of success on it.[21] Later in the battle, German reinforcement and reorganisation challenged Entente air superiority. This was partly a question of forming dedicated fighter squadrons with improved aircraft and specially trained pilots. As described in Chapter 1, all aviation-related assets were brought together as a separate arm of service under one command. These developments undoubtedly benefited German air operations but did not lead to complete superiority: there was a resurgence of the British air effort in late autumn and early winter 1916.[22]

The Development of Doctrine

Responding to the challenges of Verdun and the Somme, in autumn 1916, OHL drafted a new doctrine for combined arms battle. In an important circular setting the context, OHL explained that when trench warfare began, better training, discipline and drill had given the German army the upper hand. However, the British and French had in some ways learned more quickly and had begun to overtake the Germans. Developments since 1914 had changed warfare. These included new infantry weapons; more artillery together with increasing ranges and expenditure of ammunition; and a large air force. Such new means would allow the army to compensate for the infantry's declining perform-ance. An unwanted side-effect, however, was the numerous technical experts who were responsible for their specialities but not for the bigger picture; the consequence was an 'ever-increasing fragmentation' of battle. The person best placed to co-ordinate the whole was the general staff officer, but to do this he needed a thorough knowledge of all arms. Finally, in a war of attrition the measure of success was not gaining or losing ground, but the balance of losses in men and matériel. All planning must take into account the need to cause substantial damage to the enemy while minimising German losses.[23]

The new doctrine did not emerge from a void. Falkenhayn had issued guidance on trench warfare in autumn 1915, and in 1916 he launched the significantly titled 'Regulations for Trench Warfare for All Arms' series of manuals (Table 7.1). When Hindenburg and Ludendorff took over from Falkenhayn, they began a considerable expansion of this series to improve combined arms tactics (Table 7.2). The new doctrine was intended to

---

[21] Reichsarchiv, *Weltkrieg*, 11:110 and 12:35.
[22] Duffy, *Through German Eyes*, 312–13.
[23] OHL circular, 'Kriegführung und Generalstab'.

Table 7.1 *Doctrinal manuals issued under Falkenhayn, April–August 1916*

Mine Warfare
Illuminants
Field Fortifications
Close-Range Weapons
Infantry Liaison Aircraft and Balloons
Communications Equipment

Table 7.2 *Doctrinal manuals issued under Hindenburg/Ludendorff, August 1916–March 1917*

Artillery Liaison Aircraft
General Principles of Field Fortifications (2nd ed.) and two related manuals
Mortars
Principles for the Conduct of the Defensive Battle in Trench Warfare
Communications Equipment (2nd ed.)
Infantry Liaison Aircraft and Balloons (2nd ed.)
Close-Range Weapons (2nd ed.)
Artillery Liaison Aircraft (2nd ed.)
Principles for the Conduct of the Defensive Battle in Trench Warfare (2nd ed.)

eliminate damaging friction caused by differing views on tactics and procedures; to enable uniform training of commanders and units; and to give commanders and especially general staff officers all the information they needed to understand the different arms of service and combined arms battle.[24] The main manual was 'Defensive Battle', issued in December 1916; linked to it was 'General Principles of Field Fortifications' from the month before.[25]

To recap, 'Defensive Battle' covered the handling of the whole battle and not just tactics. It included instructions on top-down defensive organisation, intelligence, communication, all-arms co-operation, individual arms of service, reserves and the management of attrition. The section 'General Conduct of the Battle' stated that the defence should exhaust the attacker and bleed him to death while conserving German forces.[26] The division

---

[24] Reichsarchiv, *Weltkrieg*, 12:38–9; OHL to AOK 3, II Nr. 38642 op., 3 November 1916 and Oberstleutnant Bauer message to HDK, 13 November 1916, both on BArch, PH3/28, f. 22. The principal manuals in Tables 7.1, 7.2 and 7.3 are in bold. Single-arms regulations outside this series were issued in spring 1917 on infantry, artillery and aviation.

[25] In German '*Allgemeines über Stellungsbau*', which revised an earlier manual.

[26] '*Abwehrschlacht*', March 1917, 6.

became the main unit for fighting the battle, the commanders of the front divisions were responsible for handling the combined arms battle in their sector and defence was to be mobile, in depth and offensive.

Much of this doctrine was codification of best practice that had developed in 1915 and 1916 rather than a radical new departure; indeed, some of the changes had been discussed before the war.[27] Units were soon referring to 'Defensive Battle' to explain, simplify and supplement their orders.[28] Nevertheless, there was considerable resistance, especially over permission to give up ground in the mobile battle and over control of artillery. This was not just the effect of military conservatism: each of the options involved genuine difficulties. As an expression of this resistance and in contradiction to 'Defensive Battle', new infantry doctrine and the semi-doctrinal First Army Somme report, both issued in early 1917, stressed the need for the infantry to hold out to the last man rather than withdraw.[29] Foley cites evidence that OHL deliberately instigated differences of opinion to test the new defensive doctrine.[30] But if so, this should have been done at an earlier stage. In a wartime army, and particularly given concerns about declining expertise in divisional staffs, actually promulgating contradictions in doctrine sowed confusion and complicated co-ordination of the combined arms battle.

In the short term, resistance to withdrawal was bought off by changes in the second edition of 'Defensive Battle', issued in March 1917 and therefore the doctrine in force at the time of the spring offensive. Teams of experienced officers and the Army Group Rupprecht divisional command course contributed to the new edition. It was considerably longer than its predecessor, with greater clarification of principles, and couched more in the form of orders than recommendations. This approach may reflect confidence that the principles were correct, as well as the need to give firm guidance to inexperienced command teams. The edition stressed that any temporary movement to avoid enemy fire should be made forwards, not backwards. It also moved responsibility for authorising more permanent withdrawals upwards to *Gruppe* or Army – as noted in Chapter 2, an erosion of mission command.[31]

---

[27] Robert T. Foley, 'Horizontal Military Innovation', 813–14; Raths, *Vom Massensturm zur Stoßtrupptaktik*, 203–18. For a detailed description of the evolution of doctrine, see Tony Cowan, 'The Introduction of New German Defensive Tactics in 1916–1917', *British Journal for Military History*, vol. 5, no. 2 (October 2019), 81–99.

[28] AOK 7 to its Gruppen, 'Vorbereitungen für die Abwehrschlacht', Ia Nr. 155/Dez. 16, 28 December 1916, GLAK, F1/374.

[29] Kriegsministerium, *Ausbildungsvorschrift für die Fußtruppen im Kriege (A.V.F.)* (Berlin: Reichsdruckerei, 1917), 178 and 226; AOK 1, 'Erfahrungen', 63.

[30] Foley, 'Learning War's Lessons', 503.   [31] '*Abwehrschlacht*', March 1917, 6b and 15.

In contrast, the edition definitively devolved control of most artillery downwards to division. Both before and during the war, many experts believed that corps should control artillery: only this could guarantee maximum concentration of fire, and many divisional staffs were not capable of co-ordinating large amounts of artillery.[32] The problem with such centralised control was that it depended on good communications, which Chapter 6 showed could not be guaranteed in battle. This thorny question became acute on the Somme in September 1916. An OHL officer reported that both artillery–infantry and field–heavy artillery co-operation had failed; in fact the defence suffered from an unbelievable lack of artillery organisation. This was when OHL called in Maximilian von Höhn, an artillery expert then commanding a division on the Somme, to produce an initial draft of 'Defensive Battle'.[33] Artillery problems were therefore the immediate impetus for the new doctrine.

The 'Defensive Battle' section on artillery comprised nearly one third of the new edition, leaving no doubt that the arm was a crucial component of the defence. Divisions on major battle fronts were now allocated a divisional artillery commander with a small staff. He would command all artillery, both field and heavy, whether an organic part of or temporarily allocated to the division. Wherever possible, artillery command staffs should be a mix of field and heavy artillery officers.[34] Senior artillery officers at *Gruppe* and Army level would control tasking involving more than one division or longer-range targets. The German army also carefully defined artillery tasks as well as the different types of fire, guns and ammunition needed to carry them out. The Germans knew that the Entente's favoured tactic was 'the artillery conquers, the infantry occupies'. German artillery's first task was therefore counter-battery work. OHL strongly encouraged offensive types of fire, the aim being to pre-empt or prevent the enemy assault. It constantly tried to dissuade the infantry from excessive calls for defensive barrage fire, viewed as passive, ineffective and wasteful. To improve co-operation on such issues, artillery and infantry command posts should be co-located.[35]

---

[32] Gallwitz, *Erleben im Westen*, 31 and 87–8.

[33] Mertz von Quirnheim's seventh report to the Bavarian Kriegsminister, 30 September 1916, NARA, Mertz von Quirnheim papers, M958-1; Bauer, *Große Krieg*, 118–19.

[34] Kriegsministerium circular, Nr. 445/17.g.A4, 16 February 1917, BArch, PH1/10, ff. 144–53.

[35] '*Abwehrschlacht*', March 1917, 22 and 27; 'Die vorbereiteten Feuerarten', 'Die verschiedenen Kaliber und ihre taktische Verwendung in der Abwehrschlacht' and 'Die Artillerie in der Abwehrschlacht', lectures to the second divisional command course in Sedan, 21–7 March 1917, HSAS, Urach Nachlass, GU117 Bü 362.

Closely linked to artillery performance was support from aviation. Given the ranges involved, air reconnaissance, photography and observation were essential for the Entente artillery to 'conquer', and equally for the German artillery's counter-efforts. 'Defensive Battle' stressed the need to gain air superiority, even if only temporary and local, to prevent enemy and enable German air reconnaissance and observation.[36] When the Germans captured the new French attack doctrine in February 1917, instructions on countermeasures placed particular importance on using air assets to identify the enemy threat and direct pre-emptive artillery fire onto it. OHL underlined the need for close co-ordination between aviation and formation headquarters. The best way of increasing mutual understanding was to subordinate complete aviation units to divisions early on; Armies and *Gruppen* should retain as few as possible for their own use. Aviation staffs should be co-located with infantry and artillery staffs.[37] To control all this, aviation commanders were allocated to every Army headquarters and to *Gruppen* on the attack fronts. These officers had transferred into the air force from other arms of service, bringing with them much useful experience of their parent branch to the benefit of all-arms co-operation.[38]

An increasingly prominent feature of battle at the operational and tactical levels during this period was its depth, the effect of long-range artillery fire and bombing. The Germans shelled Dunkirk at a range of some forty kilometres from 1915, and bombing had begun early in the war. The intensity of these activities by both sides was now increasing. There was a general demand for longer range guns, and by early 1917 the German army was introducing new field artillery to satisfy this. It was also developing very long-range artillery: in spring 1917, preparations were under way in the Seventh Army area to install one of the guns that shelled Paris the next year.[39] This was intended to have strategic effect but other guns under development throughout 1917 were for use at the operational level. The aim was to hit targets up to fifty kilometres away, such as Army headquarters, major transport nodes and munitions facilities.[40] Similarly,

---

[36] '*Abwehrschlacht*', March 1917, 32 and 36–7.

[37] OHL circular, II Nr. 48626 op./Nachr.Abtlg., 28 February 1917, HSAS, Soden Nachlass, M660/038 Bü 17, f. 19.

[38] Hauptmann Walther Stahr, for example, Seventh Army's aviation commander in spring 1917, had some thirteen years' field artillery service before transfer.

[39] Henry W. Miller, *The Paris Gun: The Bombardment of Paris by the German Long-Range Guns and the Great German Offensives of 1918* (London: Harrap, 1930), 46–7; General der Infanterie a.D. Eduard von Liebert, *Aus einem bewegten Leben* (Munich: J. F. Lehmanns, 1925), 220.

[40] HDK to OHL, 'Zusammenstellung von Zielen für 38 cm E.-B. Geschütze', Ia/Artl. Nr. 9615, 27 November 1917, BArch, PH3/502, f. 133.

bombing of both strategic and operational-level targets increased. 'Defensive Battle' stated that systematic bombing of large camps, new aerodromes, ammunition dumps and unloading points could considerably delay and disrupt the enemy attack.[41]

Despite the greatly increased roles of the artillery and aviation by 1917, the German army still saw the infantry as the main arm of service.[42] Writers such as Bruce I. Gudmundsson admire the tactical sophistication of German infantry at this period. The Germans themselves thought their infantry had declined in quality in 1916, but remained superior to the enemy.[43] Updated regulations for infantry were issued in spring 1917. Specially selected and instructed storm battalions were used to train ordinary infantry units, with the aim of raising their overall tactical performance. Such training was the primary function of storm battalions; however, they also took part in tactically important attacks, for which they were allocated in sub-units organised according to the particular mission. Each Western Front Army had a storm battalion, which it kept under its control: this high-level subordination itself shows how few (and valuable) these units were.[44]

Case Study: Learning the New Doctrine

A unit's combat value depends on the level of its training.[45]

OHL was well aware that training was needed to convert the new defensive doctrine into tactical reality. In February 1917, it established divisional command courses in Army Group Rupprecht, and next month Army Group Crown Prince followed suit. These one-week courses comprised classroom briefing and practical demonstrations of the new combined arms battle doctrine for divisional commanders and their chief staff officers, and for other divisional infantry and artillery commanders. They were also intended to test the whole of the new doctrine – 'Defensive Battle', the new principles for field fortifications and the other regulations in the series. Otto von Moser designed and ran the first three of these courses. His account of this work well illustrates how the effectiveness or otherwise of learning in the German army depended on a combination of factors, including personality, personal relationships, experience, doctrine, organisation and events.

As the case study in Chapter 4 showed, Moser was a good choice to establish these courses, with a talent for teaching, extensive general staff

---

[41] '*Abwehrschlacht*', March 1917, 33.   [42] 'Einleitender Vortrag des Kursleiters', 23.

[43] Sophistication: Gudmundsson, *Stormtroop Tactics*, xiv; though dated, this remains the best account of German infantry tactics. Declining quality: Boehn memorandum, October 1916. Still superior: AOK 1, 'Erfahrungen', 23.

[44] Gruss, *Sturmbataillone*, 60–1.   [45] '*Abwehrschlacht*', March 1917, 53.

experience and active service on different fronts. In particular, he had recently commanded one of the best divisions in the army in a successful defensive action on the Somme, for which he had been awarded a high Prussian decoration. As with Höhn and the drafting of 'Defensive Battle', he therefore lent credibility to what might otherwise have been seen as an academic exercise. His staff were equally experienced. He had personally asked for his chief staff officer, *Hauptmann* Walter Wever, who had been serving as a general staff officer in his division (and in the 1930s became the *Luftwaffe*'s first chief of staff). The other course officers were drawn from the main arms of service required for combined arms battle – field and heavy artillery, infantry, machine guns, engineers and signals.[46]

Moser ensured that in addition to formal tuition in the classroom, wargaming and practical demonstration on the exercise ground, there were plenty of opportunities for informal learning. He knew many of the students from previous postings or from training, and he lunched with different groups every day. Most of the students had rich experience in different theatres, but while engaged at the front had lacked the time and inclination for learning. The course gave them both, with the result that a mass of proposals arose from the free exchange of views between students and with the course staff, on the ground or in relaxed situations. Naturally, the courses were also excellent for networking. No doubt with some exaggeration, Moser said that he gradually got to know the whole of the German generalship. He used personal meetings with senior visitors, including Ludendorff, Crown Prince Rupprecht and Fritz von Below, both to learn about what was going on in the wider war and to put over his own concerns.

It is less easy to reach a judgement on the actual effect of the courses. On the one hand, many OHL officers attended, including the chief doctrine writer, *Hauptmann* Hermann Geyer. This helped them keep up to date with best practice, facilitating rapid exploitation of proposals and, where appropriate, conversion into doctrine. Also, after the first course, participants came not only from sectors where Entente attacks were expected but also quiet sectors, the Eastern Front and the allies. All this helped spread best practice uniformly. Some 500–600 officers could have been trained by the time the Entente spring offensive opened, and they would at least all be working from the same knowledge base. Furthermore, tuition could be quickly adapted with the acquisition of new intelligence or experience, an example being the shift to teaching how to counter the French assault doctrine referred to in Chapter 5.

---

[46] Moser, *Feldzugsaufzeichnungen*, 267–8; on Höhn, see Cowan, 'Introduction of New German Defensive Tactics', 86.

On the other hand, these courses did not all run smoothly. In particular, Army Group Crown Prince may not have taken them as seriously as Army Group Rupprecht. The latter's courses were commanded by a *Generalleutnant*, averaged some 100 students and employed a demonstration division reinforced for major defensive battle. In contrast, Army Group Crown Prince's courses were commanded by an *Oberstleutnant* succeeded by a *Major*, they averaged sixty students and the demonstration unit was a reinforced regiment.[47] Moser was concerned that his Army Group Rupprecht courses made too great demands on the students. But after attending an Army Group Crown Prince course, Paul von Kneußl recorded that the content was more suitable for officer cadets than divisional commanders; his *Ia*, Wilhelm von Leeb, agreed with him. Some of the surviving briefing material supports these views, such as a rather basic talk on the role of infantry in the defensive battle.[48] The different approaches may reflect the fact that Hermann von Kuhl, Army Group Rupprecht's chief of staff, was the moving force behind establishing the courses – their patron in Fox's terminology – and as a result the army group gave Moser excellent support. We can speculate that Army Group Crown Prince's different methods may have been another example of the 'not invented here' syndrome, or doing things 'our way'.

We can also question the effectiveness of the courses in terms of battlefield performance. Moser stressed the crucial role of the divisional commander and *Ia* in handling combined arms battle, particularly the need to think systematically about the employment of artillery and not just infantry as before. He had met resistance from corps and heavy artillery representatives to the new doctrine of devolving control to divisions. He believed he had persuaded them to accept this devolution without simply strong-arming them into obeying. However, in practice infantry–artillery co-operation remained a problem throughout the year. A more general question relates to the short time between the establishment of these courses in February and the opening of the Entente offensive in early April. Was it in fact possible to implement the lessons from the courses properly, especially given that Army Group Rupprecht was distracted by the withdrawal to the Hindenburg Line until late March,

---

[47] Moser, *Feldzugsaufzeichnungen*, 266–78; on the reinforced Army Group Rupprecht demonstration division, see HKR army group order, Ic/1998 geh., 13 January 1917, KAM, HKR neue Nr. 31. The best documentary sources for these courses are HSAS, Urach Nachlass, GU117 Bü 362 and M635/2 Bü 544–8.

[48] Stachelbeck, *Militärische Effektivität*, 182; 'Die Infanterie in der Abwehrschlacht', lecture drafted for a divisional command course in Sedan, 2 April 1917, HSAS, Urach Nachlass, GU117 Bü 362.

and Army Group Crown Prince was frantically preparing its defences against the obviously impending French attack?

However, even if not completely successful these courses were an imaginative attempt to rapidly train divisional-level commanders and staff officers on new combined arms doctrine and so to improve lagging German performance. Strikingly, the British had no such training for their equivalent officers, so-called 'Senior Officers' courses covering battalion command only.[49] There is no doubt OHL took the divisional command courses seriously. Ludendorff praised the value of the first course, instructed Moser to organise the second in the same way and attended a day of it. After running three courses, Moser was appointed corps commander, a further sign of approval for his work. In July, OHL asked army groups for the names of general staff officers who had not yet been on a course.[50] And despite his criticisms, even Kneußl applauded the outstanding achievement of producing good doctrine to guide the employment of the impressive forces assembled against the Entente spring offensive. The army would go into the coming battle with completely different material and intellectual equipment than at the start of the battle of the Somme under 'Falkenhayn and Co. with their absolute anarchy'.[51]

The field formations of the army would require extensive training at unit level and above if they were to adopt the new tactics successfully. Divisions coming from the Eastern Front were in particular need of this because of the more advanced combat techniques in the west: in April 1917, 11th Bavarian Infantry Division's field artillery regiment practised firing with air observation for the first time.[52] OHL and army groups attempted to ensure that divisions all got at least three weeks' training. However, many factors disrupted the programme including the continuation of the battle of the Somme into late November 1916, the defeat at Verdun in December, the severity of the winter, the withdrawal to the Hindenburg Line and frequent calls for labour on defences.

'Weltkrieg' assessed that a considerable number of divisions on the Western Front and a few of those arriving from the east did receive three weeks rest and training.[53] This generalisation concealed a wide variety of experience. 3rd Bavarian Infantry Division and others which had acted as demonstration units for the command courses were in a good

---

[49] Peter E. Hodgkinson and William F. Westerman, "Fit to Command a Battalion": The Senior Officers' School 1916–18', *Journal of the Society for Army Historical Research*, vol. 93, no. 374 (summer 2015), 120–38.
[50] Moser, *Feldzugsaufzeichnungen*, 273 and 275; HKR to OHL, IIa No. 22131, 15 July 1917, KAM, HKR alte Nr. 98.
[51] Stachelbeck, *Militärische Effektivität*, 182.   [52] Ibid., 193.
[53] Reichsarchiv, *Weltkrieg*, 12:55–6.

state of training. But a battalion commander in 21st Infantry Division complained in early April about

> the complete lack of training opportunities for our men. They are not *soldiers* any more, they are just *earth workers*. For months now my regiment has had no decent opportunity for training. What use are grenade throwers, mortars or light machine guns if I cannot train my men on them at all. There are men who cannot apply and release the safety catch of their rifle. Even if one is the resting battalion for six days, one has to work on local defences and *at night* develop the rearward lines.

This officer had previously served in IIIb and was writing to Walter Nicolai, who passed the letter to the head of the Operations Department – a good example of informal learning and networking. At the time he wrote, the division was assessed as needing two to three weeks training and it is probably no coincidence that it suffered very heavy casualties, particularly men captured, when the French assault opened shortly after.[54]

Inadequate training of the field artillery was a particular concern. OHL believed the problem arose from the arm's rapid expansion coupled with the decreasing number of active officers with regiments. It called for more even distribution of experienced officers, especially to new units.[55] During 1917, at least seven training manuals for both branches of the artillery were issued.[56] This theoretical doctrine was backed up by an array of training establishments: at the peak, there were eight field and five heavy artillery schools on the Western Front. To ensure that the whole system provided unified training, in spring 1917 a General Inspection of Schools of Gunnery was set up, with an Inspection of Foot Artillery Schools of Gunnery subordinate to it.[57]

Test of Battle: The Glass Half Full

After the spring fighting, there was much praise for the contribution of 'Defensive Battle' to victory, because it had guaranteed a uniform approach without restricting commanders' freedom of action.[58] But this

---

[54] Epkenhans, *Nicolai*, 366–7 (emphasis in the original); AOK 7 weekly reports to HDK, 'Kampfwert der Divisionen', 7 and 14 April 1917, GLAK, F1/335 and 336. See next chapter for 21st Infantry Division's casualties.

[55] OHL to Chef des Militär-Kabinetts, Ic Nr. 44611 op., 15 January 1917, BArch, PH1/10, f. 96.

[56] See Ludendorff, *Urkunden der Obersten Heeresleitung*, 592–3 for a list, and Raths, *Vom Massensturm zur Stoßtrupptaktik*, 176–84 for details.

[57] 'Organisation und Gang der Ausbildung der Offiziere und Mannschaften des deutschen Heeres während des Krieges von 1914 bis 1918', unpublished Reichsarchiv research paper, BArch, RH61/1011, Anlage 8; General der Artillerie a.D. Bansi, 'Ersatz', in Kaiser, *Ehrenbuch der Deutschen Schweren Artillerie*, 101.

[58] HDK, 'Zusammenstellung einiger Lehren aus der Doppelschlacht Aisne-Champagne', 1.

was not the whole picture, as illustrated by an after-action report from 17th Infantry Division in Gruppe Vimy.[59] Early on 23 April, the division lost the village of Gavrelle. On 23 and 24 April, the *Gruppe* ordered three counter-attacks, all of which failed. In its report, the division accused the *Gruppe* of contravening the principles of 'Defensive Battle': the *Gruppe* had not released reserves early enough to the division so that it could command the battle properly, and had then mishandled and micro-managed them. In this account, the *Gruppe* had also erred in mounting a premature counter-attack on 24 April rather than a better-prepared one later.

Although generally 17th Infantry Division thought it had received good artillery support, infantry–artillery co-operation had been faulty. In the first two counter-attacks, artillery preparation of the objective was insufficient. The third time, the preparation was good and the assault troops entered the village. However, they were then shelled out again by unsuppressed British artillery. The division had carried out systematic counter-battery work, but its effectiveness had been reduced by bad weather and inadequate communications as well as lack of gas and other appropriate ammunition. On the plus side, German aviation had performed excellently. Despite numerical inferiority it had absolute control of the air, enabling it to limit British air observation and artillery effectiveness. It had also supported assaulting infantry well by strafing British positions and by informing the divisional headquarters quickly about progress.

Reflecting this praise of German aviation, April 1917 is known in British historiography as 'Bloody April', when the Royal Flying Corps suffered its heaviest casualties of the war.[60] The French air force too faced difficult problems, with many obsolescent aircraft and concerns about pilot quality. In addition, as Chapter 5 described, the French initially held back most of their fighter squadrons to prevent their concentration giving away the area of attack; this interrupted air observation, seriously affected artillery fire and aided German reconnaissance. Not surprisingly, many German divisions were positive about the support they received from their air force. Perhaps the most enthusiastic was 1st Guard Infantry Division, facing the French, which thought that German aviation deserved special recognition: it was the

---

[59] 17.ID, 'Erfahrungen der 17. Infanterie-Division aus den Kämpfen bei Arras vom 11.–25.4.1917', Ia Nr. 1565 Geheim, 28 April 1917, KAM, AOK 6 Bd. 419, ff. 82–7. As Chapter 6 recounted, Gruppe Vimy vigorously disputed parts of this report when forwarding it to Sixth Army.

[60] Jones, *War in the Air*, 3:370.

reason why even under the heaviest fire units never fell into such a desperate state of morale as during the Somme.[61]

All this needs to be seen in perspective. British numerical superiority and aggressive tactics meant that the Germans were able to impede but not stop their air reconnaissance and observation. Army Group Rupprecht subsequently commented on the excellent support British aviation had given its artillery.[62] In Champagne, one of 58th Infantry Division's regiments recorded many French aircraft directing fire on almost every day up to the assault and after; on one particular day, so few German aircraft were present that the infantry seemed to be offered up as victims.[63] A post-war *Reichsarchiv* paper suggests the uneven nature of performance against both the British and French. German fighters had effectively prevented the enemy's air reconnaissance and facilitated their own. As OHL had stressed during the battle, the work of the artillery and infantry liaison aircraft was of extraordinary importance: air battle was not an end in its own right but a means of enabling this work. Air reconnaissance had generally been successful in identifying enemy artillery, but counter-battery work using air observation had produced limited results. Infantry co-operation, including ground attack and calling for defensive fire, had been very successful.[64]

German air superiority was therefore never absolute over either the British or French. A major factor in German success in April was the technical edge enjoyed by their fighters. Conditions changed against them in May, when the British and French introduced fighters that outperformed the Germans. By concentrating greater numbers, the French regained air superiority; this enabled them to prevent German reconnaissance and artillery observation, and to carry out their own effective counter-battery work. Senior German commanders urgently requested fighters to replace heavy losses, but OHL was initially unable to provide them owing to strikes and production bottlenecks in Germany. Sixth Army estimated that by 6 May it had only 55 per cent of its aircraft establishment. Later in the month, fighter supply gradually improved. Otto von Below commented this was not before time: loss of air

---

[61] Kriegswissenschaftliche Abteilung der Luftwaffe comments on draft *Weltkrieg*, vol. 12 chapters, n.d., BArch, RH61/1901, 2.

[62] OHL to Western Front army groups and AOKs, II. Nr. 54446 geh.op., 6 May 1917, GLAK, F1/523. On the British air effort at Arras, see Mike Bechthold, 'Bloody April Revisited: The Royal Flying Corps at the Battle of Arras, 1917', *British Journal for Military History*, vol. 4, no. 2 (February 2018), 50–69.

[63] Reinhardt, *Infanterie-Regiment Nr. 107*, 334–51.

[64] 'Die Tätigkeit der Fliegerverbände der 6. Armee in der Zeit vom 14.–22. April', unpublished Reichsarchiv research paper, BArch, RH61/737, 1, quoting an OHL circular of 22 April 1917.

superiority had led to the German artillery suffering heavy casualties in men and matériel.[65]

The German official history stated that the artillery had made a decisive contribution to defeating both British and French attacks.[66] This is doubtful. Based on prisoner statements, OHL assessed that German artillery fire against French infantry was not always in proportion to the huge deployment of guns and ammunition. In a sign that the army had not fully absorbed the new doctrine, OHL re-stressed that offensive fire was preferable to defensive barrages.[67] One post-war German account even describes artillery as an important gap in 'Defensive Battle' because of the limited damage they did to the French attackers.[68] This goes too far, but British and French accounts also downplay the German artillery's role. The British commented that the German artillery were more effective in the later phases of the battle of Arras, but they were generally more struck by German infantry skills in infiltration and small-scale counter-attacks. The French too noted the violence of German counter-attacks, but believed the main reason for the failure of the offensive was the inadequacy of their own artillery preparation. In particular, it had not suppressed the German machine guns, which had paralysed the attack.[69]

Lower down the chain the results of artillery support varied, not surprisingly given the different sectors and enemies involved. An infantry regiment in 19th Reserve Division on the Chemin des Dames stated that co-operation with the artillery during the initial phase of the French assault was better than ever before, helped by co-location of infantry and artillery command posts.[70] The next month however, 33rd Reserve Division in the neighbouring *Gruppe* reported that its artillery allocation was too weak for the width of sector and the enemy infantry easily penetrated the thin barrage; it was the division's machine guns which stopped the attack.[71] At Arras, the artillery had initially given poor support to the infantry, but many divisions reported favourably on their subsequent performance. 3rd Bavarian Infantry Division thought that the German artillery were definitely superior to the British in the more mobile warfare which emerged after the initial phase of the battle.[72]

[65] Reichsarchiv, *Weltkrieg*, 12:379; Otto von Below diary, 6 and 18 May 1917.
[66] Reichsarchiv, *Weltkrieg*, 12:274 and 406.   [67] 'Sonderheft', 23.
[68] Fortmüller, 'Heeresgruppe Deutscher Kronprinz', 196.
[69] BOH 1917, 1:555; AFGG, V/2, 73–5; Rolland, *Nivelle*, 222.
[70] RIR.92, 'Meldung über Erfahrungen betr. die gegenwärtige Schlacht an der Aisne', T.-B. Nr. I/383 geh., 22 April 1917, GLAK, F1/523.
[71] 33.RD after-action report to Gruppe Vailly, no reference, c. 22 May 1917, GLAK, F1/523.
[72] 3.BID, 'Erfahrungen', 38–40.

The German artillery's primary task had been counter-battery fire. Despite the problems of the British and French artillery, German accounts record the heavy fire falling on their own positions: this demonstrates that German counter-battery work was not effective, a point made explicitly in 17th Infantry Division's report. Reasons included the limited success of aircraft in directing fire, and continued attempts to physically destroy rather than neutralise enemy batteries. As the Germans themselves knew, this was extraordinarily difficult to achieve given the small size of the target. One German battery received 2,000–3,000 shells on some days but was well protected and suffered little loss.[73]

Poor standards of technical artillery work also affected accuracy. In early 1917, much of the German artillery was only beginning to allow for the 'error of the day' (the effect of weather, barrel wear and other factors on the trajectory of a shell). The difference between where a shell was aimed and where it actually landed could vary from nothing to over 1,500 metres.[74] Lack of accuracy as well as confused battle conditions also caused 'friendly fire' incidents, to use a modern term. German infantry accounts of this period complained about it frequently, sometimes with black humour. A regiment at Arras referred to a well-known speech by the Kaiser in 1914:

> 'The artillery are following the Kaiser's word too closely!'
> 'What do you mean?'
> 'I recognise no parties, only Germans.'[75]

But it was a serious issue: 2nd Foot Guard Regiment on the Aisne was not alone in reporting that frequent short shooting by the artillery was bad for morale.[76]

Deep battle developed further during the spring offensive. German bombing in April had concentrated on the French zone, with attacks on railway facilities, battery positions, localities and camps. From the beginning of May, night bombers also systematically attacked major camps and bivouacs in the Arras area.[77] At the same time, the strategic bombing of Britain affected operations in France by causing the withdrawal of two of the Royal Flying Corps' best squadrons. This led to more aggressive

[73] Generalmajor a.D. Mummenhoff, 'Doppelschlacht Aisne-Champagne', in Kaiser, *Ehrenbuch der Deutschen Schweren Artillerie*, 435–6.
[74] OHL circular, II Nr. 60336 op., 20 July 1917, KAM, XV.BRK 184.
[75] Hans von Felgenhauer and Wilhelm Müller-Loebnitz, eds., *Das Ehrenbuch der Rheinländer: Die Rheinländer im Weltkrieg* (Stuttgart: Oskar Hinderer, n.d.), 309–10.
[76] Generalmajor a.D. Gottfried von Brauchitsch, *Das 2. Garde-Regiment zu Fuß* (Oldenburg: Gerhard Stalling, 1922), 75.
[77] Reichsarchiv, *Weltkrieg*, 12:532; 'Verwendung der Fliegerverbände der 6. Armee', unpublished Reichsarchiv research paper, BArch, RH61/737, 7.

German air activity in the period between the battle of Messines and the opening of the Flanders offensive in late July.[78] Entente bombing was having an effect too. Over a three day period in early May the British tried to bomb Sixth Army headquarters but missed, and the French set fire to First Army's main railway station, destroying large quantities of rations and artillery ammunition.[79] Bombing and long-range shelling of Laon badly hit the forward vehicle workshop there, responsible for maintaining much of Seventh Army's motor transport; it was forced to move.[80]

The increasing depth of the battlefield greatly complicated positioning headquarters and reserves. As noted in Chapter 6, sharp orders were issued to prevent the tendency of headquarters at all levels to edge backwards out of the heaviest fire. Location of reserves was even more difficult. If held too far forward, they would suffer severe casualties from enemy fire; if too far back, they might not arrive soon enough to intervene effectively. As 'Defensive Battle' pointed out, timely release of the reserves was key to success. But this was not easy to achieve. Many calls for help from the front were unjustified or premature; deploying reserves in response wasted their combat value and led commanders to man the forward lines too thickly.[81] A further problem in the Sixth Army sector was that the deepening battlefield reduced the locations where troops could be quartered in an area which was anyway poor in villages and cover.[82] The Army was heavily criticised for not having brought reserves forward in good time before the 9 April attack. It had made a judgement call of all the factors involved, including not interrupting training prematurely. Its decision was probably wrong, but it was not stupid.

Like the artillery and aviation, German infantry performance during the battle was mixed. The specially formed storm battalions were the foremost exponents of German tactical expertise at this period but were a small part of the whole infantry. There was a concern that excessive focus on special assault detachments gave the impression that only they made attacks, while other troops merely occupied the ground they captured.[83] Some German tactics during the spring fighting were up to storm troop standards, others were not. The British admired 1st Guard Reserve Division's use of infiltration. But a counter-attack against the French by another Guards formation was a flagrant example of tactical

[78] Jones, *War in the Air*, 4:134–5.
[79] Otto von Below diary, 2 and 4 May; Gruppe Reims war diary, 1–3 May 1917, HSAS, Soden Nachlass, M660/038 Bü 33.
[80] Kommandeur der Kraftfahr-Truppen to AOK 7, [part of ref missing] 14336/IIa, 17 April 1917, GLAK, F1/251.
[81] 'Abwehrschlacht', March 1917, 16.   [82] Xylander diary, 8 April 1917.
[83] 11.BID, 'Erfahrungen an der Aisne-Front', Nr. 1451/Ia, 18 June 1917, GLAK, F1/523.

backwardness: 'It was a magnificent sight. The company commanders were on horseback in front of their companies, and the Guard Ersatz Brigade advanced as if on the exercise ground, with drums beating and bugles blowing.' This account may seem incredible: but it was written by a neighbouring battalion commander, one of whose companies took part. Amazingly, the counter-attack succeeded.[84]

A further reason for mixed German infantry performance was the different degrees of resistance encountered. 3rd Bavarian Infantry Division found that the combat value of the British infantry in the four divisions it faced was very limited and that there was a striking willingness to surrender even by troops from formations known to the Germans as particularly good. In contrast, 3rd Guard Infantry Division reported that the British advanced with more determination than on the Somme; they displayed great toughness and skill in hand grenade fighting, and exemplary use of their numerous light machine guns.[85]

Three general and linked issues affected infantry performance – firepower, manpower and counter-attacks. Chapter 3 showed that increased firepower did not compensate for decreased manpower, as called for in the new defensive doctrine; the consequence was a constant need to reinforce the front divisions piecemeal by drawing on the counter-attack divisions to the rear. The German army believed that immediate counter-attacks by even the smallest groups could have disproportionate success, and the British official history stressed the important role they played in the outcome of the battle.[86] But there were problems. First, the troops counter-attacking suffered serious casualties, and the loss of officers was of particular concern.[87] Second, the immediacy of the counter-attack, meaning before the enemy had consolidated, was crucial. Since late 1915, regulations had repeatedly stressed that if an immediate counter-attack was impossible, time must be left to mount a full-scale, carefully prepared operation: attacks which fell between these two stools almost always failed. This was linked to

[84] BOH 1917, 1:555; Otto Schwalm and Oberstleutnant a.D. Ahlers, eds., *Das königlich preußische Infanterie-Regiment Landgraf Friedrich I. von Hessen-Kassel (I. Kurhessisches) Nr. 81 im Weltkriege 1914–1918* (Frankfurt: Blazek & Bergmann, 1932), 240. 6th Infantry Division's attack on 19 April was also accompanied by drums and bugles: Hauptmann a.D. Cordt von Brandis, *Die vom Douaumont: Das Ruppiner Regiment 24 im Weltkrieg* (Berlin: Wilhelm Kolk, 1930), 317.

[85] 3.BID, 'Erfahrungen', 30–1; 3.GID, 'Erfahrungen der 3. Garde-Inf.Division aus den Kämpfen bei Bullecourt (4.5–18.5.17)', [no reference and n.d.], KAM, AOK 6 Bd. 419, f. 55.

[86] BOH 1917, 1:555.

[87] 18.ID, 'Erfahrungen aus dem Einsatz der 18. Inf.-Division bei Arras', Ia Nr. 3391, 27 April 1917, KAM, AOK 6 Bd. 419, ff. 92–3; Otto von Below diary, 23 May 1917.

a frequent mistake in the spring fighting noted earlier, not allowing enough time for orders to reach all units involved.[88]

Senior commanders feared that one of the tactics advocated in 'Defensive Battle', the large-scale counter-attack from the rear, would come into just this intermediate category.[89] Experience in the spring battles produced mixed results, with some counter-attacks from the rear succeeding at least partially. But there were numerous repetitions of falling between two stools, like the operations at Gavrelle criticised by 17th Infantry Division. The worst case was a counter-attack in Champagne by three divisions on 19 April. A battalion commander who took part recorded that his men had to advance against an unshaken enemy, in daylight, without artillery preparation. He believed that this blunder, with its 'completely useless and heavy sacrifice', stemmed from the controlling *Gruppe's* failure to recognise the difference between immediate and prepared counter-attacks. More judiciously, Ludendorff agreed that the divisions had been committed too hastily, causing the attack to fail.[90] Shortly after, the corps headquarters running the *Gruppe* was replaced.

Learning from the Entente Spring Offensive and Persisting Problems

> I have learned from my mistakes, and I am sure I can repeat them exactly.[91]

The German army learned from the spring battles as soon as they began. It circulated lessons from Arras on 9 April within three days, and formations about to face the French on the Aisne had started to apply them before the day of the assault. Both army groups involved controlled the subsequent after-action report process by issuing detailed questionnaires. These naturally reflected their different experiences. Army Group Rupprecht's questions included the consequences of Sixth Army's inadequate positions, location of the reserves, the effect of both British and German artillery fire, countering tanks and any significant changes in

---

[88] OHL circular 'Erfahrungen aus den letzten Kämpfen', Nr. 17411 Op., October 1915, BArch, PH3/1901, Section b.4.

[89] Gallwitz, *Erleben im Westen*, 168.

[90] Major a.D. Isenburg, *Das Königs-Infanterie-Regiment (6. Lothring.) Nr. 145 im Großen Kriege 1914–1918*, vol. 1, *Von der Mobilmachung bis zum Abtransport zur Cambraischlacht (21. November 1917)* (Berlin: Klasing, 1922), 299 and 306; Ludendorff, *My War Memories*, 425.

[91] The late comedian Peter Cook, quoted by Charles Nevin, 'Outstanding Mistakes of All Time', BBC blogpost, 14 June 2013, www.bbc.co.uk/news/blogs-magazine-monitor-22 902556 (accessed 15 January 2022).

British methods.[92] Army Group Crown Prince wanted to know about the effect of offensively handling artillery and infantry before the battle, the combat value of the troops, the principle of fighting around the first position and the most effective ways of doing so, reserves and different forms of counter-attack, various types of outpost position and fixed defences.[93]

Despite the overlap in these questions, the different concerns of the army groups are clear; not surprisingly, the answers varied considerably too. 45th Reserve Division stressed that the lessons it drew from its experience on the Aisne were influenced by the unusual topography there. The vital Chemin des Dames ridge position required a firm defence, since if it was lost counter-attacks to retake it would be impossible. All necessary forces and matériel had to be close to the front, leading to thick manning of the forward zone and no real defence in depth. Other situations would require other tactics. Faced with completely different circumstances at Arras – more rolling terrain and few fixed defences – 3rd Bavarian Infantry Division had conducted a mobile defence from improvised shell-hole positions which was later used as a model example of implementing 'Defensive Battle'. But this division too stressed the impossibility of generalising from its experience.[94]

Strongly held views for and against prepared defensive positions divided opinion both within and between the two army groups. In Army Group Rupprecht, 50th Reserve Division believed that though improvised shell-hole positions were adequate in the short term, during a long battle lack of shelter led to high casualties and damaged discipline and morale.[95] In Army Group Crown Prince, 113th Infantry Division preferred shell-hole to prepared defences, as it had since its experience on the Somme.[96] But First Army – which had issued a famous order on the Somme that the enemy were to advance only over the corpses of the defenders – rejected the view that forward units were most secure in craters as 'feeble passivity'. Shell-hole positions no doubt gave good protection against shell fire, but they lacked defensive strength because they eliminated the personal influence of the commander on his men; they must all be connected up by continuous trenches.[97]

---

[92] HKR to its AOKs, Ic No. 2881 geh., 25 April 1917, KAM, AOK 6 Bd. 419.

[93] HDK to its AOKs, 'Gefechtserfahrungen', Ia/Ic No. 2671, 13 May 1917, GLAK, F1/523.

[94] 45.RD, Tagebuch No. 3590 geh., 26 July 1917, HSAS, Schall Nachlass, M660/037 Bü 85; 3.BID, 'Erfahrungen', 1.

[95] 50.RD to Gruppe Vimy, I Nr. 1712/17, 3 June 1917, KAM, AOK 6 Bd. 419.

[96] 113.ID to HDK, Ia No. 1 geh., 17 May 1917, GLAK, F1/523. Somme: Foley, 'Learning War's Lessons', 487.

[97] AOK 1 to its Gruppen, Ia Nr. 407 geheim, 22 May 1917, HSAS, Glück Nachlass, M660/091 Bü 16.

These differing views were reflected at army group level. At Arras, 3rd Bavarian Infantry Division's regiments had persuaded the divisional commander, Karl von Wenninger, to adopt a more mobile form of defence – a good example of bottom-up learning – and the division's excellent defensive performance persuaded Army Group Rupprecht. The army group first arranged for Wenninger to lecture on mobile defence, accompanied by a demonstration on the ground. It then submitted a report based on the division's experiences, which recommended further development of tactics. Given the new power of the enemy artillery, the battle should be fought in a still more mobile fashion, over a greater depth, than even 'Defensive Battle' called for; more use should be made of shell-hole positions and less of properly constructed defences.[98] Army Group Crown Prince commented on these proposals that the methods adopted at Arras made sense in the circumstances there but were not valid everywhere. If it had used the same tactics, it would have had to abandon its main positions. The defensive battle must be for the forward position, not least because formations must know what ground they had to hold.[99]

The potential chaos of these varying opinions demonstrates the problem with Foley's argument that after-action reports rather than formal doctrine drove tactical innovation. Both were needed, and OHL took steps to bring them into line. In June it banned lateral circulation of reports except in special circumstances. It would process and issue reports as appropriate, thus avoiding swamping formations with theoretical material or having to adapt to new tactical orders, some contradicting regulations, each time they changed sector.[100] Continuing the more restrictive line, OHL insisted that every manual in the 'Regulations for Trench Warfare for All Arms' series was absolutely binding. It justified this radical departure from the traditionally flexible conception of doctrine on the basis that it was required to secure 'the urgently needed uniformity in the army'.[101] It backed up interim instructions with a special supplement [Sonderheft] to 'Defensive Battle', followed by full-scale new editions of the manual on field fortifications in August and 'Defensive Battle' in September. Overall, OHL stressed the need for a mobile defence, combining thin manning of the front with aggressive use of reserves held close up. The forward lines should be treated as

---

[98] OHL to Western Front army groups and AOKs, II. Nr. 54446 geh. op., 6 May 1917, GLAK, F1/523, forwarding Army Group Rupprecht's report.
[99] CGS HDK to OHL, Ia/Ib Nr. 2605, 8 May 1917, GLAK, F1/523.
[100] OHL circular, II Nr. 57804 op., 16 June 1917, HSAS, Soden Nachlass, M660/038 Bü 17.
[101] 'Sonderheft', 27.

advanced positions which could be given up if necessary. However, well-developed defences were still needed to shelter reserves and delay the enemy.[102]

Between June and December 1917, OHL issued eleven new manuals in the 'Regulations for Trench Warfare for All Arms' series (Table 7.3). Half of these were second or third editions, testifying to the maturity of the doctrine writing process. The doubling of the section on the air force in 'Defensive Battle' and three of the new manuals – on ground attack aircraft, fighter squadrons and superheavy artillery – illustrate the emphasis placed on aviation and deep battle, though a notable absence here was a manual for bombing. The continually growing importance of communications, described in Chapter 6, is reflected by the inclusion of two manuals on the subject.

Martin Samuels has suggested that the German defensive doctrine that had emerged at the end of this process was 'a masterpiece of flexibility, perfectly suited to the system of attack used against it'.[103] Many senior German commanders in 1917 would have disagreed. As they saw it, the German army had become the anvil rather than the hammer. The hopes originally placed in 'Defensive Battle' had only been fulfilled to a limited extent, and the new violence of enemy methods had defeated carefully thought-out tactics.[104] The German army's mixed performance on the Western Front after the Entente spring offensive bears this out. It won a strategic victory in defeating the British offensive at Ypres, and the initial failure at Cambrai was more than compensated for by the quickly

Table 7.3 *Doctrinal manuals issued under Hindenburg/Ludendorff, June–December 1917*

Special Supplement to the Regulations on Trench Warfare
Signals
Mortars (2nd ed.)
General Principles of Field Fortifications (3rd ed.) and a related manual
Principles for the Conduct of the Defensive Battle in Trench Warfare (3rd ed.)
Infantry Liaison Aircraft and Balloons (3rd ed.)
Ground Attack Aircraft
Fighter Squadrons
Superheavy Artillery
Communications Equipment (3rd ed.)

---

[102] Ibid., 3–4.   [103] Samuels, *Command or Control?*, 196.
[104] Fortmüller, 'Die Heeresgruppe Deutscher Kronprinz', 224.

mounted counter-attack. But it also suffered six serious local defeats.[105] Their cause was partly skilful Entente adaptation to German tactics – the dynamic equilibrium at work – and partly the persistence of certain weaknesses in central aspects of mobile defence, including problems over withdrawal, counter-attacks and combined arms battle.

'Defensive Battle' authorised withdrawal rather than make costly and ultimately futile attempts to hold unfavourable positions. But as we saw in Chapter 2, failure to make pre-emptive withdrawals was a major factor in three of the six defeats (Messines, Verdun and Malmaison). In each case, withdrawal had been considered but rejected for a mixture of practical, emotional and propaganda reasons that linked strategic, operational and tactical issues. The weaknesses of mission command contributed to these three defeats: the two army groups involved had advocated withdrawal but let themselves be overruled by local objections.

A linked problem was whether to hold the forward zone which was now part of doctrine. 'Defensive Battle' stated that positions could be evacuated temporarily provided they were retaken by the end of the battle. It was for local commanders to decide how long to defend the forward zone, and this was recognised to be a difficult decision.[106] Kneußl believed that given the circumstances of 11th Bavarian Infantry Division's defence on the Chemin des Dames, any move to the rear with the intention of subsequently retaking the position was too dangerous. Right to the end of the war, some senior officers questioned the whole idea of flexible defence, which was nicknamed the 'withdrawal bacillus' [*Ausweich-Bazillus*]. For them, the ordinary soldier's only thought should be to hold his position to the death. Gerhard Tappen, a divisional commander at Third Ypres, was a particularly vigorous opponent of what he sarcastically called the 'victorious retreats' of 1917–18. There was also a view, shared by Rupprecht, that a higher provision of infantry on active battle fronts would prevent enemy successes, avoiding the need for costly counter-attacks.[107]

After the August defeat at Verdun, OHL's Hermann Geyer stated bluntly that though immediate counter-attacks by small groups could still produce good results, larger-scale counter-attacks from the rear had failed. This was partly because they were 'a new and apparently attractive

[105] Messines (June), Verdun (August), Menin Road (September), Polygon Wood (September), Broodseinde (October) and Malmaison (October).
[106] '*Abwehrschlacht*', September 1917, 6c and 39.
[107] 11.BID, 'Erfahrungen', 6; Geyer, 'Einige Gedanken über Verteidigung', 1; Oberstleutnant a.D. Hans Jäger, *Das K.B. 19. Infanterie-Regiment König Viktor Emanuel III. von Italien* (Munich: Max Schick, 1930), 307; Tappen, 'Kriegserinnerungen', f. 34; Rupprecht, *Kriegstagebuch*, 2:79–80 (10 January 1917); 18.ID, 'Erfahrungen', f. 92.

form of the previously frowned-upon overhasty counter-attack'. In addition, deep enemy standing barrages caused serious delay, confusion and casualties. One alternative, moving the counter-attack divisions forward whenever a threat developed, exhausted the men and led to casualties. Another, manning the main battle zone more thickly, caused even heavier casualties. Geyer therefore proposed greater willingness to cede ground, and later wrote that First Army's general insistence on rigid defence had seriously impeded conduct of the war.[108] But suggesting ceding ground risked arousing the criticism aimed at Kuhl the Self-Preserver for lack of offensive spirit. It certainly led to the objections to withdrawal mentioned earlier, even though such reluctance increased casualties and the ground was lost anyway. These irresolvable problems worsened at Ypres in the autumn.

Geyer pointed out in April and again in autumn that after-action reports and briefings made little reference to artillery, inferring that German command teams still thought too much in infantry terms and too little in artillery.[109] Ludendorff commented that artillery was far less effective than it should be given the vast amounts of ammunition expended and the excellent modern guns now available. Causes included continuing failure to implement modern artillery techniques fully, in turn caused by inadequate training of senior gunner commanders. In addition, Germany was still undoubtedly behind the enemy in air observation for artillery.[110] All this echoes Hindenburg's comments about the German army pre-war and implies that despite three years' experience and the updating of doctrine, understanding of combined arms battle was still not ingrained in the army.

One reason for poor infantry–artillery co-operation was inter-arm rivalry. This form of departmentalism was a problem before the war, and vituperative remarks about the artillery by Kneußl, an infantryman, suggest that it remained strong in 1917. He commented, perhaps in a moment of frustration, that despite all the attention lavished on the artillery, they were ineffective and even cowardly.[111] But a further reason for inadequate infantry–artillery co-operation was probably the continued

---

[108] Geyer memorandum, 'Vortragsnotizen zu den Verdun-Berichten (20.8. Toter Mann – 304)', n.d. (hereafter, 'Vortragsnotizen'); draft OHL letter to Western Front general staff officers, 16 November 1917; both from BArch, Geyer Nachlass, RH61/924, ff. 62–4 and 101; Matthias Strohn, *The German Army and the Defence of the Reich: Military Doctrine and the Conduct of the Defensive Battle, 1918–1939* (Cambridge: Cambridge University Press, 2011), 55.

[109] Geyer memorandum, 'Zur Reise 13.4.', n.d., and 'Vortragsnotizen', BArch, Geyer Nachlass, RH61/924, ff. 47 and 62.

[110] OHL circular, II Nr. 66830 op., 8 October 1917, KAM, ID (WK) 4388.

[111] Brose, *Kaiser's Army*, 5–6, 198–9 and 224; Kneußl diary, 10 May 1917.

predominance of infantry officers in crucial positions and of all-infantry command teams described in Chapter 2. As noted there, OHL's increasingly rigorous instructions on training general staff candidates focused on acquiring knowledge of the infantry and artillery. Given OHL's views that the general staff officer was central to handling combined arms battle, this was a clear admission that more needed to be done to improve understanding of such a fundamental tactical issue.

Conclusions

> In war everything *used to be* simple.[112]

The lead-in to this chapter argued that an army at war learns for a purpose, to improve performance in the battle that it actually faces, so performance must be the measure of effective learning; in the context of 1917, the focus is on combined arms as the key to tactical success. A summary of the chapter's findings will help answer the question of how learning – the fourth command task – affected performance against the Entente spring offensive.

Pre-war and 1914–16 doctrine stressed the importance of all-arms co-operation, but in both peace and war, implementation was uneven at best. By the Somme, the German army had fallen behind the French and British in co-ordinating infantry, artillery and aviation. The Third OHL took vigorous steps to correct this problem, by codifying best practice in new doctrine on combined arms battle and by a major training programme for staffs and formations. Progress was mixed, especially on training, but much was accomplished in a relatively short space of time before the Entente offensive. After-action reports commented positively on the new doctrine, and German combined arms co-operation had certainly improved enough to defeat the offensive: 3rd Bavarian Infantry Division's model defensive action exemplified the standards well-trained formations had reached. Doctrine and training were subsequently adapted further to take spring 1917 experience into account. However, important aspects of tactics remained problematic throughout this period, including withdrawals, handling of reserves and counter-attacks, and reliable infantry–artillery co-operation.

This summary shows that learning did improve German performance on the battlefield but many weaknesses remained. Illustrating the

---

[112] Kneußl note from November 1917, quoted in Stachelbeck, *Militärische Effektivität*, 218 (emphasis in the original). He was presumably referring to Clausewitz's well-known comment that 'Everything in war is very simple, but the simplest thing is difficult': *On War*, book 1, chapter 7, 119.

improvement, the British official history commented that the new defensive methods were an important factor in the results of battle in 1917 and even that they prevented the collapse of the German army.[113] Part of the reason why learning did not improve performance more is the effect of external factors cited by Fox such as terrain, weather and the enemy. In addition, learning was particularly difficult in 1917 given the sheer complexity of battle. Tactically, ensuring effective all-arms co-operation was no easy task and the operational level added problems such as deep battle, logistics and intelligence. Command teams were faced with cutting-edge technical questions, especially relating to artillery and aviation. Introducing even a simple weapons system such as the light machine gun was challenging. Moreover, learning did not take place in a vacuum. Not only were the enemy on an equal cultural and technical level, but they had numerical and material superiority. They innovated at least as fast as the German army; in fact faster, according to OHL in 1916. The resulting dynamic equilibrium faced all armies with the need for constant learning at a faster rate than in peacetime.

In this context, how the German army learned affected the conversion of what it learned into performance. Foley is right that it made more extensive use than the British of formal processes, particularly after-action reports recording what had and had not worked in battle. However, there is also good evidence for Fox's networked approach to learning, connecting formal and informal, individual and organisational and bottom-up as well as top-down approaches. In particular, individuals played an important role, as the contributions by officers such as Kuhl, Moser and Höhn illustrate. Informal and semi-formal transmission of knowledge was commonplace, examples noted earlier including the battalion commander writing to Nicolai, higher-level headquarters inviting officers to discuss lessons learned and Urach corresponding with his friend the Württemberg Minister of War. Training courses deliberately encouraged exchanges of experience and opinions between students and with directing staff. Even formal aspects of the system, including doctrine, ultimately depended on individuals such as the teams of experienced officers contributing to drafting 'Defensive Battle'. The building block of the formal system was the after-action report. Its content was decided by the command teams who wrote the reports, with commanders having the final say – further proof of their continuing importance.[114]

The German army also adopted Fox's 'external' approach to learning, particularly from enemies and civilians. The whole purpose of intelligence was of course to learn about the enemy, both to help counter their

---

[113] BOH 1917, 1:553–4.   [114] Stachelbeck, *Militärische Effektivität*, 353.

methods and where appropriate to learn from them – thus following Clausewitz's dictum quoted at the start of the chapter. The German army has usually received a bad press for learning from civilians, and as we saw key functions such as the general staff remained a closed shop. But we also saw greater flexibility elsewhere, especially the hundreds of civilians in intelligence. This was mirrored in organisations such as the governments of the occupied territories, the War Raw Materials Department [*Kriegsrohstoffabteilung*] and later the War Office [*Kriegsamt*], all of which were heavily staffed by civilian experts.[115] Scientists too were extensively involved in the war effort. As just one example, the renowned chemist Fritz Haber enthusiastically co-operated in developing gas warfare, briefed senior commanders such as Gallwitz and observed or took part in gas operations. Even he, with all his pre-war scientific achievements and status, found his military rank as a reserve *Hauptmann* important because it increased his standing with the army.[116]

Underlying how, and how effectively, the German army learned is the question of whether it embodied 'institutionalised innovation' as Foley and others have suggested. The spring 1917 battles produced evidence both for and against this proposition. Evidence for includes the army's by now well-established lessons learned–doctrine–training–performance–lessons learned cycle. The original custom of circulating after-action reports freely, including those that were disputed, speaks well of intellectual openness in the army. The downside, the potential for friction arising from radically differing views on best practice, could be ironed out in the doctrine creation and training phases. The generous provision of opportunities on courses for students and staff to exchange experiences and thinking also demonstrates intellectual openness. Evidence against institutionalised innovation includes OHL's decision to restrict free circulation of after-action reports and make doctrine more binding. This shifted the balance away from open-minded debate towards uniformity of approach, paralleling the shift in the first command task from decentralisation towards control. Ludendorff's micro-management and the pressures to conform noted in Chapter 6 strengthened this tendency.

[115] Holger H. Herwig, *The First World War: Germany and Austria-Hungary 1914–1918* (London: Arnold, 1997), 167; Watson, *Ring of Steel*, 378–9. BArch, PH30-I/124, a draft history of the Banking Department of the General Government of Belgium, exemplifies the use of civilian experts in the administration of occupied territories, many holding reserve military rank.

[116] L. F. Haber, *The Poisonous Cloud: Chemical Warfare in the First World War* (Oxford: Oxford University Press, 1986), 2, 27 and 355 fn. 64; Gallwitz, *Erleben im Westen*, 208. Generalmajor a.D. Ernst von Wrisberg, *Wehr und Waffen 1914–1918* (Leipzig: K. F. Koehler, 1922), 117 gives some statistics on employment of civilian experts in military organisations.

Experience in spring 1917 and later shows that 'Defensive Battle', though welcomed, was no magic weapon. Some of the reasons for this echo pre-war problems, suggesting that they were too deep-seated to be easily removed. These include the gap between doctrine and implementation; the preponderance of infantry officers in senior positions and command teams; and a resulting preponderance of infantry thinking at the expense of combined arms thinking. The repeated mistake of the premature counter-attack was the product of these long-term factors and illustrates Fox's point that an army's organisational culture and ethos deeply affect learning. It was a reversion to the pre-war 'mad rush to attack' and it happened even though doctrine and experience had warned against it since at least 1915. Armies could forget as well as learn.

The 1917 evidence for and against the German army as an example of institutionalised innovation exemplifies its dual nature outlined in the Introduction: thinking and non-thinking. The combination of performance improved through learning and persisting weaknesses also supports Christian Stachelbeck's thesis that the army clung to old methods, but would accept new ones if they seemed necessary and effective. This ambivalence, together with the constant dialectic between local initiative and centralised uniformity, explains the uneven fulfilment of the fourth command task.

8   Performance

Whatever you do, you lose a lot of men.[1]

The final command task, the end to which the first four were the means, was winning the battle. In early 1917, the German army divided this task into two, preventing an Entente breakthrough and managing attrition by inflicting maximum casualties on the enemy while preserving its own forces. The result of both sub-tasks depended on the relative performance of the opposing armies, an example of Clausewitz's continuous interaction of opposites. The German army did not have to be perfect or even good, it just had to be better than the enemy. This means that assessing its performance in early 1917 entails assessing its enemies' performance too. Performance depends on the fighting power of an army, or rather the relative fighting power of opposing armies. To quote Allan R. Millett and Williamson Murray, fighting power is 'the ability to destroy the enemy while limiting the damage that he can inflict in return'.[2]

Fighting power is nowadays seen as having three components: conceptual, moral and physical. The conceptual component is essentially the command function; the moral, all those things required to motivate men to fight; and the physical, the means to fight, including equipment.[3] The German army recognised these three components of fighting power but traditionally viewed the moral component as key and this remained true in war. First Army's Somme report stated that although matériel and numbers seemed to dominate, what was in fact decisive was the individual with strong willpower. It also commented that fighting power depended on the state of training. This point is reflected in the divisional report cited

---

[1] [Charles] Mangin, *Lettres de Guerre 1914–1918* (Paris: Librairie Fayard, 1950), 112.

[2] Allan R. Millett and Williamson Murray, eds., *Military Effectiveness*, vol. 1, *The First World War* (Boston, MA: Allen & Unwin, 1988), 2. For a general discussion of fighting power, see Sarkesian, *Combat Effectiveness*.

[3] Ministry of Defence, *British Defence Doctrine*, chapter 4. I am grateful for an exchange with Major General (retd) Mungo Melvin, which has helped clarify the differences between modern and early-twentieth-century German thinking on fighting power.

later in this chapter and was explicitly stated in the 'Defensive Battle' manual, illustrating the argument that good training was central to German powers of resistance in both world wars.[4] Experience in the spring 1917 fighting led to the introduction of reporting on the conceptual component, command, in the form of the assessments described in Chapter 2 on performance of the division, its commander and his *Ia*. Separate reports already covered the third component, the physical, including details of the numbers of machine guns, trench mortars and anti-tank guns available; senior officers discussed such questions during their regular visits to divisions.[5]

As in other areas, at this period the German army had not defined what it meant by fighting power. In fact it did not even use one term, but five. Sometimes it merely referred to the condition [*Zustand*] of the troops. The more frequent terms, however, were *Kampfwert* and *Gefechtswert*, both meaning fighting or combat value; and *Kampfkraft* and *Gefechtskraft*, both meaning fighting or combat power. It used each pair interchangeably, but the most common were *Kampfwert* and *Kampfkraft*. These two were also used interchangeably; if there was any difference, *Kampfwert* referred to the internal strength of a unit, and *Kampfkraft* to the external effect it produced on the enemy or, in a general sense, the overall capability of the army. Linguistically, *Kampfkraft* is closer to our modern term 'fighting power'. However, the Germans used *Kampfwert* more often, and this chapter therefore adopts the term 'combat value'. This may seem an over-literal translation but has the advantage of reminding us that the early-twentieth-century German view of fighting power was not precisely the same as our modern one.

Chapter 1 recounted OHL's increasing concern in late 1916 about the damage the army had suffered, and its call that November for weekly reports on the combat value of every division. Explaining this order, '*Weltkrieg*' commented:

It was true that almost all German divisions were gradually becoming quite similar in their organisation, numerical strength, weaponry and equipment. But this was not so of their combat value. Nowhere near all divisions were suited for major battle, and the capability of even those which in principle were suited continually changed.[6]

---

[4] AOK 1, 'Erfahrungen', 24 and 27; '*Abwehrschlacht*', March 1917, 53; Hew Strachan, 'Ausbildung, Kampfgeist und die zwei Weltkriege', in Bruno Thoß and Hans-Erich Volkmann, eds., *Erster Weltkrieg – Zweiter Weltkrieg: Ein Vergleich. Krieg, Kriegserlebnis, Kriegserfahrung in Deutschland* (Paderborn: Schöningh, 2002), 265–86.

[5] Generalkommando 64 circular, 'Übersicht über Gefechtsstärken, Nahkampfmittel, Reserven', Ia 33 geh., 15 February 1917, HSAS, M34 Bü 7; AOK 6 memorandum, 'Meldung ueber Fahrt mit dem O.B. am 10.5.17.', 11 May 1917, KAM, AOK 6 Bd. 369.

[6] Reichsarchiv, *Weltkrieg*, 11:481.

Two points emerge from this. First, because of their composition, many divisions had too low a combat value ever to engage in major battle. Second, the combat value of those divisions that were in principle suited for major battle constantly fluctuated depending on their recent engagements. Here, these two qualities are called 'intrinsic combat value' and 'current combat value' respectively. The difference between them is illustrated by the modern sporting saying, 'Form is temporary, class is permanent.' It reflects Clausewitz's distinction between 'the real spirit of an army' [*Geist des Heeres*] and its changeable 'mood' [*Stimmung*].[7] German intelligence usage developed in 1917 to evaluate enemy formations also adopted this distinction.

Intrinsic and Current Combat Value

> Armies do not win wars by means of a few bodies of super-soldiers but by the average quality of their standard units.[8]

> ...in war a battalion is sometimes stronger than a division and sometimes weaker than a company. The relative strengths of bodies of troops can never be known to anyone.[9]

The quality and homogeneity of German formations, in other words their intrinsic combat value, became an issue immediately on the outbreak of war. The peacetime army comprised the 'active' divisions in which conscripts did their military service. On mobilisation, these were supplemented with reserve, *Ersatz* [reinforcement] and *Landwehr* divisions. Reserve divisions were expected to fulfil the same tasks as active divisions in the initial campaign, but their lesser scale of equipment meant they did not have the same intrinsic combat value over the longer term. *Ersatz* divisions comprised men who were supernumerary, including replacements for casualties. Neither they nor *Landwehr* divisions, composed of older men and intended for static defence, were suited for full-scale operations against a first-class enemy in the open field.[10] From August 1914 on, these divisions were joined by an array of new formations raised in different ways. The example of reserve divisions shows some of

---

[7] Clausewitz, *On War*, book 3, chapter 5, 189.

[8] Field-Marshal Sir William Slim, *Defeat into Victory* (London: Cassell, 1956), 529.

[9] Tolstoy, *War and Peace*, quoted in Julian Jackson, *The Fall of France: The Nazi Invasion of 1940* (Oxford: Oxford University Press, 2003), 7.

[10] Cron, *Geschichte des Deutschen Heeres*, 95–106 for changes to the number and composition of divisions; see also Gudmundsson, 'Learning from the Front', chapter 2. Weakness of the *Ersatz* divisions: Generalmajor a.D. van den Bergh to Reichsarchiv, 28 January 1927, BArch, RH61/893. *Landwehr*: Reichsarchiv, *Weltkrieg*, vol. 1, *Die Grenzschlachten im Westen* (Berlin: E. S. Mittler, 1925), 23.

Table 8.1 *Types of reserve division*

Date formed	Composition	Number
2 Aug. 1914	Formed as planned on mobilisation from trained troops who had completed their active military service	31
Aug.–Oct. 1914	Consisted mainly of untrained wartime volunteers	13
Oct. 1914	39th Reserve Division. Mixture of Bavarian and Prussian *Ersatz* and *Landwehr* units; 39th Bavarian Reserve Division from Feb. 1916	1
Nov. 1914–Jan. 1915	Formed from trained recruits, war-experienced officers and men, and existing artillery units	9
Sept. 1916	9th Bavarian Reserve Division. Formed from existing Bavarian reserve, *Ersatz* and *Landwehr* regiments	1
Total		55

the methods used to create new formations and suggests why assessing intrinsic combat value was both important and difficult. Despite having the same title there were in fact five different types (Table 8.1).

Not surprisingly, divisions of different types performed differently. On 1 July 1916, the Württemberg 26th Reserve Division, belonging to the first type, stopped the assault of five British divisions. It was clearly a higher-quality and stronger formation than the 39th Bavarian Reserve Division, similarly titled but from the third type. This division was manned on the basis that it would only engage in trench warfare on quiet fronts; it had no experience of major battle; and it stated frankly in autumn 1916 that it was not fit to be deployed to Verdun. Nevertheless it was deployed there and 'completely failed' during the successful French attack in December. One corps commander wrote that the defeat proved it was self-deceit to describe 39th Bavarian Reserve Division as a reserve division and to expect it to perform well at Verdun.[11] The army made constant efforts to eradicate the differences in intrinsic combat value exemplified by these two divisions, but as '*Weltkrieg*' commented even by late 1916 this had not been achieved. If anything, the problem became worse because the new defensive tactics were believed to place heavier demands on a lower-quality army.[12]

Despite its importance, few reports on intrinsic combat value survive. The system for evaluating it was informal rather than formal, and there

---

[11] Reichsarchiv, *Weltkrieg*, 11:151–2; Kuhl, 'Kriegstagebuch', 19 December 1916; Maximilian von Höhn letter to Mertz von Quirnheim, 17 December 1916, NARA, Mertz von Quirnheim papers, M958-1.

[12] Wrisberg, *Heer und Heimat*, 13; Hindenburg, *Out of My Life*, 262–3.

was certainly no classification into assault and line-holding divisions as in early 1918. Anecdotal and statistical evidence demonstrates how the system worked. In keeping with the army's generally pragmatic approach, the main factor was performance in battle. There are many references to 'proven' [*bewährt*], 'capable' [*tüchtig*] and 'combat-tested' [*kampferprobt*] formations, or if less good, 'average' [*durchschnittlich*]. In early 1917, Army Group Rupprecht gave 'reliable' [*erprobt*] divisions priority in training, suggesting an emphasis on quality rather than quantity; slightly later, it sorted divisions roughly into good and second-class.[13] Sometimes experience in battle was listed: when Gruppe Sissonne rated 5th Bavarian Reserve Division as its best formation, the first reason it gave was the division's combat-experienced status, having fought in the 1915 battle of Arras and twice on the Somme. Negative assessments followed the same pattern. Otto von Below commented that one of 15th Reserve Division's regiments which failed at Fresnoy had done so before. Nor were such judgements purely subjective, an example being OHL's decision not to deploy 22nd Reserve Division to Arras because it had performed badly at Verdun.[14]

A second factor in assessing intrinsic combat value was the regional origin of divisions. Echoing British martial race theory (and the way in which German intelligence assessed enemy divisions), German commanders had definite views on the combat value of troops from different areas. Before the war, the army had a general preference for recruits from agricultural regions.[15] As VII Corps commander, Karl von Einem thought highly of his men, who were mainly from agricultural and industrial areas in Westphalia. Similarly, Albrecht von Thaer commented on the toughness of IX Reserve Corps' north German soldiers. Views on troops from other areas were less positive. Concerns about the loyalty of men from Alsace-Lorraine and Polish-speaking communities are well-known, though Alexander Watson suggests that the latter at least were militarily effective.[16] There had been widespread doubts

---

[13] Reichsarchiv, *Weltkrieg*, 12:55; HKR, 'Liste des Einsatzes und der Verluste der Divisionen in der Schlacht bei Arras bis 20.5.1917', Abtlg. Ic, 27 April 1917 [sic], KAM, HKR alte Nr. 150.

[14] Höhn letter to the Bavarian Kriegsministerium, 'Einsatz des Gen. Kdos. an der Aisne', No. 401/4/25 geh., 30 April 1917, KAM, XV.BRK 89; Otto von Below diary, 3 May 1917; Rupprecht, unpublished diary, 12 April 1917.

[15] Manfred Messerschmidt, 'Preußens Militär in seinem gesellschaftlichen Umfeld', in H. J. Pühle and H.-U. Wehler, eds., *Geschichte und Gesellschaft*, Sonderheft 6, *Preußen im Rückblick* (Göttingen: Vandenhoeck & Ruprecht, 1980), 69. For martial race theory, see Tan Tai Yong, *The Garrison State: The Military, Government and Society in Colonial Punjab, 1849–1947* (New Delhi: Sage Publications, 2005), especially chapter 2.

[16] Einem, *Erinnerungen*, 165; Thaer, *Generalstabsdienst*, 91–2. Alsace-Lorrainers: Alan Kramer, '*Wackes* at War: Alsace-Lorraine and the Failure of German National Mobilization, 1914–1918', in John Horne, ed., *State, Society and Mobilization in Europe during the First World War* (Cambridge: Cambridge University Press, 1997), 105–21.

before the war about the reliability of Rhineland troops. Adding to the complexity, by 1917 the non-Prussian contingents enjoyed different combat reputations: the Württembergers were very well regarded, the Bavarians had a mixed reputation – some units were good, some bad – and there were growing concerns about the Saxons.[17]

High intrinsic combat value was a prerequisite of participation in major battle, and the deployment of divisions therefore helps understand how commanders assessed it. Statistical analysis of five battles from early 1916 to early 1918 is revealing. The five are Verdun, the Somme, the spring 1917 Entente offensive, Third Ypres that autumn and the German offensive of March 1918. As the example of reserve divisions showed, it is not possible to analyse the quality of divisions simply based on nomenclature. The analysis here therefore categorises divisions into three types: active divisions; those formed on mobilisation following detailed peacetime planning; and those formed after mobilisation, all more or less improvised. It then calculates both the percentage each category contributed to the army as a whole and the percentage it formed of the total forces engaged in the five battles. Figure 8.1 illustrates the difference between the two. So for instance, in spring 1917 active divisions formed 21 per cent of the army but 32 per cent of divisions engaged against the Entente offensive. They can therefore be described as 'over-represented' by 11 per cent.[18]

Active divisions were over-represented in all five battles, reaching nearly 25 per cent in March 1918. These are arresting statistics given that active divisions' proportion of the whole decreased as the army expanded. They apparently represent OHL's confidence in the intrinsic combat value of these divisions compared with the rest. The 1918 attack divisions for instance were given special treatment in terms of equipment, manning and training. The high proportion of active divisions must therefore represent a conscious decision by OHL, presumably building on perceived superior performance in the earlier battles.[19] Divisions formed on mobilisation were on the opposite trajectory, over-representation in the first four battles becoming under-representation in spring 1918.

Ethnic Poles: Alexander Watson, 'Fighting for Another Fatherland: The Polish Minority in the German Army, 1914–1918', *English Historical Review*, vol. 126, no. 522 (October 2011), 1137–66.

[17] Cowan, 'A Picture of German Unity?', 148–54.
[18] The figures for 21 March 1918 cover attack divisions [*Angriffs-Divisionen*] engaged in the battle, not all divisions engaged as in the other four cases.
[19] See Reichsarchiv, *Weltkrieg*, 14:40–3 for the attack divisions.

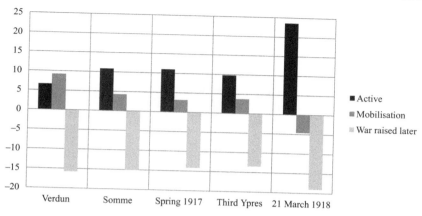

Figure 8.1 Difference between percentage of army and percentage of formations engaged in battle, by category of formation

All divisions raised after mobilisation were under-represented in all the battles. Given that by spring 1917 they formed 61 per cent of the whole army, this needs further investigation. We can identify four groups of divisions whose intrinsic combat value was apparently assessed at that time as too low for major battle on the Western Front. They are *Landwehr* divisions; those deployed on a long-term basis to the Eastern Front; a miscellaneous group on the Western Front about which OHL clearly had doubts; and divisions only recently formed. Divisions raised after mobilisation formed a big proportion of the first three categories and all of the last.

By the end of the Entente spring offensive in May 1917, there were thirty-three *Landwehr* divisions, twenty-nine of them formed after mobilisation: fifteen were on the Western Front, fifteen in the east and three moved from west to east. When formally assessed, the western divisions were categorised as 'only fit for trench warfare', which is to say their intrinsic combat value was too low to do more than hold the line in what the German army called 'normal trench warfare'. Only two *Landwehr* divisions fought in the spring battles. One was on the periphery but the after-action report from the other, 13th Landwehr Division, shows why it was unfit for major battle. The troops, who were from older manpower classes, were brave enough. But they lacked the skill and training to operate successfully the core features of the new tactics, particularly making immediate counter-attacks.[20]

---

[20] 60.LIB, 'Erfahrungen über die Zeit vom 19.III. bis 9.V.17', Br.B. No. Ia 93/6 17 geh., 4 June 1917, GLAK, F1/523.

The second group of divisions with low intrinsic combat value comprised those deployed long-term on the Eastern Front.[21] In 1915, this front had been Germany's main theatre of operations. But from the start of the Verdun offensive in February 1916, the Western Front took priority. Hindenburg commented that though Russian forces had definite qualities, the Germans were unquestionably superior: they could use formations on the Eastern Front whose combat value would have prevented employment in the west except in emergencies. Crown Prince Rupprecht recorded in November 1916 that all units which were less effective in battle were now being sent east. Conversely, by spring 1917 the best divisions had long been removed from there.[22] Excluding *Landwehr*, forty-three divisions served on the Eastern Front for all or almost all of 1917. Of these, thirty-seven (86 per cent) were war-raised, and many of them only ever served in the east.

The third group comprised twenty-three divisions of various types which OHL evidently regarded as unfit for major Western Front battle, including twelve that had aroused performance concerns in 1916.[23] The proportion of divisions raised after mobilisation is relatively low, at 57 per cent. The final group of divisions not fit for Western Front combat is different, because their low intrinsic combat value was temporary. These were the thirteen divisions formed in early 1917 to be ready for action by March. Numerically, these new divisions represented a 6 per cent increase in the total available. In terms of quality, although they were assessed as not yet ready for major battle, they could free up combat-capable units. Given time, there was no reason why they should not become effective formations, and in fact several took part in subsidiary actions and in the later stages of the spring battles.

The 228 formed infantry divisions available when the spring offensive opened on 9 April 1917 had increased to 236 by its end. The 33 *Landwehr* divisions were by definition not suitable for major battle. To this we can add 43 divisions that were on the Eastern Front long term, 23 that though theoretically suitable for major battle were not used or should not have been used, and the 13 new divisions that were temporarily unsuitable. This comes to 112 divisions, or 47 per cent. So in early 1917, nearly half

---

[21] For simplicity, 'Eastern Front' includes Rumania and the Balkans.

[22] Hindenburg, *Out of My Life*, 133; Rupprecht, unpublished diary, 3 November 1916; Reichsarchiv, *Weltkrieg*, 12:546.

[23] The twenty-three divisions were 8th, 12th, 15th, 16th, 117th, 123rd, 212th, 219th, 228th, 255th, 301st and 10th Bavarian Infantry Divisions; 5th, 11th, 22nd, 24th, 53rd, 30th Bavarian and 39th Bavarian Reserve Divisions; 5th and 19th Ersatz Divisions; 1st and 2nd Naval Divisions. Chapter 1 noted the divisions of concern in late 1916.

the German divisions in the field were intrinsically not up to the demands of major battle on the Western Front.

Given their relative scarcity, it was essential to make most efficient use of those divisions that *were* intrinsically fit for major battle. The principal management tool for this was the system of weekly reports on current combat value. Shortly before the Entente offensive, OHL issued orders that reports should divide divisions into three categories: fully fit for combat [*vollkampfkräftig*]; needing a specified number of weeks' training; and only fit for trench warfare.[24] Although no unified regulations were sent out on what points to cover, 5th Guard Infantry Division's report after its engagement against the French in April 1917 is typical. Titled 'State of Training and Combat Value', its largest section was on infantry, and within that the part on training was longer than the one on combat value. The report also covered casualties, the quality of replacements, morale [*Stimmung*] and health. The infantry, which had suffered heavy casualties in certain specified categories, were fit for immediate deployment on a quiet front, but not on a battle front. The training and combat value of the artillery, engineers and other units were generally good.[25] Higher up the chain of command, reports also considered factors like overall divisional strength, casualties, average battalion strength and length of time in the front line.[26]

Assessing current combat value honestly and accurately was recognised to be a difficult task. Underestimating it meant that units were relieved prematurely, draining the crucial pool of fresh reserves. Overestimating it meant that a division might crack when attacked. The Army Group Crown Prince report on the December 1916 defeat at Verdun commented that reasons for the defeat included over-optimistic assessment of combat value; to avoid similar reverses in future, 'ruthless clarity' was required.[27] Ludendorff insisted in his memoirs that from time to time OHL reminded the army to report only objective truth, unfavourable as well as favourable.[28] A divisional command course lecturer believed the question of how long divisions could hold out was so important that staffs should if necessary bypass the chain of command to interrogate regiments directly.[29] Hermann von Kuhl wrote convincingly about measures to ensure that his staff understood the state of units by visits and by inviting

[24] AOK 7 telegram to its Gruppen, Ia Nr. 40/April 17, 5 April 1917, GLAK, F1/250.

[25] 5.GID to AOK 7, 'Ausbildungsstand und Gefechtswert der 5. Garde-Inf.-Division', Ia B. Nr. 1582/V, 3 May 1917, GLAK, F1/257.

[26] HKR lists, 'Liste des Einsatzes und der Verluste der Divisionen in der Schlacht bei Arras bis 20.5.1917' and 'O.H.L.- und H.Gr.-Reserven', c. 7 May 1917, both on KAM, HKR alte Nr. 150.

[27] Reichsarchiv, *Weltkrieg*, 11:171.   [28] Ludendorff, *My War Memories*, 21.

[29] 'Organisation des Divisionsstabes in der Abwehrschlacht', 5.

front officers to headquarters; also, many senior commanders were friends, and they told him about the condition of their troops.[30]

It is clear then that there was much honest reporting and that genuine efforts were made to assess units accurately. But this was not easy, given the number of variables and the difficulty of factoring in likely enemy action. Chapter 6 explained the physical and bureaucratic obstacles to contacting forward troops to assess their condition. Another potential obstacle to accurate reporting was operational and personal pressure to exaggerate divisions' current combat value. Operationally, the shortage of formations intrinsically fit for major battle forced staffs to maintain divisions in the line for as long as possible. In April 1917, Army Group Crown Prince stated that divisions which had been deployed for months in a quiet sector should normally be assessed as fit for major battle.[31] This order to relax standards when judging current combat value clearly filtered down. Otto von Moser commented that many reports on units were written by general staff officers; the younger and less experienced they were, the more optimistic. It was also alleged that the report 'The division is fought out' was always unwelcome higher up, and might be greeted with the reply, 'Perhaps under another general staff officer it would not be?'[32] This was symptomatic of the personal pressure to adopt a can-do attitude described in Chapter 6.

Test of Battle: Pyrrhic Victory?

But the most worrying thing was the destructive effect of the huge battles lasting for months on end, in which our troops were overwhelmed by superior force and bit by bit crushed physically and morally. The wastage of capable officers, NCOs and well-trained men was enormous. Many competent regimental and battalion commanders had succumbed to the psychologically corrosive effects of the defensive battle ... [and to] the increasing difficulty of constantly having to reconstruct their units each time they were shot to bits, with inadequate material and without being able to weld them together in a long period of rest, with good rations and far from combat. We could not fight many more Aisne-Champagne battles.[33]

As we saw, the German army divided its final command task, winning, into two parts: first, to stop the enemy breaking through, and second, to manage attrition by inflicting maximum casualties while economising on

---

[30] Kuhl, *Generalstab*, 191 and 207–8.
[31] HDK to AOK 1, Ib Nr. 1753 geh., 16 April 1917, GLAK, F1/374.
[32] Moser, *Ernsthafte Plaudereien*, 54; Anon, *Das alte Heer*, 78.
[33] Schulenburg, 'Erlebnisse', 150–1.

German forces. In overall terms, the German army fulfilled both parts of the task and OHL was naturally delighted with the result. Georg Wetzell commented after the war that the German army had achieved something 'absolutely extraordinary' in defeating the gigantic Entente spring offensive.[34] However, as the quote from Army Group Crown Prince chief of staff Friedrich Graf Schulenburg shows, the reality is that the army paid a high price in resources and casualties. Also, its success was by no means entirely due to its own performance.

To fulfil the first sub-task, preventing a breakthrough, the Germans needed ultimately to retain control of the battlefield. This was a traditional measure of success and therefore important in morale and propaganda terms. 'Defensive Battle' covered this requirement: it allowed troops to move flexibly to avoid enemy action, but stressed that they must end up in possession of their original positions. However, potential problems arose from its instructions that in order to avoid unnecessary casualties, commanders were not to hold ground rigidly. They must consider whether retaking lost positions was worth the likely casualties and expenditure of ammunition. If they decided not to retake the ground, they must ensure that the new positions were favourable to the defence, if necessary by withdrawal.[35]

The Germans lost up to eight kilometres of ground in the central part of the Arras battlefield, most of it in the initial British assault and the subsequent withdrawal. They also lost some tactically valuable positions, especially Vimy Ridge and the high ground at Monchy-le-Preux. The biggest French advance, six or seven kilometres on a twelve kilometre front, followed a German withdrawal on the western flank of the Aisne sector. Elsewhere the French moved forwards four to five kilometres in some areas, capturing tactical features such as the commanding Plateau de Californie and the heights in western Champagne; Ludendorff called losing the latter a severe blow.[36] These British and French gains came nowhere near a breakthrough, but in 1916–17 terms did represent considerable advances.

German reactions varied in the two sectors, mainly because of differing terrain. At Arras, Sixth Army was able to adopt the flexible approach recommended in 'Defensive Battle'. As described in Chapter 3, it recaptured Fresnoy, which tactically it could not afford to lose; but it cancelled an operation to retake the village of Roeux as unnecessary. The situation in Army Group Crown Prince, with its important ridge positions, was very different. The French had captured some points that enabled them to inflict heavy casualties by observed artillery fire. The Germans could

---

not tolerate such losses in the long term and could solve the problem either by withdrawing or by attacking to regain the original positions. Any withdrawal meant retiring to the next ridge. On the Chemin des Dames this was up to five kilometres away, so a withdrawal would cede considerable terrain to the enemy. This was unacceptable on propaganda grounds: the French would be able to claim success, which would help restore morale in the French army and people and so undo a large part of the gain from the German victory.[37] The Entente had exploited the withdrawal to the Hindenburg Line in precisely this way to 'prove' they had won the battle of the Somme.

The alternative solution, attacking, was more to the taste of the aggressively minded German army. Throughout the summer, Seventh Army launched a series of assaults to recapture its original positions. German battle nomenclature recognised fifteen separate actions from 1 June to mid-July, most at German initiative; a total of thirteen divisions were involved. In June, the Army was losing 500 casualties a day, and not many fewer subsequently. From Army Group Rupprecht's point of view, these attacks were 'useless scrapping': they simply wasted troops and ammunition better deployed in Flanders against the coming British offensive. Because of the resources required, OHL too considered these operations 'highly unwelcome' and ordered the army group to keep them to a minimum. But it did not forbid them, a sign of the difficulty it had balancing the powerful interests represented by army groups.[38]

This leads to the second German sub-task, to inflict maximum casualties while economising on German forces. Though no full statistics are available, as Table 8.2 shows, the Germans certainly inflicted more casualties than they suffered.[39] But the German army was also badly damaged. German casualties in spring 1917 were lighter than in the most intense phase of the Somme but much worse than during the first three full months of Verdun and worse than in summer–autumn 1917 during Third Ypres, the second battle of Verdun and Malmaison (Figure 8.2).[40] 'Weltkrieg' described casualties in spring 1917 as very heavy

---

[37] Reichsarchiv, Weltkrieg, 12:561.

[38] Fortmüller, 'Heeresgruppe Deutscher Kronprinz', 197–8; Kuhl, 'Kriegstagebuch', 24 June and 1 November 1917; Reichsarchiv, Weltkrieg, 13:39.

[39] German: Reichsarchiv, Weltkrieg, 13:22. French: Reichsarchiv, Weltkrieg, 12:410 fn. 1 which quotes a French publication stating French losses 'for the whole battle' as 271,000. British: BOH 1917, 1:556 gives 'probably rather under 150,000' for Arras, which I have taken as 148,000; and BOH 1917, 2:87–8 gives 25,000 for Messines. The resulting total of 444,000 does not include French and British casualties incurred outside the main fighting. McRandle and Quirk, 'Blood Test', table 12, calculates German and French/British casualties for 1 April to 31 July 1917 as 469,000 and 635,000, respectively.

[40] McRandle and Quirk, 'Blood Test', table 6. The July 1916 figures must include some Verdun casualties before the German offensive there ended.

Table 8.2 *German and Entente casualties on the Western Front, April–June 1917*

| German | 384,000 |
| British and French | 444,000 |

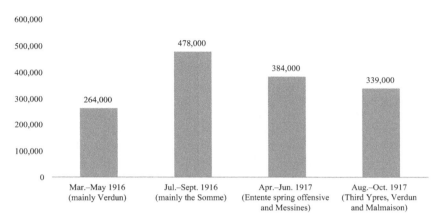

Figure 8.2 Comparison of German Western Front casualties in 1916–17

in places, adding that the army's fighting power had again declined considerably.[41] Also, despite the failure of the French offensive, one significant indicator in a war of attrition had continued to move in the French favour. The ratio between casualties suffered and casualties inflicted by the French had been 1:0.86 in the December attack at Verdun but rose to 1:0.96 during the Nivelle offensive, the best the French army had achieved so far.[42]

Statistics from the divisional level bear out the severity of the German casualties. In twenty-one days of battle in May and early June – when the main part of the Entente offensive was over – 242nd Infantry Division lost 3,100 men, one-third of its infantry establishment.[43] At least twenty-two other divisions suffered similar or heavier casualties in the two battles, or at least one-fifth of divisions engaged. Within two days of the opening of the French offensive, the combined fighting strength of 21st Infantry

---

[41] Reichsarchiv, *Weltkrieg*, 13:22–3.
[42] François Cailleteau, *Gagner la Grande Guerre* (Paris: Economica, 2008), 107 and tableau 5.
[43] General der Infanterie a.D. Freiherr von Soden to the Kriegsgeschichtliche Forschungsanstalt des Heeres, 27 February 1939, BArch, RH61/1901.

Division's three infantry regiments had been reduced to 1,260, less than half the pre-battle average for one regiment. One of 2nd Guard Infantry Division's regiments lost twenty-nine officers and 1,228 men, most of them in six days.[44] These examples are probably at the high end of the scale, but they illustrate how heavily losses could hit individual units.

Although historical attention and controversy has focused on such raw casualty figures, more helpful to understanding attrition are two other series of statistics: the actual strength [*Iststärke*] of the field army and its total wastage [*Gesamtausfall*]. The latter term meant men who were permanently or long-term unavailable for field service and therefore needed replacement. It covered killed and missing together with those wounded and sick who could not be treated with their units or in field hospitals and needed lengthy care in Germany. The difference between actual strength and total wastage represents the attrition of the German army. Figure 8.3 sets out how it evolved throughout 1916 and 1917.[45]

Several important points emerge from this chart. The left scale (bars) shows that actual strength of the field army increased more or less steadily from January 1916 until June 1917, when it reached its height of just over 5.2 million men. The right scale (line) shows that the decline in wastage from a peak in summer 1916 contributed to and was perhaps the primary factor in the increase. This underlines the extent to which Entente inability to mount continuous, large-scale operations over winter 1916–17 let the German army off the attritional hook. The serious damage inflicted on the army by the Entente spring offensive is also clear.

Separating the same statistics by front as in Figure 8.4, we can see that at its height the offensive was causing nearly as much wastage as the battles of Verdun and the Somme together, and much more than Third Ypres. Once again, Entente inability to maintain operations at the same intensity let the German army off the hook. That said, the spring offensive caused or contributed to the fall in field army strength which set in from June 1917. Indeed, by late July, there was a severe manpower crisis, created by casualties from the spring fighting and simultaneous increased requirements for labour to feed the war economy.[46] Ironically, part of this increase was for the Hindenburg Programme, designed to produce matériel to replace manpower. Figure 8.4 also explains why the Eastern Front mattered to

---

[44] Reichsarchiv, *Weltkrieg*, 12:344; Generalleutnant von Winterfeldt, *Das Kaiser Franz-Garde-Grenadier-Regiment Nr. 2 1914–1918* (Oldenburg: Gerhard Stalling, 1922), 51.

[45] Reichskriegsministerium, *Sanitätsbericht über das Deutsche Heer (Deutsches Feld- und Besatzungsheer) im Weltkriege 1914/1918*, vol. 3, *Die Krankenbewegung bei dem Deutschen Feld- und Besatzungsheer* (Berlin: E. S. Mittler, 1934), tables 148–50. The 1916 total wastage parts of Figures 8.3 and 8.4 first appeared, in slightly different format, as Figures 1 and 2 in Cowan, 'Muddy Grave?'

[46] Reichsarchiv, *Weltkrieg*, 13:25–6.

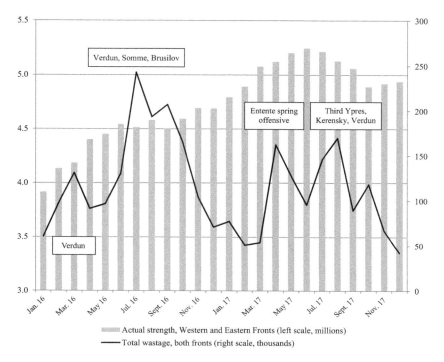

Actual strength, Western and Eastern Fronts (left scale, millions)
Total wastage, both fronts (right scale, thousands)

Figure 8.3 Actual strength and total wastage of the field army, January 1916–December 1917

the Entente: German wastage in spring 1917 was much less than it would have been if the Entente had succeeded in co-ordinating operations on the two fronts. It was only the revival of the front at the time of the Kerensky offensive and German-Austro-Hungarian counter-offensive in July and August that saw total wastage reach the same level as in spring.

Seventh Army's experience facing the French illustrates the workings of attrition and how the system of assessing current combat value helped counter it. The Army's rather anecdotal current combat value returns in April and May 1917 fall naturally into five categories rather than the three ordered by OHL. Broadly, they described divisions as fully fit for combat; still fit for combat though of reduced combat value; needing two to four weeks rest and training but if necessary still fit for defensive tasks; needing four to eight weeks training; and fought out or only fit for trench warfare. The Army's strength varied between twenty and twenty-seven divisions. Figure 8.5 shows the percentage of divisions in different categories of combat value. For clarity, it looks only at the top two and bottom two

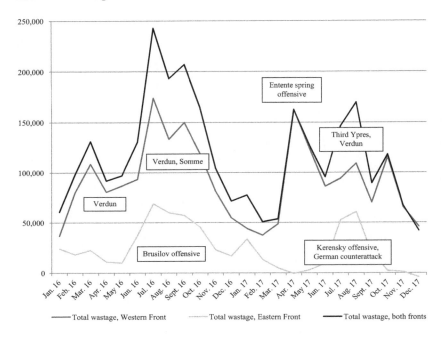

Figure 8.4 Total wastage by front, January 1916–December 1917

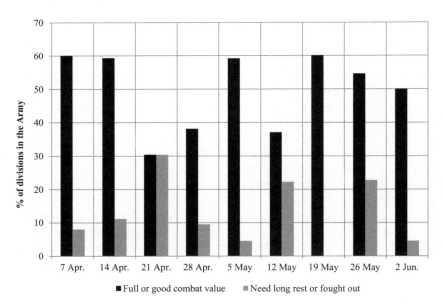

Figure 8.5 Current combat value of Seventh Army's divisions as a percentage of its total strength

categories, aggregated; in other words, the most and least combat-capable divisions.[47]

For French attrition tactics to have worked at this level, the percentage of divisions needing a prolonged rest or fought out would have had to exceed those with full or good combat value. As Figure 8.5 makes clear, even at the period of maximum damage inflicted by the French – the first few days of the offensive from 16 April – the percentages of the two categories were only equal. For most of April and May, divisions in the higher category comfortably outweighed those in the lower. The rise in the lower category on 12 and 26 May reflected in particular the relatively large French local attacks of 4–6 and 20–25 May, but nowhere near reached dangerous levels. This indicates that the system for handling reserves and relieving front divisions on the basis of their current combat value worked well enough.

Generalleutnant Richard Wellmann's 20th Infantry Division demonstrates this at divisional level. It joined Seventh Army in mid-March, initially in OHL reserve. Shortly before the French infantry assault it was successively released to Army and then *Gruppe* control, becoming counter-attack division to Gruppe Liesse on the Chemin des Dames. It first supported the front division during the initial attack and then replaced it from 17 April, itself being replaced as counter-attack division by Kneußl's 11th Bavarian Infantry Division. With the latter's support, it beat off major French attacks on 4 and 5 May and held the front till 7 May when its relief began. During its deployment it lost some 3,900 men. It left Seventh Army in mid-May, had a spell in a quiet sector and then moved east for the counter-attack after the Kerensky offensive.[48]

Table 8.3 summarises the weekly assessment by Seventh Army of 20th Infantry Division's current combat value.[49] In his submission for the 5 May summary, the *Gruppe* commander expressed confidence that once relieved the energetically led division would soon become fully fit for combat again. After the relief, Wellmann reported that the troops were very tired but had in no way suffered in moral strength. The division needed time to integrate its many replacements and would then be fit for major battle again.[50]

[47] 'Kampfwert der Divisionen' section of AOK 7 weekly reports to HDK of the relevant dates, GLAK, F1/334, F1/335 and F1/336. Note that on 19 May no divisions were in the bottom two categories.

[48] Reichsarchiv, *Weltkrieg*, 12:314, 333, 366 and Beilage 1a; 20.ID to Gruppe L[iesse], Ia Nr. 5471, 11 May 1917, GLAK, F1/257.

[49] AOK 7 'Kampfwert der Divisionen' reports, GLAK, F1/335 and F1/336; ten-day casualty reports, GLAK, F1/639.

[50] Gruppe L[iesse] to AOK 7, 'Kampfwert der Truppe', Ia Nr. 363 op., 3 May 1917 and 20. ID to Gruppe L, Ia Nr. 5471, 11 May 1917, both on GLAK, F1/257.

Table 8.3 *20th Infantry Division's current combat value, April–May 1917*

7 Apr.	Fully fit for combat
14 Apr.	Fully fit for combat
21 Apr.	Fit for combat. Has already suffered perceptible casualties (total 851 casualties by 20 Apr.)
28 Apr.	No longer in top condition but still able to engage in defensive action. Has suffered quite heavy casualties so will soon need relief. After fourteen days rest and training will probably be fit for deployment again including on the Seventh Army front (total 1,829 casualties by 30 Apr.)
5 May	Combat value reduced by serious casualties but with the support of the counter-attack division will be able to withstand an enemy attack. Its relief has been initiated. After some three weeks rest and training, expected to be fully deployable again, including on the Seventh Army front (total 3,876 casualties to c. 7 May when relief started)
12 May	Requires eight weeks training on a quiet front and will then be fully fit for combat again

Given that the division's losses amounted to over 40 per cent of its infantry establishment, in not relieving it sooner senior commanders certainly displayed the 'hardness' expected of them. In fact, one of its regiments subsequently alleged that current combat value reports had not accurately depicted the poor state of the units.[51] This suggests that the division's reporting was over-optimistic or even fudged in the sense Chapter 6 described. The division's move to the Eastern Front is also significant. First, it may indicate that higher command realised its current combat value was weaker than stated by Wellmann. Second, like most divisions it only did one tour in the spring fighting. This explains the main reason why Seventh Army always had divisions with good enough current combat value available – French inability to keep up the pressure.

Nevertheless as '*Weltkrieg*' commented, defeating the Entente spring offensive had required an 'extraordinarily high' consumption of troops, especially because of the continual early commitment of fresh reserves, and this could only be maintained temporarily. By the end of the offensive, the number of German divisions committed and more or less used up was about the same as British and French. As early as 2 May, Army Group Crown Prince informed Seventh Army that for the time being OHL could provide no further divisions as reinforcements; economy of the forces available was therefore all the more necessary, and front divisions must not be relieved prematurely. Ten days later, it told Armies that this was the last time it could allocate fresh counter-attack divisions;

---

[51] Viereck, *Infanterie-Regiment Nr. 77*, 395–6.

in future only divisions which had already been engaged would be available.[52]

The strain showed itself in other ways too, with OHL intervening ever more closely in local operations. By early July, Ludendorff wanted to be informed beforehand about minor Seventh Army actions to improve its positions, on the basis that 'the fewer of them we can get by with, the more this accords with the general situation'.[53] Such infringements of mission command were understandable given that OHL had few reserves available to deal with impending Entente attacks in Flanders, Italy and the east. The maximum force it could initially send to deal with the Kerensky offensive was six divisions, all of which had suffered heavy casualties in the west; sending more would have meant making withdrawals on the Western Front.[54]

This shortage of fresh reserves both increased the importance of accurate assessment of current combat value and made it more difficult for commanders to be objective. As described earlier, Army Group Crown Prince gave orders to relax standards when judging current combat value; Army Group Rupprecht exerted pressure not to relieve divisions too soon. One of the accusations against Sixth Army was that it had not reported accurately on the condition of its divisions, some of which then failed at Arras on 9 April.[55] In this instance, the Army probably did make mistakes. But equally, the division that failed worst – 14th Bavarian Infantry Division – was an average, war-raised formation which was hit by one of the most effective attacks the British ever mounted. No system of assessing current combat value, however conscientiously implemented, could have allowed for this.

The period of greatest strain for the German army in 1917, usually dated to autumn, in fact began that spring. From April, millions of letters started to arrive from the front complaining about the almost unbearable strain and losses in the unbroken chain of battles.[56] By May, Albrecht von Thaer was worrying about extensive political agitation among men on leave and wounded, who were openly discussing the need for revolution after victory.[57] Thousands of soldiers wrote supporting the Social Democratic Party's new policy of peace without annexations or reparations, almost certainly reflecting the views of many others. Some months before, OHL had begun propaganda efforts, known as 'information work'

---

[52] Reichsarchiv, *Weltkrieg*, 12:408–9 and 565; HDK telegram to AOK 7, 1 ab 2542, 2 May 1917, GLAK, F1/249.
[53] Reichsarchiv, *Weltkrieg*, 13:39.   [54] Ibid., 38 and 159.
[55] HKR to its AOKs, 'Erfahrungen u. Folgerungen aus den Kämpfen bei Arras am 9.4.17', Ia No. 2853 geh., 21 April 1917, BArch, RH61/1890; Sheldon, *Vimy Ridge*, 336–7.
[56] Moser, *Ernsthafte Plaudereien*, 201.   [57] Thaer, *Generalstabsdienst*, 122.

[*Aufklärungsarbeit*], to counter such views, and later in the year this developed into a systematic programme of 'patriotic instruction' [*Vaterländischer Unterricht*].[58]

But nothing could stop the erosion of the military machine. In early July, Kneußl bemoaned the much reduced quality of 11th Bavarian Infantry Division, which he felt was common to all formations: 'It is terribly depressing when one sees the sword in one's hand gradually being blunted in this way.'[59] Illustrating the continuous strain, in September 1917, 15th Infantry Division – which had acquired such a bad reputation on the Somme – was said to be utterly run-down and to have failed everywhere.[60] The navy too was in a poor way. Particularly worrying for the high command was a series of 'strikes' among surface warships, during which some 5,000 sailors signed a document supporting the Independent Social Democratic Party's peace conditions.[61] By then, the political situation had also reached breaking point, with the forced resignation of Chancellor Bethmann Hollweg in July and a few days later the *Reichstag*'s passing of a resolution calling for peace without annexations.

The Other Side of the Hill

Everyone has a plan 'till they get punched in the mouth.[62]

We cannot understand the failure of the Entente spring offensive without assessing British and French performance at the different levels of war. Lack of a unified Anglo-French high command, poor civil–military relations in both countries and problematic command structures all impeded the smooth formulation and execution of grand strategy, strategy and operations. The friction and suspicion arising from Lloyd George's plot to subordinate the British to the French army not only poisoned the relationship between the two but delayed the offensive by weeks.[63] Once agreement was reached, although the relationship remained scratchy the two armies were able to co-operate sufficiently well to mount the offensive. For example, Haig was flexible on timing of the assaults in order to fit changing French requirements. The problem at this level was now the state of civil–military relations, particularly for

---

[58] Lipp, *Meinungslenkung*, 62–89; Benjamin Ziemann, *War Experiences in Rural Germany 1914–1923*, trans. Alex Skinner (Oxford: Berg, 2007), 66–71 and 151.

[59] Stachelbeck, *Militärische Effektivität*, 298.   [60] Tappen, 'Kriegserinnerungen', f. 191.

[61] Watson, *Ring of Steel*, 483–4.

[62] Former heavyweight boxer Mike Tyson, quoted in Lawrence Freedman, *Strategy: A History* (Oxford: Oxford University Press, 2013), ix.

[63] Doughty, *Pyrrhic Victory*, 335.

Nivelle after Painlevé's arrival at the Ministry of War. To quote Sir William Robertson, Nivelle went into action 'with a rope round his neck. It is a horrible predicament for a Commander.'[64]

Nivelle was clearly overwhelmed by his task, not surprisingly since he was handling many inter-allied issues as well as planning the offensive. Though not young, he lacked experience at this level and Joffre's moral authority. He failed to ease his burden by giving Alfred Micheler, also inexperienced at his level, full powers as Reserve Army Group commander, making him a 'delegate' instead. Compounding this problem, Micheler and Charles Mangin at Sixth Army despised each other. They clashed openly in February, and Nivelle's efforts to smooth things over merely demonstrated his weakness. In particular, he made little or no attempt to impose his will on the headstrong Mangin. Indeed, some came to see the offensive as 'Mangin's battle', since his ideas for the offensive were fed into GQG and from there into orders to the army group. There were quarrels over Micheler's right to intervene in Sixth Army's affairs, but more importantly he and Mangin had different conceptions of the offensive: Micheler wanted a slower-paced attack, Mangin fast. Such arguments were replicated at GQG, where Colonel Renouard, head of the Third Bureau (Operations), disagreed with Nivelle's *chef de cabinet*, Lieutenant-Colonel Audemard d'Alançon, about the form the offensive should take.[65] As in the German army, these personal clashes reflected genuine and strongly held differences of opinion over real military issues.

On the British side, once a working arrangement with the French was reached, the struggle between the military and civilians entered a lull. Command relationships in the British army were less fraught than in the French, but it was unhelpful that Haig and Third Army commander Sir Edmund Allenby did not see eye to eye. Indeed, there was said to be a rivalry between them dating back to their time together at Staff College. At conferences attended by Army commanders, Haig often more or less ignored Allenby's views. He turned down Allenby's imaginative artillery tactics, intended to achieve surprise at Arras, and told him shortly before the attack that his plan of battle seemed faulty. This poor relationship was one of the reasons Allenby was selected in June for command of the forces in Palestine. He was dismayed at his apparent sacking for unsatisfactory

---

[64] Robertson to Haig, 14 April 1917, in David R. Woodward, ed., *The Military Correspondence of Field-Marshal Sir William Robertson, Chief of the Imperial General Staff, December 1915–February 1918* (London: Army Records Society, 1989), 171.
[65] Colonel Émile Herbillon, *Le Général Alfred Micheler (1914–1918): De la Meuse à Reims* (Paris: Librairie Plon, 1933), 133–9; Rolland, *Nivelle*, 97, 120–5 and 135.

performance at Arras, but achieved great victories in the easier circumstances of the Middle East.[66]

As Chapter 1 described, the Entente were well aware of the need to maintain pressure on the Germans, and their grand strategy was therefore to mount synchronised offensives on the Eastern and Western Fronts, including in Italy, as early as possible in 1917. Ludendorff was in no doubt that the failure to execute this grand strategy was the key factor in defeating the Anglo-French offensive:

I could not help considering what our position must inevitably have been had the Russians attacked in April and May and met with even minor successes. We should then, as in the autumn of 1916, have had a desperate struggle. Our supply of munitions would have been diminished to an alarming extent. If the Russian successes of July had occurred in April and May I do not see, as I look back, how [OHL] could have mastered the situation. During these two months of 1917, in spite of our Aisne-Champagne victory, it was the Russian Revolution alone that saved us from serious trouble.[67]

Three factors at the strategic level contributed to the defeat. Chronologically, the first was the good German intelligence work and poor French security, which stripped the French offensive of the crucial element of surprise. Both French and Germans agreed this was another principal reason why the Nivelle offensive failed.[68] The second factor was the withdrawal to the Hindenburg Line in March. Chapter 1 explained the disadvantages as well as advantages for the Germans. The most beneficial effect was to disrupt part of the British attack and almost all of the French attack on the Oise, both aimed at drawing in German reserves before the main French assault. The greatly reduced scale of the Oise attack clearly damaged French prospects, though not in such a decisive way as the loss of surprise.[69]

The third and most important of the strategic factors was changing French and British priorities. The failure of the initial French breakthrough attempt soon led to conversion of the offensive into a series of bite-and-hold attacks. Faced with little progress at the cost of mounting casualties, the French government reined in the scale of operations. When Pétain replaced Nivelle, he initially intended to carry out several major

[66] General Sir Archibald Wavell, *Allenby: A Study in Greatness* (London: Harrap, 1940), 170–85; Newton, 'Anatomy of British Adaptation', 21–4 and 53. Newton offers a balanced picture of Allenby's strengths and weaknesses as a senior commander on the Western Front. On Allenby's artillery plan, see Trevor Harvey, 'Arras, Allenby and Artillery: The Decision for a Four-Day Preliminary Bombardment', *Journal of the Society for Army Historical Research*, vol. 94, no. 380 (winter 2016), 314–35.
[67] Ludendorff, *My War Memories*, 426–7.
[68] Reichsarchiv, *Weltkrieg*, 12:403; AFGG, V/2:66–72.
[69] BOH 1917, 1:171–2 and 485–6.

bite-and-hold operations, but had to cancel them because of the mutinies. As the French effort faded, the British turned their attention to an offensive in Flanders. This forced them to continue using the same divisions at Arras rather than feed in new ones. The current combat value of the British troops there sank, and in the later stages of the battle depleted British formations such as 34th Division faced fresh German ones.[70] Figure 8.3 shows graphically how attritional pressure on the German army plummeted as a result of Entente inability or unwillingness to sustain the offensive.

At the operational level, Nivelle's muddled thinking further endangered success. In his original January agreement with Haig, the offensive was to consist of three stages – strong attacks phased to draw in German reserves, the main, rapid breakthrough and exploitation. His final orders, issued on 4 April, divided the offensive into two stages: a prolonged battle leading to breakthrough, followed by exploitation; there was now no reference to phasing, apparently because he feared the Germans might withdraw.[71] Yet in briefing politicians, Nivelle constantly referred to a very short battle of twenty-four or forty-eight hours duration, followed by exploitation; if he had not achieved decisive success in forty-eight hours at most, he would stop the battle. It has been argued that nobody really believed in victory in forty-eight hours, and that Nivelle spoke in these terms to avoid the government cancelling the offensive or the troops losing their high morale.[72] But the orders issued by GQG were clearly for a rapid breakthrough, as the II Colonial Corps example showed. To quote Lloyd George, 'General Nivelle in December was a cool and competent planner. By April he had become a crazy plunger.'[73]

After the successful opening of the battle of Arras, mistaken judgements and shortcomings in staff work prevented the British army preparing, co-ordinating and phasing operations in the most effective manner.[74] In the French sector, there were also repeated problems of co-ordinating attacks: much of the fighting became piecemeal rather than full-scale and well-integrated operations.[75] German deployment of reserves in depth gave the flexibility to counter any likely British or French thrust, and as we have seen attrition of these forces, though severe, never reached levels which would have endangered the defence.

[70] Ibid., 550.
[71] BOH 1917, 1: appendix 7; AFGG, V/1:457–60; Spears, *Prelude to Victory*, 257.
[72] Rolland, *Nivelle*, 148 and 166–7.
[73] David Lloyd George, *War Memoirs of David Lloyd George* (London: Nicholson & Watson, 1934), 3:1518.
[74] BOH 1917, 1:548–52.   [75] For example, attacks on 8–9 May: AFGG, V/1:764–5.

Two basic factors affecting both operational and tactical levels were the weather and the terrain. Of course bad weather affected both sides, but it apparently caused more problems for the attackers. It prevented British air reconnaissance spotting German reserves moving up to counter-attack the initial success at Arras. It also added to problems of road repair and hence transport; in addition, it contributed to delaying the second phase of operations.[76] In the French sector, the weather badly disrupted Sixth Army's artillery fire because of its effect on air observation. Nivelle delayed the infantry assault three times in an effort to improve the results of the preliminary bombardment, in vain as it turned out.[77]

At Arras, some parts of the terrain favoured the British, some the Germans. British operational choices on where to make their main effort failed to make the most of terrain advantages.[78] In the French sector, the terrain had both advantages and disadvantages for the Germans. The sharp slopes of the ridge positions meant that limited withdrawals were not possible and that local reserves had to be kept closer to the front than desirable. But the numerous large caverns allowed secure accommodation of the reserves. And the broken nature of the ground caused serious problems for the attacker's infantry and artillery, especially in the Chemin des Dames area. Pétain had commented on the extremely difficult terrain during the initial reconnaissance of December 1916, and the French later came to see this as a significant factor in their defeat.[79] As recounted in Chapter 1, there were good strategic reasons for choosing the Aisne and Champagne as the location for the French offensives. But the failure to consider the operational and tactical problems of the terrain was a major error.

At the tactical level, the very ambitious French objectives compounded this error. The French general Marie-Émile Fayolle had accurately described the tactical dilemma of the attack in trench warfare in 1916. Each enemy position required organisation of a new operation with fresh artillery preparation. Attacks should succeed each other as quickly as possible but, as Fayolle explained, 'If you go too quickly, you risk defeat. If you go too slowly, the enemy has time to reconstruct his successive positions. That is the problem and it is extremely difficult.'[80] Nivelle's tactical objectives ignored this hard-won experience, calling for the attackers to break through all the German positions and advance up to fifteen kilometres on the first day. No army on the Western Front had achieved

---

[76] BOH 1917, 1:274, 379–82 and 540; AFGG, V/1:603.
[77] AFGG, V/1:570 and 619–21.   [78] BOH 1917, 1:549–50.
[79] AFGG, V/1:613–14 and V/2:67.
[80] Maréchal Fayolle, *Cahiers Secrets de la Grande Guerre*, ed. Henry Contamine (Paris: Librairie Plon, 1964), 142.

this since trench warfare set in. Nivelle's methods were based on his successful attacks at Verdun in late 1916, but they were on a completely different scale. In October, four divisions had made a maximum advance of two-and-a-half kilometres; and in December, four divisions had advanced, on part of the attack front only, to a maximum depth of three-and-a-half kilometres. These were therefore not good models for a general offensive.[81]

The Verdun successes had relied largely on heavy and accurate artillery preparation. This too proved inadequate in the Nivelle offensive. The number of guns and mortars per metre of front was greater than in earlier battles, but the depth and complexity of the German defences meant that artillery fire per unit of trench was less dense than on the Somme. Some parts of the terrain could not be properly engaged by artillery at all. Even if the infantry had made better progress, failure to produce the planned number of modern guns and tractors would have prevented the artillery moving forward as required to achieve the objectives. The effectiveness of the artillery also suffered from the inexperience of some battery commanders; lack of co-ordination between the aviation and artillery units; and inadequate joint training.[82] Nor could French tanks, which had a difficult debut on 16 April, make up for the deficiencies of the artillery.[83]

The Germans viewed the French army as tactically more experienced and skilled than the British. However, the centralised training programme launched by Pétain as soon as he became commander-in-chief suggests that there were also considerable shortcomings in the French army.[84] Based on experience in the Somme campaign, the British army had made great progress in developing more effective doctrine and the training to go with it. The success on the first days of Arras and Messines showed how far it had come in mounting set-piece attacks. But in the subsequent more open warfare at Arras, poor staff work, inexperience and rigid methods prevented exploitation or even recognition of tactical opportunities.[85]

This litany of British and French difficulties and shortcomings lends an air of inevitability to the Entente defeat, but in fact the picture is more nuanced. On the one hand, concerns about the French part of the

---

[81] AFGG, IV/3, *Bataille de la Somme (fin). Offensives françaises à Verdun (3 septembre–fin décembre 1916)* (Paris: Imprimerie Nationale, 1935), chapters 7 and 8.

[82] 'Rapport sur les conditions dans lesquelles s'est effectuée la préparation d'artillerie pour l'attaque du 16 avril'; AFGG, V/2:76–83, 90 and 92–9.

[83] Tim Gale, *The French Army's Tank Force and Armoured Warfare in the Great War: The Artillerie Spéciale* (Farnham: Ashgate, 2013), chapter 2.

[84] On the training programme, see Greenhalgh, *French Army and the First World War*, 220–5.

[85] BOH 1917, 1:544–52.

offensive in particular were not entirely hindsight. They started with Pétain's reservations of December 1916 and culminated in the stormy meeting between government leaders and the most senior French generals at Compiègne on 6 April. While still Minister of War, Lyautey was said to have likened Nivelle's plan to a comic opera.[86] On the other hand, even after the event it was possible to defend the offensive. Proponents, including Mangin, argued that it could have produced decisive results, and perhaps even an earlier end to the war, if politicians had not prematurely halted it from fear of the growing casualties.[87]

More plausibly, French commanders in the sector where the initial assault made most progress – against Gruppe Sissonne – believed that better handling of reserves would have led to greater success. One later wrote that by 0800 on 16 April his division had advanced three kilometres. The weakness of the German defence was evident throughout the morning, and fresh troops could have made easy progress. The German counter-attack that afternoon recaptured some lost ground but was 'literally destroyed' by massed defensive fire and further progress could then have been made. He reported this up the chain of command, but no reserves arrived and the opportunity was lost.[88]

The course of events on the German side lends credibility to this. The three divisions in the front line in this sector were badly hit, suffering an average of 3,000 casualties. The two counter-attack divisions supporting them were brought to a halt in the afternoon with their missions only partly accomplished. Large elements of the two divisions in OHL reserve further back also became engaged late on 16 April, and even Seventh Army's precious storm battalion was deployed as a back-stop. When yet another division was brought forward the next day (making a total of eight in the sector), Army Group Crown Prince told OHL that this was now the last available reserve behind Seventh Army; no more would arrive till 18 April.[89]

These German deployments were sufficient to hold the French attack in this sector on 17 April and subsequent days, but the Entente were chewing through German reserves at a rapid pace. French intelligence assessed that by the end of April fresh divisions in reserve behind Army Group Rupprecht and Army Group Crown Prince had dropped from about twenty each to six.[90] Statistical analysis suggests that OHL only had available eleven divisions which were in principle fit for major combat but

---

[86] Smith, *Between Mutiny and Obedience*, 180.   [87] Rolland, *Nivelle*, 302–7.

[88] Ibid., 229–30, quoting a letter to Nivelle from General Martin Gadel dated 1 June 1917; Gadel commanded French 9th Infantry Division during the offensive.

[89] Reichsarchiv, *Weltkrieg*, 12:328; 5.BRD, 'Gefechtsbericht'.

[90] GQG Deuxième Bureau memorandum, 'L'usure allemande depuis les attaques franco-anglaises d'avril, mai, juin 1917', 23 June 1917, AFGG, V/2: Annexe 563.

were not in fact deployed to face the Entente offensive.[91] Growing German alarm about reserves is clear from the evidence discussed earlier, such as pressure to drop standards when assessing current combat value and to keep divisions in the line as long as possible; Army Group Crown Prince having to allocate as counter-attack divisions formations that had already been through the battle rather than fresh ones; and OHL's desire to retain control of the few reserves available to cope with expected Entente attacks in different theatres.

Against this background, we can counterfactually imagine a situation in which different French operational and tactical choices would have led to greater success, even if not the longed-for breakthrough. These would have included a more limited attack in the very difficult Chemin des Dames sector, with the aims of seizing or at least blinding German observation points, pushing back the artillery and pinning reserves. The *Schwerpunkt* of the offensive would then have been in the French Fifth Army area, which had excellent ground observation for artillery fire and was good tank country, as the defending Gruppe Sissonne had noted. Also, an attack could be made earlier in this sector, denying the Germans valuable preparation time.[92]

This could profitably have been combined with different command arrangements. The Fifth Army commander, General Olivier Mazel, was criticised by the official board of inquiry for lack of grip preparing and executing the offensive in his sector, and particularly for failure to exercise initiative in deploying reserves to exploit success (corroborating the divisional commander from earlier). In addition, he had no experience preparing an attack, either as a corps or Army commander.[93] A better choice would have been Fayolle, who had commanded French Sixth Army on the Somme, or if a more thrusting general was preferred, Mangin. It might also have made sense to adopt the structure originally considered for the supreme command, with Joffre remaining as commander-in-chief and Nivelle under him as Western Front theatre

---

[91] The eleven were 2nd, 7th, 24th, 28th, 40th, 192nd, 204th and 4th Bavarian Infantry Divisions; 12th, 23rd and 25th Reserve Divisions. The reserve situation would ease in June once the divisions being transferred from the east had arrived and received at least the minimum training needed for the more exacting Western Front (see Chapter 1).

[92] Earlier attack in Fifth Army sector: Spears, *Prelude to Victory*, 120–1. After the war, Micheler suggested a different alternative plan, to limit the attack to taking the German first position on a front of thirty to forty kilometres. He thought this would have brought 'a magnificent success' for minimal casualties, with at least 30,000–40,000 prisoners, 700–800 guns captured or destroyed and a huge moral effect on France and its army, its allies and the enemy: Herbillon, *Micheler*, 174.

[93] Brugère Report, 27.

commander. Joffre would have supplied the moral authority and experience, Nivelle the dash and imagination.[94]

All these choices were within French control and therefore realistic possibilities. We could also take the counterfactual further into the hypothetical. First is the British contribution. If the French had made better progress with the main offensive, they might have persuaded the British – still under their command – to concentrate on Arras rather than switch to Flanders. Haig could then have deployed fresh divisions to maintain the offensive. He might usefully have inserted a new command team of General Sir Herbert Plumer and his chief of staff Major-General Charles Harington, who inflicted three severe local defeats on the German army in the autumn. With or without them, the British army did now understand how to co-ordinate attacks properly as 9 April itself proved. Had it got its act together after the opening phase, the Arras offensive might have fulfilled its operational role of attracting German reserves from the French sector.

Most speculative is what might have happened if the Russians had synchronised their offensive with the western allies as planned. Figure 8.6 tests Ludendorff's comments on the ensuing crisis by adding the actual German total wastage from the Kerensky offensive and

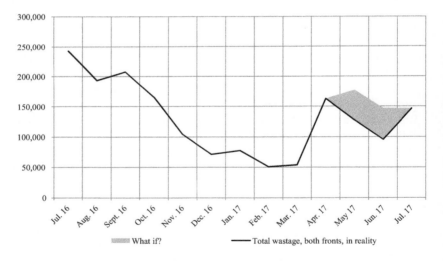

Figure 8.6 Total wastage if the Kerensky offensive had taken place in May–June 1917

[94] Spears, *Prelude to Victory*, 29.

subsequent counter-offensive to the wastage from the Entente spring offensive; it assumes that the Russians attacked in May, as originally promised, rather than April, as Ludendorff feared. In effect if Entente grand strategy had worked as intended, for three or more months German total wastage would have equalled that caused by the Somme. Adding to the crisis, and not shown on the chart, would have been the Italian offensive in May, which drew in Austro-Hungarian reserves from the Eastern Front; and also higher expenditure of ammunition, already problematic as Ludendorff pointed out.

Given the colossal strain thrown on the German army by the Entente spring offensive with all its faults, a better-executed and longer Anglo-French attack alone could well have produced a serious defeat, especially because of the limited German reserves available. As we saw, the Germans sent six divisions from the Western Front to face the Kerensky offensive, all they could initially afford without making withdrawals in the west. These divisions had suffered heavy casualties in the Nivelle offensive and were only despatched east in late June and early July, once the western fighting had died down. So if the British and French had continued launching heavy attacks, would the Germans have been able to send them? And if they had not, what would have happened when the Russians launched the Kerensky offensive, either counterfactually in May–June or actually in July? Of course, we cannot know the answer, but as Ludendorff said, the German army would indeed have faced a general crisis.

Conclusions

> Strategic victory in a battle of attrition was undoubtedly a chimera – hoped for, planned for, even on occasion apparently imminent, but unrealisable.[95]

In April–May 1917, the German army fulfilled its fifth command task with a clear victory, in both preventing an Entente breakthrough and inflicting more casualties than it suffered. But the losses it did sustain were heavy, and for the first time the strength of the field army began to fall. Much of the army had too low an intrinsic combat value to participate in major battle, so the attrition of those divisions that *could* participate was serious. The assessments of current combat value, despite the difficulties in making them, undoubtedly contributed to the army's ability to survive this attrition. But its victory was only partly the result of its own performance. Problems on the Entente side at the different

---

[95] Philpott, *Bloody Victory*, 383.

levels of war were at least as important a factor: foremost were grand strategic failure to synchronise offensives in different theatres, the loss of surprise and unwillingness or inability to maintain the joint Anglo-French assaults.

The huge gap between the Entente's aspirations and the outcome may suggest that the offensive was always doomed to defeat. The quote heading this section, remarks such as Lyautey's as well as the catalogue of Entente problems and shortcomings strengthen this impression. But the scale of OHL's preparations show that the German army took the offensive seriously, especially the French assault. Max von Boehn, fighting his first battle as an Army commander, wrote: 'I cannot deny that I took up my new post with some concerns. The impending battle was seen by everyone at the time as the deciding event of the war. And the size of my task also alarmed me.'[96] At least one formation, 19th Reserve Division on the Chemin des Dames, reconnoitred artillery positions to the rear in case it had to retreat. Even in June, after the defeat of the offensive and during the French mutinies, Army Group Crown Prince ordered construction of the *Hunding/Brunhild* position behind its front as a precaution.[97]

Further evidence comes from the focus in the important divisional command courses on defeating the new French operational and tactical methods. Lectures to the courses demonstrate considerable respect for these methods, which paralleled German thinking throughout the war on how to carry out an offensive.[98] The severe and lasting damage suffered by the German army also shows that its defeat of the offensive was no walkover. Apart from the heavy casualties, over four-fifths of divisions which could meet the demands of major battle were committed. At the start of the offensive, German commanders were horrified that divisions were being consumed at a faster rate than on the Somme.[99] As we have seen, by its end, almost as many German divisions had been used up as British and French. Of equal worry to OHL was the huge expenditure of ammunition, which for lengthy periods considerably outstripped production. This extraordinarily high consumption of troops and ammunition could only be maintained for a short period.[100] When the Kaiser visited the Western Front in late May,

---

[96] Boehn, 'Kriegserlebnisse', 5.

[97] GQG Deuxième Bureau memorandum, 'Renseignements sur les attaques tirés des interrogatoires des prisonniers', 13 May 1917, AFGG, V/2: Annexe 193; Reichsarchiv, *Weltkrieg*, 12:553.

[98] See Boff, *Haig's Enemy*, 94 for a 1916 example of German offensive thinking.

[99] Rupprecht, *Kriegstagebuch*, 2:138 (10 April 1917).

[100] Reichsarchiv, *Weltkrieg*, 12:408–9 and 564–5.

top-level commanders expressed confidence in the situation but believed Germany must end the war as it could not hold out much longer.[101]

Summing up, although the German army successfully fulfilled the fifth command task in early 1917, this was only partly due to its own efforts; in addition, the cost of its defensive victory caused a considerable decline in its fighting power. As the counterfactual shows, better Entente decision-making would probably have inflicted a serious defeat on the German army, and possibly even have brought about a general crisis.

[101] Lyncker to his wife, 24 May 1917, in Afflerbach, *Kaiser Wilhelm II. als Oberster Kriegsherr*, 498.

Conclusion

He who has not fought the Germans does not know war.[1]

The Entente spring offensive was a severe test of the German army's command system. So far from seeing the result as a foregone conclusion, before the event OHL and senior commanders such as Max von Boehn believed it would be the decisive moment of the war. These were the first major defensive battles fought entirely under the Hindenburg/Ludendorff Third OHL, with the new command arrangements it had introduced and the new tactical doctrine it had codified. For the first time, two army groups were required to conduct the defence – an indication of the offensive's scale. Although the main operations lasted for a relatively short period, preparations beforehand and follow-up actions afterwards extended their duration to five or six months. In terms of both operations and attrition, the German army won a convincing victory, but at the cost of incurring serious and lasting damage.

The Entente spring offensive therefore makes a good case study of German operational command on the Western Front. The book has derived five main tasks as a conceptual framework for analysing command, and this raises two obvious questions: have the tasks been correctly identified, and are the findings for early 1917 valid more broadly? In deriving the tasks, the book starts from contemporary German thinking on command as well as modern works such as Anthony King's study. It takes into account the current state of research on the Entente spring offensive and on the German army as an institution. It pays particular attention to German commanders' and staff officers' views of the problems they faced and how to tackle them. Added backing is provided by systematically comparing pre-war thinking on these issues and developments in the early war period with events in 1917; and by distinguishing the German army's doctrine and reputation from what actually

[1] Cited as a British military aphorism in Russell F. Weigley, *Eisenhower's Lieutenants: The Campaign of France and Germany 1944–1945* (London: Sidgwick & Jackson, 1981), un-numbered title page.

happened. The command tasks are therefore solidly founded, which is not to say uncontroversial. But even scholars disputing them will hopefully find the supporting evidence in the book useful to their own research.

This last chapter summarises the findings on the five tasks and then addresses the validity issue. Here, it is worth pointing out that one advantage of the command task framework is to allow full exploration of the complexity of modern battle in the First World War. There were often no right and wrong solutions, there was simply an 'option of difficulties' as the British General Wolfe put it in 1759.[2] The question of withdrawal is an example, as Chapters 7 and 8 showed. What should have been purely tactical or at most operational decisions also involved strategic and even grand strategic issues of attrition, military and national morale, propaganda and international standing. The relationship between these issues illustrates Gerhard P. Groß's point that the levels of war are interdependent.[3] The resulting complexity was further increased by the dynamic equilibrium arising from the opposing armies' constant striving for tactical, technological and organisational advantage. This complexity of Western Front decision-making is the reason why older accounts by writers such as Trevor N. Dupuy, G. C. Wynne or Martin Samuels and even modern ones such as King's do not provide a sufficient explanation of German command and need supplementing.

***

The first command task, co-ordinating a mass army, involved striking a balance between decentralisation and control of the forces concentrated for a major defensive battle. Many commentators have seen decentralisation, in the form of mission command, and its implementation through the partnership between commanders and their chief general staff officers as perhaps the most distinctive German principles of command. But in 1917, though mission command could still be employed in low-level tactics, its use from division upwards was limited and infringements of the principle were common. Furthermore, the first phase of Arras and the battle of Messines demonstrated that granting formations freedom of action was risky. On the Western Front therefore, conditions compelled the German army to move the balance away from decentralisation towards control. One consequence was the greater authority acquired by the general staff, distorting the traditional relationship between commanders and their chief staff officers. Nevertheless, commanders remained important and the army continued to place value in creating

---

[2] Boff, *Winning and Losing*, 248–9 is illuminating on the 'almost infinite number of different problems' the British army faced during the 1918 Hundred Days campaign.
[3] Groß, *Mythos und Wirklichkeit*, 17.

effective command teams. At divisional level, it was reasonably successful in terms of these teams' duration; it had less success in achieving the best balance between arms of service, with negative consequences for the conduct of combined arms battle.

Not surprisingly given Western Front conditions, principles relating to control, especially establishing a *Schwerpunkt* and maintaining the chain of command, were essential for the concentration of forces needed to fight a major defensive battle. However, the organisation through which these principles were implemented changed radically. Commentators such as Wynne, Samuels and Timothy T. Lupfer misunderstand these changes: they wrongly downplay the role of higher-level formations, in particular corps/*Gruppen*, and consequently exaggerate the greater independence accorded to divisions by the new tactical doctrine. Overall, in spring 1917 the German army carried out the first command task successfully in the French sector, preparing a strong defence that defeated the attempt to break through from the start. Performance against the British was patchier, partly because Army Group Rupprecht struck the wrong balance between decentralisation and control of its Armies: this was one cause of serious defeats on 9 April and at Messines.

It is often assumed that in a war of masses and matériel, individuals and personality played little part. This was certainly not true of the German army. Personal relationships and personal motivations affected all aspects of command, including implementation of mission command, how well command teams worked together and the actual authority exercised by a formation. Networks and informal contacts had a major influence on the exchange of information and decision-making. Personal contact was crucial to accurate assessment of a formation's current combat value, and personal career motives were one reason why such assessments were not always accurate. Even if physically distant a commander could still exert his personality by telephone, contributing to its role as the principal means of communication. In other words, human realities of personality and personal relationships played a much greater role in the exercise of command than Michael Geyer's thesis on the Third OHL's cult of mechanisation and efficiency would allow.

The German army well understood the influence of personality and made determined efforts to meet its second command task, selecting the right men for the job. It operated the seniority tempered by merit principle for appointing and promoting officers, based on a carefully structured though flawed confidential reporting system. During the war, it strove continuously if not always successfully to select good and weed out unsuitable commanders and general staff officers. There were, however, limits on its ability to post officers freely, especially because of the conservatism of and constraints on the Military Cabinet. Operating a completely objective system was impossible and the suggestion – perhaps derived from modern *Bundeswehr* practice – that function automatically overrode rank is therefore wide of the mark.[4] There was always the possibility of friction in such cases, exemplifying the effect of personal factors such as reputation, honour, ambition, pay and strain. Personal relationships, sometimes developing into cliques, interacted with objective professional considerations and influenced the conduct of operations as well as the subsequent historiography.

The German army traditionally viewed war as the realm of constant uncertainty that both offered opportunities and created problems. Reducing it to an acceptable level where it could be exploited was the third command task. Various means were available to meet this task such as achieving superiority by establishing a *Schwerpunkt* and taking the initiative, thus passing the burden of uncertainty to the enemy. But at the start of 1917, though manpower in the field was still rising, the German army stood on the defensive and was inferior to its enemies in both numbers and matériel. Intelligence on enemy plans became critical to optimum deployment of scarce resources; so too was the ability to understand the situation of German forces and control them through effective communication.

German intelligence has a poor reputation as illustrated by Citino's damning claim that it was 'among the worst in European military history'. Intelligence performance in early 1917, though mixed, was certainly better than this suggests. True, at the grand strategic level, despite much effort German intelligence failed to produce reporting of value on economic and political issues. But good intelligence on French intentions enabled timely concentration of forces and thus played a central role in the resulting strategic victory against the main effort of the Entente offensive. Other results were not so good: uncertainty about British plans was a major factor in delaying defensive preparations, leading to the severe defeat at the start of the battle of Arras. And faulty assessment of the British mining threat at Messines was an important cause of German failure to make a pre-emptive withdrawal there.

Communication was central to German command methods, and the army had evolved a mixture of organisational, personal and technical means to handle it. Though personal contact remained essential, 1917 conditions led to ever-greater reliance on technical communications and these were continually developed. At the higher level of command between OHL and division, the communications system worked

---

[4] *Bundeswehr*: Millotat, *Generalstabssystem*, 45 and 114.

effectively during the spring fighting. Between division and the front line it was more problematic but generally functioned at least adequately: a significant contributory factor here was the slow tempo achieved by the Entente attackers. However, the unstoppable growth of bureaucracy was a danger signal that the urge to reduce uncertainty had got out of hand. The linked problem of distorted reporting, which often related to over-optimistic assessments of formations' combat value, actually increased uncertainty.

In overall terms, the German army completed the third command task at least adequately by means of intelligence and communication. The mix of positive and negative performance demonstrates the close links between the first three command tasks. Better intelligence at Arras and Messines would have strengthened Army Group Rupprecht's ability to impose its authority on its Armies; personality and personal ability affected both the extent to which mission command could be implemented and the way in which superior officers communicated with their subordinates; and as a final example, good technical communications were both cause and effect of the limited application of mission command.

The geographical stagnation of the Western Front conceals the continuous changes introduced by the opposing armies, and learning was therefore the fourth German command task. The army had a networked approach to learning, connecting formal and informal, individual and organisational and bottom-up as well as top-down approaches. Informal and semi-formal transmission was commonplace, and individuals, including civilians, played an important role. As in peacetime, the spring 1917 fighting produced evidence for and against institutionalised innovation in the German army. The establishment of an effective lessons learned-doctrine-training-performance-lessons learned cycle and willingness to circulate dissenting opinions speak well of the army as a thinking organisation and even its intellectual openness. But in spring 1917, OHL exerted a tighter grip on this process, limiting the circulation of after-action reports and making doctrine more binding. Increasing pressure to conform and the 'can-do' mentality also strengthened the move away from open debate.

The main concern of the learning process was combined arms battle, key to tactical success and an area in which the German army had fallen behind its enemies. Following vigorous steps by the Third OHL to make improvements, performance was certainly good enough to defeat the Anglo-French assault. But important aspects of tactics remained problematic throughout this period, including withdrawals, handling of reserves and counterattacks, and reliable infantry-artillery co-operation.

These problems echo pre-war issues such as the preponderance of infantry thinking at the expense of combined arms co-operation, suggesting that they were too deep-seated to be easily removed. The combination of performance improved through learning and persisting weaknesses supports the argument that the army clung to old methods, but would accept new ones if they seemed necessary and effective. This ambivalence, together with the constant dialectic between localised initiative and centralised uniformity, explains why fulfilment of the fourth command task was patchy.

The final and overarching command task was winning the battle. In April–May 1917, the German army fulfilled this task with a clear victory, in both preventing an Entente breakthrough and inflicting more casualties than it suffered. But even though the balance of attrition was in its favour, its losses were heavy. Given that over four-fifths of divisions which could meet the demands of major battle were committed, this attrition was especially serious. Two factors helped the German army survive. First, the relatively new system of assessing current combat value undoubtedly helped it get the most out of divisions without letting them become 'burned to cinders' as the expression was. Second, problems on the Entente side at the different levels of war prevented the infliction of maximum attrition on the German army. The loss of surprise was a big factor in the Entente defeat. Even more important were the linked issues of grand strategic failure to synchronise offensives in different theatres and strategic unwillingness or inability to maintain the joint Anglo-French assaults. Better Entente decision-making would probably have caused a serious German defeat and possibly even a major crisis.

Various general points can be made about the German army's command tasks in spring 1917. First, they were not new; however, their implementation had been extensively moulded by developments in warfare since 1914, such as major changes to organisation. Next, they should not be seen in isolation from each other. They interacted to a greater or lesser extent, perhaps the second (selecting the right men) most of all. These linkages both reflected and increased the complexity of the war discussed earlier. Third, the German army's performance of all the tasks was mixed – certainly not disastrous, but not perfect either. This mundane but important point is discussed further later.

***

How far is this analysis of the German army's command tasks applicable beyond the Western Front in early 1917? The answer is more obvious in the case of some tasks than others. For instance, certain problems relating to the second task, selecting the right men, continued throughout the war as shown clearly by issues about seniority. Hindenburg was chosen to command Eighth Army in August 1914 with Ludendorff as his chief of staff because as a *Generalmajor* Ludendorff would lack authority over senior corps commanders like *General der Infanterie* Hermann von François.[5] In February 1915, *Generalleutnant* Gustav Freiherr von Hollen, commanding 3rd Infantry Division, claimed that serving under an officer junior in rank was incompatible with his honour. He gave in, but later that year Maximilian von Höhn, then Third Army chief of staff, refused to serve under Konstantin Schmidt von Knobelsdorf, who was junior to him.[6] Seniority lay behind the serious friction between Army commanders Max von Gallwitz and Fritz von Below on the Somme in July 1916: indeed, this was one of the reasons for establishing independent army groups. In July 1918, as the *Reich* was entering its death throes, François resigned rather than serve under a less senior commander.[7] The book's finding that function did not simply override rank therefore applies throughout the war.

Part of the answer to how far we can generalise from the findings here depends on whether trench warfare was an aberration which only arose because of conditions specific to the time and place; OHL certainly hoped this was the case. In the important document of November 1916 acknowledging the problems of modern battle and faster Anglo-French learning about it, OHL suggested that 'the correct image' of warfare was seeking a decision through large-scale, mobile and offensive operations: this was 'our military ideal of the future' to which the German army must return when possible.[8] The implication was that anything which departed from the ideal, such as trench warfare, was an incorrect image. To paraphrase one modern British general, such labels are a euphemism to avoid acknowledging that your enemy is not playing to your strengths and you are not winning.[9]

As head of the post-war German army [*Reichsheer*], Hans von Seeckt thought that what had caused trench warfare was the phenomenon of the mass army. His solution was a smaller, more professional and mobile army able to beat numerically superior enemies.[10] His analysis implied that mass armies inevitably produced situations like the Western Front. This question was clearly a preoccupation of the *Reichsheer*: Walther

---

[5] Epkenhans, *Nicolai*, 112.
[6] Gallwitz, *Meine Führertätigkeit*, 209; Foley, *German Strategy*, 176.
[7] Kuhl, 'Kriegstagebuch', 2 August 1918, quoting a letter from François.
[8] OHL circular, 'Kriegführung und Generalstab'.
[9] Rupert Smith, *The Utility of Force: The Art of War in the Modern World* (London: Penguin Books, 2006), 4. He was writing about the phrase 'asymmetric warfare'.
[10] Citino, *German Way of War*, 242–3; Strohn, *Defence of the Reich*, 95–6.

Reinhardt, chief of staff to Seventh Army in 1917–18 and Seeckt's predecessor as head of the *Reichsheer*, was by no means alone in believing that future war would be a war of masses and would inevitably lead to trench warfare. Right up to spring 1940, many senior German officers believed that a campaign against the French might well bog down early; at best it would be protracted, with extremely heavy casualties, and it could turn into trench warfare. Even the priorities of Hitler's greatly expanded ammunition programme of late 1939 reflected these expectations.[11] Summing up, 1917-style trench warfare might not be ideal but nor was it an aberration.

Looking at this question another way, were there different command tasks in offensive and defensive warfare, or at least were they implemented differently? There could, for instance, have been greater scope for mission command in fluid situations during the mobile phases in the west or on the Eastern Front where force/space ratios were more favourable to manoeuvre. Indeed, Samuels suggests that extensive decentralisation of command was one of the main reasons for German success on 21 March 1918.[12] He may well be right, especially as he is discussing actions below divisional level where, as Chapter 2 explained, there was scope for mission command in 1917 too. But, again as in 1917, performance was uneven. Schulenburg, chief of staff to Army Group Crown Prince, recorded that many front-line commanders waited for hours having reached their objectives in spring 1918, because they did not know what to do next. An after-action report at the same period from 79th Reserve Division referred frankly to its infantry advancing in thick masses, waiting for artillery to deal with British machine guns that had brought them to a halt, and failing to use their own initiative to solve the problem.[13] This is particularly striking as the division was one of the formations specially equipped and trained for the assault.

Christian Stachelbeck's analysis of 11th Bavarian Infantry Division in June 1918 shows that higher levels of command limited the division's freedom of action; the division controlled its own units by a mixture of strict regulation and a measure of independence. In the June offensive, after initial success its progress was slowed and eventually halted by imperfect all-arms co-operation coupled with ammunition supply and

---

[11] Groß, *Mythos und Wirklichkeit*, 150–1; Karl-Heinz Frieser, *The Blitzkrieg Legend: The 1940 Campaign in the West*, trans. John T. Greenwood (Annapolis, MD: Naval Institute Press, 2005), 9–10, 19 and 33–4; Adam Tooze, *The Wages of Destruction: The Making and Breaking of the Nazi Economy* (London: Penguin Books, 2007), 328–9 and 340–1. I am grateful to Dr Daniel Whittingham for the Tooze reference.

[12] Samuels, *Command or Control?*, 266–7.

[13] Schulenburg, 'Erlebnisse', 184; 79. RD after-action report, [no ref], 12 April 1918, BArch, Geyer Nachlass, RH61/924, ff. 183–5.

communications problems.[14] There are similarities and dissimilarities with early 1917 here. Faulty implementation of combined arms battle was common to both; in 1917, OHL's concerns about ammunition production and supply inhibited major offensive but not defensive actions; and in a situation where the enemy's attacks only attained limited tempo, communications had been at least adequate.

Finally, Jonathan Boff's research on the German defence in the final campaign of the war shows the recurrence of problems from 1917, including excessive intervention from above, resistance to conducting mobile defence, unwillingness to withdraw, premature and badly supported counter-attacks, and difficulty inculcating uniform tactical doctrine. By that stage, sackings and other pressure were discouraging realistic debate and hindering the free flow of information. Boff concludes that the rigidity of the German command system played a major role in the army's ultimate defeat.[15]

The question whether the command tasks also apply to the British and French armies goes beyond the scope of this book and cannot be treated fully here. Both armies faced the same problems as the Germans on the Western Front, not least because of its dynamic equilibrium, and some of their solutions were similar. Approaching the first command task, co-ordinating a mass army, General Ferdinand Foch had argued since before the Somme that the balance of command must move away from decentralisation towards control; this became the basis of what was known as the 'methodical battle' [bataille conduite]. As Chapter 3 recorded, the British and French armies both changed the composition of corps in similar ways to the Germans and for the same reasons. Denis Rolland has described the problems faced by the French army in fulfilling the second task, selecting the right men, as well as the friendships and enmities between senior officers and the serious consequences of personality clashes. He also records French complaints about the growing burden of bureaucracy.[16] On the fourth command task, learning, the French army, like the Germans, circulated dissenting opinions; Aimée Fox's research demonstrates the importance and difficulty of learning in the British army, and as we saw earlier, there were many similarities between the British and German approaches.[17]

What all this shows is that the command tasks remained the same in different situations, as did many or most of the factors which affected their

---

[14] Stachelbeck, *Militärische Effektivität*, 155–61.
[15] Boff, *Winning and Losing*, chapters 6 and 8 and 246–7.
[16] Rolland, *Nivelle*, especially 10–12, 92–7 and 120–5.
[17] I am grateful to Dr Tim Gale for the information on Foch and on French circulation of dissenting opinions.

implementation. But the interplay between the tasks and how things turned out of course varied. Adapting the fifth command task, winning, to the German spring 1918 offensives, for example, the sub-task to prevent an Entente breakthrough translates directly into the requirement to break through. The other part of the task, inflicting more casualties than suffered, remained relevant too: indeed the heavy German casualties in these offensives were a major factor in the army's final defeat.[18]

***

The findings from this case study of the fighting in spring 1917 are therefore more broadly applicable to German command in the First World War. The army that emerges is not the picture of military excellence which Citino suggests is such a firmly rooted notion in modern history. But nor is it a gang that couldn't shoot straight, an army stultified by its rigidity and shortcomings. Analysing its command tasks and how well it fulfilled them produces a more rounded and indeed more humanly recognisable picture of German command and of the army as an institution, warts and all. This in turn helps understand better its contribution to Germany's ability to hold out for over four years. In early 1917, the army was a tiring giant, flawed, battered and under increasing strain, but still able to think, innovate and operate effectively. It remained a formidable opponent to the Entente, too formidable indeed for them to defeat despite their numerical and material superiority.

The German army's victory in spring 1917 did not depend on any genius for war, but on competently carrying out its command tasks. Performance of the tasks was patchy and even victory came at a great price. The army did not need to be perfect, though, or even good, it just had to be better than the enemy, including carrying out its command tasks better. And this it did – it held out.

---

[18] David Stevenson, *With Our Backs to the Wall*, 281–3.

Bibliography

Note: the ranks and posts stated in entries for personal files and *Nachlässe* are those held in April 1917.

Primary Material

A. Unpublished

(i) Official Documents

Bayerisches Hauptstaatsarchiv/Abteilung IV Kriegsarchiv, Munich (KAM)

AOK 6 Bd. 369	'Chef Besprechungen'
AOK 6 Bd. 409	'Abwehrschlacht', September 1916–August 1917
AOK 6 Bd. 419	'Erfahrungen', May 1915–December 1917
HKR alte Nr. 98	'Lehrgänge 1917/18'
HKR alte Nr. 150	'Einsatz und Verluste von eigenen Divisionen 1917–1918; Kampfwert der O.H.L. und Heeresgruppen-Reserven', August 1916–December 1917
HKR neue Nr. 31	'Verschiedenes, Schlachtenbezeichnungen, Geschäftsordnung 1916/1918'
HKR neue Nr. 113	'Verpflegung- und Gefechtsstärke, Verluste 1915/1918'
HKR neue Nr. 378	'HGr IIa Persönlich (Qual.Berichte u.s.w.), September.16–Jan.18'
HKR neue Nr. 382	'Qualifikationsberichte über Offiziere', December 1916–September 1918
ID (WK) 4388	10. bayerische Infanterie-Division, 'Nachrichtendienst – Verschiedenes', 1915–1918
Kriegsministerium 2211	'Stellenbesetzung im Kriege 1914/1918 Bund 31', April 1917
OP 54	General der Artillerie Maximilian Ritter von Höhn, commander XV. bayerisches Reserve-Korps (Gruppe Sissonne), personal file

OP 18705	Major Rudolf Ritter von Xylander, Ia 6. Armee, personal file
XV.BRK 11	'Kriegstagebuch', 28 February–18 April 1917
XV.BRK 89	'Anlage 4 zum Kriegstagebuch: Doppelschlacht an der Aisne', April 1917
XV.BRK 171	'Einsatz an der Aisne: Befehle an Divisionen, grundsätzliche Verfügungen, Berichte an Armee-Oberkommando, Mitteilungen an Nachbargruppen', March–April 1917
XV.BRK 174	'Nachrichten', March–April 1917
XV.BRK 184	'Verfügungen und Berichte', 1917–1918
XV.BRK 185	'Überzählige Verfügungen', 1917–1918

Bundesarchiv/Militärarchiv, Freiburg im Breisgau (BArch)

PH1/3	'Akten des königlichen Militär-Kabinetts Abteilung I betreffend Mobilmachung 1914. 1. Allgemeines. Band 1a von August 1914 bis Dezember 1914'
PH1/9	'Akten des königlichen Militär-Kabinetts Abteilung I betreffend Mobilmachung 1914. 1. Allgemeines. Band 6 von Juli 1916 bis Dezember 1916'
PH1/10	'Akten des königlichen Militär-Kabinetts Abteilung I betreffend Mobilmachung 1914. 1. Allgemeines. Band 7 von Januar 1917 bis September 1917'
PH2/500	'Stärkenachweisungen für Dienststellen und Formationen im Zusammenhang mit Aufstellungen, Umformierungen und Auflösungen', July 1915–September 1918
PH3/4	'Verzeichnis der Fernsprechteilnehmer im Grossen Hauptquartier. Stand Mai 1917'
PH3/25	'Kriegführung und Generalstab: Ausbildung von Generalstabsoffizieren und Organisation der Zusammenarbeit der höheren Stäbe mit der Truppe', October 1916–July 1917
PH3/28	'Herstellung einer neuen Ausbildungsvorschrift für die Infanterie (A.V.I.)', November 1916
PH3/310	'Organisation und Tätigkeit des Stellvertretenden Generalstabes der Armee', 1914–1919
PH3/502	'Schwerste Artillerie, Bd. 9:1917–Jan. 1918'
PH3/602	'Allgemeiner Schriftverkehr (Postüberwachung, Personalien und Aufklärungsmeldungen) zwischen dem Nachrichtenoffizier beim AOK 5, der Abt. IIIb und anderen Abteilungen im Nachrichtendienst', 1914–1916
PH3/1901	'Gesichtspunkte für den Stellungskrieg', October 1915
PH5-II/370	AOK 3, 'Armeebefehle. Bd. 4', January 1917

PH30- I/124	'Die Bankabteilung des General-Gouvernements in Belgien', 1914–1916
R43/2466i	'Die Kriegsakten des Vertreters der Reichskanzlei im Großen Hauptquartier. Allgemeine Militär- und Marineberichte aus dem Großen Hauptquartier. Bd. 4: Febr.–Juni 1917'
RH61/737	'Die Verwendung der Fliegerverbände in der Arras-Schlacht Frühjahr 1917'. Preparatory papers for *Weltkrieg*, 12 by the Kriegswissenschaftliche Abteilung der Luftwaffe
RH61/893	'Generalmajor a.D. van den Berghs Stellungnahme für das Reichsarchiv als ehemaliger Mobilmachungsreferent im preußischen Kriegsministerium'
RH61/ 1011	'Organisation und Gang der Ausbildung der Offiziere und Mannschaften des deutschen Heeres während des Krieges von 1914 bis 1918'
RH61/ 1091	'Schlachten und Gefechte des Großen Krieges 1914–1918. Nachträge'
RH61/ 1645	'Theobald von Schäfer, "Die Entwicklung der Gesamtlage an der deutschen Front vom Herbst 1916–Frühjahr 1917". Drafts for *Weltkrieg*, 11
RH61/ 1655	'Die Entwicklung der Stimmung im Heere im Winter 1916/17'
RH61/ 1886	'Die Schlacht bei Arras. Korrespondenz, Bd. 1', 1938–1939
RH61/ 1890	'Die Schlacht bei Arras vom 1.2.-Ende Mai 1917. Aktenauszüge, Bd. 2'
RH61/ 1891	'Die Aisne-Champagne-Schlacht einschließlich der Vorbereitungskämpfe von Febr.-Ende Mai 1917'. Preparatory papers for *Weltkrieg*, 12 by Werner von Stünzner
RH61/ 1901	'Die Aisne-Champagne-Schlacht 1917. Korrespondenz', 1938–1939
RM5/273	'Organisation, Zuständigkeit und Personal des Admiralstabs, Bd. 3', 1900–1907
RM120/ 66	Marinekorps Flandern, 'Feindbeobachtung, Bd. 1', July 1916–April 1917

Generallandesarchiv Karlsruhe, 456 military series (GLAK)

E/8877	Hauptmann Rudolf Pattenhausen, general staff officer X. Reserve-Korps, personal file
E/9729	Generalmajor z.D. Justus Roeder, commander 30. Reserve-Infanterie-Brigade, personal file
F1/171	AOK 7, 'Kriegstagebuch A.O.K. 7, 5. Buch', 16 July 1916–17 May 1917
F1/246	AOK 7, 'Operationsakten', 16 February–30 April 1917
F1/249	AOK 7, 'Operationsakten', 23 April–10 May 1917

F1/250	AOK 7, 'Operationsakten', 25 March–13 April 1917
F1/251	AOK 7, 'Operationsakten', 11–22 April 1917
F1/257	AOK 7, 'Operationsakten', 1 May–7 June 1917
F1/334	AOK 7, 'Tagesmeldungen vom 30.V.17–4.VII.17'
F1/335	AOK 7, 'Tagesmeldungen vom 14.IV.17–29.V.17'
F1/336	AOK 7, 'Tagesmeldungen vom 6.III.17–13.IV.17'
F1/374	AOK 7, 'Grundlegende Befehle der O.H.L. und des A.O.K. von dauernder Bedeutung, Vorschriften über Organisation und Ausbildung, Band III, 2', 1 December 1916–30 April 1917
F1/430	AOK 7, 'Untersuchung des negativen Verhaltens der 15. Infanterie-Division während der Somme-Schlacht', 10 October 1916–25 March 1917
F1/431	AOK 7, 'Verhalten der 15. Infanterie-Division an der Somme', 10 October 1916–16 March 1917
F1/432	AOK 7, 'Berichte mit Stellungnahmen zum Verhalten verschiedener Einheiten während der Somme-Schlacht (mit Inhaltsverzeichnis)', 21 September 1916–22 February 1917
F1/523	AOK 7, 'Erfahrungen verschiedener Einheiten der 7. Armee aus der Doppelschlacht an der Aisne und in der Champagne 6.4.-27.5.1917', 25 April–1 July 1917
F1/525	AOK 1, 'Erfahrungen der 1. Armee in der Sommeschlacht 1916, I: Taktischer Teil'
F1/536	AOK 7, 'Sammlung beachtenswerter Erfahrungen der 7. Armee und anderer Einheiten', June 1917–November 1918
F1/547	AOK 7, 'Verhalten der 16. Infanterie-Division an der Somme (Bericht und Schriftwechsel der Heeresgruppe Kronprinz von Bayern mit dem A.O.K. 7)', October–November 1916
F1/639	AOK 7, 'Verlustlisten', 2 October 1916–23 December 1917
F3/650	Armee-Abteilung B, 'Sammlung von Vorgängen über die feindlichen Kräfteverteilungen, Kriegsgliederungen und Uniformen sowie nachrichtendienstliche Erhebungen', December 1914–October 1918
F6/72	XIV. Armee-Korps, 'Allgemeine Verfügungen und Personalangelegenheiten', September 1915–October 1918
F108/188	Armee-Nachrichtenkommandeur 7, 'Tagesmeldungen', May–December 1917

Hauptstaatsarchiv Dresden (HSAD)

11250–056	Sächsischer Militärbevollmächtigter im Großen Hauptquartier, 'Berichte', January–March 1917
11355–0268	AOK 3, 'Beurteilungen der Divisionskommandeure, Generalstabsoffiziere und Artilleriekommandeure', 15 May 1917–29 August 1918

Hauptstaatsarchiv Stuttgart (HSAS)

M1/4 Bü 1543	Württemberg Kriegsministerium Abteilung für die allgemeine Armee- und für persönliche Angelegenheiten, 'Nachrichtenoffizier', June 1916–September 1919
M1/6 Bü 1116	Württemberg Kriegsministerium Verwaltungsabteilung, 'Kriegsbesoldung, Kriegsbesoldungsvorschrift, Gebührnisnachweisungen, Kriegsjahres- und Mobilmachungsetat, Kriegsbeihilfen für Nicht-Heeresbeamte im Allgemeinen', January 1917–May 1918
M30/1 Bü 334	Heeresgruppe Albrecht Abteilung II, 'Beurteilungen, Beschwerden, Versetzungen und Nachweisungen von Offizieren', March–November 1917
M33/2 Bü 423	XIII. Armee-Korps, 'Generalstabsdienst', 31 December 1915–22 December 1917
M33/2 Bü 536	XIII. Armee-Korps, 'Feindliche Kriegsgliederungen und Gruppierungen', 24 May 1916–12 January 1918
M34 Bü 7	Generalkommando 64, 'Geheime Befehle und Verfügungen, Berichte betr. u. a. Formationsänderungen, Kartenwesen, Gefechtsführung', 19 February 1917–24 April 1918
M430/2 Bü 2044	Hauptmann Kurt Spemann, Ia 5. Infanterie-Division, personal file
M635/2 Bü 111	'Die Stimmung im französischen Heere und Volk', 30 June 1917
M635/2 Bü 544	'II. Übungskurs Sedan; mit Anleitungen, Karten', March 1917
M635/2 Bü 545	'VI. Übungskurs Sedan; mit Anleitungen, Karten', May 1917
M635/2 Bü 546	'XIII. Übungskurs Sedan; mit Anleitungen, Karten', July 1917
M635/2 Bü 547	'XV. Übungskurs Sedan; mit Anleitungen, Karten', August 1917
M635/2 Bü 548	'V. Lehrgang Valenciennes; mit Anweisungen und Karten', April 1917

Service historique de la Défense (SHD)

GR/5/ N/255	'Rapport de la Commission d'Enquête instituée par Lettre Ministérielle N° 18.194, du 14 Juillet 1917' (the Brugère Report)

US National Archives and Records Administration (NARA)

Publication Number T77 L, Rolls 1439–1440 and 1507–1509	Generalmajor a.D. Friedrich Gempp, 'Geheimer Nachrichtendienst und Spionageabwehr des Heeres', 15 vols., 1928–42 (the Gempp report)

(ii) Private Papers and *Nachlässe*

Archiv des Hauses Württemberg (AHW)

G331   Generalfeldmarschall Herzog Albrecht von Württemberg, commander Heeresgruppe Albrecht

Bayerisches Hauptstaatsarchiv/Abteilung III Hausarchiv, Munich (HAM)

Generalfeldmarschall Kronprinz Rupprecht von Bayern, commander Heeresgruppe Rupprecht

Bayerisches Hauptstaatsarchiv/Abteilung IV Kriegsarchiv, Munich (KAM)

Generalleutnant Paul Ritter von Kneußl, commander 11. bayerische Infanterie-Division
Major Rudolf Ritter von Xylander, Ia 6. Armee

Bundesarchiv/Militärarchiv, Freiburg im Breisgau (BArch)

N12	General der Infanterie Magnus von Eberhardt, commander X. Reserve-Korps (Gruppe Brimont)
N21	Generaloberst z.D. Ludwig Freiherr von Falkenhausen, commander 6. Armee
N58	Oberst Friedrich Graf von der Schulenburg-Tressow, chief of staff Heeresgruppe Deutscher Kronprinz
N87	General der Infanterie Otto von Below, commander 6. Armee
N187	Generalleutnant Martin Chales de Beaulieu, commander XIV. Armee-Korps (Gruppe Prosnes)
N306	General der Infanterie z.D. Max von Boehn, commander 7. Armee
N710	General der Artillerie Max von Gallwitz, commander 5. Armee
N882	Major Curt Liebmann, Ia 302. Infanterie-Division
N2214	Major Walther Obkircher, Ia 9. Armee
RH61/924	Hauptmann Hermann Geyer, OHL chief doctrine writer
RH61/970	Generalleutnant Hermann von Kuhl, chief of staff Heeresgruppe Rupprecht, 'Persönliches Kriegstagebuch', November 1915– November 1918
RH 61/986	Generalmajor Gerhard Tappen, commander 5. Ersatz-Division, 'Meine Kriegserinnerungen'

Hauptstaatsarchiv Stuttgart (HSAS)
GU117   General der Kavallerie Wilhelm Herzog von Urach,
               commander Generalkommando 64
M660/031   Generalleutnant Otto von Moser, commander XIV.
               Reserve-Korps (Gruppe Quéant)
M660/037   Hauptmann Karl Schall, Ib 14. Infanterie-Division (in
               Gruppe Liesse)
M660/038   General der Infanterie z.D. Franz Freiherr von Soden,
               commander VII. Reserve-Korps (Gruppe Reims)
M660/091   Oberst Eugen Glück, commander 242. Infanterie-Brigade
               (in Gruppe Reims and Gruppe Prosnes)
M660/197   Generaloberst z.D. Richard von Schubert, recently
               removed commander 7. Armee

University of Leeds Special Collections
LIDDLE/WW1/   Franz Benöhr letters to Peter Liddle, February and
GE/29/05   March 1973

US National Archives and Records Administration (NARA)
Publication Number   Oberst Hermann Ritter Mertz von Quirnheim, section
M958   head in OHL

B.   Published

(i)   Official Published Material

France
Ministère de la Guerre, *Les Armées françaises dans la grande guerre*, 103 vols. (Paris: Imprimerie Nationale, 1922–37).

Germany
Bayerisches Kriegsministerium, *Militär-Handbuch des Königreichs Bayern* (Munich: Im Verlage der Lithographischen Offizin des Kriegs-Ministeriums, 1831–1914).
Bayerisches Kriegsministerium, *Rangliste der Offiziere der Königlich Bayerischen Armee* (Munich: Bayerisches Kriegsministerium, 1918).
Behrmann, Franz, *Die Osterschlacht bei Arras 1917*, 2 vols., Schlachten des Weltkrieges 28–29 (Oldenburg: Druck und Verlag von Gerhard Stalling, 1929).
Bose, Thilo von, *The Catastrophe of 8 August 1918*, trans. and ed. David Pearson, Paul Thost, and Tony Cowan (Newport, NSW: Big Sky Publishing, 2019).

Originally published as *Die Katastrophe des 8. August 1918*, Schlachten des Weltkrieges 36 (Oldenburg: Druck und Verlag von Gerhard Stalling, 1930).

Chef des Generalstabes des Feldheeres, *Anlage kleiner Angriffs-Unternehmungen bei Gruppe Vailly (XI. Korps) im Mai/Juni 1917* (GHQ: Druckerei des Chefs des Generalstabes des Feldheeres, 1917).

Chef des Generalstabes des Feldheeres, *Das französische Angriffsverfahren nach der unter dem 16. Dezember 1916 von der franz. O.H.L. herausgegebenen 'Anweisung über Ziel und Vorbedingungen für eine allgemeine Offensive'* (GHQ: Druckerei des Chefs des Generalstabes des Feldheeres, 1917).

Chef des Generalstabes des Feldheeres, *Vorschriften für den Stellungskrieg für alle Waffen*, Teil 1a, *Allgemeines über Stellungsbau: Vom 15. August 1917* (Berlin: Reichsdruckerei, 1917).

Chef des Generalstabes des Feldheeres, *Vorschriften für den Stellungskrieg für alle Waffen*, Teil 1b, *Einzelheiten über Stellungsbau: Vom 15. Dezember 1916* (Berlin: Reichsdruckerei, 1916).

Chef des Generalstabes des Feldheeres, *Vorschriften für den Stellungskrieg für alle Waffen*, Ergänzungsheft zum Teil 1b, *Betonbauten: Vom 15. November 1917* (Berlin: Reichsdruckerei, 1917).

Chef des Generalstabes des Feldheeres, *Vorschriften für den Stellungskrieg für alle Waffen*, Teil 3, *Nahkampfmittel: Vom 1. Januar 1917* (Berlin: Reichsdruckerei, 1917).

Chef des Generalstabes des Feldheeres, *Vorschriften für den Stellungskrieg für alle Waffen*, Teil 5, *Verwendung und Tätigkeit der Artillerieflieger im Stellungskrieg: Vom 10. Februar 1917* (Berlin: Reichsdruckerei, 1917).

Chef des Generalstabes des Feldheeres, *Vorschriften für den Stellungskrieg für alle Waffen*, Teil 6, *Verbindung der Infanterie mit Fliegern und Fesselballonen: Vom 1. Januar 1917* (Berlin: Reichsdruckerei, 1917).

Chef des Generalstabes des Feldheeres, *Vorschriften für den Stellungskrieg für alle Waffen*, Teil 6, *Der Infanterieflieger und der Infanterieballon: Vom 1 September 1917* (Berlin: Reichsdruckerei, 1917).

Chef des Generalstabes des Feldheeres, *Vorschriften für den Stellungskrieg für alle Waffen*, Teil 7, *Die Minenwerfer: Vom 15. November 1916* (Berlin: Reichsdruckerei, 1916).

Chef des Generalstabes des Feldheeres, *Vorschriften für den Stellungskrieg für alle Waffen*, Teil 7, *Die Minenwerfer: Vom 1. Juli 1917* (Berlin: Reichsdruckerei, 1917).

Chef des Generalstabes des Feldheeres, *Vorschriften für den Stellungskrieg für alle Waffen*, Teil 8, *Grundsätze für die Führung in der Abwehrschlacht im Stellungskriege: Vom 1. Dezember 1916. Neudruck vom 1. März 1917* (Berlin: Reichsdruckerei, 1916 [sic]).

Chef des Generalstabes des Feldheeres, *Vorschriften für den Stellungskrieg für alle Waffen*, Teil 8, *Grundsätze für die Führung der Abwehrschlacht im Stellungskriege: Vom 1. September 1917* (Berlin: Reichsdruckerei, 1917).

Chef des Generalstabes des Feldheeres, *Vorschriften für den Stellungskrieg für alle Waffen*, Teil 9, *Nachrichtenmittel und deren Verwendung: Vom 15. Dezember 1917* (Berlin: Reichsdruckerei, 1917).

Chef des Generalstabes des Feldheeres, *Vorschriften für den Stellungskrieg für alle Waffen*, Teil 10, *Signalordnung: Vom 15 Juni 1917* (GHQ: Druckerei des Chefs des Generalstabes des Feldheeres, 1917).

Chef des Generalstabes des Feldheeres, *Vorschriften für den Stellungskrieg für alle Waffen*, Teil 11, *Schwerstes Flachfeuer: November 1917* (Berlin: Reichsdruckerei, 1917).

Chef des Generalstabes des Feldheeres, *Vorschriften für den Stellungskrieg für alle Waffen*, Teil 12, *Verwendung und Einsatz von Schlachtfliegern: Vom 15. Oktober 1917* (GHQ: Druckerei des Chefs des Generalstabes des Feldheeres, 1917).

Chef des Generalstabes des Feldheeres, *Vorschriften für den Stellungskrieg für alle Waffen*, Teil 13, *Weisungen über den Einsatz von Jagdstaffeln: Vom 25. Oktober 1917* (Berlin: Reichsdruckerei, 1918 [sic]).

Chef des Generalstabes des Feldheeres, *Sonderheft zum Sammelheft der Vorschriften für den Stellungskrieg: Vom 10. Juni 1917* (GHQ: Druckerei des Chefs des Generalstabes des Feldheeres, 1917).

Chef des Generalstabes des Feldheeres Nachrichten-Abteilung, *Kurze Zusammenstellung über die französische Armee*, 4th ed. (Hauptquartier Mézières-Charleville: Druckerei des Chefs des Generalstabes des Feldheeres, 1917).

Gold, Ludwig and Schwencke, Alexander, *Die Tragödie von Verdun 1916*, 3 vols., Schlachten des Weltkrieges 13–15 (Oldenburg: Druck und Verlag von Gerhard Stalling, 1926–9).

Großer Generalstab, ed., *Moltkes Militärische Werke*, 14 vols. (Berlin: Ernst Siegfried Mittler und Sohn, 1892–1912).

Großer Generalstab, *Anhaltspunkte für den Generalstabsdienst* (Berlin: Reichsdruckerei, 1914).

Großer Generalstab, *Die Schlachten und Gefechte des Großen Krieges 1914–1918* (Berlin: Verlag von Hermann Sack, 1919).

Kommandierender General der Luftstreitkräfte, *Weisungen für den Einsatz und die Verwendung von Fliegerverbänden innerhalb einer Armee* (GHQ: Druckerei des Chefs des Generalstabes des Feldheeres, 1917).

Königliches Ministerium des Innern, *Adreß-Kalender für die Königl. Haupt- und Residenzstädte Berlin und Potsdam sowie Charlottenburg auf das Jahr 1914* (Berlin: Carl Heymanns Verlag, 1914).

Kriegsministerium, *Rangliste der Königlich Preußischen Armee und des XIII. (Königlich Württembergischen) Armeekorps* (Berlin: Ernst Siegfried Mittler und Sohn, 1867–1914).

Kriegsministerium, *D.V.E. Nr. 291. Bestimmungen über Personal- und Qualifikations-Berichte (P. u. Q. Best.) vom 19. Juni 1902* (Berlin: Reichsdruckerei, 1902).

[Kriegsministerium], *Dienstalters-Liste der Offiziere der Königlich Preußischen Armee und des XIII. (Königlich Württembergischen) Armeekorps* (Berlin: Ernst Siegfried Mittler und Sohn, 1907/1908, 1912/1913, 1917, 1918 and 1919).

Kriegsministerium, *Felddienst-Ordnung (F.O.)* (Berlin: Ernst Siegfried Mittler und Sohn, 1908).

Kriegsministerium, *Exerzier-Reglement für die Infanterie. (Ex.R.f.d.I.) Vom 29. Mai 1906: Neuabdruck mit Einfügung der bis August 1909 ergangenen Änderungen (Deckblatt 1–78)* (Berlin: Ernst Siegfried Mittler und Sohn, 1909).

Kriegsministerium, *D.V.E. Nr.219a. Stärkenachweisungen der Behörden und Truppen in der Kriegsformation (St. N.) (Beiheft zum Mobilmachungsplan vom 1. Juli 1907): Neuabdruck vom 1. Juni 1911* (Berlin: Reichsdruckerei, 1911).

Kriegsministerium, *D.V.E. Nr.102. Gebührnisnachweisungen (Beiheft zur Kriegsbesoldungsvorschrift vom 29. Dezember 1887): Vom 6. Januar 1912* (Berlin: Reichsdruckerei, 1912).

Kriegsministerium, *D.V.E. Nr.53. Grundzüge der höheren Truppenführung: Vom 1. Januar 1910* (Berlin: Reichsdruckerei, 1913).

Kriegsministerium, *D.V.E. Nr.101. Kriegs-Besoldungs-Vorschrift (K. Besold. V.) Vom 29. Dezember 1887: Neuabdruck 1914* (Berlin: Reichsdruckerei, 1914).

Kriegsministerium, *Vorschriften für den Stellungskrieg für alle Waffen*, Teil 1, *Stellungsbau: Vom 20. Juni 1916* (Berlin: Reichsdruckerei, 1916).

Kriegsministerium, *Vorschriften für den Stellungskrieg für alle Waffen*, Teil 2, *Minenkrieg: Vom 19 April 1916* (Berlin: Reichsdruckerei, 1916).

Kriegsministerium, *Vorschriften für den Stellungskrieg für alle Waffen*, Teil 4, *Leuchtmittel: Vom 31 Mai 1916* (Berlin: Reichsdruckerei, 1916).

Kriegsministerium, *Ausbildungsvorschrift für die Fußtruppen im Kriege (A.V.F.)* (Berlin: Reichsdruckerei, 1917).

Lepsius, Johannes, Bartholdy, Albrecht Mendelssohn and Thimme, Friedrich, eds., *Die Große Politik der Europäischen Kabinette 1871–1914: Sammlung der Diplomatischen Akten des Auswärtigen Amtes*, 40 vols. (Berlin: Deutsche Verlagsgesellschaft für Politik und Geschichte, 1922–7).

Militärgeschichtliches Forschungsamt, ed., *Germany and the Second World War*, 13 vols. (Oxford: Clarendon Press, 1990–2014). Originally published as *Das Deutsche Reich und der Zweite Weltkrieg*, 13 vols. (Stuttgart: Deutsche Verlags-Anstalt, 1979–2008).

Reichsarchiv, *Der Weltkrieg 1914 bis 1918: Die militärischen Operationen zu Lande*, 14 vols. (Berlin: E. S. Mittler und Sohn, 1925–56).

Reichskriegsministerium, *Sanitätsbericht über das Deutsche Heer (Deutsches Feld- und Besatzungsheer) im Weltkriege 1914/1918 (Deutscher Kriegssanitätsbericht 1914/1918)*, 3 vols. (Berlin: E. S. Mittler und Sohn, 1934–38).

Reichswehrministerium, *Führung und Gefecht der verbundenen Waffen (F.u.G.): Vom 1. September 1921* (Berlin: Verlag Offene Worte, Charlottenburg, 1921).

Sächsisches Kriegsministerium, *Rangliste der Königlich Sächsischen Armee* (Dresden: Druck der C. Heinrich'schen Buchdruckerei, 1871–1914).

Great Britain

Edmonds, Brigadier-General Sir James E., ed., *Military Operations: France and Belgium*, 14 vols. (London: Macmillan and Co. and HMSO, 1922–48).

General Staff, *S.S. 135: Instructions for the Training of Divisions for Offensive Action* (London: Harrison & Sons, 1916).

House of Commons, *Review of Intelligence on Weapons of Mass Destruction* (London: The Stationery Office, 2004).

Ministry of Defence, *British Defence Doctrine (Joint Warfare Publication 0–01)*, 2nd ed. (London: Ministry of Defence, 2001).

Ministry of Defence, *Army Doctrine Publication: Operations* (London: Ministry of Defence, 2010).

Raleigh, Walter and Jones, H. A., *The War in the Air: Being the Story of the Part Played in the Great War by the Royal Air Force*, 7 vols. (Oxford: Clarendon Press, 1922–37).

United States

Headquarters, Department of the Army, *Field Manual No. 6–0: Mission Command: Command and Control of Army Forces* (Washington, DC: Department of the Army, 2003).

United States War Office, *Histories of Two Hundred and Fifty-One Divisions of the German Army which Participated in the War (1914–1918)* (London: London Stamp Exchange, 1989). Originally published as War Department Document No. 905, 1920.

(ii)   Articles, Books, Diaries, Memoirs and Unit Histories

Afflerbach, Holger, ed., *Kaiser Wilhelm II. als Oberster Kriegsherr im Ersten Weltkrieg: Quellen aus der militärischen Umgebung des Kaisers 1914–1918* (Munich: R. Oldenbourg Verlag, 2005).

Alten, Georg von, ed., *Handbuch für Heer und Flotte: Enzyklopädie der Kriegswissenschaften und verwandter Gebiete*, 8 vols. (Berlin: Deutsches Verlagshaus Bong, 1909–12).

Ammon, Major a.D., 'Das Nachrichtenwesen', in Max Schwarte, ed., *Die Technik im Weltkriege* (Berlin: Ernst Siegfried Mittler und Sohn, 1920), 245–71.

Anon., *Das alte Heer, von einem Stabsoffizier* (Charlottenburg: Verlag der Weltbühne, 1920).

Balck, Colonel William, *Tactics*, vol. 1, *Introduction and Formal Tactics of Infantry*, 4th ed., trans. Walter Krueger (Fort Leavenworth, KS: US Cavalry Association, 1915). Originally published as Balck, William, *Taktik*, 6 vols. (Berlin: Verlag von R. Eisenschmidt, 1897–1904).

Balck, Generalleutnant z.D. William, *Entwickelung der Taktik im Weltkriege*, 2nd ed. (Berlin: Verlag von R. Eisenschmidt, 1922).

Bauer, Oberst Max, *Der große Krieg in Feld und Heimat*, 3rd ed. (Tübingen: Osiander'sche Buchhandlung, 1922).

Behr, Major Hugold von, *Bei der fünften Reserve-Division im Weltkriege* (Berlin: Ernst Siegfried Mittler und Sohn, 1919).

Bernhardi, Friedrich von, *Deutschland und der nächste Krieg*, 6th ed. (Stuttgart: I. G. Cotta'sche Buchhandlung Nachfolger, 1913).

Bielenburg, P. E., 'Erfahrungen mit der l.F.H. 16', *Artilleristische Monatshefte*, vol. 15, nos. 169/170 (January–February 1921), 19–26.

Binding, Rudolf, *A Fatalist at War*, trans. Ian F. D. Morrow (London: George Allen & Unwin, 1929). Originally published as *Aus dem Kriege* (Frankfurt: Literarische Anstalt Rütten & Loening, 1925).

Bismarck, Oberstleutnant a.D. Busso von, 'Der Militärattaché im Nachrichtendienst', in Generalmajor von Lettow-Vorbeck, ed., *Die Weltkriegsspionage* (Munich: Verlag Justin Moser, 1931), 104–10.

Brandis, Hauptmann a.D. Cordt von, *Die vom Douaumont: Das Ruppiner Regiment 24 im Weltkrieg* (Berlin: Verlag Tradition Wilhelm Kolk, 1930).

Brauchitsch, Generalmajor a.D. Gottfried von, *Das 2. Garde-Regiment zu Fuß* (Oldenburg: Druck und Verlag von Gerhard Stalling, 1922).

Bronsart von Schellendorff, Major, *Der Dienst des Generalstabes*, 4th ed. (Berlin: Ernst Siegfried Mittler und Sohn, 1905).

Clausewitz, Carl von, *On War*, trans. and ed. Michael Howard and Peter Paret (Princeton, NJ: Princeton University Press, 1976).

Cron, Hermann, *Geschichte des Deutschen Heeres im Weltkriege 1914–1918* (Berlin: Militärverlag Karl Siegismund, 1937).

Cron, Hermann, Volkmann, Erich Otto, and Immanuel, Friedrich et al., eds., *Ruhmeshalle unserer alten Armee*, 2 vols., 5th ed. (Berlin: Verlag für Militärgeschichte und deutsches Schrifttum, c. 1934).

Degener, Herrmann A. L., ed., *Wer ist's? Unsere Zeitgenossen*, 7th ed. (Leipzig: Verlag von H. A. Ludwig Degener, 1914).

Degener, Herrmann A. L., ed., *Wer ist's? Unsere Zeitgenossen*, 8th ed. (Leipzig: Verlag von H. A. Ludwig Degener, 1922).

Deutelmoser, Major a.D. Adolf, *Die 27. Infanterie-Division im Weltkrieg 1914–18* (Stuttgart: Berger's Literarisches Büro und Verlagsanstalt, 1925).

Deutscher Offizier-Bund, ed., *Ehren-Rangliste des ehemaligen Deutschen Heeres auf Grund der Ranglisten von 1914 mit den inzwischen eingetretenen Veränderungen*, facsimile repr. of 1926 original (Osnabrück: Biblio Verlag, 1987).

Doerstling, Oberstleutnant a.D. Paul, ed., *Kriegsgeschichte des Königlich Preußischen Infanterie-Regiments Graf Tauentzien v. Wittenberg (3. Brandenb.) Nr. 20* (Zeulenroda: Bernhard Sporn, 1933).

Drees, Major a.D., 'Die Geschütz-Ausrüstung unserer Feld- und schweren Artillerie im Weltkriege', *Artilleristische Monatshefte*, vol. 15, nos. 169/170 (January–February 1921), 62–71.

Eberhardt, General der Infanterie Magnus von, *Kriegserinnerungen* ([Neudamm]: Verlag J. Neumann-Neudamm, 1938).

Einem, Generaloberst Karl von, *Erinnerungen eines Soldaten 1853–1933* (Leipzig: Verlag von K. F. Koehler, 1933).

Epkenhans, Michael, Groß, Gerhard P., Pöhlmann, Markus and Stachelbeck, Christian, eds., *Geheimdienst und Propaganda im Ersten Weltkrieg: Die Aufzeichnungen von Oberst Walter Nicolai 1914 bis 1918* (Berlin: Walter de Gruyter, 2019).

Fayolle, Maréchal, *Cahiers Secrets de la Grande Guerre*, ed. Henry Contamine (Paris: Librairie Plon, 1964).

Felgenhauer, Hans von and Müller-Loebnitz, Wilhelm, eds., *Das Ehrenbuch der Rheinländer: Die Rheinländer im Weltkrieg* (Stuttgart: Vaterländische Verlagsanstalt Oskar Hinderer, n.d.).

Fortmüller, Generalleutnant August, 'Die Heeresgruppe Deutscher Kronprinz 1917 bis März 1918', in Max Schwarte, ed., *Der Weltkampf um Ehre und Recht*, vol. 3 (Leipzig: Alleinvertrieb durch Ernst Finking, n.d.), 159–228.

Freytag-Loringhoven, Oberstleutnant Hugo Freiherr von, *Die Macht der Persönlichkeit im Kriege: Studien nach Clausewitz* (Berlin: Ernst Siegfried Mittler und Sohn, 1905).

Freytag-Loringhoven, General der Infanterie a.D. Hugo Freiherr von, *Menschen und Dinge wie ich sie in meinem Leben sah* (Berlin: Ernst Siegfried Mittler und Sohn, 1923).

Frobenius, Hermann, ed., *Militär-Lexikon. Handwörterbuch der Militärwissenschaften* (Berlin: Verlag von Martin Oldenbourg, 1901).

Gallwitz, Max von, *Meine Führertätigkeit im Weltkriege 1914/1916: Belgien – Osten – Balkan* (Berlin: Ernst Siegfried Mittler und Sohn, 1929).

Gallwitz, Max von, *Erleben im Westen 1916–1918* (Berlin: Ernst Siegfried Mittler und Sohn, 1932).

Geyer, Hermann, 'Einige Gedanken über Verteidigung, Ausweichen und dergleichen', *Militärwissenschaftliche Mitteilungen*, vol. 1 (November 1921).

Gleich, Generalmajor Gerold von, *Die alte Armee und ihre Verirrungen: Eine kritische Studie* (Leipzig: Verlag von K. F. Koehler, 1919).

Goes, Gustav, *Chemin des Dames*, Das Heldenlied des Weltkrieges 3 (Hamburg: Hanseatische Verlagsanstalt, 1938).

Goßler, Conrad von, *Erinnerungen an den Großen Krieg dem VI. Reservekorps gewidmet* (Breslau: Verlag von Wilh. Gottl. Korn, 1919).

Gruss, Hellmuth, *Die deutschen Sturmbataillone im Weltkrieg: Aufbau und Verwendung* (Berlin: Junker und Dünnhaupt Verlag, 1939).

Haldane, Viscount, *Before the War* (London: Cassell and Company, 1920).

Harms, Heinrich, *Die Geschichte des Oldenburgischen Infanterie-Regiments Nr. 91* (Oldenburg: Druck und Verlag von Gerhard Stalling, 1930).

Heidrich, Fritz, *Geschichte des 3. Ostpreußischen Feldartillerie-Regiments Nr. 79* (Oldenburg: Druck und Verlag von Gerhard Stalling, 1921).

Herbillon, Colonel Émile, *Le Général Alfred Micheler (1914–1918): De la Meuse à Reims* (Paris: Librairie Plon, 1933).

Hindenburg, Marshal Paul von, *Out of My Life*, trans. F. A. Holt (London: Cassell and Company, 1920). Originally published as *Aus meinem Leben* (Leipzig: S. Hirzel Verlag, 1920).

Hoeppner, General der Kavallerie Ernst von, *Deutschlands Krieg in der Luft: Ein Rückblick auf die Entwicklung und die Leistungen unserer Heeres-Luftstreitkräfte im Weltkriege* (Leipzig: Verlag von K. F. Koehler, 1921).

Immanuel, Hauptmann Friedrich, *Handbuch der Taktik* (Berlin: Ernst Siegfried Mittler und Sohn, 1905).

Immanuel, Oberst Friedrich, *Siege und Niederlagen im Weltkriege: Kritische Betrachtungen* (Berlin: Ernst Siegfried Mittler und Sohn, 1919).

Isenburg, Major a.D., *Das Königs-Infanterie-Regiment (6. Lothring.) Nr. 145 im Großen Kriege 1914–1918*, 3 vols. (Berlin: Verlag von Klasing, 1922–39).

Jäger, Oberstleutnant a.D. Hans, *Das K.B. 19. Infanterie-Regiment König Viktor Emanuel III. von Italien* (Munich: Verlag Max Schick, 1930).

Jünger, Ernst, *Kriegstagebuch 1914–1918*, ed. Helmuth Kiesel (Stuttgart: Klett-Cotta, 2010).

Kaiser, Franz Nikolaus, ed., *Das Ehrenbuch der Deutschen Schweren Artillerie* (Berlin: Verlag Tradition Wilhelm Kolk, 1931).

Kirchbach, Arndt von, *Pietate et Armis: Erinnerungen aus dem Leben von Arndt v. Kirchbach*, ed. Esther von Kirchbach and Ernst Kähler, 5 vols. (Göppingen-Jebenhausen: Self-Publication, 1987).

Kuhl, Hermann von, *Der deutsche Generalstab in Vorbereitung und Durchführung des Weltkrieges*, 2nd ed. (Berlin: Verlag von Ernst Siegfried Mittler und Sohn, 1920).

Kuhl, Hermann von, *Der Weltkrieg 1914–1918*, 2 vols. (Berlin: Verlag Tradition Wilhelm Kolk, 1929).

Liebert, General der Infanterie a.D. Eduard von, *Aus einem bewegten Leben* (Munich: J. F. Lehmanns Verlag, 1925).

Litzmann, General der Infanterie a.D. Karl, *Lebenserinnerungen*, 2 vols. (Berlin: Verlag R. Eisenschmidt, 1927–28).

Lloyd George, David, *War Memoirs of David Lloyd George*, 6 vols. (London: Ivor Nicholson & Watson, 1933–6).

Loßberg, Fritz von, *Meine Tätigkeit im Weltkriege 1914–1918* (Berlin: E. S. Mittler und Sohn, 1939).

Ludendorff, General Erich, *My War Memories 1914–1918* (London: Hutchinson & Co., 1919). Originally published as *Meine Kriegserinnerungen 1914–1918* (Berlin: Ernst Siegfried Mittler und Sohn, 1919).

Ludendorff, Erich, *Urkunden der Obersten Heeresleitung über ihre Tätigkeit 1916/18*, 2nd ed. (Berlin: Verlag von E. S. Mittler und Sohn, 1921).

Mangin, [Charles], *Lettres de Guerre 1914–1918* (Paris: Librairie Arthème Fayard, 1950).

Manstein, Generalfeldmarschall Erich von, *Verlorene Siege* (Bonn: Athenäum-Verlag, 1955).

Marder, Arthur J., ed., *Fear God and Dread Nought: The Correspondence of Admiral of the Fleet Lord Fisher of Kilverstone*, 3 vols. (London: Jonathan Cape, 1952–9).

Marx, Generalleutnant a.D. Wilhelm, 'Zur Psychologie der deutschen Kriegskritik', *Militär-Wochenblatt*, vol. 119, no. 5 (4 August 1934), 174–6.

Marx, Generalleutnant a.D. Wilhelm, 'Die entschwindende Führerromantik', *Militär-Wochenblatt*, vol. 119, no. 27 (18 January 1935), 1052–5.

Meyer, Georg, ed., *Generalfeldmarschall Wilhelm Ritter von Leeb: Tagebuchaufzeichnungen und Lagebeurteilungen aus zwei Weltkriegen* (Stuttgart: Deutsche Verlags-Anstalt, 1976).

Möller, Hanns, ed., *Geschichte der Ritter des Ordens 'pour le mérite' im Weltkrieg*, 2 vols. (Berlin: Verlag Bernard & Graefe, 1935).

Möller, Hanns, *Fritz v. Below, General der Infanterie: Ein Lebensbild* (Berlin: Verlag Bernard & Graefe, 1939).

Morgen, Curt von, *Meiner Truppen Heldenkämpfe* (Berlin: Ernst Siegfried Mittler und Sohn, 1920).

Moser, Otto von, *Die Führung des Armeekorps im Feldkriege* (Berlin: Ernst Siegfried Mittler und Sohn, 1910).

Moser, Otto von, *Ausbildung und Führung des Bataillons, des Regiments und der Brigade: Gedanken und Vorschläge*, 4th ed. (Berlin: Ernst Siegfried Mittler und Sohn, 1914).

Moser, Otto von, *Ernsthafte Plaudereien über den Weltkrieg* (Stuttgart: Chr. Belser A.G., Verlagsbuchhandlung, 1925).

Moser, Otto von, *Feldzugsaufzeichnungen 1914–1918 als Brigade-, Divisionskommandeur und als kommandierender General*, 3rd ed. (Stuttgart: Chr. Belser A.G. Verlagsbuchhandlung, 1928).

Neumann, Major a.D. Georg Paul, ed., *Die deutschen Luftstreitkräfte im Weltkriege* (Berlin: Ernst Siegfried Mittler und Sohn, 1920).

Nicolai, Walter, *Nachrichtendienst, Presse und Volksstimmung im Weltkrieg* (Berlin: Ernst Siegfried Mittler und Sohn, 1920).

Ranke, Leopold von, *Geschichten der romanischen und germanischen Völker von 1494 bis 1514*, 3rd ed. (Leipzig: Verlag von Duncker & Humblot, 1885).

Rauch, Oberst a.D. Leopold von, 'Der Deutsche Nachrichtendienst im Weltkriege', *Deutscher Offizier-Bund*, vol. 6, no. 20 (1927), 848–50.

Reinhardt, Major Georg Hans, Hauptmann, Hauptmann a.D. Fritz, Hartmann, Hauptmann Rudolf et al., eds., *Das kgl. Sächs. 8. Infanterie-Regiment "Prinz Johann Georg" Nr. 107 während des Weltkrieges 1914–1918* (Dresden: Verlag der Buchdruckerei der Wilhelm und Bertha v. Baensch Stiftung, 1928).

Rodenberg, Oberst a.D., 'Militär-Kabinett', in General der Infanterie a.D. Ernst von Eisenhart Rothe, ed., *Ehrendenkmal der deutschen Armee und Marine 1871–1918* (Berlin: Deutscher National-Verlag Aktiengesellschaft, 1926), 52–66.

Rupprecht von Bayern, Kronprinz, *Mein Kriegstagebuch*, ed. Eugen von Frauenholz, 3 vols. (Munich: Deutscher National Verlag A.G., 1929).

Schneider, Paul, *Die Organisation des Heeres* (Berlin: Verlag von E. S. Mittler und Sohn, 1931).

Schoenaich, Paul Freiherr von, *Mein Damaskus. Erlebnisse und Bekenntnisse*, 2nd ed. (Hamburg-Bergedorf: Fackelreiter-Verlag, 1929).

Schwalm, Otto and Ahlers, Oberstleutnant a.D., eds., *Das königlich preußische Infanterie-Regiment Landgraf Friedrich I. von Hessen-Kassel (I. Kurhessisches) Nr. 81 im Weltkriege 1914–1918* (Frankfurt: Blazek & Bergmann, 1932).

Schwarte, Max, ed., *Die Technik im Weltkriege* (Berlin: Ernst Siegfried Mittler und Sohn, 1920).

Schwarte, Max, ed., *Der Weltkampf um Ehre und Recht*, 8 vols. (Leipzig: Alleinvertrieb durch Ernst Finking, n.d.).

Schwertfeger, Bernhard, *Die großen Erzieher des deutschen Heeres: Aus der Geschichte der Kriegsakademie* (Potsdam: Akademische Verlagsgesellschaft Athenaion, 1936).

Seeckt, General Hans von, *Thoughts of a Soldier*, trans. Gilbert Waterhouse (London: Ernest Benn, 1930). Originally published as *Gedanken eines Soldaten* (Berlin: Verlag für Kulturpolitik, 1929).

Shakespear, Lieutenant-Colonel John, *The Thirty-Fourth Division 1915–1919: The Story of Its Career from Ripon to the Rhine* (London: H. F. & G. Witherby, 1921).

Sheffield, Gary and Bourne, John, eds., *Douglas Haig: War Diaries and Letters 1914–1918* (London: Weidenfeld & Nicolson, 2005).

Slim, Field-Marshal Sir William, *Defeat into Victory* (London: Cassell and Company, 1956).

Spears, Brigadier-General Edward L., *Prelude to Victory* (London: Jonathan Cape, 1939).

Steltzer, Theodor, *Sechzig Jahre Zeitgenosse* (Munich: Paul List Verlag KG, 1966).

Stosch, Major von, 'Beiträge zum Wiederaufbau des deutschen Heeres', *Militär-Wochenblatt*, vol. 103, no. 115 (29 March 1919), 2095–8.

Thaer, Albrecht von, *Generalstabsdienst an der Front und in der O.H.L: Aus Briefen und Tagebuchaufzeichnungen 1915–1919*, ed. Siegfried A. Kaehler (Göttingen: Vandenhoeck & Ruprecht, 1958).

Tschischwitz, General der Infanterie a.D. Erich von, ed., *General von der Marwitz: Weltkriegsbriefe* (Berlin: Ernst Steiniger Druck- und Verlagsanstalt, 1940).

Viereck, Oberleutnant a.D. Helmut, *Das Heideregiment. Königlich Preußisches 2. Hannoversches Infanterie-Regiment Nr. 77 im Weltkriege 1914–1918* (Celle: Druck und Verlag August Pohl, 1934).

Wellmann, Generalleutnant a.D. Richard, *Mit der Hannoverschen 20. Infanterie-Division in Ost und West: Oktober 1916 bis Dezember 1917* (Hannover: Druck von Edler & Krische, 1923).

Wilkinson, Spenser, *The Brain of an Army: A Popular Account of the German General Staff*, 2nd ed. (Westminster: Archibald Constable & Co., 1895).

Winterfeldt, Generalleutnant von, *Das Kaiser Franz-Garde-Grenadier-Regiment Nr. 2 1914–1918* (Oldenburg: Druck und Verlag von Gerhard Stalling, 1922).

Woodward, David R., ed., *The Military Correspondence of Field-Marshal Sir William Robertson, Chief of the Imperial General Staff, December 1915– February 1918* (London: The Bodley Head for the Army Records Society, 1989).

Wrisberg, Generalmajor a.D. Ernst von, *Heer und Heimat 1914–1918* (Leipzig: Verlag von K. F. Koehler, 1921).

Wrisberg, Generalmajor a.D. Ernst von, *Wehr und Waffen 1914–1918* (Leipzig: Verlag von K. F. Koehler, 1922).

Zwehl, Hans von, *Maubeuge, Aisne – Verdun. Das VII. Reserve-Korps im Weltkriege von seinem Beginn bis Ende 1916* (Berlin: Verlag Karl Curtius, 1921).

Zwehl, Hans von, *Generalstabsdienst im Frieden und im Kriege* (Berlin: E. S. Mittler und Sohn, 1923).

Later Works

(i)   Books and Reviews

Afflerbach, Holger, *Auf Messers Schneide: Wie das Deutsche Reich den Ersten Weltkrieg verlor* (Munich: Verlag C. H. Beck oHG, 2018).

Allport, Alan, *Britain at Bay 1938–1941: The Epic Story of the Second World War* (London: Profile Books, 2020).

Beach, Jim, *Haig's Intelligence: GHQ and the German Army, 1916–1918* (Cambridge: Cambridge University Press, 2013).

Beckett, Ian F. W., *A British Profession of Arms: The Politics of Command in the Late Victorian Army* (Norman, OK: University of Oklahoma Press, 2018).

Boff, Jonathan, *Winning and Losing on the Western Front: The British Third Army and the Defeat of Germany in 1918* (Cambridge: Cambridge University Press, 2012).

Boff, Jonathan, *Haig's Enemy: Crown Prince Rupprecht and Germany's War on the Western Front* (Oxford: Oxford University Press, 2018).

Boff, Jonathan, Review of *Command: The Twenty-First-Century General* by Anthony King, *Journal of Military History*, vol. 84, no. 1 (January 2020), 343–5.

Boghardt, Thomas, *Spies of the Kaiser: German Covert Operations in Great Britain during the First World War Era* (Basingstoke: Palgrave Macmillan, 2004).

Bradley, Dermot, Hildebrand, Karl-Friedrich, and Roevekamp, Marcus, eds., *Deutschlands Generale und Admirale*, Teil 4, *Die Generale des Heeres 1921–1945*, 7 vols. (Osnabrück: Biblio Verlag, 1993–2004).

Brose, Eric Dorn, *The Kaiser's Army: The Politics of Military Technology in Germany during the Machine Age, 1870–1918* (Oxford: Oxford University Press, 2001).

Buchheit, Gert, *Der deutsche Geheimdienst: Geschichte der militärischen Abwehr* (Munich: Paul List Verlag KG, 1966).

Bucholz, Arden, *Moltke, Schlieffen and Prussian War Planning* (New York: Berg, 1991).

Buckley, John, *Monty's Men: The British Army and the Liberation of Europe, 1944–5* (New Haven, CT: Yale University Press, 2013).

Burke, Edward, *An Army of Tribes: British Army Cohesion, Deviancy and Murder in Northern Ireland* (Liverpool: Liverpool University Press, 2018).

Cailleteau, François, *Gagner la Grande Guerre* (Paris: Economica, 2008).

Chickering, Roger, *Imperial Germany and the Great War, 1914–1918*, 2nd ed. (Cambridge: Cambridge University Press, 2004).

Citino, Robert M., *The German Way of War: From the Thirty Years' War to the Third Reich* (Lawrence, KS: University Press of Kansas, 2005).

Coopersmith, Jonathan, *Faxed: The Rise and Fall of the Fax Machine* (Baltimore, MD: John Hopkins University Press, 2015).

Creveld, Martin van, *Command in War* (Cambridge, MA: Harvard University Press, 1985).

Deist, Wilhelm, ed., *Militär und Innenpolitik im Weltkrieg 1914–1918*, 2 vols. (Düsseldorf: Droste Verlag, 1970).

Demeter, Karl, *The German Officer-Corps in Society and State 1650–1945*, trans. Angus Malcolm (London: Weidenfeld and Nicolson, 1965).

Doughty, Robert A., *Pyrrhic Victory: French Strategy and Operations in the Great War* (Cambridge, MA: The Belknap Press of Harvard University Press, 2005).

Doughty, Robert A., Review of *The Battle of the Frontiers: Ardennes 1914* by Terence Zuber, *Journal of Military History*, vol. 72, no. 3 (July 2008), 965–6.

Duffy, Christopher, *Through German Eyes: The British and the Somme 1916* (London: Weidenfeld & Nicolson, 2006).

Dupuy, Trevor N., *A Genius for War: The German Army and General Staff, 1807–1945* (London: Macdonald and Jane's, 1977).

Echevarria II, Antulio J., *After Clausewitz: German Military Thinkers Before the Great War* (Lawrence, KS: University Press of Kansas, 2000).

Erfurth, Waldemar, *Die Geschichte des deutschen Generalstabes von 1918 bis 1945* (Göttingen: Musterschmidt-Verlag, 1957).

Farr, Don, *A Battle Too Far: Arras 1917* (Warwick: Helion & Company, 2018).

Ferguson, Niall, *The Pity of War* (London: Allen Lane The Penguin Press, 1998).

Ferris, John, ed., *The British Army and Signals Intelligence during the First World War* (Stroud: Alan Sutton Publishing, 1992).

Ferris, John Robert, *Intelligence and Strategy: Selected Essays* (Abingdon: Routledge, 2005).

Foley, Robert T., trans. and ed., *Alfred von Schlieffen's Military Writings* (London: Frank Cass, 2003).

Foley, Robert T., *German Strategy and the Path to Verdun: Erich von Falkenhayn and the Development of Attrition, 1870–1916* (Cambridge: Cambridge University Press, 2005).

Fox, Aimée, *Learning to Fight: Military Innovation and Change in the British Army, 1914–1918* (Cambridge: Cambridge University Press, 2018).

Freedman, Lawrence, *Strategy: A History* (Oxford: Oxford University Press, 2013).

Frieser, Karl-Heinz, *The Blitzkrieg Legend: The 1940 Campaign in the West*, trans. John T. Greenwood (Annapolis, MD: Naval Institute Press, 2005).

Gale, Tim, *The French Army's Tank Force and Armoured Warfare in the Great War: The Artillerie Spéciale* (Farnham: Ashgate Publishing Limited, 2013).

Geile, Willi, *Die im 'Militär-Wochenblatt' und im 'Marineverordnungsblatt' veröffentlichten preußischen und fremdstaatlichen (deutschen und außerdeutschen) Ordensverleihungen an Offiziere der preußischen Armee und der kaiserlichen Marine von 1914 bis 1918* (Konstanz am Bodensee: Phaleristischer Verlag Michael Autengruber, 1997).

Geyer, Michael, *Deutsche Rüstungspolitik 1860–1980* (Frankfurt: Suhrkamp Verlag, 1984).

Görlitz, Walter, *Der Deutsche Generalstab: Geschichte und Gestalt 1657–1945* (Frankfurt: Verlag der Frankfurter Hefte, 1950).

Gooch, John, *The Italian Army and the First World War* (Cambridge: Cambridge University Press, 2014).

Goya, Michel, *La chair et l'acier: L'armée française et l'invention de la guerre moderne (1914–1918)* (Paris: Tallandier Éditions, 2004). Translated as Goya, Michel, *Flesh and Steel during the Great War: The Transformation of the French Army and the Invention of Modern Warfare*, trans. Andrew Uffindell (Barnsley: Pen & Sword Military, 2018).

Grawe, Lukas, *Deutsche Feindaufklärung vor dem Ersten Weltkrieg: Informationen und Einschätzungen des deutschen Generalstabs zu den Armeen Frankreichs und Russlands 1904 bis 1914* (Paderborn: Verlag Ferdinand Schöningh, 2017).

Greenhalgh, Elizabeth, *Victory through Coalition: Britain and France during the First World War* (Cambridge: Cambridge University Press, 2005).

Greenhalgh, Elizabeth, *The French Army and the First World War* (Cambridge: Cambridge University Press, 2014).

Griffith, Paddy, *Battle Tactics of the Western Front: The British Army's Art of Attack 1916–18* (New Haven, CT: Yale University Press, 1994).

Groß, Gerhard P., *Mythos und Wirklichkeit: Geschichte des operativen Denkens im deutschen Heer von Moltke d.Ä. bis Heusinger* (Paderborn: Ferdinand Schöningh, 2012). Translated as Gross, Gerhard P., *The Myth and Reality of German Warfare: Operational Thinking from Moltke the Elder to Heusinger*, ed. David T. Zabecki (Lexington, KY: University Press of Kentucky, 2016).

Gudmundsson, Bruce I., *Stormtroop Tactics: Innovation in the German Army, 1914–1918* (New York: Praeger, 1989).

Haber, L. F., *The Poisonous Cloud: Chemical Warfare in the First World War* (Oxford: Clarendon Press, 1986),

Hackl, Othmar, *Die bayerische Kriegsakademie (1867–1914)* (Munich: C. H. Beck'sche Verlagsbuchhandlung, 1989).

Hall, Brian N., *Communications and British Operations on the Western Front, 1914–1918* (Cambridge: Cambridge University Press, 2017).

Hannagan, Tim, *Management: Concepts and Practices*, 4th ed. (London: FT Prentice Hall, 2005).

Harris, Paul, *The Men Who Planned the War: A Study of the Staff of the British Army on the Western Front, 1914–1918* (London: Routledge, 2016).

Hart, Peter, *Bloody April: Slaughter in the Skies over Arras, 1917* (London: Weidenfeld & Nicolson, 2005).

Hayes, Geoffrey, Iarocci, Andrew and Bechthold, Mike, eds., *Vimy Ridge: A Canadian Reassessment* (Waterloo, ON: Laurier Centre for Military Strategic and Disarmament Studies and Wilfrid Laurier University Press, 2007).

Heinl, Jr, Robert Debs, *Dictionary of Military and Naval Quotations* (Annapolis, MD: United States Naval Institute, 1966).

Herwig, Holger H., *'Luxury' Fleet: The Imperial German Navy 1888–1918* (London: George Allen & Unwin, 1980).

Herwig, Holger H., *The First World War: Germany and Austria-Hungary 1914–1918* (London: Arnold, 1997).

Herwig, Holger H., *The Marne, 1914: The Opening of World War I and the Battle that Changed the World* (New York: Random House, 2009).

House, Jonathan M., *Combined Arms Warfare in the Twentieth Century* (Lawrence, KS: University Press of Kansas, 2001).

Hughes, Daniel J., *The King's Finest: A Social and Bureaucratic Profile of Prussia's General Officers, 1871–1914* (New York: Praeger, 1987).

Hughes, Daniel J., trans. and ed., *Moltke on the Art of War: Selected Writings* (Novato, CA: Presidio Press, 1993).

Hughes, Daniel J. and DiNardo, Richard L., *Imperial Germany and War, 1871–1918* (Lawrence, KS: University Press of Kansas, 2018).

Jackson, Julian, *The Fall of France: The Nazi Invasion of 1940* (Oxford: Oxford University Press, 2003).

Jäger, Helmut, *Erkundung mit der Kamera: Die Entwicklung der Photographie zur Waffe und ihr Einsatz im 1. Weltkrieg* (Munich: Venorion VKA, 2007).

Jahr, Christoph, *Gewöhnliche Soldaten: Desertion und Deserteure im deutschen und britischen Heer 1914–1918* (Göttingen: Vandenhoeck & Ruprecht, 1998).

Jones, Spencer, ed., *The Darkest Year: The British Army on the Western Front 1917* (Warwick: Helion & Company, 2022).

Jung, Jakob, *Max von Gallwitz (1852–1937): General und Politiker* (Osnabrück: Biblio Verlag, 1995).

King, Anthony, *Command: The Twenty-First-Century General* (Cambridge: Cambridge University Press, 2019).

Kitchen, Martin, *The German Officer Corps 1890–1914* (Oxford: Clarendon Press, 1968).

Knox, MacGregor, *Common Destiny: Dictatorship, Foreign Policy, and War in Fascist Italy and Nazi Germany* (Cambridge: Cambridge University Press, 2000).

Lipp, Anne, *Meinungslenkung im Krieg: Kriegserfahrungen deutscher Soldaten und ihre Deutung 1914–1918* (Göttingen: Vandenhoeck & Ruprecht, 2003).

Loez, André and Mariot, Nicolas, eds., *Obéir/désobéir: Les mutineries de 1917 en perspective* (Paris: Éditions La Découverte, 2008).

Loez, André, Review of *Nivelle: L'inconnu du Chemin des Dames* by Denis Rolland, *Vingtième Siècle*, no. 116 (October–December 2012), 176.

Lupfer, Timothy T., *The Dynamics of Doctrine: The Changes in German Tactical Doctrine During the First World War* (Fort Leavenworth, KS: Combat Studies Institute, U.S. Army Command and General Staff College, 1981).

Meisner, Heinrich Otto, *Militärattachés und Militärbevollmächtigte in Preußen und im Deutschen Reich: Ein Beitrag zur Geschichte der Militärdiplomatie* (Berlin: Rütten & Loening, 1957).

Melvin, Mungo, *Manstein: Hitler's Greatest General* (London: Weidenfeld & Nicolson, 2010).

Merridale, Catherine, *Lenin on the Train* ([London]: Allen Lane, 2016).

Militärgeschichtliches Forschungsamt, ed., *Untersuchungen zur Geschichte des Offizierkorps: Anciennität und Beförderung nach Leistung* (Stuttgart: Deutsche Verlags-Anstalt, 1962).

Militärgeschichtliches Forschungsamt, ed., *Handbuch zur deutschen Militärgeschichte 1648–1939*, 13 vols. (Munich: Bernard & Graefe Verlag für Wehrwesen, 1964–1981).

Miller, Henry W., *The Paris Gun: The Bombardment of Paris by the German Long-Range Guns and the Great German Offensives of 1918* (London: George G. Harrap, 1930).

Millett, Allan R. and Murray, Williamson, eds., *Military Effectiveness*, 3 vols. (Boston, MA: Allen & Unwin, 1988).

Millotat, Christian E.O., *Das preußisch-deutsche Generalstabssystem: Wurzeln – Entwicklung – Fortwirken* (Zurich: vdf Hochschulverlag, 2000).

Möller-Witten, Hanns, *Festschrift zum 100. Geburtstag des Generals der Infanterie a.D. Dr. phil. Hermann von Kuhl* (Berlin: Verlag E. S. Mittler und Sohn, 1956).

Mohr, Eike, *Heeres- und Truppengeschichte des Deutschen Reiches und seiner Länder 1806 bis 1918: Eine Bibliographie* (Osnabrück: Biblio Verlag, 1989).

Mombauer, Annika, *Helmuth von Moltke and the Origins of the First World War* (Cambridge: Cambridge University Press, 2001).

Müller, Klaus-Jürgen, *Generaloberst Ludwig Beck: Eine Biographie* (Paderborn: Ferdinand Schöningh, 2008).

Murphy, David, *Breaking Point of the French Army: The Nivelle Offensive of 1917* (Barnsley: Pen & Sword Military, 2015).

Muth, Jörg, *Command Culture: Officer Education in the U.S. Army and the German Armed Forces, 1901–1940, and the Consequences for World War II* (Denton, TX: University of North Texas Press, 2011).

Nicholls, Jonathan, *Cheerful Sacrifice: The Battle of Arras 1917* (London: Leo Cooper, 1990).

Oetting, Dirk W., *Auftragstaktik: Geschichte und Gegenwart einer Führungskonzeption* (Frankfurt: Report Verlag, 1993).

Offenstadt, Nicolas, ed., *Le Chemin des Dames: De l'événement à la mémoire* (Paris: Éditions Stock, 2004).

Paret, Peter, ed., *Makers of Modern Strategy from Machiavelli to the Nuclear Age* (Princeton, NJ: Princeton University Press, 1986).

Pedroncini, Guy, *Les Mutineries de 1917*, 4th ed. (Paris: Presses Universitaires de France, 1999).

Pethö, Albert, *Agenten für den Doppeladler: Österreich-Ungarns Geheimer Dienst im Weltkrieg* (Graz: Leopold Stocker Verlag, 1998).

Philpott, William, *Bloody Victory: The Sacrifice on the Somme and the Making of the Twentieth Century* (London: Little, Brown, 2009).

Philpott, William, *Attrition: Fighting the First World War* (London: Little, Brown, 2014).

Pöhlmann, Markus, *Kriegsgeschichte und Geschichtspolitik: Der Erste Weltkrieg: Die amtliche deutsche Militärgeschichtsschreibung 1914–1956* (Paderborn: Ferdinand Schöningh, 2002).

Raths, Ralf, *Vom Massensturm zur Stoßtrupptaktik: Die deutsche Landkriegtaktik im Spiegel von Dienstvorschriften und Publizistik 1906 bis 1918* (Freiburg: Rombach Verlag KG, 2009).

Rolland, Denis, *Nivelle: L'inconnu du Chemin des Dames* (Paris: Éditions Imago, 2012).

Rosinski, Herbert, *The German Army*, ed. Gordon A. Craig (London: Pall Mall Press, 1966).

Samuels, Martin, *Command or Control? Command, Training and Tactics in the British and German Armies, 1888–1918* (London: Frank Cass, 1995).

Sarkesian, Sam C., ed., *Combat Effectiveness: Cohesion, Stress and the Volunteer Military* (Beverly Hills, CA: Sage Publications Inc., 1980).

Schmidt-Bückeburg, Rudolf, *Das Militärkabinett der preußischen Könige und deutschen Kaiser: Seine geschichtliche Entwicklung und staatsrechtliche Stellung 1787–1918* (Berlin: Verlag von E. S. Mittler und Sohn, 1933).

Schmidt-Richberg, Wiegand, *Die Generalstäbe in Deutschland 1871–1945: Aufgaben in der Armee und Stellung im Staate* (Stuttgart: Deutsche Verlags-Anstalt, 1962).

Schulte, Bernd-Felix, *Die deutsche Armee 1900–1914: Zwischen Beharren und Verändern* (Düsseldorf: Droste Verlag, 1977).

Sheffield, Gary and Todman, Dan, eds., *Command and Control on the Western Front: The British Army's Experience 1914–1918* (Staplehurst: Spellmount Limited, 2004).

Sheldon, Jack, *The German Army on Vimy Ridge 1914–1917* (Barnsley: Pen & Sword Military, 2008).

Sheldon, Jack, *The German Army in the Spring Offensives 1917: Arras, Aisne and Champagne* (Barnsley: Pen & Sword Military, 2015).

Sheldon, Jack, *Fighting the Somme: German Challenges, Dilemmas and Solutions* (Barnsley: Pen & Sword Military, 2017).

Showalter, Dennis E., *Tannenberg: Clash of Empires* (Hamden, CT: Archon Books, 1991).

Sigg, Marco, *Der Unterführer als Feldherr im Taschenformat: Theorie und Praxis der Auftragstaktik im deutschen Heer 1869 bis 1945* (Paderborn: Ferdinand Schöningh, 2014).

Simpson, Andy, *Directing Operations: British Corps Command on the Western Front 1914–18* (Stroud: Spellmount Limited, 2006).

Smith, Leonard V., *Between Mutiny and Obedience: The Case of the French Fifth Infantry Division during World War I* (Princeton, NJ: Princeton University Press, 1994).

Smith, Rupert, *The Utility of Force: The Art of War in the Modern World* (London: Penguin Books, 2006).

Smithson, Jim, *A Taste of Success: The First Battle of the Scarpe. The Opening Phase of the Battle of Arras, 9–14 April 1917* (Solihull: Helion & Company, 2017).

Stachelbeck, Christian, *Militärische Effektivität im Ersten Weltkrieg: Die 11. Bayerische Infanteriedivision 1915 bis 1918* (Paderborn: Ferdinand Schöningh, 2010).

Stevenson, David, *1914–1918: The History of the First World War* (London: Penguin Books, 2005).

Stevenson, David, *With Our Backs to the Wall: Victory and Defeat in 1918* (London: Allen Lane, 2011).

Stevenson, David, *1917: War, Peace, and Revolution* (Oxford: Oxford University Press, 2017).

Strachan, Hew, Review of *Command or Control? Command, Training and Tactics in the British and German Armies, 1888–1918* by Martin Samuels, *Journal of Military History*, vol. 60, no. 4 (October 1996), 778–9.

Strachan, Hew, *The First World War*, vol. 1, *To Arms* (Oxford: Oxford University Press, 2003).

Strachan, Hew, *The First World War: A New Illustrated History* (London: Pocket Books, 2006).

Strohn, Matthias, *The German Army and the Defence of the Reich: Military Doctrine and the Conduct of the Defensive Battle, 1918–1939* (Cambridge: Cambridge University Press, 2011).

Tan, Tai Yong, *The Garrison State: The Military, Government and Society in Colonial Punjab, 1849–1947* (New Delhi: Sage Publications, 2005).

Tooze, Adam, *The Wages of Destruction: The Making and Breaking of the Nazi Economy* (London: Penguin Books, 2007).

Travers, Tim, *The Killing Ground: The British Army, the Western Front and the Emergence of Modern Warfare, 1900–1918* (London: Unwin Hyman, 1990).

Trumpener, Ulrich, Review of *The King's Finest: A Social and Bureaucratic Profile of Prussia's General Officers, 1871–1914* by Daniel J. Hughes, *International History Review*, vol. 10, no. 4 (November 1988), 643–6.

Walker, Jonathan, *The Blood Tub: General Gough and the Battle of Bullecourt, 1917* (Staplehurst: Spellmount, 1998).

Warner, Philip, *Auchinleck: The Lonely Soldier* (London: Cassell and Company, 2001).

Watson, Alexander, *Enduring the Great War: Combat, Morale and Collapse in the German and British Armies, 1914–1918* (Cambridge: Cambridge University Press, 2008).

Watson, Alexander, *Ring of Steel: Germany and Austria-Hungary at War, 1914–1918* (London: Allen Lane, 2014).

Wegner, Günter, *Stellenbesetzung der deutschen Heere 1815–1939*, vol. 1, *Die höheren Kommandostellen 1815–1939* (Osnabrück: Biblio Verlag, 1990).

Weigley, Russell F., *Eisenhower's Lieutenants: The Campaign of France and Germany 1944–1945* (London: Sidgwick & Jackson, 1981).

Woodward, David R., *Trial by Friendship: Anglo-American Relations, 1917–1918* (Lexington, KY: University of Kentucky Press, 2003).

Wynne, Graeme C., *If Germany Attacks: The Battle in Depth in the West*, ed. Robert T. Foley (Brighton: Tom Donovan Editions, 2008). First published by Faber and Faber in 1940.

Zabecki, David T., ed., *Chief of Staff: The Principal Officers Behind History's Great Commanders*, 2 vols. (Annapolis, MD: Naval Institute Press, 2008).

Ziemann, Benjamin, *War Experiences in Rural Germany 1914–1923*, trans. Alex Skinner (Oxford: Berg, 2007).

Zuber, Terence, *The Mons Myth: A Reassessment of the Battle* (Stroud: The History Press, 2010).

(ii)   **Articles, Chapters in Edited Books and Papers to Conferences**

Afflerbach, Holger, 'Wilhelm II as Supreme Warlord in the First World War', *War in History*, vol. 5, no. 4 (1998), 427–49.

Bariéty, Jacques, 'L'Allemagne et les problèmes de la paix pendant la première guerre mondiale à propos d'une publication récente', *Revue Historique*, vol. 233, no. 2 (1965), 369–92.

Bechthold, Mike, 'Bloody April Revisited: The Royal Flying Corps at the Battle of Arras, 1917', *British Journal for Military History*, vol. 4, no. 2 (February 2018), 50–69.

Bock, Fabienne, 'Le secret est-il compatible avec le régime parlementaire? L'exemple de la Grande Guerre', *Matériaux pour l'histoire de notre temps*, vol. 58 (2000), 40–4.

Bourne, John, 'Hiring and Firing in the BEF on the Western Front, 1914–1918', Paper presented to the military history seminar of the Institute of Historical Research, 6 October 2009.

Brückner, Hilmar-Detlef, 'Schluga von Rastenfeld', *Newsletter of the International Intelligence History Study Group*, vol. 6, no. 2 (winter 1998), 1–5.

Brückner, Hilmar-Detlef, 'Germany's First Cryptanalysis on the Western Front: Decrypting British and French Naval Ciphers in World War I', *Cryptologia*, vol. 29, no. 1 (January 2005), 1–22.

Brückner, Hilmar-Detlef, 'Die deutsche Heeres-Fernmeldeaufklärung im Ersten Weltkrieg an der Westfront', in Jürgen W. Schmidt, ed., *Geheimdienst, Militär und Politik in Deutschland* (Ludwigsfelde: Ludwigsfelder Verlagshaus, 2008), 199–246.

Cowan, Tony, 'The Basis of Our Own Plans and Operations? German Intelligence on the Western Front, 1917', Paper presented to the military history seminar of the Institute of Historical Research, 26 February 2013.

Cowan, Tony, 'A Picture of German Unity? Federal Contingents in the German Army, 1916-1917', in Jonathan Krause, ed., *The Greater War: Other Combatants and Other Fronts, 1914–1918* (London: Palgrave Macmillan, 2014), 141–60.

Cowan, Tony, 'Muddy Grave? The German Army at the End of 1916', in Spencer Jones, ed., *At All Costs: The British Army on the Western Front 1916* (Warwick: Helion & Company, 2018), 451–73.

Cowan, Tony, 'The Introduction of New German Defensive Tactics in 1916-1917', *British Journal for Military History*, vol. 5, no. 2 (October 2019), 81–99.

Deist, Wilhelm, 'Zur Geschichte des preußischen Offizierkorps, 1888-1918', in Hanns Hubert Hofmann, ed., *Das deutsche Offizierkorps, 1860–1960* (Boppard am Rhein: Harald Boldt, 1980), 39–57.

Deubner, Christian, 'Ludwig Deubner: A Professor from Königsberg and the Birth of German Signal Intelligence in WWI', *Journal of Intelligence History*, vol. 18, no. 2 (2019), 164–98.

Echevarria II, Antulio J., 'Clausewitz's Center of Gravity: It's Not What We Thought', *Naval War College Review*, vol. 61, no. 1 (winter 2003), 108–23.

Fantauzzo, Justin, 'Dead Sea Fruit: Edmund Allenby, the First World War and the Politics of Personal Loss', *First World War Studies*, vol. 7, no. 3 (November 2016), 287–302.

Förster, Stig, 'The Battlefield: Towards a Modern History of War', Lecture to the German Historical Institute London (London: German Historical Institute, 2008).

Foley, Robert T., 'Institutionalized Innovation: The German Army and the Changing Nature of War 1871–1914', *RUSI Journal*, vol. 147, no. 2 (April 2002), 84–90.

Foley, Robert T., 'Easy Target or Invincible Enemy? German Intelligence Assessments of France Before the Great War', *Journal of Intelligence History*, vol. 5, no. 2 (winter 2005), 1–24.

Foley, Robert T., 'The Other Side of the Wire: The German Army in 1917', in Peter Dennis and Jeffrey Grey, eds., *1917: Tactics, Training and Technology* (Canberra: Australian History Military Publications, 2007), 155–78.

Foley, Robert T., 'Learning War's Lessons: The German Army and the Battle of the Somme 1916', *Journal of Military History*, vol. 75, no. 2 (April 2011), 471–504.

Foley, Robert T., 'A Case Study in Horizontal Military Innovation: The German Army, 1916-1918', *Journal of Strategic Studies*, vol. 35, no. 6 (December 2012), 799–827.

Foley, Robert T., 'Dumb Donkeys or Cunning Foxes? Learning in the British and German Armies during the Great War', *International Affairs*, vol. 90, no. 2 (March 2014), 279–98.

Fox, Aimée, 'The Secret of Efficiency? Social Relations and Patronage in the British Army in the Era of the First World War', *English Historical Review*, vol. 135, no. 577 (December 2020), 1527–57.

Gale, Tim, '1917: The 'Dark Days' of the Tank', in Spencer Jones, ed., *The Darkest Year: The British Army on the Western Front 1917* (Warwick: Helion & Company, 2022), 483–504.

Geyer, Michael, 'The Past as Future: The German Officer Corps as Profession', in G. Cocks and K. H. Jarausch, eds., *German Professions 1800–1950* (Oxford: Oxford University Press, 1990), 183–212.

Geyer, Michael, 'Rückzug und Zerstörung 1917', in Gerhard Hirschfeld, Gerd Krumeich and Irina Renz, eds., *Die Deutschen an der Somme 1914–1918: Krieg, Besatzung, Verbrannte Erde* (Essen: Klartext Verlag, 2006), 163–201.

Gordon, Andrew, 'Ratcatchers and Regulators at the Battle of Jutland', in Gary Sheffield and Geoffrey Till, eds., *The Challenges of High Command: The British Experience* (Basingstoke: Palgrave Macmillan, 2003), 26–33.

Grawe, Lukas, 'German Secret Services before and during the First World War – A Survey of Literature and Recent Research', *Journal of Intelligence History*, vol. 18, no. 2 (2019), 199–219.

Grawe, Lukas, 'Albion an Holsteins Küsten? Der preußische Generalstab und die Furcht vor einer britischen Landung in Norddeutschland und Dänemark, 1905–1914', *Militärgeschichtliche Zeitschrift*, vol. 79, no. 1 (May 2020), 26–64.

Hahlweg, Werner, 'Lenins Reise durch Deutschland im April 1917', *Vierteljahrshefte für Zeitgeschichte*, vol. 5, no. 4 (1957), 307–33.

Hall, Brian N., 'The British Army, Information Management and the First World War Revolution in Military Affairs', *Journal of Strategic Studies*, vol. 41, no. 7 (2018), 1001–30.

Hampton, Meleah, 'Especially Valuable? The I Anzac Corps and the Battles of Bullecourt, April-May 1917', in Spencer Jones, ed., *The Darkest Year: The British Army on the Western Front 1917* (Warwick: Helion & Company, 2022), 337–59.

Harvey, Trevor, 'Arras, Allenby and Artillery: The Decision for a Four-Day Preliminary Bombardment', *Journal of the Society for Army Historical Research*, vol. 94, no. 380 (winter 2016), 314–35.

Herwig, Holger H., 'Imperial Germany', in Ernest R. May, ed., *Knowing One's Enemies: Intelligence Assessment before the Two World Wars* (Princeton, NJ: Princeton University Press, 1984), 62–97.

Hieber, Hanne, '"Mademoiselle Docteur": The Life and Service of Imperial Germany's Only Female Intelligence Officer', *Journal of Intelligence History*, vol. 5, no. 2 (winter 2005), 91–108.

Hirschfeld, Gerhard, 'Mata Hari: die größte Spionin des 20. Jahrhunderts?', in Wolfgang Krieger, ed., *Geheimdienste in der Weltgeschichte: Von der Antike bis heute* (Cologne: Anaconda Verlag, 2007), 179–202.

Hodgkinson, Peter E. and Westerman, William F., '"Fit to Command a Battalion": The Senior Officers' School 1916–18', *Journal of the Society for Army Historical Research*, vol. 93, no. 374 (summer 2015), 120–38.

Hümmelchen, Gerhard, 'Otto von Moser: Ein württembergischer General', *Wehrwissenschaftliche Rundschau*, vol. 31, no. 6 (1982), 196–202.

Kramer, Alan, '*Wackes* at War: Alsace-Lorraine and the Failure of German National Mobilization, 1914–1918', in John Horne, ed., *State, Society and Mobilization in Europe during the First World War* (Cambridge: Cambridge University Press, 1997), 105–21.

Leistenschneider, Stephan, 'Die Entwicklung der Auftragstaktik im deutschen Heer und ihre Bedeutung für das deutsche Führungsdenken', in Gerhard P. Groß, ed., *Führungsdenken in europäischen und nordamerikanischen Streitkräften im 19. und 20. Jahrhundert* (Hamburg: Verlag E. S. Mittler und Sohn, 2001), 175–90.

Löbel, Uwe, 'Neue Forschungsmöglichkeiten zur preußisch-deutschen Heeresgeschichte: Zur Rückgabe von Akten des Potsdamer Heeresarchivs durch die Sowjetunion', *Militärgeschichtliche Mitteilungen*, vol. 51, no. 1 (1992), 143–9.

McColl, General Sir John, 'Modern Campaigning: From a Practitioner's Perspective', in Jonathan Bailey, Richard Iron and Hew Strachan, eds., *British Generals in Blair's Wars* (Farnham: Ashgate Publishing, 2013), 109–17.

McRandle, James H. and Quirk, James, 'The Blood Test Revisited: A New Look at German Casualty Counts in World War I', *Journal of Military History*, vol. 70, no. 3 (July 2006), 667–701.

Martin, Gregory, 'German and French Perceptions of the French North and West African Contingents, 1910–1918', *Militärgeschichtliche Mitteilungen*, vol. 56, no. 1 (1997), 31–68.

Messerschmidt, Manfred, 'Preußens Militär in seinem gesellschaftlichen Umfeld', in H. J. Pühle and H.-U. Wehler, eds., *Geschichte und Gesellschaft*, Sonderheft 6, *Preußen im Rückblick* (Göttingen: Vandenhoeck & Ruprecht, 1980), 43–88.

Neitzel, Sönke, 'Zum strategischen Mißerfolg verdammt? Die deutschen Luftstreitkräfte in beiden Weltkriegen', in Bruno Thoß and Hans-Erich Volkmann, eds., *Erster Weltkrieg – Zweiter Weltkrieg: Ein Vergleich. Krieg, Kriegserlebnis, Kriegserfahrung in Deutschland* (Paderborn: Ferdinand Schöningh, 2002), 167–92.

Olivera, Philippe, 'La bataille introuvable?', in Nicolas Offenstadt, ed., *Le Chemin des Dames: De l'événement à la mémoire* (Paris: Éditions Stock, 2004), 36–46.

Pöhlmann, Markus, '"Daß sich ein Sargdeckel über mir schlösse": Typen und Funktionen von Weltkriegserinnerungen militärischer Entscheidungsträger', in Jost Dülffer and Gerd Krumeich, eds., *Der verlorene Frieden: Politik und Kriegskultur nach 1918* (Essen: Klartext Verlag, 2002), 149–70.

Pöhlmann, Markus, 'Towards a New History of German Military Intelligence in the Era of the Great War: Approaches and Sources', *Journal of Intelligence History*, vol. 5, no. 2 (winter 2005), i–viii.

Pöhlmann, Markus, 'German Intelligence at War, 1914–1918', *Journal of Intelligence History*, vol. 5, no. 2 (winter 2005), 25–54.

Pöhlmann, Markus, 'Une occasion manquée? Les mutineries de 1917 dans la stratégie et l'historiographie allemandes', in André Loez and Nicolas Mariot, eds., *Obéir/désobéir: Les mutineries de 1917 en perspective* (Paris: Éditions La Découverte, 2008), 385–98.

312   Bibliography

Pöhlmann, Markus, 'A Portrait of the Soldier as a Young Man: Ernst Jünger at Fresnoy, April 1917', *Journal of Military and Strategic Studies*, vol. 18, no. 2 (2017), 105–17.

Pöhlmann, Markus, 'The Evolution of the Military Intelligence System in Germany, 1890-1918', in Simon Ball, Philipp Gassert, Andreas Gestrich and Sönke Neitzel, eds., *Cultures of Intelligence in the Era of the World Wars* (Oxford: Oxford University Press, 2020), 145–65.

Rolland, Denis, 'Un ciel allemand?', in Nicolas Offenstadt, ed., *Le Chemin des Dames: De l'événement à la mémoire* (Paris: Éditions Stock, 2004), 121–36.

Samuels, Martin, 'Ludwig Föppl: A Bavarian Cryptanalyst on the Western Front', *Cryptologia*, vol. 40, no. 4 (2016), 355–73.

Sanderson, Harry, 'Black Day of the British Army: The Third Battle of the Scarpe 3 May 1917', in Spencer Jones, ed., *The Darkest Year: The British Army on the Western Front 1917* (Warwick: Helion & Company, 2022), 360–86.

Showalter, Dennis E., 'Even Generals Wet Their Pants: The First Three Weeks in East Prussia, August 1914', *War & Society*, vol. 2, no. 2 (1984), 61–86.

Soutou, Georges-Henri, 'Poincaré, Painlevé et l'offensive Nivelle', in Jean-Claude Allain, ed., *Des Étoiles et des Croix* (Paris: Economica, 1995), 91–109.

Stachelbeck, Christian, '"Lessons learned" in WWI: The German Army, Vimy Ridge and the Elastic Defence in Depth in 1917', *Journal of Military and Strategic Studies*, vol. 18, no. 2 (2017), 118–35.

Strachan, Hew, 'Ausbildung, Kampfgeist und die Zwei Weltkriege', in Bruno Thoß and Hans-Erich Volkmann, eds., *Erster Weltkrieg – Zweiter Weltkrieg: Ein Vergleich. Krieg, Kriegserlebnis, Kriegserfahrung in Deutschland* (Paderborn: Ferdinand Schöningh, 2002), 265–86.

Strachan, Hew, 'Clausewitz and the First World War', *Journal of Military History*, vol. 75, no. 2 (April 2011), 367–91.

Stützel, Hermann, 'Geheimschrift und Entzifferung im Ersten Weltkrieg', *Truppenpraxis*, July 1969, 541–45.

Trumpener, Ulrich, 'War Premeditated? German Intelligence Operations in July 1914', *Central European History*, vol. 9, no. 1 (March 1976), 58–85.

Watson, Alexander, 'Fighting for Another Fatherland: The Polish Minority in the German Army, 1914–1918', *English Historical Review*, vol. 126, no. 522 (October 2011), 1137–66.

Wehler, Hans-Ulrich, 'Der Aufbruch in die Moderne 1860–1890. Armee, Marine und Politik in Europa, den USA und Japan', in Michael Epkenhans and Gerhard P. Groß, eds., *Das Militär und der Aufbruch in die Moderne 1860 bis 1890* (Munich: R. Oldenbourg Verlag, 2003), xxi–xxix.

Wiens, Gavin, 'Guardians and Go-betweens: Germany's Military Plenipotentiaries during the First World War', *Journal of Military History*, vol. 86, no. 2 (April 2022), 344–71.

Ziemann, Benjamin, 'Le Chemin des Dames dans l'historiographie militaire allemande', in Nicolas Offenstadt, ed., *Le Chemin des Dames: De l'événement à la mémoire* (Paris: Éditions Stock, 2004), 341–9.

(iii)   Theses

Gudmundsson, Bruce I., 'Learning from the Front: Tactical Innovation in France and Flanders, 1914–1918', unpublished D.Phil. thesis, University of Oxford, 2009.

Hoffmann, Jan, 'Die sächsische Armee im Deutschen Reich 1871 bis 1918', unpublished PhD thesis, University of Dresden, 2007.

Meyer, Bradley J., 'Operational Art and the German Command System in World War I', unpublished PhD thesis, Ohio State University, 1988.

Newton, Christopher, 'An Anatomy of British Adaptation on the Western Front: British Third Army and the Battles of the Scarpe, April–June 1917', unpublished PhD thesis, King's College London, 2019.

Rezsöhazy, Élise, 'De la protection du secret militaire à l'occupation des populations civiles: Les polices secrètes allemandes derrière le front Ouest (1914–1918)', unpublished PhD thesis, Université catholique de Louvain, 2020.

Wiens, Gavin, 'In the Service of Kaiser and King: State Sovereignty, Nation-Building and the German Army, 1866–1918', unpublished PhD thesis, University of Toronto, 2019.

(iv)   Online Resources

Anon., *La Chanson de Craonne*, http://crid1418.org/espace_pedagogique/documents/ch_craonne.htm.

Bavarian *Kriegsranglisten*, www.ancestry.co.uk, under 'Bavaria, Germany, World War I Personnel Rosters, 1914–1918'.

Bayerische Akademie der Wissenschaften, *Neue Deutsche Biographie*, www.ndb.badw-muenchen.de/ndb_baende.htm.

'Combat Boot' twitter account, https://twitter.com/combat_boot.

Cowan, Tony, 'German Army Command and Control in the Late Nineteenth and Early Twentieth Centuries', unpublished research paper, 2010, https://independent.academia.edu/CowanTony/Papers.

Echevarria II, Antulio J., 'Optimizing Chaos on the Nonlinear Battlefield', *Military Review*, vol. 77, no. 5 (September/October 1997), http://cgsc.contentdm.oclc.org/cdm/ref/collection/p124201coll1/id/429.

Great War Forum, 'Meaning of "Mebus" in WW1 Recollection', www.greatwarforum.org/topic/265830-meaning-of-mebus-in-ww1-recollection/.

Kleist family genealogy, www.v-kleist.com/FG/fgn093.htm.

McMeekin, Sean, 'Was Lenin a German Agent?', *The New York Times*, 19 June 2017, www.nytimes.com/2017/06/19/opinion/was-lenin-a-german-agent.html.

Nevin, Charles, 'Outstanding Mistakes of All Time', BBC blogpost, 14 June 2013, www.bbc.co.uk/news/blogs-magazine-monitor-22902556.

Offenstadt, Nicolas, 'La Grande Guerre des régions', *Le Monde* online, 12 May 2014, www.lemonde.fr/centenaire-14-18/article/2014/05/12/la-grande-guerre-des-regions_4415168_3448834.html.

Index